J. G. FRAZER
HIS LIFE AND WORK

Portrait of J.G. Frazer by H. Macbeth Raeburn, 1883

J. G. FRAZER
HIS LIFE AND WORK

ROBERT ACKERMAN

Director of Humanities,
University of the Arts, Philadelphia

The right of the
University of Cambridge
to print and sell
all manner of books
was granted by
Henry VIII in 1534.
The University has printed
and published continuously
since 1584.

CAMBRIDGE UNIVERSITY PRESS

CAMBRIDGE

NEW YORK   PORT CHESTER

MELBOURNE   SYDNEY

Published by the Press Syndicate of the University of Cambridge
The Pitt Building, Trumpington Street, Cambridge CB2 1RP
40 West 20th Street, New York, NY 10011, USA
10 Stamford Road, Oakleigh, Melbourne 3166, Australia

First published 1987
Reprinted 1988 (twice)
Canto edition 1990

Printed in Great Britain by
Billings & Sons Ltd, Worcester

British Library cataloguing in publication data
Ackerman, Robert
J.G. Frazer : his life and work.
1. Frazer, *Sir* James George   2. Mythology
I. Title
291.1'3'0924   BL310.F713

Library of Congress cataloguing in publication data
Ackerman, Robert, 1935–
J.G. Frazer : his life and work.
Bibliography
Includes index.
1. Frazer, James George, Sir, 1854–1941.
2. Anthropologists – England – Biography. I. Title.
GN21.F65A27   1987   301'.092'4   [B]   87-9343

ISBN 0 521 34093 4 hardback
ISBN 0 521 39825 8 paperback

CONTENTS

List of illustrations   *page* vi

Acknowledgments   vii

Introduction: Frazer and intellectual biography   1

1 Childhood and youth   5

2 Trinity undergraduate   17

3 The vista of anthropology   35

4 Pausanias and Robertson Smith   53

5 Mythography and ambivalence   70

6 *The Golden Bough*   95

7 Smith dies; Frazer marries   111

8 *Pausanias's Description of Greece*   127

9 Baldwin Spencer, Andrew Lang, and Edmund Gosse   143

10 The second edition   164

11 The Hebrew world   180

12 *Lectures on Kingship* and Liverpool   197

13 Frazer and his critic Marett   221

14 The third edition   236

15 Honor to the king   258

16 Return to the classics   278

17 Aftermath   301

Appendix 1 Additions to Besterman's bibliography   309

Appendix 2 Frazer's notebooks   311

Bibliographic notes   313

Abbreviations   314

Notes   315

Index   341

ILLUSTRATIONS

Portrait of J.G. Frazer by H. Macbeth Raeburn, 1883   *frontispiece*

FOLLOWING PAGE 126

1   J.G. Frazer, his brother Samuel, and his sister Christine
2   J.G. Frazer with his brother and his mother, Mrs Katherine
    Frazer, in the family home in Garelochhead
3   The "intense" teenager
4   *En famille:* with his mother, father, sister Isabella, and an
    unidentified family friend
5   Playful: with Christine and Isabella and a Mr Edwards
6   With an unidentified scientific friend at Cambridge, 1880s
7   As a young Fellow of Trinity College, 1880s
8   Receiving an honorary degree: Frazer with M. Paul-Emile
    Appell (Rector of the Sorbonne) and Rudyard Kipling, 1921
9 and 10   Sir James and Lady Frazer, annual dinner of the
            Royal Literary Fund, London, 1930
11   The blind old man, mid-1930s

ACKNOWLEDGMENTS

No book of this kind can be written without the help of many people and institutions, and it is my great pleasure to acknowledge their assistance. First I wish to thank the Master and Fellows of Trinity College, Cambridge, holders of copyright and literary executors of the Frazer estate. I am especially grateful to the following people in Trinity College: Dr Philip Gaskell, Fellow and former Librarian; Dr Timothy Hobbs, Sub-Librarian; Dr R.H. Glauert, Junior Bursar; Mr T.C. Nicholas, Fellow; and the late Sir J.R.M. Butler, Fellow; among past and current Wren Library staff, Ms Helen Clifford, Ms Rosemary Graham, Mr Trevor Kaye, and Mr Alan Kucia.

I wish to thank Margaret, Viscountess Long, for her courtesy in permitting me to see and use her Frazer memorabilia; Professor William M. Calder III, of the University of Colorado, for friendship, support, and information over many years; and Dr Alan Findlay, of Churchill College, Cambridge, who initiated me into the mysteries of word processing and whose unfailing assistance made it possible for me to produce this book on the computer.

Next, there is the National Endowment for the Humanities, for a fellowship for Independent Study and Research, and the Institute for Advanced Study, Princeton, for a fellowship, during which I wrote an early draft of part of this book; and the American Council of Learned Societies, for a fellowship that permitted me to gather and edit most of Frazer's letters.

I am grateful to Dr Leon Botstein and Dr Dimitri Papadimitriou, president and executive vice-president of Bard College and Simon's Rock of Bard College, and Mr Robert B. Strassler, chairman of the Board of Overseers of Simon's Rock of Bard College – all three of whom made it possible for me to enjoy a fellowship in Britain from the Bard College Center, during which I completed most of this work.

I also wish to thank the following persons who generously answered my questions or helped in other ways: Ms A.S. Adams, Mr A.A. Allan, Revd Peter G. Baker, the late Mr Theodore Besterman, Mr M.A.F. Borrie, Mr R.T. Brown, Mrs Clare (Cornford) Chapman, Mr Alan Clodd, Mr Nigel Cross, Miss A. Darvell, Mr Rodney G. Dennis, Mr R. Angus Downie, Ms Elizabeth Edwards, Mr T.M. Farmiloe, Sir Raymond Firth, Mr F.J. Friend, Professor Ernest Gellner, Professor Wynne Godley, Mrs Elizabeth Gotch, Professor Christian Habicht, Professor Robert Alun Jones, Mrs Jean Kennedy, Professor Sir Edmund Leach, Professor Peter Levi, Dr Alan Macfarlane, Sir Robert Marett, Miss E. McNeill, Professor Margaret Mead, Mr Paul Naiditch, Dr Dorothy M. Owen, Mrs Jean Pace, Mrs A. Payne, Drs Herbert and Ellen Peyser, Dr David W. Phillipson, Dr A. Raspin, Sir John Rothenstein, Mr Clive Rouse, Dr Malcolm Ruel, Mr Menahem Schmelzer, Mr C. D. W. Sheppard, Professor Robert Skidelsky, Mr Robert N. Smart, Mr Anthony Mackenzie Smith, Dr I. Stolzenberg, Mr Christopher Stray, Ms Saundra Taylor, Professor Homer Thompson, Mrs L. A. Tinkler, Mrs Helena Wayne (Malinowska), Provost Bernard Williams, Mr P. R. Williams, and Professor R. E. Wycherley.

I wish to offer special thanks to Michael Black, Kevin Taylor, and Christine Lyall Grant, of Cambridge University Press, for their inestimable assistance in turning a manuscript into a book.

I owe much to all those institutions that graciously allowed me to read, photocopy, and use their letters by and to Sir James Frazer. Heading the list must come the two largest and most important collections – those in the Wren Library, Trinity College, Cambridge, and in the British Library (Macmillan Company papers). There are, in addition, Frazer letters or other material in the following libraries and archives:

Great Britain: Macmillan Company Archives, Basingstoke; King's College, Cambridge; University Museum of Archaeology and Anthropology, Cambridge; University Library, Cambridge; University of Dundee Library; Eastbourne Public Library; National Library of Scotland, Edinburgh; Glasgow University Library; Brotherton Collection, University of Leeds; University of Liverpool Archives; British Academy; British Library of Political and Economic Science (LSE); Drapers' Company, London; Royal Geographical Society; Royal Anthropological Institute; W. H. Heinemann & Co.; Royal Botanical Society; Royal Society; University College Library, London; British Library; Balfour Library, Pitt-Rivers Museum, Oxford; Bodleian Library, Oxford; St Andrews University Library.

Europe and Australia: Abo Akademis Bibliotek, Finland; Preussischer Kulturbesitz Staatsbibliothek, Berlin; Universitaetsbibliothek, Bonn; Bayerische Staatsbibliothek, Munich; Tübingen University Library; Uppsala University Library; University of Victoria Library, Melbourne.

United States: University of California at Los Angeles Library; Yale University Library; Lilly Library, Indiana University, Bloomington, Indiana; Houghton Library, Harvard University; Library of the Jewish Theological Seminary of America, New York; Temple University Library; Harry Ransom Humanities Research Center, University of Texas at Austin; Library of Congress; Smithsonian Institution Archives.

I wish to thank the following persons and institutions for permitting me to print hitherto unpublished material: British Academy; British Library Board, British Library of Political and Economic Science (LSE); Brotherton Collection, University of Leeds; University Museum of Archaeology and Anthropology, Cambridge; University Library, Cambridge; Houghton Library, Harvard University; W.H. Heinemann & Co.; Library of the Jewish Theological Seminary of America, New York; Lilly Library, Indiana University, Bloomington, Indiana; The Macmillan Press Limited; University of St Andrews; Staatsbibliothek, Berlin; Harry Ransom Humanities Research Center, University of Texas at Austin; University College London Library; Mrs Clare Chapman; Sir Robert Marett; Mrs Helena Wayne (Malinowska).

The editor of the *Journal of the History of Ideas* has given me permission to quote from my essay, "Frazer on Myth and Ritual," in vol. 36 (1975), 115–34.

FOR MY BELOVED WIFE PATRICIA

INTRODUCTION: FRAZER AND INTELLECTUAL BIOGRAPHY

FRAZER is an embarrassment. The man who has had more readers and who was arguably a better writer than any other anthropologist writing in English does not appear in any of the professional lineages that anthropologists acknowledge today. The reason for this is plain enough: he wrote vast, assured tomes about primitive religion and mythology without ever leaving the library. He based his comprehensive theories on the often crude and ethnocentric reports of explorers, missionaries, and traders. He lacked the idea of culture as the matrix, both conscious and unconscious, that gives meaning to social behavior and belief, and thus had no qualms about comparing items of culture from the most disparate times and places. He was a hard-line rationalist who used ethnographic facts to try and knock the last nail in the coffin of religion in the name of objective science. If from time to time he achieved a kind of prophetic power, it is because he was the spokesman for an imperialist confidence that has now been swept away. It is no wonder that no one wants him for a professional ancestor.

The other great men of the two generations of British anthropology preceding the First World War, who as contemporaries must have shared at least some of Frazer's failings, have found friends. E. B. Tylor, who was of the same rationalist and intellectualist persuasion as Frazer, receives the honor properly due the Founder, and in addition he did succeed in establishing the academic study of anthropology. Lewis Henry Morgan rightly receives credit for understanding the importance of the classificatory system in the study of kinship, and besides he has been taken up by Marxists and other materialists, so he is not in need of supporters. J. F. McLennan was largely responsible for dragging the red herring of totemism across the intellectual scene, but at least he understood the development of religion in sociological terms and not as the intellectual product of a few great minds. He was also to some extent the intellectual begetter of William Robertson Smith. Smith, Frazer's friend and mentor, furthered the sociological study of primitive religion, besides being a world-class Orientalist, and he went on to influence Durkheim, so he too belonged to the future.

But Frazer has no one. All he did was read and write, and he never went anywhere wilder than Greece, so he had no adventures – hardly even any anecdotes – such as are the birthright of any anthropologist who ventures into the field. The wall of books bound in dark green just seemed to grow and grow,

1

and as it did it blocked any view of the little man behind them, working away tirelessly at his desk. Even blindness, which came to him in his seventy-eighth year, did not stop him; with the aid of amanuenses he continued to work for a further decade. At the very end one of them, R. Angus Downie, was commissioned by Lady Frazer to write a life. But she literally read over his shoulder as he wrote, and she was unwilling to permit even the slightest hint of criticism.

She wished the world to believe, as Downie wrote in 1940, that "The facts of Frazer's life consist essentially of a list of his works."[1] Which of course is evasive nonsense – books do not write themselves, and Frazer was heir to the same uncertainties and confusions and anxieties as the rest of us. Thirty years later Downie wrote a memoir of his years with the Frazers that is valuable mainly for the anecdotes he preserves.[2] But he was no more a scholar in 1970 than in 1940; the memoir contains many mistakes, and as a study of Frazer's work and ideas is simply inadequate.

That is all there is, except for the obituaries and the obligatory brief accounts of Frazer in the various histories of anthropology.[3] Because these histories have been mainly whiggish and polemical exercises, and because no historian has had an interest in claiming Frazer as a member of the great tradition that inevitably leads up to and justifies himself and his own theoretical position, Frazer has received a poor press indeed. It was therefore not until 1962 that Frazer's ideas first received serious study, and then not by an anthropologist but by a literary critic. The relevant section of Stanley Edgar Hyman's *The Tangled Bank*, good as it is, has three shortcomings: he knows no more about Frazer's life than the standard sources recount;[4] he focuses on Frazer's metaphors, which is intelligent but is not sufficiently powerful as a method for tracing the development of his ideas; and he is writing about Frazer in order to further the fortunes of his own critical position (myth and ritual criticism), which he traces back to Frazer. Later in the 1960s I. C. Jarvie and T. H. Gaster in their different ways argued that Frazer was not hopeless and that his work might be rehabilitated, but their work was generally not well received.[5] Aside from a conventional influence study of the impact of *The Golden Bough* on modern literature in 1973, and a few scattered articles by various scholars, that is essentially all.[6]

This will not do. Embarrassment though he may be, Frazer was immensely important in his own time and through the first half of this century. Even if he leads nowhere in anthropology as it is currently configured, anthropology is not the only field that he touched. Along with the several dozen volumes of speculations on the history of religion for which he is best known, he did more first-rank classical work than many classical scholars accomplish in a lifetime; he is still cited by historians of religion, among whom the comparative method was never totally eclipsed, as it was for the anthropologists; and as the example of Hyman indicated, he remains a presence, diffused but real enough, in literary criticism. Aside from the now virtually extinct myth-and-ritual group, he was admired by critics as different, if equally distinguished, as Northrop Frye and Lionel Trilling.[7]

More important still than these academic effects, he was appreciated by thousands of ordinary readers for his literary power, which fundamentally changed the way they saw themselves and some of their social and religious institutions. After the First World War certain Frazerian images became part of the intellectual and emotional landscape for anyone aspiring to a critical attitude to life. In this sense his influence has been immense if diffused, and he received hundreds of unsolicited letters from readers thanking him for opening their eyes and changing their lives.

It is time for me to declare my interest. Like Stanley Edgar Hyman I am a literary historian, but unlike him I am not a true-believing ritualist, so this biography is not trying to offer Frazer as "relevant" today. I first came to Frazer through a study of four classical scholars, now largely out of favor with their own professional descendants, called the Cambridge Ritualists: Jane Ellen Harrison, Gilbert Murray, F.M. Cornford, and A.B. Cook. They attempted at the turn of this century to use anthropology to elucidate the old and vexed problem of the origin of tragedy. They proposed that the source of the structure of tragedy was to be found in the rituals of agricultural fertility magic common to the cultures of the eastern Mediterranean in prehistoric times. They therefore depended heavily on Frazer; although he was friendly with all of them he was not part of the group but rather their intellectual parent.

When in the early 1970s I came to Cambridge – specifically, to the Wren Library of Trinity College, where Frazer was a Fellow for sixty-two years – on the trail of the Ritualists, I found an immense mass of Frazer's papers. Although Jane Harrison was undoubtedly more interesting as a person, Frazer was undoubtedly more important from a historical and intellectual point of view. In attempting to trace the connections between Frazer and the Ritualists I realized the need for a biography and therefore decided to write one. As I was not an anthropologist, the dismal state of his reputation made him, if anything, rather more interesting than otherwise. What did dissuade me for a long while, however, was the number of hostages I would be giving. I could hope for readers in anthropology, history of religion, classics, and literary criticism, in each of which my readers knew Frazer's work perhaps better than I did but might not know what he had done in the others. That is, there would always be readers for whom the information required more scene-setting because they were encountering it for the first time. I hope that I have managed to do this without condescension.

My approach is chronological. Because most of the events in Frazer's adult life were publications, I have discussed all the important ones in terms of their

3

ideas, at the same time setting them in the context of his life, which is largely unknown. Because it is unknown, I have quoted extensively from the original sources. I have made a sustained effort to describe the shadowy figure responsible for the flood of words and shelves of books. I have unearthed, collected, and edited many hundreds of his unpublished letters, along with a number of his diaries and other manuscripts; spoken with elderly men and women in Cambridge and elsewhere who remember him (and especially remember Lady Frazer); and found his only living descendant, a great-grandniece who fortunately turned out to possess the Frazer family photograph album (the source of many of the illustrations in the book). For all that, believing as I do that the intellectual and nonintellectual aspects of life are not separable, I could have used more evidence about the quality of his personal life; to the end Frazer has remained somewhat elusive.

One reason for his elusiveness is that because he worked so hard and because he seems to have been a kind and generous man but of a retiring temperament, not many firsthand descriptions of him have come down to us. Those that do exist – I think especially of the one by Bronislaw Malinowski – have therefore been inordinately influential in fixing his image in the mind of his intellectual posterity. That image is clear: Frazer as the consummate solitary library drudge, virtually helpless in everyday life and unable even to take part in ordinary conversation. That description is to an important degree inaccurate and must be modified. This is a complicated matter, for on the one side he may well have become such a person in middle age, but on the other Malinowski's words must be weighed in the light of his own ambivalent relationship to Frazer, his patron. Frazer was, however, until well into his forties when he underwent a personal crisis, quite lively, with many friends, and a member of intellectual networks in Cambridge and beyond.

His inner life, however, still seems somewhat thin and remote: he was not notably introspective, and except on rare occasions both his joys and his anxieties tended to be muffled in their expression, even by the standards of his more reticent times. Further, his emotional range and style as a private person seem to have narrowed in later years. His sense of humor was vestigial – it appears usually as sarcasm – and he was only rarely given to any redeeming irony about himself.

Otherwise, although virtually anything about Frazer must be an essay in rehabilitation, I should declare that I am not arguing that he was "right" and that those who have rejected him are "wrong." I am aware that the revolutions undergone by anthropology mean that Frazer's approach to religion is virtually meaningless in terms of contemporary practice. Not only are his answers superseded, but more important his questions likewise are no longer relevant. But even though his time and mental outlook are not ours, several of his metaphors have been influential, on writers and on general readers alike, in the creation of the modern spirit. He merits and repays the respect and attention that a biography implies.

1 · CHILDHOOD AND YOUTH

AMONG THE MANY HONORS received by Sir James George Frazer in a long life, few seemed to have pleased him more than the award, on 22 April 1933, of the freedom of his native city of Glasgow. Perhaps because it represented recognition from "one's own," who are proverbially the last to see the light, Frazer in response composed an address that looked back fondly on his youth some seventy-five years earlier. That talk he later supplemented with a sequel that proved to be one of his last original published pieces, "Memories of My Parents"; [1] together these supply us with some of the facts of Frazer's childhood and youth and also give some idea of what he felt, many years later, about his upbringing.

He was born on 1 January 1854, the eldest in a family of four children. [2] Three previous children had died at birth; we may assume that James was a child whom his parents wanted and cherished. [3] It is not surprising that he showed some of the traits frequently seen in first or only children: a precocious maturity, in the form of early adoption of an adult manner, which in Frazer's case may account for some of the marked resemblances between himself and his father, and a highly developed sense of seriousness and responsibility. He was a son of the middle class, for his father Daniel was a druggist (in Scottish usage "druggist" and "chemist" coexist), who was a partner in what was to become a leading firm of Glasgow pharmacists, Frazer & Green.

His father was reticent about his family, and Frazer has little information on them; his mother had no such reserve, so that more than half of "Memories of My Parents" is given over to the results of his mother's keen interest in genealogy. She traced a connection to royalty in the persons of James I and II of Scotland and, in a collateral line, to what is nearly as good as royalty in some circles in Scotland, Oliver Cromwell. Frazer offers this information simply as fact. Such lofty connections may have been part of his romantic daydreams when he was a boy, but he is not family-proud.

His memories of his early years are pleasant, even idyllic. In the well-run household of Daniel Frazer (1821–1900) and Katherine Frazer (died 1899) young James George grew up in comfort and security. His parents were all that solid, respectable, God-fearing Victorian Scots were supposed to be: his father highly esteemed by all as a man of rectitude and honor; his mother sociable, cheerful, and musical. The family lived the normal parochial life of the mid-nineteenth-century pious Scot, complete with rigorous sabbatarian observance.

James strongly resembled his father in many respects, so it is worth looking

5

at what he tells us about him. The first and most obvious of Daniel Frazer's legacies to his eldest child was shortness of stature. Neither stood more than three inches above five feet; both were abstemious and shared good health and long life. More important, Daniel Frazer found time to do some writing. He published (privately) three short works: a pamphlet called *Paper, Pens and Ink* (1878), devoted to a description and history of the materials of writing,[4] and thus full of curious lore (like most of his son's compositions); in 1883 a lecture that he had given to the Chemists' and Druggists' Association of Glasgow on *The Pharmacy Acts Amendment Bill of 1883*; and in 1885, his "magnum opus," a 104-page book called *The Story of the Making of Buchanan Street: With Some Reminiscences of the Past Half Century*. In this memorial Daniel Frazer offers an extraordinarily circumstantial account of the public events of his own life, which (like his son's) was largely peaceful and uneventful, along with an equally detailed account of the growth of Buchanan Street as a commercial center of Glasgow. Notable here are the elder Frazer's obsessive efforts to be accurate,[5] which are so extreme as to defeat any narrative impulse the reminiscences might have. He seems to have had a double dose of his son's Shandyan willingness to digress in order to pursue secondary matters.[6] After relating in detail how he had been apprenticed to his elder brothers and gradually risen to partnership in the firm, and after supplying us with a history of the growth of Frazer & Green, he digresses widely to relate in great detail some of the remarkable events he had seen during his forty years on Buchanan Street. His ramblings are otherwise unremarkable except in the matter of the style, which is stiff and oratorical; Daniel Frazer was given to mouth-filling phrases like "deserving a full meed of approbation," and seems wholly to have lacked humor. The reader of his son's works will recognize a certain family style.

I am not cutting James down to the size of his provincial parent when I note in both a compulsive drive for accuracy; an interest in fact for its own sake, along with the literalness that often is its accompaniment; no humor; a certain formality of style and a reserve that takes the form of rigorous adherence to the public dimension of events and a general eschewing of emotion. The father is a caricature of the son, and he totally lacks the erudition, the irony, and the vision that characterize Frazer's achievement.

There exists another account, of interest in itself, and even more for the light it casts on the portrait of the father by the son. The considerable obituary of Daniel Frazer that appeared in *The Chemist and Druggist* for 20 January 1900 acts as a valuable complement and to some extent even a corrective to "Memories of My Parents."[7] From it we learn of the sheer eminence of the man in the pharmaceutical trade: "He was one of the most remarkable pharmacists of modern times, for the business of Frazer & Green in Buchanan

Street, Glasgow, with its three associated branch-pharmacies, was one of the best of its kind in Europe."

More important psychologically, we read of the passionately activist character and temperament of Daniel Frazer. He was political throughout his life, in both the professional and larger social sense of the word. The son tells us in a single sentence that the father was a confirmed Gladstonian Liberal, but here we learn of Daniel's extensive involvement in professional politics. Early on he became a member of the council of the Pharmaceutical Society, first in its North British (that is, Scottish) branch and later on the national level. "But the Council did not give scope to his remarkable qualities of opposition. He was essentially a controversialist, and a thorough Radical, with keen appreciation of legal rights." He pressed unceasingly for a "more liberal policy and greater sympathy with the retail pharmacy as a trade than the Council had hitherto exercised. He was one of the most strenuous advocates for the Council-meetings being open to the Press." James played up his father's piety, his honorable dealings, and his high standing in the community, but from his version one would never guess that his father was a substantial and effective businessman, a political partisan and advocate of unpopular causes, and in general a mover of men and affairs. Though James chose to emphasize the continuities and resemblances between himself and his father, we must be struck by the way in which the son established his identity seemingly from earliest times in contradistinction and even to some extent in opposition to the father.

From boyhood James retreated inwards, and was always bookish; not only did he read prodigiously, but he became a professional student of that least practical of subjects, classics; he shunned public life and that share of the limelight that became his with the growing celebrity he attained after the First World War. He seems always to have been of retiring temperament, a tendency that was doubtless heightened during his undergraduate years at Glasgow and Cambridge, where he worked extremely hard and seems to have had no time for student hijinks. In middle and later life, this inclination was reinforced by his crushing self-imposed workload and by his wife's resolve not to permit the world to disturb him.

The letters show that Frazer feared the loss of time and concentration that involvement in public life would bring, and accordingly refused a number of honors. That said, one notes immediately that he did not refuse the highest ones – fellowship of the Royal Society and British Academy, knighthood, membership in the exclusive Order of Merit. He accepted these marks of preferment largely at his wife's urging, and to gratify her. Unlike professional activity, which often requires large amounts of time and effort, these were largely ceremonial and some involved attendance one time only, at the installation. Of all the bodies of which he was a member, only in the Royal Society – and then only when he sought support for his friend John Roscoe's anthropological expedition – was he active.

Most scholars are not averse to recognition of their work and would sympathize with, or least understand, this point of view. But those who knew him personally (albeit in the second half of his life) testify to his discomfort in ordinary social relationships, which is something more than a scholar's unwillingness to waste time. Somehow Frazer gradually changed during his forties from an admittedly shy man but one with numbers of friends to a withdrawn man not much at home in society. There exist a number of testimonies to this middle period, when Frazer was extremely quiet and inward. Then, in the 1920s, when the Frazers were abroad and traveling much of the time and he lacked access to his library, he seems to have come out of himself once again.

Downie speaks of Frazer's excessive formality and total lack of ease in conversation. Although his evidence should be discounted in part because he knew Frazer only in the latter's extreme old age and in the status of an employee, the same cannot be said for Bronislaw Malinowski, who knew Frazer for the last thirty years of his life. Malinowski speaks of his inability to converse easily with others or to think on his feet.[8] In this light perhaps his polished prose was not only the felicitous vehicle for his thought but also increasingly his principal channel to the social world.

Son of a controversialist father, Frazer was awkward in society and he positively loathed public meetings. Thus the obituary is important for its clear depiction of Daniel Frazer – a masterful man, one to whom others always listened respectfully and often deferred, a battler and a partisan, a politician, a Justice of the Peace – in short, a list of attributes that is about as far as possible from describing the life, public or private, of James George Frazer.

We return to "Memories of My Parents" with a new sense of how problematic that document may be. It is the sole source for information and attitudes concerning his youth and as such is important. But the obituary has permitted us to penetrate Frazer's characteristic smooth surface; its hints about his personal development remain to be developed.

If Daniel Frazer was not much of a writer, he did like books, and he accumulated a good library, from which the young James profited.[9] Along with the predictable Walter Scott and John Calvin, other favorites of both father and son included *Don Quixote* and *The Arabian Nights*. And "in his library there was also a fine edition of Moore's *Lalla Rookh*, which I read with youthful enthusiasm, reciting the verses aloud to the accompaniment of an old lute or guitar" (134). The photographs of young James certainly permit us to believe in his enthusiasm; like many another bookish young man, he seems "serious" and "intense." Characteristically, Frazer can say nothing about his father's literary tastes beyond an enumeration of his books, because the latter

8

"was not given to speaking much about it." In short, if Daniel Frazer's taste, formed in classically oriented Scotland in the early nineteenth century (we hear nothing of Wordsworth, Carlyle, or Dickens), offers few surprises, it did provide his elder son with solid reading. I call attention to the young Frazer reading Scott, Cervantes, and *The Thousand and One Nights*, for the romanticism of the young man strumming the guitar and declaiming Tom Moore went underground in the work of the mature man, but never totally disappeared. Because, as Frazer tells us, his father knew no foreign languages, young James had to wait until he went to Germany before he encountered Heine; when he did, however, he found his poet of choice. Heine became the voice for a range of emotions that Frazer was never otherwise able to articulate.

His parents were pious. His father (and, one assumes, his mother as well) was a "staunch Presbyterian and Free Churchman." Like the Church of England, but for quite different reasons, the 1830s and 1840s were a time of travail for the northern Establishment. In Scotland the church was convulsed by a bitter dispute concerning the system of patronage, or the assignment of clergy to parishes. The state insisted on its right in principle to overrule the choice of local congregations, and a large number of clergy and laity regarded this as intolerable interference. Finally, the dissidents, who were mainly the puritanical and evangelical party, seceded in 1843 and founded the Church of Scotland Free, or "Free Church," as it was and is generally called. As in the Wesleyan movement in the preceding century, the reformers drew their strongest support from the lower middle class – shopkeepers, artisans, smallholders. The rising young pharmacist Daniel Frazer was a typical adherent.[10]

His son tells us that Daniel and Katherine Frazer had a large clerical acquaintance who frequented their house. In so many homes in mid-Victorian Britain, "family worship formed part of the daily routine"; when Daniel Frazer "conducted it, as he usually did, he always read a portion of Scripture without comment and prayed extempore, the whole family and the servants kneeling devoutly" (132). The Frazer family was strenuous in its version of the Scottish Sunday, with its exclusive diet of divine service and edifying books. Frazer says that he liked it: "I never found this observance of the Sabbath irksome or wearisome. On the contrary, I look back to those peaceful Sabbath days with something like fond regret, and the sound of Sabbath bells, even in a foreign land, still touches a deep chord in my heart" (133). His final remark about his parents' religion is perhaps the most curious: "I should add that though both my father and my mother were deeply and sincerely pious they never made a parade of their religion; they neither talked of it themselves nor encouraged us children to do so; the subject was too sacred for common conversation" (133).[11]

Here Frazer, the lifelong professional student of religion, becomes silent too. It is hard to believe that he was uninterested; perhaps for a private, rather old-fashioned person like him, unused to baring his soul, in a sense the entire subject "was too sacred for common conversation," and he could not or would not proceed in this public discourse. All happy families are famously alike; to the extent that this is true, the family experience of the young A.C. Haddon (1855–1940) might be invoked, however tentatively, to flesh out Frazer's sketch and give us a better sense of the emotional tone of his early years.[12] Haddon was Frazer's nearly exact coeval and his friend and contemporary at Cambridge, and they both sprang from middle-class Nonconformist households; except that Haddon was English and Frazer Scottish, the similarities are remarkable. Haddon and Frazer both grew up in happy families, with whom they stayed connected life-long.

The main use of the parallel is to dispel the image of such evangelical homes as bastions of narrowmindedness, bigotry, and philistinism, derived from a few justly famous savage accounts in autobiographies and novels. This is not to deny the Philip Pontifexes, the Philip Gosses, or the Margaret Ruskins their existence or their due. But it is important to see the other side, which we get from Haddon's life. There we see a young man growing up immersed in religion, earnestness, moral uplift, and good works (and in Haddon's case straitened economic circumstances as well) and loving it all; he thrived in this environment and portrayed his world as neither stuffy nor smothering nor hateful. On the contrary, young Haddon seems to have had no important points of conflict with his family, except that they could not understand his interest in collecting and dissecting zoological specimens, and were always trying to get him to go into his father's stationer's business. Both Frazer and Haddon, after they had made the crucial move to the university, which was not part of the expectation of their class or background, remained good and dutiful sons. Neither underwent that characteristically Victorian experience of "deconversion," thereby disavowing their families and their religious upbringings by identifying them with ignorance, superstition, hypocrisy, and the dead hand of the past.

The main difference between them was in their aptitudes and in their general orientation toward intellectual work. Like all anthropologists of that time, both were trained in something else – Haddon in zoology, Frazer in classics. Haddon was an activist by nature, already in his boyhood exploring his environment and carrying out simple biological experiments, as well as reading as much as he could; his all-in-all was science and facts, which he perceived as fundamentally opposed to literary grace and style, identified as somehow factitious. Frazer seems never to have been boisterous and awkward; he tells us of no interest in natural history or indeed of any outdoor pursuit beyond walking. (Downie says that Frazer as a young man also fenced and enjoyed horseback riding;[13] this last would stand him in good stead when he had to ride on horse and mule all over Greece in the 1890s.) Putting it in an

10

extreme but justifiable form, he seems never to have been very interested in objects as such, and he later recognized this tendency himself.[14]

For Frazer the phenomena that counted were words and thoughts, his own and those of others; he was always self-consciously literary, a tendency that was accentuated in university. Now and again he experienced a centripetal pull, as when he traveled twice through Greece in the 1890s in connection with his work on Pausanias, or when he toyed with the notion of going out to New Guinea (with Haddon) in 1895, which notion was firmly put to rest by the pressure of work at home and by his marriage and consequent new family responsibilities in 1896.[15] For Frazer intellectual life seems generally to have taken him inward, into his own mind, whereas for Haddon the movement was outward, into the world. Alternatively, Frazer's shyness may have steered him toward an intellectual life characterized mainly by reading and writing books, whereas Haddon, who was gregarious, always enjoyed fieldwork and meeting people as much as the more bookish side of his science.

Returning to Frazer and his pious upbringing, one may conclude that, as sometimes with vaccination, religion in Frazer's case simply did not "take" (there is a parallel in the life of Frazer's friend Edmund Gosse, where the dose was administered – and rejected – much more forcefully). So far from there having been any trauma in Frazer's youth to explain his turning away from religion, there are only the warm memories recounted above. It seems fair to conclude that however much domestic piety was a reality among the Frazers as a family it seems never to have involved young James. He learned his Shorter Catechism and never questioned orthodoxy, he says, but when he began to read and think for himself, his reading and thinking were entirely along utilitarian and Spencerian lines, and the observance of his youth dropped away quietly and forever.

Yet he spent most of his adult life reading, writing, and thinking about religion. His choice of subject matter must therefore be allowed some symbolic value. He makes it clear that although his family had a definite and powerful religious commitment, the heart of the matter was too private and "too sacred" for anyone, and especially the children, to talk about. Perhaps for Frazer as a boy, religion, insofar as he thought about it, was something for the adults, and in his patriarchal family, especially for his father. This sort of speculation is suggestive when considered in the light of Frazer's lifelong fascination with religion. Though he seems to have been an atheist from early on, the label does not do justice to his to-ings and fro-ings.[16] His remarkable lecture of 1909 called *Psyche's Task*, where he speaks explicitly as a devil's advocate *on behalf of* religion (which he nevertheless calls "superstition"), arguing that it has had a generally salutary influence on the development of human institutions, is a work of the years that also produced the great third edition of *The Golden Bough*, that *summa* of rationalism and anticlericalism.

Frazer makes it clear that he respected his father but loved his mother. He

11

ascribes to her a saintly sweetness, along with all the other attributes that add up to the best Victorian idea of "Mother." Frazer's thin description of his mother makes it plain that he was his father's boy, for he had neither her sociability nor her musicality.[17]

Frazer first went to school at Larchfield Academy in Helensburgh, whither Daniel Frazer had moved his growing family to escape the first stage of industrialization in Glasgow. The school had been founded in 1858 by a Congregational minister to give the growing Nonconformist middle-class community a place to send its sons for a good education. Frazer says that the headmaster, Alexander Mackenzie, taught him the rudiments of Latin and Greek and instilled in him "the taste for classical studies which I have retained ever since" (120). From Larchfield he went to the University of Glasgow, where he matriculated in November 1869, two months before his sixteenth birthday. Of the Glasgow experience he says, sixty years later, that "it laid the foundation for my whole subsequent career" (120).

Scottish universities have always differed from those in England. Throughout the nineteenth century students were admitted at a much younger age than at Oxford and Cambridge. Fifteen-year-olds like Frazer were numerous because students in Scotland advanced strictly in terms of their academic achievement, irrespective of age. Further, because Scotland has never had anything analogous to the network of classically oriented English public schools that drew on the same upper social classes for both students and masters and therefore turned out a largely homogeneous, self-selected, and academically superior student body for Oxbridge, students at the Scottish universities tended to be more heterogeneous socially and less well prepared academically than their southern counterparts.[18]

Education has always been respected in Scotland, but in the nineteenth century a degree was never regarded as the mandatory entry ticket to the professions or to upper-class social life. The University of Glasgow, when Frazer entered it, offered what by today's standards would be called a good secondary education. Scottish graduates desirous of, and able to afford, further education went on to Oxbridge, as Frazer did.

Here is Frazer's description of the Glasgow curriculum a century ago:

In my time no option whatever was allowed to a student preparing for the Master's degree [the first degree]. Every one without exception had to study and satisfy the examiners in precisely the same subjects, which were Greek and Latin, Mathematics, Natural Philosophy (which meant Physics), Logic and Metaphysics, Moral Philosophy, and English Literature (121).

The differences between this course of study and what prevailed at still generally unreformed Cambridge (or even at Eton) in the early 1870s are striking, the main ones being the presence of English literature and natural philosophy.

Frazer mentions three men who influenced him at Glasgow; of these, only one was a classical scholar, the others being a philosopher and a physicist. Because an English boy of his time and class would very likely not have come in contact with either a philosopher or a physicist in the course of his secondary schooling (nor indeed in his university work either, unless he was reading those subjects), it seems reasonable to infer that Frazer recognized that his Scottish education made an important difference.

The first of the three was George Gilbert Ramsay (1839–1921), Professor of Humanity (that is, Latin) from 1863 to 1906: "to him more than any one else I owe the powerful impulse which directed the current of my thoughts and studies for many years to the classics of antiquity" (122). Frazer also dedicated to Ramsay his six-volume monumental translation of, and commentary on, Pausanias (1898), which the older man acknowledged as the greatest honor he had ever received in his life.[19]

Ramsay was responsible to a large extent for instilling in the young man the comprehensive view of antiquity that he came to have, though Frazer adopted his distinctively comparativist and folkloristic approach a decade after he had left Glasgow. Ramsay certainly must have had much to do with Frazer's extraordinarily deep and broad preparation in Latin.

The second influence Frazer acknowledges was John Veitch (1829–94), Professor of Logic and Metaphysics at Glasgow, a historian of philosophy and a literary critic. For Frazer, Veitch was the last practitioner of philosophy as conducted in the old manner. Frazer implies that when Edinburgh was "the Athens of the North" its citizens seemed to feel the pressure of thought in their daily lives somewhat as the fifth-century Athenians were supposed to have done; the Scottish philosophers, Frazer writes, were notable for "the clearness, simplicity, and literary finish with which they expounded their doctrines. They wrote like gentlemen in the language of polished society, and not like pedants in the uncouth jargon of the schools" (123).[20]

Frazer admired Veitch because he was an exemplar of the time when philosophy (which to Veitch would have included speculative psychology as well as literary criticism) was one of the humanities. Its practitioners were gentlemen; like the poet in Wordsworth's Preface to *Lyrical Ballads* of 1798, the philosopher is a man speaking to men. Along with logic and metaphysics Veitch taught rhetoric. In this capacity he appealed both to Frazer's love of sonorous diction and to what I have called his "underground" romanticism. Frazer mentions being impressed by Veitch's "true poetical feeling" and "the quiet but deep enthusiasm with which he recited verses of Wordsworth and of the fine old Scottish ballad 'Sir Patrick Spens'" (123).

In histories of philosophy Veitch is no more than a footnote because he devoted himself largely to a belligerent critique of metaphysical (that is, intuitionist or anti-utilitarian) tendencies then current in Britain, without offering any synthesis or theory of his own. The *Dictionary of National Biography* notes that this attitude of opposition to what he saw as pernicious in

13

philosophy isolated Veitch and made him a person of no moment in British academic circles, although many were impressed by his personal qualities.[21]

His *Knowing and Being* (1889) consists of the lectures he gave to his advanced philosophy class at Glasgow in 1888–9. It contains a sustained critique of metaphysics in its Hegelian and neo-Kantian forms, which were then enjoying a brief and unnatural vogue in Britain. His main criticism of such transcendental metaphysics is that they put the epistemological cart before the psychological horse – that before any valid answer to the question of what we can know is possible, we must first examine and analyze what and how we do know.

In a word, we must have Psychology – that is, a study of consciousness in its widest sphere – before we can have Metaphysics, or the science of reality; and we must further have psychology in all its fulness before we can have what is called the Theory of Knowledge, for the simple reason that you cannot give the theory of a thing before you know what that thing is, and is in all its completeness.[22]

Frazer concludes his notice of Veitch by saying that his teaching "opened up an intellectual vista of which I had never dreamed before." It seems reasonable to assume that this vista contained two elements: a view of the possibility that the mind itself might be analyzed, which may well never have occurred earlier to the teenage boy; and an elevated style and tone that attracted the young Frazer.

The third member of the trio at Glasgow, and certainly the most illustrious man in the entire university, was the Professor of Natural Philosophy, Sir William Thomson, later Lord Kelvin (1824–1907), after Clerk Maxwell and along with Faraday the greatest physical scientist Britain had produced since Newton.[23] Frazer had singled out Ramsay and Veitch for their outstanding qualities as men and as teachers. They inspired because they showed their students thrilling and elevating "intellectual vistas." Kelvin was not a good teacher because he paid his students the supreme compliment of not talking down to them but instead of addressing them about whatever work he had in hand. Thus they were in the position of being in the vanguard of knowledge, seeing science advanced literally before their eyes by one of its most eminent practitioners, but unable to understand what they were seeing because Kelvin was too immersed in his work to explain it properly. This was especially true for those who, like Frazer, were not talented mathematically. What Frazer did take away from Kelvin's lectures was

a conception of the physical universe as regulated by exact and absolutely unvarying laws of nature expressible in mathematical formulas. The conception has been a settled principle of my thought ever since, and now in my old age I am not disposed to change it for that conception of matter which appears to find favour with some modern physicists, though to me, in my ignorance, it seems to cut straight at the very root of science by eliminating causality and thereby implicitly denying the possibility of a rational explanation of the universe (123–4).[24]

In many ways such rationalistic scientism was "in the air" in the optimistic 1870s; a seeming analogy in historiography is Von Ranke's endlessly quoted contemporary dictum about the goal of history being the recovery of "*wie es eigentlich gewesen*." The important distinction between Von Ranke and Kelvin on the one side and Frazer on the other, however, is that the physicist and the historian both assume the objective existence of a world of "facts" that are "out there"; the young Frazer was not at all sure of the out-thereness of the world, for he was soon to enter a period of radical subjectivism, in which the world was entirely subsumed in sensation and mind. Kelvin's optimism that the universe is ultimately rational and therefore expressible mathematically suits perfectly with Frazer's analogous idea that the mind, at least in its evolved, "civilized" form, is an equally ordered, comprehensible, and describable "place," with its own rules of development and operation.

Another of Frazer's judgments – this time negative – on one of his professors at Glasgow has survived. Writing on 27 June 1927 to his good friend the Oxford anthropologist R. R. Marett Frazer added this sardonic postscript: "I have just reconciled my three theories of totemism in a higher unity, as Edward Caird would have said in his Hegelian jargon, which used to make me sick at Glasgow."[25]

Caird (1835–1908) was the idealist Professor of Moral Philosophy at Glasgow from 1866 to 1893, who wrote on Kant, Hegel, and Comte. From Glasgow he was translated to Oxford, where he became Master of Balliol. He was a leader in the attempt in the last quarter of the nineteenth century to construct an intuitionist ethics, an effort as unsuccessful as that on the part of the agnostic utilitarians to create a "scientific" ethics that dispensed with supernatural sanctions. Once the initial shock of Darwin's bombshell had stopped reverberating, the struggle between the two camps became the central philosophical issue in the 1870s and 1880s – that is, during and after Frazer's undergraduate days at Cambridge. Here one may say, on the basis of his visceral reaction to Caird, that Frazer was a convinced and even a passionate utilitarian from an early age.

Frazer did brilliantly at Glasgow, winning honors galore.[26] But he knew in his own mind when he graduated in 1874 that his academic preparation was incomplete. Having chosen classics as his subject, he had to go south, to an English university. He thought of competing for the Snell Exhibition, which had sent a stream of bright young Scotsmen, from Adam Smith to Andrew Lang, to Balliol College. His father, who no doubt would have preferred his son to carry on the family business but who recognized James's academic talent, had different ideas. To Daniel Frazer Balliol meant Oxford, and Oxford meant High Church, and perhaps even a hint of Newman and Rome of thirty years earlier: "fearing to expose me to the contagion he sent me to Cambridge instead" (124). His university having been chosen for him in such an accidental and, so to speak, sentimental manner, his college was determined when his father's close friend, John William Burns, suggested Trinity, having himself been an undergraduate there a generation earlier. So Frazer duly sat for, and won, a minor entrance scholarship in December 1873, became a pensioner (that is, a fee-paying student) on 9 January 1874, and at Michaelmas (October) 1874, aged nearly twenty-one (and thus one of the oldest in his year), James George Frazer was entered upon the books of Trinity College, which would be a home, both actual and spiritual, to him for the rest of his life.

2 · TRINITY UNDERGRADUATE

IN CHAPTER 1 social "forces" and similar abstractions – the evangelicalism of Frazer's parents, his family's middle-class status, the differences between English and Scottish educational systems – were invoked not only because they are an effective conventional means of setting the historical scene, and not only because in some ultimately mysterious sense they did "determine" the general outline of Frazer's youth, but also because detailed information about his childhood, like that of most people, is scanty. In the natural course of things as Frazer grew older he generated more records, which permit a fuller and more accurate assessment of his interaction with the larger social tendencies.

Before we plunge young Frazer into university, it seems reasonable to ask what the Cambridge of the day was like, both because Frazer was a Trinity man for his entire adult life and because he was to a large measure shaped by Cambridge ideas on the classics. The university that Frazer entered in 1874 was in the midst of a prolonged ferment that had been going on since at least 1860. From the middle of the century both ancient English universities had been repeatedly and increasingly attacked as citadels of medieval privilege and intellectual irrelevancy, and there had been a number of efforts at reform. The outstanding issue in political terms had been the abolition of religious tests; the disabilities of non-Anglicans were gradually relaxed over the years. But there was also agitation from within the universities themselves for academic reform through the introduction of new subjects and courses of study.

Changes were also demanded in classics and mathematics, the traditional heart of Cambridge education, and especially the Tripos (the examination for honors degrees). Increasingly in the 1860s it was argued that the classical Tripos, which had remained virtually unchanged since 1822, did not test true scholarship, as its upholders alleged, and that it was an examination of skill, not knowledge. As is so often the case in academic controversy, the battle was waged over an arbitrary, symbolic issue – in this case, verse writing. Because the social goal of classical education had been the formation of the discriminating taste needed by a gentleman, the writing of verses in Greek and Latin had long been important. Its supporters imputed to it salubrious effects on the mind as well as on the style. On the other side, the reformers pointed out that the Tripos unfairly rewarded the student possessing a talent for this

17

pleasant but irrelevant skill whereas it ignored and therefore penalized the student with the ambition and intelligence to undertake the large course of reading needed to grasp the true spirit of antiquity, as manifested in ancient history or philosophy. In response to this argument, and after much controversy, a single nonphilological exception had been introduced in 1849 – a compulsory paper on Ancient History. But this had satisfied no one – the conservatives felt that the history paper had adulterated the true (that is, purely philological) nature of the examination and in any case had encouraged cramming (which it had), whereas the reformers felt that the incorporation of nonlinguistic elements had hardly begun, and the Tripos still did not examine what it should.

In the 1850s the first of many subsequent proposals was made to divide the examination into two parts, with one devoted entirely to demonstrating mastery of Greek and Latin as languages, whereas the other would cover history, philosophy, rhetoric, and the like; but such efforts at a divided Tripos were strenuously resisted and finally beaten back. As a sample of the heat of the debate, here is a polemical contribution from a reformer, Henry Jackson of Trinity, later Frazer's good friend:

He must go back for a time, to the old Tripos which came to an end in 1872, the golden age according to Mr [T.E.] Page, the age of "pure scholarship." What their "pure scholarship" meant was this. They read Thucydides, but not Grote; they studied the construction of the speeches, but did not confuse themselves by trying to study their drift. They read the *Phaedrus*, but did not know what Plato was driving at or what Protagoras meant. They read twenty or thirty letters of Cicero – they took care to read selected letters – but they did not look into a Roman history in connection with them.[1]

The situation was exacerbated by the fact that classical students competing for the university's highest academic honor, the Chancellor's Medal, were still required to have attained at least a second class in the mathematical Tripos (the justification being that mathematics was necessary to develop the reasoning faculties), with the result that the medal frequently went not to the best or second-best classicist but instead to a lesser man who happened to have a facility for mathematics as well. Finally, after several rebuffs on the part of the University Senate, the reformers put through a compromise in 1869 by which the verse composition paper was retained, but to the Tripos were added three new papers – one on philology and two on philosophers and rhetoricians.

The Tripos then consisted of fourteen three-hour papers, written over nine days. It included four papers in composition (English to, respectively, Latin prose, Greek prose, Latin verse, and Greek verse), six in translation, one in ancient history, one in classical philology, one on the philosophers and rhetoricians for translation, and one on the "subject matter" of these same philosophers and rhetoricians (who were specified as Plato and Aristotle, Cicero, Lucretius, and Quintilian). This, then, was the Tripos for which Frazer

18

sat in 1878, since the divided Tripos ("double honors") that is the ancestor of the examination given today was finally accepted only in 1879.

On a less insistently institutional level, the point to be made about education at Cambridge in the 1870s was that it was available, but only to those who pursued it. Reminiscences of the period 1860–80 are unanimous in emphasizing the separation between the several distinct groups of students, which was much greater then than now.[2] The majority was composed of "poll" or pass men, who were at the university not out of academic interest but because their family and social class dictated that they spend the three years from age eighteen to age twenty-one there; prominent among them were the athletes and the "bloods," or those interested in what used to be called, in those calmer days, "fast" living. Frazer, needless to say, was one of the ever-present but never-numerous group of men interested in learning for its own sake, the "reading men."[3]

The system for imparting education, even to those eager to acquire it, was also very different from what it is now. Here is the testimony of Thomas Thornely, who was nearly an exact contemporary of Frazer's, entering Trinity Hall in 1873:

The best work was done in the privacy of our own rooms, for the college lectures were indisputably poor, and regarded more as a form of discipline than as a means of advancing knowledge. "University lecturers" had not yet been created, and inter-Collegiate lecturers were rare, while professors catered only for the more advanced students, if indeed they condescended to lecture at all. To supplement this inadequate teaching, private tuition was largely resorted to by those who could afford that luxury.[4]

The abilities of the lecturers varied from college to college, and Frazer was more fortunate than Thornely in attending the larger, wealthier, and more prestigious Trinity College, which was able to attract more (and perhaps) better students and therefore more (and perhaps) better Fellows and tutors, but overall the system was everywhere the same.[5] Students were free to do what they liked so long as they satisfied the relatively small number of requirements for the degree, such as the "Previous Examination" (more familiarly, the "Little Go"), taken at the end of the first year, in which one demonstrated knowledge of the rudiments of the classical languages, mathematics, and Scripture (which included Paley's *Evidences*). And of course one crammed as much as one wished or thought necessary for the Tripos, which completely determined the degree one received (as it does today).

Much is known or can be reconstructed of Frazer's career as an undergraduate. His most important activity (so far as his future work was concerned) was his reading, which was voluminous. The first document is an autograph list of his classical reading, dated October 1875 (that is, at the start of his second year), that, in its breadth, is worth reproducing in full.[6] The superscription, in the hand of his tutor J.M. Image (1842–1919), is "J.G. Frazer has read":

GREEK
1. *Verse*
    Homer (Iliad, Odyssey)
    Hesiod (except Fragments)
    Pindar „ „
    Aeschylus „ „
    Sophocles „ „
    Euripides „ „
    Aristophanes „ „
    Theocritus „ „
    Theognis, Tyrtaeus and the rest of the poets in Bergk's Poet. Lyr. Gr. up to p. 569, part II, ed. 3d (XIV in no.) Also a no. of the poems of the Pseudo-Anacreon.
2. *Prose*
    Herodotus
    Thucydides
    Xenophon (Hellenica, and between 3 and 4 bks (about) of Anabasis)
    Plato (Apol., Crito, Phaedo, Gorgias, Phaedrus, Republic, Protagoras)
    Aristotle (Politics)
    Aeschines (In Ctesiphontem)
    Demosthenes (Olynthiacs, Philippics, De Pace, De Halonneso, Περὶ τῶν ἐν Χερσονήσῳ; Πρὸς τὴν ἐπιστολήν; Ἐπιστολὴ Φιλίππου; Περὶ συντάξεως, Περὶ τῶν συμμορίων, Pro libertate Rhod., Pro Megalop., Περὶ τῶν πρὸς Ἀλεζάνδρου συνθήκων, De Cor., De fals. legat., Advers. Lept., In Mid., In Androt., In Aristocratem, Advers. Phormionem, πρὸς τὴν Λακρίτου παραγραφήν, Παραγραφὴ πρὸς πανταίνετον, Adversus Boeotum de nomine, Adversus Boeotum de dote, Adversus Dionysodorum)
    Isocrates (ad Demonicum, and Panegyric)

Latin
1. *Verse*
    Virgil, Horace, Lucretius, Juvenal, Persius, Propertius, Tibullus, Terence, Plautus (Mostellaria and Persa), Ovid (Fasti, Heroides 1–14, Metam. 1–5 and extracts)
    Prose
    Cicero (Verrine, Philippic, and Catilinarian Orat., Pro Cluentio (except some chapters), a little of the De Nat. Deorum, and a few Epistles)
    Livy (I–X, XI–XIV)
    Tacitus (Annals, Agricola, Germania)
    Caesar (Some of the Gallic War, amount uncertain)
    Sallust (Jugurtha, between 60 and 70 chapters, probably; Catiline – amount uncertain)
    Pliny (Epistles)
    Augustine (De Civ. Deo lib I)
Many of these books I have read twice or oftener, e.g. Thucydides, Virgil, Horace. Besides these I have read a little of Diodorus Siculus, Lucan, Martial, Quintilian, and Tertullian.

[signed]

James G. Frazer
Oct 1875

Classicists will make their own judgment, but nonclassicists will be struck by the length of the list, both the number of authors covered and the thoroughness with which Frazer has read them. It is most impressive that by the age of twenty-one he had read *all* of Plato, *all* of Euripides, *all* of Pindar. From the list one cannot tell whether he preferred Latin or Greek, for they are about equally represented. To have done this much at age twenty-one means that his goal for many years was to read as widely as possible. In addition, the list contains many late authors, which was unusual for the time even if, as is possible, Frazer read them in school editions. In the words of a historian of classical scholarship, at that time "such late authors [as Diodorus Siculus, Tertullian, Lucan, and Quintilian] were rarely read or even worked on by scholars at the time. Mostly it was Homer through Demosthenes for Greek and Plautus/Terence through Ovid for the Romans, with Tacitus of course."[7]

An instructive general comparison may be made with what Frazer's slightly older German contemporary Ulrich von Wilamowitz-Moellendorff (1848–1931), the premier Hellenist of the age, had read at about the same stage in his career. Each had read exceptionally widely by the time he was twenty-one, but, as his biographer W.M. Calder notes:

In general Wilamowitz's reading [in Greek] especially at school [Pforte] was more "classical." Hesiod and Theocritus among the poets he would not have read except in fragments cited in the secondary sources. Frazer is way ahead in the prose, especially Demosthenes and Aeschines, and I don't know when Wilamowitz first read Aristotle, *Politics*. At school Wilamowitz and Nietzsche read only Plato, *Symposium*, and that they both read on their own, probably partially at least for prurient reasons. In Latin Wilamowitz would not have read at eighteen and probably not at twenty-one Ovid, *Fasti* and *Heroides*, Augustine *De Civ Deo* I, and probably not more than very few of Pliny *Epp*. That Frazer had read any Diodorus Siculus and Tertullian, not to speak of Lucan and Quintilian, I find remarkable.[8]

As for Plato, Frazer's having read seven dialogues bespeaks something more than adolescent tingling. Give his seriousness, his extensive early reading of Plato should be seen as an extension of his interest in psychology and epistemology, which had been aroused by Veitch in Glasgow, and which was to be followed up directly: first, in his 1879 fellowship essay on platonic epistemology, next in his unpublished notes on "Philosophy," and finally and massively, in *The Golden Bough* and the other volumes of speculative intellectualist anthropology for which he is best known.

Finally, note the characteristic scruple in Frazer's last sentence, where he distinguishes those authors he had read more than once and those in whom he had read but "a little." This is to be read literally, as fact not as boast. Not only did he not want Image to think his reading extended where it did not, but he was compulsive in his need to represent facts as such. This trait becomes important where doubts about his scrupulousness in the handling of evidence have been raised.

More is known about his reading because in 1907 he had a catalogue prepared of his personal library.[9] Although any inferences based on it must be advanced with caution, the catalogue obviously furnishes a *terminus ad quem* for items that appear on it. It shows that by 1907 Frazer had long since got into the habit, to which Lady Frazer testified later, of buying any book that he needed, for in that year his library consisted of nearly five thousand titles, many running to more than one volume, an immense number for a college Fellow with a family and without extensive private means. Although the catalogue does not permit us to be certain when Frazer bought or read a particular volume, the presence of clusters of books by an author, all with dates of publication within a few years, is suggestive.

The best example of the utility of the catalogue, and one particularly relevant to any discussion of Frazer as an evolutionary thinker, is Herbert Spencer. Spencer was extremely popular throughout the English-speaking world in the 1870s, when Frazer was an undergraduate. The catalogue lists no fewer than ten titles, and except for the posthumously published *Autobiography*, all with publication dates from 1875 to 1880 (roughly, his Trinity undergraduate years). In the case of Spencer, however, we can go further, for we have the following from a letter by Frazer to his patron Francis Galton (1822–1911), dated 8 March 1885. The letter accompanied the submission to Galton, president of the Anthropological Institute, of the text of Frazer's first significant anthropological essay, a paper that he read to the Institute entitled "On Certain Burial Customs as Illustrative of the Primitive Theory of the Soul." He writes:

I shall always esteem it a high privilege and honour to have been allowed to read a paper before the Anthropological Institute. I am deeply sensible of the honour done me by the intention or wish of yourself and the other distinguished men whom you mention to hear my paper. That Herbert Spencer should be one of them is more gratifying to me than I care to say, for my intellectual debt to his writings is deep and will be life long. That I should be able even in prospect to interest one from whom I have derived such keen intellectual pleasure and enlightenment is to me almost affecting.[10]

For Spencer at least, the catalogue is a reliable instrument for deciding when Frazer read the books in his library.

The other important item from this period, an edition of *English Poems by Milton* (1876), signed and dated 31 May 1877, bears as much on his writing as his reading. That someone with Frazer's literary training and inclination should have read Milton is of course not remarkable. What is significant is his additions to the volume. On the end papers he has copied a whole page of "poetic-sounding" compound epithets from Milton;[11] on the page opposite the half-title he has penciled in long lists of adjectives, nouns, and verbs, again all of a florid or unusual kind. From these lists we may infer that Frazer's boyhood love of high-sounding rhetoric, reinforced in Glasgow by Veitch, was thriving in Cambridge. One imagines a studious and somewhat compulsive young writer setting himself rhetorical exercises in a quest for literary excellence based on the "best" models. The volume shows that, as one might have supposed, his style, often elaborate and frequently gorgeous, was, at least in early days, the product of sedulous application.

Frazer, for reasons of temperament, decided early on to take as models the great writers of the preceding century. His great masters were Addison and Gibbon, who may be said to exemplify the two aspects of his style. Most of his work is written in the pellucid Addisonian, or plain, mode, in which his meaning is never in doubt. He tends to affect the Gibbonesque, with its conscious latinity and sententiousness, when he seeks to soar or impress. This latter element echoes Milton (sometimes directly) and ultimately the ciceronian strain of much of Renaissance humanism.

So much for his private work and interests. Apart from his excellent record, there is a fact to be remarked about his undergraduate career: namely, its length.[12] He came up to Trinity in October 1874 and remained in residence until he took the Tripos in March 1878: eleven terms, fully three and a half years. At that time the statutory residential requirement for eligibility to sit for the Tripos was nine terms (each academic year containing three), and most students took nine or ten terms. It is likely that he stayed longer at his tutor's suggestion in order to improve his already excellent preparation. Such extra terms were not uncommon when a tutor thought one of his students was a real academic high-flyer, with a chance not merely of a First Class degree but of the Chancellor's Medal or others of the highest honors. His academic performance was outstanding, and would have been in any time and place; he was, however, competing in the Tripos against men about three years younger, which gave him an added advantage.

For he certainly continued the prize-winning ways of Glasgow: in his first, second, and third years (1875, 1876, and 1877) his name appears on the list of those receiving "first class" in the annual internal college examinations.[13] But these were as nothing compared to the Tripos. When he had to do his best, he did; he was second classic in 1878,[14] and next to his name on the honors list in *The Historical Register of the University of Cambridge* is "highly distinguished in the examination for the Chancellor's Medal."

It is worth dwelling for a moment on the Tripos. Because everything rode (and rides) on Tripos results, one always hears or reads about the Tripos or its Oxford analogue (Mods and Greats), but such statements tend not to have much meaning (especially to the non-English reader) unless one has some sense of the nature and content of the examination.

The first thing any observer notices about the Tripos is its length. Because these were the days of the undivided Tripos, the work of the entire three years was examined at once. Before all else, then, one who would do well in preparing for and taking the examination needs good mental and physical health (which Frazer enjoyed lifelong, except for his eyesight). The conditions resemble those of a championship chess tournament, in which only those in the very best condition can hope to go the distance.

The question papers themselves reinforce the idea of the Tripos as ordeal. Whether the paper is philological or historical, whether it involves translation or verse writing, one is struck by the extraordinary number of the questions and the consequent need for the student above all to be quick. To do outstandingly in such an examination meant that the student knew the material so thoroughly that he could write virtually without having to think, for there was no time to engage in thought. A good example is afforded by the questions in the first paper, on the *Gorgias* and the first three books of *De rerum natura*. There are no trick questions, but there are five on Plato and seven on Lucretius, each with several parts, many requiring some translation, and the student must answer all. However little or much the student knew, he must have it on call; speed and glibness were at a premium and no marks were awarded for analysis or depth. To know too much might be fatal; twelve questions in three hours means an average of fifteen minutes per response. And so it went in the other papers as well: Classical Philology, part I, contained fifteen questions, many with several parts, that range from "Criticise the scientific method pursued respectively by Buttman, Bopp, and G. Curtius, and describe the advances in philological science due to each of them" to "Classify the uses of the ablative case in Latin, and show how the functions performed by the Latin ablative are distributed among the cases of the Greek noun."

Given the relentless pace demanded by the length of each paper, it seems fair to say that the Tripos primarily tested stamina and the will to survive; by comparison, the intellectual mastery it required was not excessive. Frazer's coming second, then, is impressive mainly as demonstrating that he had internalized the examination's peculiar constraints and adjusted himself to them better than all but one of the other students of his year. In fact his learning was real – extensive and deep – but he had not much chance to show it in this examination.[15]

An outstanding record such as Frazer's, in those pre-Ph.D. days, would ordinarily have led either to a fellowship of his college or, failing that, to a career as a schoolmaster. We find Frazer in a letter to Image dated 11 April 1878, that is, after the Tripos and just before he took his degree, saying that "As I should like to be a little more independent of my father, and the only certain way of becoming so seems to be to take pupils, I should be obliged if you could send me some for next term" [that is, for the summer, or Long Vacation]. And then, underlining the importance to Frazer of Image in at least his last difficult Tripos days: "I wish to thank you for the kind help and sympathy you have constantly given me, and of which I am very sensible."[16]

But his plans changed, for the next letter to Image, dated 30 June 1878, is addressed from Hamburg.[17] His progress in German had been slow and he had found so little time for classical work that he had abandoned the idea of submitting a fellowship dissertation. He had hoped to continue with his own work in "modern philosophy," but that too would have to wait until he returned home.

Taking pupils, then, was plainly a makeshift, to gain financial independence, while he prepared to try for a fellowship. "Modern philosophy" refers to his intention at the time of doing academic work in that subject, a long-time interest that lapsed only when he began working on Pausanias and ethnography in the mid-1880s.

Frazer probably went to Germany for a holiday; the strain of the Tripos was great, and his father probably gave him the trip as a reward for his outstanding performance. There was the added pleasure of traveling with a friend, Joseph Shield Nicholson.[18] Nicholson (1850–1927), later Professor of Economics in the University of Edinburgh for forty-five years, had read moral sciences from 1873 to 1876 at Trinity, where they met and became friends. But even in the company of a friend, to one so genuinely in love with learning, and to one so driven by the need to work as was Frazer, all holidays were working holidays, and he used the trip to improve his German. In the course of doing so he came to know and love the poetry of Heine.

Having concluded that he lacked the time that summer to prepare a dissertation, he decided to wait. He then competed for and won one of the four fellowships awarded the next year (1879) at Trinity. Fortunately, because of the completely unrelated but controversial question of whether Henry Sidgwick might be re-elected to a Senior Fellowship at that time, Henry Jackson composed a circumstantial account of the meeting in which the fellowships were decided in 1879.[19] It shows clearly that Frazer was seen by the electors as the best man in the group.

His dissertation was entitled "The Growth of Plato's Ideal Theory." In 1930 it was published unaltered as an act of homage to Frazer, then seventy-six years old; the preface he wrote to this volume is of some interest. He tells us that "Plato was an old love of mine, and that I had read the whole of his works in the original before I took my first degree at Cambridge in 1878." And although he had long since turned from Plato to matters of quite a different kind, "reviewing my youthful essay after the lapse of half a century I am encouraged to believe that it truly represents the rise and fall of the Ideal Theory in Plato's mind; hence I venture to publish it exactly as I wrote it."[20]

The Growth of Plato's Ideal Theory is Frazer's first substantial piece of work (it runs to 107 printed octavo pages, composed with generous margins and spacing). Readers of his later books, who may sometimes find themselves surfeited by his excessive use of examples that only tenuously exemplify, would breathe a sigh of delight here. The book is an essay, not an encyclopaedia; moreover, no doubt because Frazer soon thereafter deserted philosophy for ethnography, it is one of his few scholarly essays that did not later swell into, or become part of, a compendium. To those who are curious, then, about how Frazer manages a single-stranded argument of some length, the answer is – very competently. Leaving to one side the submissions of the others who competed for fellowships in 1879, it is easy to see why the examiners liked this one. It is enterprising, it has a real subject that is pursued with intelligence and verve, and it is well written.

The work has two announced purposes. The first is to take on the ghost of Plato as an equal, as one philosopher arguing with another; there is no undergraduate tentativeness here. The issue is the one that Frazer regards as the central development in Plato's epistemology, the way in which Plato misunderstood Socrates' theory of knowing and accordingly converted it into his own mistaken theory of being – Frazer calls it Plato's "splendid error." The second aim of the essay, which flows from the first, is to venture a theory, on the basis of the rise and fall of the Ideas, on the perennial question of the order in which the dialogues were written.

Beyond the psychological subject, the most notable feature of the work in terms of Frazer's overall development is the style. *Plato's Ideal Theory* is remarkable for being among the small number of Frazer's sizable compositions to be virtually without irony. It is not that he felt irony would be out of place in a fellowship essay but that only when he came upon anthropology as subject and comparison as method did he assume, or perhaps was forced into, irony. In 1879 his eyes had not yet been opened by the extraordinarily bizarre behavior of our ancient and primitive cousins. When faced with the implicit challenge to make sense of such data, he could have retreated into moral relativism, like most anthropologists. Frazer could not, or would not, do so and consequently adopted an ironic posture from which he never deviated or retreated.

Frazer cited few authorities; that most of them were Anglo-Saxon and empiricist cannot be surprising, for he is writing as an avowed experimentalist and nominalist against the archrealist Plato. But along with the professional philosophers we also find two references to the mentality of "savages": the first comes where Frazer is upbraiding Socrates/Plato for having misunderstood the aims and goals of physical science, and thus for abandoning physics in favor of logic. Having thus forsaken the only path that (according to Frazer) leads to truth, Plato then makes an equally futile attempt to explain phenomena by invoking the doctrine of final causes. As is well known, Plato said that "the good" is the (final) cause of all actions and all things. Here Frazer engages him:

Now it is quite true that every voluntary action of every man is directed to some good or rather to something that seems to him good. But acting thus for a good implies a mind in which there is a picture of an object to be attained. But from the fact that all our voluntary actions are prompted by this mental preconception of an object, were we to infer that every change in physical things is prompted by a striving after the good, we would be committing the same mistake into which savages fall when, from the analogy of their own acts, they ascribe the action of inanimate objects to a principle of life, thought, and feeling inherent in these objects. (66–7)

This sounds like a Tylorian description of the way savages think, but we know from Frazer himself that he did not read *Primitive Culture* until it had been brought to his attention by James Ward, the psychologist and philosopher, whom he met while an undergraduate but seems to have befriended only after he became a Fellow.[21] Thus such ideas concerning primitive thought were "in the air" in 1879 and need not, at least when expressed so generally, be ascribed to any particular source.

The other reference occurs a few pages later when Frazer is speaking of that which can, and that which cannot, be figured in the imagination even though it is readily understandable. He offers Descartes' example of the notion of a thousand-sided polygon.

No one can picture such a figure to his imagination, but every civilized man has a notion of what it is. (I say civilized man, for savages are, it is well known, often deficient in their notions of number, not altogether, but in degrees varying according to their intelligence and progress.) (70)

This could come from Spencer, whom Frazer was then reading, but again it is not necessary to attribute the idea to any single writer or work. The point surely is not the source but that not every young classical scholar in the mid-1870s would have read Spencer (or wherever he found this) on such matters and integrated what he had read into his own mind.

The fellowship meant economic security at a critical time in his life, for he was now able to pursue his scholarly work for six years without having to concern himself about earning a living. His fellowship was of the so-called Title Alpha variety under the Old Statutes of the college, and 1879 was one of the last "unreformed" years in Cambridge, when such fellowships were given out fairly freely. (These fellowships were considerably restricted as part of the university reforms of 1882.) Such awards were known as "prize fellowships" because they were given outright to those who had performed best on the annual fellowship examination and submitted the best dissertations. Their recipients were not required to perform any duties whatever, and although some did carry on scholarly work, many simply collected the stipend and went off to do other things.

The Title Alpha fellowship carried with it one dividend unit (or "modulus," in Trinity parlance). This unit varied with the return received by the college from its investments, but in any case might not exceed £250 per year, tax-free. Inasmuch as the bulk of the college's income was then in the form of rents from farmland, and Britain was in an agricultural depression during most of the quarter century preceding the First World War, in many years in that interval the modulus did not reach £250, and in some years dipped below £200.[22]

A reasonable multiplier for converting retail prices in 1880 to those in England in the mid-1980s is fifty to sixty.[23] (Such a bland statement conceals the fact that in the 1880s people paid for servants, candles, horses, and carriages; in the 1980s they buy dishwashers, video recorders, and sports cars. All that notwithstanding, the multiplier gives a general idea of Frazer's relative financial status.) This means that when the modulus reached £250, it roughly equaled in buying power a mid-1980s after-tax income of £12,500 to £15,000, which is to say that Frazer was, in comparative terms, well off. In the prewar years when the modulus hovered around £200, Frazer often found himself hard-pressed, for it was during this period that he married (and thereby became responsible for his wife's two children from her first marriage), moved house several times, and continued to buy books as unstintingly as he had in his bachelor days.

Frazer's fellowship was renewed three times, in 1885, 1890, and again in 1895; at the last renewal it became tenable for life. This meant that he would receive one modulus annually as a college pension for the rest of his life. But in 1879 of course he knew only that the next six years were secure. Inasmuch as he published nothing during the first years of his fellowship and there are practically no extant letters, it seems likely that he spent some of the time casting about for a significant scholarly project. It is impossible to know whether the unique "Philosophy" notebook of 1880 was a typical product of those years, but it seems reasonable to infer that the study of classics as it was then conducted in Cambridge, and to which he remained committed, offered little scope for his speculative tendencies.

One thing he did do during this time was to study law. On 24 October 1878, as soon as he had returned from his summer in Germany, he was admitted as a student in one of the Inns of Court – the Honourable Society of the Middle Temple. Compulsory examinations for admission to the bar had been introduced in 1872, and the Council of Legal Education, the examining body of the Inns of Court, had accordingly instituted courses of lectures for prospective lawyers. Frazer may have attended some of them; alternatively, as was customary but not compulsory, he may have spent some time in chambers as a pupil of a practicing barrister. Whatever he did, he prepared for and passed the examinations, and accordingly was called to the bar on 26 January 1882. He never practiced.

Why did Frazer study law? When he was named Honorary Bencher (governor) of the Middle Temple in 1931 he said that he had done so to satisfy his father. Daniel Frazer wished his son to have a profession and thus proposed that Scottish favorite, the law.[24] Perhaps Frazer himself did not especially relish the prospect of schoolmastering, the obvious vocation for one with a brilliant academic record like his. It is hard to say how he felt about it when he was twenty-four; certainly later on, when he had come to love the cloistered life of college Fellow, he would not willingly have embraced that of a schoolmaster or indeed even of a university lecturer. In any case, Frazer became a lawyer entirely out of filial obligation; one sees no effect whatever in his work of legal training. He pays no special attention to primitive law or legal institutions, and his methods for gathering and presenting his data are wholly derived from classical and not legal modes of study.

Aside from the blind alley that the law was to represent, not much is known about what Frazer was doing in the early eighties besides reading. His reading at this date, to judge by the library catalogue, was mainly classical, historical, literary, and philosophical, not anthropological or folkloristic. We have flashes of him in the memoir of his close friend James Ward, the psychologist, composed by the latter's daughter, Olwen Ward Campbell. Mrs Campbell is not especially clear about chronology, but it seems to be the early eighties when she describes her father, toiling by day on physiology and psychology, and devoting the evenings "to literature, reading English and Latin by himself, or Dante with Oscar Browning and J. G. Frazer."[25]

Frazer met Ward in 1875, but their friendship became close in the early eighties.[26] Not only did they participate in Oscar Browning's well-known Dante reading circle at King's College, but no doubt Ward, a man of wide interests, suggested many books to Frazer of a philosophical or psychological cast that the latter would not encounter in the usual course of classical reading. The signal example, already remarked, is Tylor's *Primitive Culture*, which Frazer tells us he read at Ward's urging. But having said that, he continues that whereas "the writings of Mr Tylor had first interested him in anthropology, and the perusal of them had marked an epoch in his life," "my interest in the subject might have remained purely passive and inert if it had not been for the influence of another Cambridge friend . . . William Robertson Smith."[27]

Two other documents illuminate this obscure period in Frazer's life. The first is an imposing set of testimonials that he collected from his senior classical colleagues at Trinity in December 1881, when the professorship of Humanity (that is, Latin) came open in the University of Aberdeen.[28] Several qualities are singled out by more than one of his referees: his industry, the soundness of his preparation and his scholarship, the breadth of his reading, the power and originality of his mind, the uprightness of his character. The comments of Dr W. H. Thompson (the Master of Trinity), and of Professor H. A. J. Munro seem based on a largely perfunctory acquaintance; the other referees, however, had been either his tutors or examiners and their letters therefore bear closer examiation. For example, E. W. Blore, the Vice-Master and Frazer's first tutor, recognizes that his stellar performance was all the more remarkable because it had been achieved despite the fact that he had not come up on the usual track of academic success – that is, through an English public school.

The most interesting, because most circumstantial, letter is from Henry Jackson. Jackson rates Frazer as one of the best classical scholars to be educated at Trinity over the preceding fifteen years. But beyond this, Jackson notices Frazer's literary attainments, and in particular the fineness of his style in translations ("His prose compositions in Greek and Latin were often masterly"). Jackson praises as well the "considerable knowledge of mental and moral philosophy" shown by Frazer on the fellowship examination, and the originality and expository power of the dissertation. He concludes on the literary note he has already struck: "I leave it to others, who have had better opportunities of forming an opinion, to speak of Mr Frazer's power of communicating his knowledge; but I should think it strange if his pupils were not stirred by his genuine enthusiasm for all that is best in literature."

Of course Frazer did not get the place, which was filled by the no doubt worthy but obscure J. Donaldson. There can be little doubt that not winning Aberdeen was the best thing that could have happened. Had he been plunged into teaching, committee work, and the social obligations that devolved upon a professor in a small university in a small city, even someone as industrious as Frazer would have been hard put to publish much. Interestingly, had he gone to Aberdeen, he probably would have met Robertson Smith there, but in 1881 and the years following Smith was much occupied with legal problems, and he was away in the Near East then as well. So it is safe to say that even if they had then met, Frazer might well have not been ready to make the move into anthropology, as he was three years later.

The other document that sheds light on Frazer's activities in the early eighties is a manuscript diary that he kept of a three-week trip to Spain that he and his friend Ward made in March 1883.[29] Mrs Campbell in her memoir of her father describes the trip as "most successful" and intimates that it was undertaken at least partly because his spirits were low at the time.[30] From Frazer's diary one would never guess any of this.

Diaries are kept for various reasons – therapy (diary as confessional), mnemonic (diary as *aide-mémoire*), literary (diary as workshop in which ideas are sketched for future development), etc. The best are probably those that draw on a number of these motives, thereby expressing more of the diarist's sensibility. Unfortunately for anyone interested in Frazer's sensibility in 1883, he seems to have regarded a journal strictly as a chronological record and as a help for his memory, which was always bad. Accordingly this volume, and those covering his trips to Greece in 1890 and 1895 and to Rome in 1900, are taken up with public events nearly entirely; they seem to have been composed on the assumption that they should contain nothing that might not be read by a stranger. Even such a resolutely bland and public narrative, however, yields something to the reader intent on detecting the stray unintentional note of personality.

Fortunately, an occasional tremor is to be detected in the marmoreal composure of Frazer the traveler. For example, he and Ward spent the first night of their trip in Paris and accordingly got tickets for the play of the moment – *Fedora*, by Sardou, with Bernhardt in the title role. After a full description of the decor of the theater, Frazer finally gets to the play. "The play itself is far from pleasing, the hero and the heroine are Russians, the play ends with the suicide of the heroine by poisoning." Then follows a synopsis of *Fedora*'s convoluted plot. He concludes: "The acting of Sarah Bernhardt was powerful and Ward was particularly struck by it. The piece was over by midnight, we walked back to the hotel."

That is, Frazer was shocked by the violence and darkness of the action, but unwilling to go beyond "far from pleasing." This impression of stolidity is heightened by a certain priggishness and self-satisfaction. An example: they are in Granada and have just visited the Alhambra. It is evening, and they watch the sunset: "There, sitting upon a stone in a ploughed field of red earth with the shrill song of the cicadas ringing in our ears we watched the sunset and the light upon the Sierra Nevadas, in the hope of seeing them turn rosy red in the evening light. In this we were disappointed: the virgin snow did not blush under our rude gaze." The coyness or archness of this last phrase is pervasive.

In the light of Frazer's later preoccupation with religion, it may be worth setting down an incident that illustrates his reaction to the violent chiaroscuro of Catholic Spain. Valencia, 24 March 1883:

After breakfast walked out to the Cathedral. This is a classical structure in the style, (sit venia dicto) of St Peter's at Rome: in the form of a cross, with a lantern over the intersection of the cross. It is an utterly uninteresting building, in bad taste, disfigured by a mass of tawdry decorations, more fitted for a beer-shop than a church. Various services went on: a stentorian voice chanted a portion of the liturgy, ending each petition with "ora pro nobis," and the people responded, also chanting "ora pro nobis." The effect at first was rather harsh, but as the ear became accustomed to it, it grew musical and even touching. The pictures were veiled, but at a particular point of the service the organ crashed out, bells pealed, and the curtain which hid the pictures behind the high altar rolled back. The effect was rather theatrical.

We are very far here from the reflex anti-Catholicism of the "Dissidence of Dissent" of the 1860s. This determinedly cool, detached account, in which Frazer is willing to admit having been touched by the liturgy and impressed by the service (all the while having seen it as theatricality), reminds us that the attitude called aestheticism was by no means the exclusive property of the Aesthetes, most of whom in 1883 were in any case in their adolescence.

By the 1880s Frazer had long been an atheist (or at least an agnostic); his remark that Kelvin taught him to see the universe as a mechanism implies that he had already arrived at this position at Glasgow. And such scientific and naturalist tendencies would have been powerfully reinforced by his total immersion in Spencer during his undergraduate years. But one's orientation toward religion is not profitably approached by reducing it to a catechism that begins: "Do you believe in God?" This diary entry reveals more about his ambivalent attitude to religion than a discussion of what might be called his "catechetical" atheism.

It is one thing to follow the course of Frazer's progress through Trinity College and the university as measured in awards and performances in examinations, another to understand what they tell us about his life. Not much has been preserved that would inform us about his social life at Trinity, although from the extant letters one can say that no one in his year except John Steggall, who became his brother-in-law, remained either a friend or correspondent in later life. We do know that the *Cambridge Review* was founded in his rooms, in 1879, which implies that he was a member of a group, probably literary in complexion.[31] He definitely had friends, but no doubt he was already a serious, quiet person. He lived quietly, his Scottishness and his modest origins and means (by Trinity's aristocratic standards) perhaps acting as deterrents to much socializing; he likely made a few acquaintances among those reading classics, and he nearly certainly spent the Long Vacations back home with the family in Scotland.[32]

One matter that does invite comment is the disparity between the subject he was reading – classics – and the subjects he seems to have been most interested in, as evidenced by the library catalogue and his early postgraduate work – philosophy, psychology, and literature. This disparity is real enough, but it should not be taken to imply that Frazer was an unwilling "prisoner" of the classics; in view of his lifelong love for the classics and his periodic reversion to them, it seems more reasonable to see his diverse interests as radiating from a literary and philosophical center, a center distinctly humanistic rather than linguistic. Although he was a competent philologist, he never thought of himself as an editor of texts or an exact linguistic scholar.[33] None of his explicitly classical work, from Pausanias to the *Fasti*, was undertaken as a philological project. He was always interested in what textual scholars have traditionally regarded as peripheral. Although he took the greatest of pains on the Pausanias, the only thing left undone was the preparation of the text, which to a classicist is the *sine qua non* of an edition. The commentary grew inordinately, from one volume to four, but only on the archaeological and folkloristic sides, not philologically.

It would be absurd, however, to adduce the narrowness of the Cambridge curriculum as a sufficient explanation of Frazer's choices. What one needs here is a view of what the intellectual context and prospects were for a relatively mature young man like Frazer, entering Trinity in 1874. When he went up to Cambridge fifteen years had elapsed since the publication of *The*

Origin of Species, which is to say that the central issue for serious men in the 1870s was that of belief. Although the great social issues throughout the century had presented themselves at least partly in religious terms, and although the tide among educated persons had been running against religion for some time, once Darwin had pronounced in 1859 the battle was joined. Despite Daniel Frazer's good intentions he could have sent his son nowhere in the realm in the 1870s more likely to act as a solvent to faith than Cambridge.

As might be expected, the universities had always taken an interest in contemporary biblical scholarship. But while Oxford, always actually or incipiently idealist, published *Essays and Reviews* in 1860 as a sign of its first troubled wrestling with the angel of historicism, Cambridge, traditionally impatient with anything nonscientific, and generally more politically liberal than Oxford, had already embraced the new religion of humanity. Sheldon Rothblatt writes:

In Cambridge in the 1860s the very air seemed full of Comtianism, an unhappy [Charles] Kingsley wrote [F.D.] Maurice. Historical method was replacing the older science of human nature with its stress on psychology and logic. Biblical and classical scholarship had become increasingly historical-minded; and anthropology and sociology too, emphasizing the state of social organization and belief in the past, helped draw attention to the historical method.[34]

One may imagine the young Frazer seeing himself as privileged to live in a second Renaissance, in which the intellectual world was to be interpreted afresh in the light of the new "Key to All Mythologies" – evolution. By 1875 the first fierce polemical salvos on evolution had already been exchanged by the older generation, who had emotional stakes in the pre-Darwinian intellectual world. Most of them had had to struggle to understand and accept the new way. But for the thinking men who were young in the 1870s (and for thinking women as well – for example, Jane Ellen Harrison and Beatrice Potter), evolution must have seemed the obvious answer to many great questions, a star to steer by at all times.[35] Everywhere around him Frazer, to the extent that he took part in those long intense conversations that are a feature of undergraduate life everywhere, must have heard his more serious contemporaries discussing "philosophy" – which in this case meant the implications of evolution – far into the night. And their consensus was clear – that the religion that had been dinned into them by parents and schools would no longer do.

Where to turn, then? There existed the examples, inspiring to many in their earnestness and moral intensity, of those prophetic figures whose work constitutes much of the best of the Victorian age – the "sages" (to use John Holloway's word) like Carlyle or Ruskin or George Eliot who were elaborating a quasi-religion of strenuous work and duty, a way of living in the world "as if" there were a God.[36] And there were the utilitarians, the rationalists, and positivists, of whom the most eminent were J.S. Mill and T.H. Huxley and who were ably represented in the younger generation by Henry Sidgwick in Frazer's own college and by John Morley, Frederic Harrison, and W. K. Clifford.

There were, as well, able men on the other side, who strove to refashion and bring up to date the older conservative religious syntheses – Edward Caird, whose "Hegelian jargon" so sickened Frazer during his days at Glasgow, was one. Frazer's library catalogue, our only evidence of his response to his intellectual situation, clearly enlists him among the rationalists. There is no complete match between the books listed and what the leading controversialists produced, but the conclusion is inescapable: half a dozen titles of Mill's, all in editions of the late 1870s, Morley and Harrison (but in the 1880s), and finally and massively Herbert Spencer. The letter to Galton quoted earlier permits us to acknowledge Spencer's influence in Frazer's own words; had it not existed we might have inferred it.

Although Spencer has emerged from obscurity and has attracted much more favorable attention in the last twenty years than he had in the preceding half century, in the seventies of the last century Spencer was acclaimed virtually as the master of those who know. To have become a Spencerian meant that the young man had enrolled himself decisively in the Party of Reason. The consequences of that enrollment, which wavered but never lapsed, may be reserved for the next chapter.

3 · THE VISTA OF ANTHROPOLOGY

WITH FRAZER POISED on the brink of anthropology, it is appropriate to offer an outline of the intellectual, social, philosophical, and historical antecedents of late Victorian British anthropology – especially of the anthropological treatment of "primitive" religion and mythology, Frazer's special subjects. Several such surveys exist.[1] There are, however, two problems with this kind of presentation: the first is that it is usually carried out from the standpoint of the present day, which means that it distorts the questions as they were understood at the time. The second problem arises from the fact that, because of the complexity of the intellectual, social, etc., synthesis embodied in late Victorian anthropology, the outline, if it is to be of manageable size, cannot shed much light on any individual scholar, such as Frazer.

Consider this assemblage of tendencies and movements:

1. The eighteenth-century interest in primitive and exotic cultures aroused by the access of quantities of new information from travelers, missionaries, and explorers in the New World, Africa, and the Orient, and the publicity given to these data by the *philosophes* in their struggle to *écraser l'infâme*;

2. Its political correlative, the great colonialist expansion in the nineteenth century that flooded the imperial capitals, especially London, with new information on the "savages" inhabiting hitherto little-known parts of the world;

3. The indigenous school of eighteenth-century Scottish conjectural historians and moral philosophers, who asserted the mental homogeneity of primitive mankind;

4. The triumph of romantic historicism and comparative philology, with their new focus on mythology as, potentially, the master science for unstanding the "primitive mind" and the primitive world;

5. The strength of the native British antiquarian and folklore movements;

6. The new idea of prehistory and ancient history afforded by archaeological discoveries in the eastern Mediterranean and elsewhere.

Such a relentlessly *zeitgeistlich* approach, however, cannot be faithful to the truth of any individual's life. Silently to equate the life of the scholar with the ideas he expounded is an inadmissible simplification, replacing as it does the actual confused existence led by a real person with the seamless history of thought. Besides giving an undesired Hegelian turn to the exposition, with reason thus seen embodying itself in the lives of succeeding generations of scholars, it undercuts the need for biography at all.

We may not, however, totally dispense with scene-setting. First, and outstandingly, something must be said about the air of intellectual crisis in which the "rise" of anthropology took place in Britain in the last third of the nineteenth century. Second, Frazer's special subject – the study of the "primitive mind," as expressed in the mythology and other beliefs of ancient and primitive peoples – has a long and complicated history, which needs some introduction. In this chapter I shall present the first of these; mythography will be reserved for Chapter 5.

Several scholars have discussed the efflorescence in the last third of the nineteenth century of "scientific naturalism," which constituted for educated people the sharpest philosophical challenge to Christianity in Britain in the nineteenth century.[2] As its name implies, this school of thought rejected supernaturalism and based itself on the methods and theories of natural science. To scientists, philosophers, and scientific publicists like T. H. Huxley, Herbert Spencer, Francis Galton, W. K. Clifford, G. H. Lewes, and Frederic Harrison, the empirical triumphs of science and the extraordinary promise held out by scientific thought and institutions for future dramatic advances in our understanding of the natural world justified a call to thinking people everywhere to renounce the confused subjectivism of religion in favor of the rigorous objectivity of science. Although Spencer's numerous publications through the 1850s constituted a significant preparation for the burst of evolutionary theorizing that was to follow throughout the next forty years, the movement as a whole understandably received its major impetus from the success of *The Origin of Species* (1859).

The orthodox immediately rose to give battle to what were usually seen, in antinomian fashion, as the forces of confusion and mischief.[3] But the aggressive claims of the scientists and their allies produced a second reaction as well among the scholars and thinkers who, although themselves intellectually and emotionally unable to remain Christians, could not or would not accept a universe in which human will and motivation were irrelevant. Accordingly this latter group, much more effectively than the religiously orthodox, took up the challenge laid down by the naturalists, and for a generation (1880–1910) contended with them for the hearts and minds of the educated in the fields of ethics, psychology, and the philosophy of science. Among the leading antinaturalists were Henry Sidgwick, Alfred Russel Wallace, F. W. H. Myers, George Romanes, Samuel Butler, and James Ward. Without rehearsing this lengthy controversy, it is significant that two of these men, Sidgwick and Ward, were Fellows of Trinity College.[4]

By the accident of his college, and then by the academic success which led to his fellowship and the friendships that ensued, Frazer as a young man was thus situated in the midst of an intellectual battleground. He was "present at the creation" when some exceedingly sharp attacks were being launched by both sides about the perennial questions, which had been redefined and pointedly posed anew in the light of evolution: Did empiricism furnish a light any brighter or more reliable than that of religion to illuminate the darkness in which humanity now found itself? Was an evolutionary ethics, eschewing intuition and employing only objective categories, possible? Might purpose be legitimately imputed to any aspect of human or natural life, or was the hope of moral progress an empty dream? Did the associationist psychology accurately represent the play of mind, or was it a radically inadmissible simplification of the complexity of inner reality?

The answers offered by both sides have been superseded. The discovery of the germ plasm as the mechanism of heredity in biology, the exploration of the concept of the unconscious in psychology, and the greater methodological rigor and the turn toward linguistic analysis in philosophy in this century have all meant that their questions are no longer ours. However, the struggle is of more than purely historical interest, for it prefigured similar intellectual conflicts later. Further, it has great human interest because, with both sides agreeing that a mortal blow had been delivered to religion as a sufficient guide to life, the publications that marked the controversy represented a series of efforts made by serious, highminded men struggling to figure out how to live their lives in a world seemingly emptied of meaning. It is against this backdrop that Frazer's achievements and renunciations ought to be seen and evaluated.

It is hard to say how all this intellectual drama affected the young James George Frazer in 1880. If some of his teachers, friends, and colleagues were major actors in it, he was never more than a minor character, and without ambitions to stardom. Although a brilliant student, he was not one of those undergraduates who before going down are already marked for promising public careers. He had opinions on the questions then attracting so much attention, but he never engaged publicly in this great philosophical battle, and he never thought of using his prestigious position as Fellow of Trinity as a springboard for launching himself or his ideas.

Even the solidest of scholars have ambitions, albeit of a rarefied and academic kind. In the early eighties Frazer sought an intellectual project (perforce in the classics, for that was all he then knew) to which he could give himself wholeheartedly; one imputes no mean motive to him in imagining that he also thought that its successful completion would make his name. We have already noted the unusual breadth of his tastes and interests, and when we look more closely at the men in Cambridge who helped form him intellectually, the fact that none was a philologist adds to the feeling that he had already grown dissatisfied with the study of the classics, for that subject was construed in the Cambridge of his day as virtually synonymous with the editing of texts. Behind these mentors, now colleagues and friends, were the personalities of the larger, stormier intellectual world, who always serve as points of attraction and repulsion for any young person entering upon independent intellectual work. In the former group the most important were Henry

Jackson, James Ward, and William Robertson Smith; in the latter, Herbert Spencer, E. B. Tylor, Heinrich Heine, and Ernest Renan.

Of the two groups, the more significant was the first because of the effect that personal example has on the bright and ambitious young graduate. Chronologically, the order in which Frazer encountered these personalities can be stated with assurance: as an undergraduate he heard Jackson's lectures and he read a great deal of Spencer. He also met Ward while an undergraduate, and their friendship grew after he won his fellowship in 1879. In early 1884 Smith came to Trinity and Frazer fell under his spell. He read Heine in 1878, but for reasons that will become clear in the next chapter, Heine is better understood in tandem with Smith. He seems to have come to Renan last of all, in the mid-eighties, when he was about to embark on *The Golden Bough*. It seems reasonable, then, to deal with them in this sequence.

Henry Jackson, Praelector in Ancient Philosophy at Trinity, later Vice-Master of the college and a member of the Order of Merit, was a leading student of Plato in Britain in the latter part of the nineteenth century; equally important, he was the social center of his college for the best part of half a century.[5] From 1864, when he gained his fellowship, through the First World War, when he was Vice-Master, Jackson's door was always open in the evening for all to enter. Many accounts attest to the importance of Jackson's soirées to the life at Trinity during those years, and Frazer's letters show that he too shared in Jackson's magnanimity and counted the older man a friend – indeed, even confided in him when personal difficulties arose.[6] The result of Jackson's perpetual hospitality and his willingness to work hard for academic and administrative reform in the college and university was that he never came to write the book on Plato he was planning all his life. His scholarly work thus consists essentially of a series of seven long articles about Plato's later theory of ideas, each considering that theory in a different dialogue, which appeared in the *Journal of Philology* from 1882 to 1897. Seen in the light of Jackson's scholarly preoccupations and publications, the title and argument of Frazer's fellowship dissertation of 1879 must be seen as an act of discipleship. Frazer's essay is not much more than a development of ideas that appear explicitly in the earlier of Jackson's articles, and which must have figured in his lectures in the mid-1870s, when Frazer heard them.

Jackson was a man of extremely wide mental culture, and when Frazer embarked upon anthropology he found Jackson both interested and informed. Perhaps he was drawn to the subject from his own work on platonic epistemology, which may have led him to consider the general question of the evolution of the human mind. In any case, from a memoir we learn that Jackson was one of the earliest readers of McLennan's work on totemism, and that he was "eagerly, not to say passionately, absorbed . . . with folk-lore and the comparative study of primitive customs. He followed with enthusiasm the investigations of McLennan, Robertson Smith, Tylor, and Sir James Frazer."[7]

In the years leading up to the writing of *The Golden Bough*, because of this knowledge and interest Jackson was able to be of real help to Frazer, acting as a sounding board for the younger man's ideas.

If the first mentor and friend was an idealist philosopher, the second was an idealist psychologist. James Ward (1843–1925), Professor of Moral Philosophy and Logic, and Jackson's nearly exact contemporary, was Frazer's friend for forty-five years.[8] It was he who had suggested that his classical friend might find *Primitive Culture* worthwhile, and he and Frazer traveled together to Spain in 1883. Ward (like Jackson and Robertson Smith) was a man whose many interests set the younger man thinking beyond classics or even anthropology. We know that he was one of the few who were close to Frazer, and that their intellectual intercourse was deep and enduring: in 1911 Frazer wrote of his friend Ward, "with whom I have walked and talked on all subjects in earth and heaven on an average of once a week for many years."[9]

Today Ward is virtually forgotten; in his day (1885–1914) he was one of the premier psychologists in the English-speaking world. Like so many other eminent Victorian intellectuals, he grew up in a religious (and financially straitened) household of Evangelical leanings, and from adolescence was destined for the ministry. He studied theology in a Congregationalist college, but when a friend went to Germany in 1869 to study theology and philosophy, Ward scraped the money together and followed. The impact on his religious and philosophical temperament of the Hegelianism he imbibed in Berlin and Göttingen soon caused him to question his early beliefs, with the result that when he returned to England and was sent as a candidate-minister to a local Nonconformist chapel in Cambridge, within a year his subtleties and doubts made clear to both him and his conservative congregation that he was unsuited to pastoral work.

At this point his life came to resemble in some ways that of the hero of *Jude the Obscure*. Like Jude Fawley, the stonecutter in love with learning who can get no closer to the university than working on its stone exterior, Ward, physically resident in Cambridge but living in the stultifying world of provincial Nonconformity, seemed light-years away from the university. When his inner turmoil quickly grew too great, friends encouraged him to follow his academic vocation. Ward, however, not being a character in Hardy, then had some good luck: he was admitted to the university as a noncollegiate student (at the age of twenty-nine), and in 1873 became a beneficiary of the efforts of the university reformers to expand and enhance the status of the recently established course of study in moral sciences. Ward won a scholarship in that subject offered by Trinity College and, like Frazer, having entered Trinity he never left, for in 1875 he was elected to the first fellowship in moral sciences ever awarded in Cambridge. His dissertation on "The Relationship of Physiology to Psychology" was one of the earliest discussions in Britain of the psychophysical investigations then being carried out by Fechner and others in

Germany. No laboratory scientist, he was the last great practitioner in Britain of the older, speculative psychology, which was inextricably bound up with philosophy. As a philosopher and psychologist he and the Frazer of 1880 spoke the same humanistic and philosophic language.

Ward's main interest – and here is the specific importance for Frazer – was epistemology, which in Britain throughout the century had been thoroughly sensationalist and empiricist in tendency. This is the line of thought, beginning with Locke and including Hartley, J. S. Mill, and Mill's follower Bain, that asserts that the mind is essentially a passive instrumentality that receives pictures of the world from stimuli that impinge on it (via the sensorium) through the action of the mechanisms of association and habit. From introspection and from the idealist impulse in his own nature that had been nourished in Germany, Ward believed this view to be profoundly mistaken, and he (along with F. H. Bradley) delivered the first serious attack on this reigning sensationalism in his seminal article "Psychology" in the ninth edition of the *Encyclopaedia Britannica* (1885).

In the article Ward argued that the mind, far from being passive, had a constitutive and interpretive function as it constructed (and not merely registered) the world that it received; and further, that association, at least as a mechanical process, was wholly inadequate to describe, much less explain, any of the so-called higher mental functions. Now Frazer was no "Wardian" in epistemology, for he always assumed some sort of associationism in his discussions of mental functioning, at least among primitive people. Rather, he was at one with the associationists (and with Tylor) in assuming that the mind's essential function was cognitive, and that the world for the primitive person (as for the modern) essentially consisted of a series of problems that are solved out of disinterested curiosity. The point is that Frazer had, "at home" in Trinity, men like Ward and Jackson vitally interested in questions central to his own work. From the fact that their protracted intellectual intercourse produced no discernible movement in Frazer, we may infer how early and how profoundly the latter was committed to his own position.

Although Herbert Spencer was in the audience when Frazer made his intellectual debut, reading a paper at a meeting of the Anthropological Institute in 1885, we know of no personal relations between the two. Inevitably, then, Spencer's effect on Frazer was expressed differently from those of Jackson and Ward. Spencer had certainly replaced Mill as the dominant intellectual presence in British philosophy in the seventies. Frazer's mind, however, was quite different in kind from Spencer's, and therefore Frazer, although powerfully impressed while a student, did not in the end take much from the older man. He had little inclination toward Synthetic Philosophy, whether Spencer's or one of his own manufacture.[10]

There were inevitably many differences in personality, training, and method between Frazer and Spencer: the former was a university scholar and a classicist with belletristic tendencies; the latter was largely self-educated, trained as an engineer, and antiliterary. Once Spencer had conceived and sketched the outlines of the Synthetic Philosophy in the 1850s, he used a conveniently timed legacy to hire assistants to read for him under his direction and cull facts that he deemed useful or relevant to support his deductions. Frazer, on the other hand, although fundamentally changed neither by friends and mentors at Trinity nor by sometime heroes like Spencer, was not essentially a deductive thinker. Unlike Spencer, who used facts primarily to illustrate his theses, Frazer's attitude toward his mountains of facts was one of humility; he was always willing to change his mind in the light of new information. Spencer was a theorist or he was nothing; Frazer recognized that his own theories and speculations were all provisional, likely to be replaced by better ones, and hoped that his works might endure as storehouses of data.[11]

Fortunately we have an unpublished document from this period that offers some insight into Frazer's philosophical position. It makes clear his intellectual affiliations (and is thus important regarding Spencer) and, even more important, because it was intended for his private use, offers us a chance to overhear him thinking. This series of abstract observations and jottings even sounds the personal note so rare in Frazer's written work. It embodies his hopes, which came to nothing, of establishing himself in the world of academic philosophy.

On 6 April 1880 the 26-year-old Frazer, newly a Fellow of Trinity College, dated a student's notebook and labeled it "Philosophy."[12] This is all that remains of an abortive effort at independent work in philosophy – specifically, in ethics and the philosophy of science. Its immediate impetus was probably the dissertation on Plato completed in the preceding year. We have no idea how long he kept the notebook going, and the striking variation in handwriting of the entries suggests that they may have been composed over a considerable period of time. As it is, although the notebook marks the dead end of Frazer's philosophical aspirations, it is an invaluable place marker in his intellectual development and permits us to see how far back the ideas go that characterize his mature work. From it we may infer something of what "philosophy" and "science" looked like to a young, classically trained Scotsman starting out in the eighties.

To anticipate, the notebook is valuable for at least four reasons: (1) it catches Frazer still searching for both subject and method; (2) it shows him, having already measured Plato and found him wanting, doing the same with his other early mentor, Spencer; (3) its contents reveal neither a flair nor a passion for analysis, which perhaps explains why Frazer put away philosophy so easily and so quietly when, in 1884, he found in anthropology a new, yet "philosophical," subject; and (4) at least one entry hints at some personal upset or trouble, which, considering his general uncertainty about the future, cannot be especially surprising.

41

The notebook contains nine entries, amounting to twenty pages in typed transcript. Some are virtual essays, written in a flowing, expansive hand and amplified with footnotes; others consist of a few paragraphs composed in a distinctly cramped hand that look as if they were squeezed in to fit the space remaining on a page. The first piece (a small, complete essay) comes to eight pages, the second (a fragment that peters out into notes) five and a half, and the remaining seven run from two pages to one sentence in length. Accordingly, most of what follows will be addressed to the first two entries.

Two main questions occupy Frazer: (1) the extent to which the analysis of human institutions ought to be reduced to the study of the human minds that produce them; and (2) the substantive and methodological interrelations of what we now call philosophy of science, psychology, sociology, and anthropology (the chief thinkers in question being Comte, Spencer, William Whewell, and J.S. Mill).

Frazer begins the first essay with a credo that amounts to a partial declaration of independence from Spencer. For although Spencer, at least in the first edition (1855) of *The Principles of Psychology*, had taken a quasi-deistic position in asserting the existence of what he termed an "Unknowable" beyond phenomena, in fact the *Psychology* along with the rest of his work has a naturalist, materialist, collectivist, and sociological cast. Frazer, on the other hand, although undoubtedly a naturalist, seems to have been idealist, individualist, and psychological from the start, so that the dose of Spencer he absorbed as an undergraduate did not change him any more than did thirty years of weekly conversations with Ward. Thus the opening paragraph of the essay, with its bold assertion that collapses physics into psychology ("the only objects of knowledge possible are the operations of [one's] own mind. The science of Nature is therefore the science of Mind"), is a clear rejection of materialism, whether Spencer's or anyone else's.

Like Mill, Frazer is not about to exchange what he saw as the clarities of positive science for the vaguenesses of intuition, and like Mill he is willing to write about science without knowing much about it in detail (he acknowledges his weak preparation and dutifully resolves to study mathematics and science – a resolution never acted upon). He proposes to use the data of modern scientific psychology (by which he means associationism) to dismiss any philosophy that lacks an adequate epistemological basis. Frazer is not among the many Victorian critics of culture (Carlyle, for example) who, having expelled the religion of their youth through the front door, reintroduce it through the back door because they cannot bear the resultant metaphysical void. Nor does he group himself with the growing number of his contemporaries who reject reason and science as the principal valid means of acquiring knowledge. It is impossible to know exactly what his objections to theism were, for he never made them explicit, even in so private a place as this notebook, but it is equally impossible to miss his objections, expressed here and ever afterwards, to materialism.

It has often been noted that the mainstream of British social thought, which can broadly be called positivist, is profoundly individualistic and psychologistic in its origins, methods, and character.[13] Beginning in the seventeenth-century analysis of those conditions that would permit an educated minority to lead lives of personal and political freedom, this tradition gradually replaced the older Christian hierarchical connections of this world and the next with a vision of an assemblage of individuals, living in this world alone, by and for themselves, guided only by a divinely instilled conscience and a divinely implanted reason. The answer to the obvious question why such a mass of atomistic selves, acting solely in and for their own interests as they understood them, did not bring about social chaos, was offered by Locke and reinforced, in a seemingly iron-clad and scientific fashion, by the classical economists: the "law" of the natural coincidence or identity of interests, whereby the efforts of each were accommodated beneficially to the good of all. Such a theory was heartening because it reduced social and economic interaction to individual motivation, which could then be studied by the convenient method of rational introspection. Understanding of institutional phenomena, then, depended upon understanding of individual psychology, and of course the staple of eighteenth-century philosophy was the inquest into human nature, which meant the intricate ways in which the passions were modified and finally controlled by the reason and the will.

John Stuart Mill had suggested that all British thought for the rest of the nineteenth century would be conducted by the intellectual descendants of either Bentham or Coleridge;[14] Frazer is unmistakably of the lineage of Bentham. Bentham begins his utilitarian explorations into morality with an analytic table of motives, to which he thinks he can ascribe all human actions. Bentham, and J. S. Mill after him, were arguing, in a way that reached back to the Renaissance, that men lived in a world that they did and could control because it was a world that they, as persons endowed with certain known psychological attributes, had made. This assumption of the primacy of motive over result, of will over matter, is deeply and powerfully ingrained as a theme in the British philosophical imagination down to the twentieth century, and Frazer was here only subscribing to a tenet held by most educated men.

In this first essay it seems reasonable to suggest that Frazer during his undergraduate years at Trinity with Jackson was seeking an intellectual accommodation between on the one hand his psychologistic and idealistic tendencies, which were a legacy of eighteenth-century Scottish philosophy, and on the other the powerful scientific–naturalistic challenge posed by Spencer, whom he read in one great rush at Cambridge. Veitch, the last straggler in the distinguished line of Scottish psychologists and moral philosophers, was undoubtedly the first to show the young man the importance and scope of epistemology, which may have appealed to him because of the habit of closely examining one's conscience that was a result of an Evangelical upbringing.

If we grant such a mental and philosophical predisposition to the young Frazer, we have next to assess the method and example of Plato (and Henry Jackson). Jackson expounded Plato not as a magnificent episode in the history of thought but as a living philosopher upon whom one might even now found one's life, and his intellectual brilliance and social ascendancy in the college through the 1870s must have made the study of Plato especially attractive to a serious-minded classical undergraduate like Frazer.

At the same time that Frazer was reading Plato, however, he was also reading contemporary philosophers, for, as the notebook shows, he still fancied himself an aspirant to their brotherhood. Contemporary philosophy in English then meant Spencer; many people with more philosophical culture than Frazer were bowled over by him.

And there was much to impress. Spencer's contemporaries were dazzled most by his claim to present an integrated view of all (scientific) knowledge. To be sure Comte and J. S. Mill had offered similar organons, but Comte had remained resolutely on the plane of the abstract, whereas Mill, who did give examples, could not present the cornucopia of illustrations that constitute such a prominent feature not merely of Spencer's style but of his work in general.

In addition Frazer's classical training reinforced his tendency to approach any subject through the patient accumulation of detail; classicists have always assumed that before one was qualified to pronounce on any scholarly question, one had to control *all* the primary and main secondary materials. It is therefore unnecessary to derive Frazer's predilection (or mania) for facts for their own sake and facts as illustrations from Spencer or anyone else.[15]

A more specific link between Frazer and Spencer was to be found in the latter's special concern with the connections between natural science (biology) on the one hand and social science (sociology) and psychology on the other. This kind of integrative power, when applied to the relationships among mind, body, and society, would ensure a deep interest from a reader with Frazer's background and interests. Thus Frazer, like all social scientists, owes a debt to Spencer for certain general notions, such as the idea of understanding societies and social arrangements as the products of complex evolutionary processes, the importance of differentiation as an index to evolutionary development, the necessity of studying psychology as it related to social institutions, and the need to think of social and psychological phenomena as systematically organized and as fulfilling functions. But beyond this overall indebtedness, common to all Spencer's contemporaries and long ago absorbed deeply into the theory and practice of social science, there is something more: Frazer had to come to terms with Spencer in order to arrive at philosophical independence and maturity. Part of this process of assimilation and rejection is being played out in the notebook before us. Obviously such a complex casting-off was not completed in the weeks or months during which the notebook was being written, but just as obviously the notebook is invaluable as an indicator not only of Frazer's position but of widespread notions about science that were "in the air" in Britain in the 1880s.

Beyond its forthright assertion of subjective or epistemological idealism (as this variant of idealism is called), the first essay is most important for the ways in which it presents an unimpeded view of the philosophical underpinnings of Frazer's anthropological work. One sees clearly here that his later subject matter neither required nor caused him to change his presuppositions at all. His idea of primitive metaphysics is entirely congenial to, and is a simple extension of, his own metaphysics. The primitives agree with Frazer when they believe, albeit in a naive way, that the world is entirely derived from mind, whether their own or that of the gods: "In other words, it has been discovered that of the phenomena which men have regarded as composing the external world, the larger number are to be referred not to the outward world but to the mind." Thus in an age of evolutionism it follows that the proper approach to the study of primitive culture is psychological, in order to trace the steps between the childhood of the race and its maturity today, in the form of the European gentleman–scholar. Again, because (to adopt Frazer's phrase) the two long-sundered sisters, Science and Metaphysics, have met and kissed once again, the focus for the proper study of social and institutional origins must shift from the historical to the epistemological. Sociology has been drastically redefined to become the origins and development of thought:

At present, the majority of our sensations are explained by science by reference to a few physical, external principles; but when it is recognised that these physical principles are themselves as much and as merely sensations as the sensations they are at present adduced to explain, then at last the circle will be complete; all sensations will be explained by reference to other sensations, probably to those of a single sense; Science and Metaphysics, those long parted, long discordant sisters, will have met and kissed.

But the origins and development of thought are fundamentally limited by anatomy and physiology, and take place within craniums and not within history, among individuals and not within cultures. It is a small step then to say that all men's minds are basically similar, and another, somewhat larger, step to say that the evolution of mind is the same everywhere because it is not fundamentally influenced by environment or culture but simply follows its own inbuilt psychological laws, which govern its unfolding.

As is so often the case when one attempts to explain an intellectual or psychological event, too many good reasons, each perhaps alone sufficient but confusing and conflicting when taken together, present themselves – what psychologists call "overdetermination." In this case, whatever Frazer's own psychological needs or predisposition, anyone familiar with the history of British thought will immediately recognize that all the themes of the 1880 notebook – the epistemological idealism, the assumption of the psychic unity

45

of mankind, the disregard for history – are typical rather than idiosyncratic and have long and well-known pedigrees. They are staples of the Scottish Enlightenment, and are particularly associated with that nation's school of speculative psychologists and philosophers: Ferguson, Hume, Adam Smith, and Dugald Stewart.

The Scotland of Frazer's day took pride in and made much of the work of its great men of the preceding century. If it was not in his father's library, then it was at the university in Glasgow – probably in the person of John Veitch again – that Frazer became acquainted with the ideas of the Scottish conjectural historians, as the group were called. The likelihood that Veitch was the source is increased when one notes that he was the biographer of Sir William Hamilton, the last, belated representative of the school (and himself the editor of Dugald Stewart), and thus intimately conversant with the history and development of thought in Scotland. Here then is Stewart, who is speaking of Adam Smith's *Dissertation on the Origin of Languages* (1761) but whose comment may in fact be applied to the assumptions and methods of all the Scottish thinkers concerning human nature and its history.

When, in such a period of society as that in which we live, we compare our intellectual acquirements, our opinions, manners, and institutions, with those which prevail among rude tribes, it cannot fail to occur to us as an interesting question, by what gradual steps the transition has been made. . . . On most of these subjects very little information is to be expected from history, for long before that stage of society when men began to think of recording their transactions, many of the most important steps of their progress have been made. A few insulated facts may perhaps be collected from the casual observations of travelers, who have viewed the arrangements of rude nations; but nothing, it is evident, can be obtained in this way, which approaches to a regular, connected detail of human improvement. In this want of direct evidence, we are under necessity of supplying a place or fact by conjecture; and when we are unable to ascertain how men may have actually conducted themselves upon particular occasions, of considering in what manner they are likely to have proceeded. . . . In such inquiries, the detached facts which travels and voyages afford us may frequently serve as landmarks to our speculations; and sometimes our conclusions *a priori*, may tend to confirm the credibility of facts, which, on a superficial view, appeared to be doubtful or credible. . . . In examining the history of mankind, as well as in examining the phenomena of the material world, when we cannot trace the process by which an event *has* been produced, it is often of importance to be able to show how it *may have been* produced by natural causes. . . . To this species of philosophical investigations, which has no appropriated name in our language, I shall take the liberty of giving the title of *Theoretical* or *Conjectural History*; an expression which coincides pretty nearly in its meaning with that of *Natural History* as employed by Mr Hume [in *The Natural History of Religion*], and with what some French writers have called *Histoire Raisonnée*. . . . [Stewart then goes on to instance Montesquieu as a practitioner of this method.] It is thus, that in his occasional elucidations of the Roman jurisprudence, instead of bewildering himself among the erudition of scholiasts and of antiquaries, we frequently find him borrowing his lights from the most remote and unconnected quarters of the globe, and combining the casual observations of illiterate travelers and navigators, into a philosophical commentary of history and of manners.[16]

What Stewart calls Montesquieu's habit of "borrowing his lights from the most remote and unconnected quarters of the globe" becomes, after Auguste Comte, the "comparative method." Now the comparative method is responsible for the first great scientific triumphs in the nineteenth century – in anatomy and philology – but in those disciplines early agreement had been reached about what was to be compared and what sorts of inferences might reasonably be drawn from the comparisons. In the case of the social sciences like anthropology in which the comparative method was to be used on a grand scale (and Frazer was only its most industrious practitioner), no such agreement was ever arrived at. Instead, in writers like Tylor or Frazer, the most diverse sorts of ethnographic data, which from our point of view have at best tenuous connections with one another, were juxtaposed.

This was felt to be legitimate because the social scientists of the last third of the nineteenth century, completely under the spell of Darwinism,[17] simply assumed the orderly and rectilinear development of the human mind, along with the rest of the organism.[18] And since they were dealing with preliterate societies, which by definition had no records to illustrate the local version of the universal and inexorable march of the growth of Mind, artifacts and items of behavior from evolutionary sequences all round the world were pressed into service to supply the dynamic element needed to move from one "stage" to the next, and thus to fill in the many missing rungs on the developmental ladder. If one assumes that mental and therefore cultural evolution did take place, and if some behavior has been observed in, say, the jungles of the Amazon but, unfortunately, not in the jungles of the Congo, and if – all-importantly – one assumes the psychic unity of mankind – then it is perfectly in order to use data from the Amazon to make a point about the Congo.

Aside from being what may thus be called a "survival" of Enlightenment conjectural history, the essay also shows us the dangers of simply placing Frazer as one of "the party of humanity" – the rationalist, secularist materialists who incarnated triumphant Benthamite social science in the last quarter of the nineteenth century. There is no doubt that Frazer was what we generally call a rationalist, and that he did share some of the characteristic Benthamite traits – he cared hardly at all for history and complaisantly replaced it with logic, as he offered speculative reconstructions of blanks in evolutionary sequences, based on what he regarded as the likeliest line of development;[19] he undoubtedly assumed that progress was the law of both life and of history. But in his idealism he was distinctly atypical. Note the distinction that Spencer himself drew rather exasperatedly between himself and Comte in a letter to G. H. Lewes:

What is Comte's professed aim? To give a coherent account of the progress of *human conceptions*. What is my aim? To give a coherent account of the progress of the *external world*. Comte proposes to describe the necessary, and the actual, filiation of *ideas*. I propose to describe the necessary, and the actual, filiation of *things*. Comte professes to interpret, as far as is possible, the genesis of the phenomena *which constitute nature*.

The one end is *subjective*. The other is *objective*. How then can one be the originator of the other?[20]

By this criterion Frazer is clearly a Comtean, and we have here yet another example of the dangers of dichotomies, for here Mill's suggestive distinction between the Benthamites and the Coleridgeans breaks down once one expands the field of reference outside Britain.

Frazer continues with his ambitious program, which is fundamentally a methodological one. By changing the emphasis from the study of the structure and development of the physical world to the structure and development of the percipient mind, he hopes to illustrate the "general course of scientific procedure" – in short, he wants to think about the best way to think and the best way to study thinking.

Frazer asserts that the general evolutionary path of the progress of thought is from the general to the particular. Generalization is what he calls "reverse or backward thinking," whereas its opposite, particularization, is progressive, or forward, thinking. The reason thought has developed from the former to the latter is, he writes in a burst of unadulterated Spencer, that

as multiplication of differences (differentiation) is the essence of particularisation, so it is the essence of the development of things, most obviously of organised beings. . . . So in particularisation; we start from a general idea consisting of a very few qualities, and proceed downwards through genera, sub-genera, species, sub-species, etc., at every step adding to the number of diverse qualities.

This last sentence is not a bad description of the organizational principle of *The Golden Bough*, although its strict Linnaean tendencies are everywhere belied by the centrifugal impulse toward excursion and digression.

This notebook is the only extant nonepistolary document from the 1880s in which we may overhear the rhythms of Frazer's thought; in that sense it resembles the dissertation on Plato, for all the rhetorical artfulness of that work, rather more than the flat diary of the trip to Spain with Ward. Thus we have a good deal, in this first entry, of Frazer talking to himself on paper – making an assertion, seeing difficulties, and adjusting his ideas accordingly. When I remarked that the notebook showed no special flair for analysis, I did not mean unfairly to compare it with published work, for had Frazer decided to let any part of it appear, he would certainly have refined it. For that reason it is all the more valuable here.

There is one last teasing detail in the first entry. Immediately following the sentence quoted above on the need to counter vulgar materialism, he counts as a secondary but nonetheless real benefit of keeping this notebook the following: "at least the inquiry, if I pursue it, may give me occupation and interest, to the exclusion of more melancholy thoughts." Inasmuch as we never again hear of these melancholy thoughts, they merit a pause. Frazer's life was, in Freudian terms, a monument to sublimation, in which all his formidable energies were channeled into work and more work. This entry in the notebook represents one of the few times when Frazer had enough time to indulge such thoughts and had enough privacy to express them. Nothing in the self ever disappears completely; even though he would soon find his subject and his method, this note of sadness will recur.

The second entry in the notebook, written in a smaller hand, is a much less considerable effort. Despite its impressive title, "[On the] Deontic sciences or ontic sciences," it peters out disappointingly. So far as it goes, it shows Frazer a wholly conventional moral thinker in the utilitarian mode. (So far as this notebook goes, Henry Sidgwick, the greatest man after J. S. Mill in utilitarian ethics, might never have existed.)

Frazer begins straightforwardly enough with the distinction between two kinds of science, those that study what is (the ontic) and those that study what ought to be (the deontic), and the relation between them. He has no doubt that what ought to be derives from what is, and that therefore our moral sciences (law, ethics, psychology) are – must be – faulty in direct proportion to the lacunae in our knowledge of the physical world on which they depend: "Thus the Deontic sciences can only progress with the progress of the Ontic; progress in the latter is a necessary *preliminary* to a true progress of the former; and on the other hand Ontic sciences only exist as a *means* to the Deontic." The final clause, however, suddenly turns the point completely around – the scientist is right to look down on the inexactitude of the philosopher, but the latter, for all that he trails behind, is focused on the subject of greatest interest – ourselves and, by implication, our selves.

With this as basis, Frazer immediately takes an unexceptionably Benthamite position: thus, "The aim which every man constantly proposes to himself at every moment of his waking life is happiness. All feelings are either pleasurable or painful. Happiness is pleasurable feeling (pleasure)." Frazer will countenance none of the difficulties that John Stuart Mill and Sidgwick wrestled with: for him happiness and pleasure are unitary and quantifiable, and we need not concern ourselves with whether it is preferable to be Socrates dissatisfied or a pig satisfied. This is distinctly Old Believer Benthamism for 1880.

At this point Frazer moves to a further consideration of the effect of the ontic on the deontic. As the ontic sciences continue to add to our knowledge of the natural world, they are also

constantly throwing light upon the origin of feelings, whose springs were previously unknown and therefore uncontrollable: and that when the causes thus revealed are not only knowable [but] also controllable by us, we are enabled by controlling these causes, to controll [*sic*] also the feelings which are the effects of these causes – we win for Man a fresh realm, fresh means of happiness, from Nature; – what was once thought *necessary* is found to be liable to the human will.

His notion of the role of the emotions in the overall economy of the self is standard empiricist–sensationalist. Feelings are the effects of stimuli that impinge from without; he has no thought about any inherent physiological capacities of the percipient that would permit him to adapt to these stimuli, no thought about innate patterns of response. Frazer's gaze is resolutely fixed on the philosophical side: as more becomes known, less is involuntary (the emphasis throughout is on "control"); the less that is involuntary, the greater the opportunity for man to exercise moral autonomy. A dramatic view, implying (in the best Victorian fashion) strenuous moral effort to reclaim the emotions for the will. This passage could have been written by a psychologist or moral philosopher in Britain at any time between 1860 and 1885 – that is, between the publication of the work on the emotions of Mill's disciple Alexander Bain and the attacks on associationism by Ward and Bradley.

The consequences of his main point – the subordination of the moral to the natural sciences – are optimistic because, as anyone could see, the ontic sciences are progressing apace, so that we might directly expect correlative advances in the deontic sciences as well. Additions to our knowledge of the natural world permit us increasingly to appreciate the interdependence of all phenomena, with less and less of human conduct construable as ethically neutral (that is, conducing to neither pleasure nor pain). This because such neutrality is really but another name for our ignorance; as we come to understand better (that is, more accurately, more scientifically) how things hang together, we shall be better able to decide on the best course of action. It is unfortunate that Frazer never offers a list of incentives or motives that would make men who know the right wish to do the right, except for the enlightened self-interest implied in the equation of happiness and pleasure. The focus throughout this entry, and indeed throughout the notebook, is the individual. Only the most passing mention is made of the effects and constraints on the individual of society; there is less Spencer here than we should expect from such a self-proclaimed Spencerian. But of course this individualistic and psychologistic emphasis is entirely in keeping with his later work in anthropology; once again one notes how little Frazer had to adjust his old preconceptions to his new subject-matter.

The essay then degenerates into a series of notes that sketch the lines for continuation, which would have been ambitious. He first would distinguish between "(1) Law with its artificial (though real) motives and sanctions, and (2) Religion with its supernatural (and unreal?) motives and sanctions." After a discussion of the conflict between various motives and sanctions, he would then have demonstrated that a perfect morality is theoretically possible when and if science completely uncovers all the secrets of nature, thus placing all life (again theoretically) under the conscious control of mankind. Finally, harking back to the Enlightenment roots of Benthamite speculation, there is "Reconcile the happiness of the Individual and of the Race," which is a larger recasting of the problem of the classical economists referred to above. In the light of this optimistic program, we may say his later investigations into the foundations of our social institutions revealed a tension between the Individual and the Race that he never imagined in 1880. Once he came upon this tension, he never made up his mind whether the needs of self and society are in fact reconcilable.

On this same subject we have a somewhat different viewpoint expressed in the fifth entry. Once again embarking from the same point – that the deontic sciences must wait upon the findings of the ontic – he sees that any system of morals must, by definition, be understood as provisional. He then turns to psychology which, because pursued introspectively, seemingly did not depend upon data from and about the physical world. But this is not the case, says Frazer. Introspection is insufficient (although he does not say why), which implies that psychology must someday be assumed into some ontic science (like neurophysiology). Although he is unclear where we ought to look for the outlines of a future psychology, he does make it clear that psychology must recognize that it depends on the achievements of physical science.

Finally, a comment on the third item. This begins with the several sciences arranged on a ladder, from those that study the simplest phenomena to those that study the most complex – a notion, as Frazer himself says, that has been "a commonplace since Comte." Once again he is interested in the interrelationships of the sciences, and once again he advances the idea of closure: "science will be complete, when the data of each special science are fully explained by the science next below it in complexity, so that the whole series of special sciences shall be run into each other without any gaps." Frazer, however, is begging the question: is it true that each science differs from the one beneath it only in terms of the greater complexity of their common elements, or is the difference qualitative as well as quantitative? In particular, is life something specific to physiology and therefore not present (or implied) in chemistry, or is life "only a new and more complex mode of combination of chemical forces?"

Although Frazer never pursued this question as it concerns the special status of life, there is no doubt that he did not agree with Mill, Bain, and the other materialists (including, later, Freud) in believing that psychology could and would be shown to be finally a special case of physiology. For Frazer, not only were the data of psychology irreducible to those of any other science, but it seems likely that he thought of psychology as the queen of the human sciences, and certainly the mother of anthropology and the study of religion. Despite the influence of Robertson Smith he never felt the need to learn more about sociology; despite his later admiration for Malinowski's work on "primitive" economics, he never thought that subject of sufficient importance to learn about it himself, much less use economic data or categories in his own analyses of primitive life; and despite the example of Tylor and of his own long-time friendship with Baron von Hügel of the Cambridge anthropological museum, he never asked whether the evolution of technology might itself have caused any important change in human attitudes. By 1880, then, Frazer at the age of 26 was a man with certain basic ideas he felt it unnecessary to re-examine; a man, moreover, marked by curiosity and erudition, dissatisfied with the ordinary prospects for one with his background and therefore ambitious enough, or at least venturesome enough, to look elsewhere should something offer itself.

4 · PAUSANIAS AND ROBERTSON SMITH

In the academic world of the early 1880s Frazer held an immensely promising position, but nothing he had touched had come to anything, and his future was uncertain. He had qualified in law but his heart was not in it and he had not pursued it; his efforts in philosophy seem to have petered out; he had tried for a classical post at Aberdeen and been rejected. But his fellowship would run until 1885, and he was under no pressure to make a move. So he continued to read omnivorously, following new interests as they appeared. Therefore, despite the lack of explicit evidence, it seems safe to say that he had begun reading anthropology before 1884. He had probably started haphazardly, his imagination piqued by the footnotes in *Primitive Culture*, which he read at this time; perhaps Henry Jackson or some other friend guided him. In any case we know that by the end of the decade his anthropological files were so extensive that William Robertson Smith credited them as an important source for *The Religion of the Semites* (1889).[1] It is most unlikely that all this reading began only after Frazer met Smith in 1884.

But although he discovered and become quickly enamored of anthropology in the mid-eighties, he did not abandon classics. He never believed that the two subjects were in conflict or that he had to choose between them. On the contrary, it was while working on Pausanias that he first began to see the power of anthropology in the exposition of a classical text. Which is to say that he was distinctly ready when he met Smith and was actively inducted into the anthropological fold. But 1884 was notable as well because it marked his first publication.

In that year the London firms of Whittaker & Co. and George Bell announced a new co-publication, in their well-known Grammar School Classics series – a second edition, revised, of Sallust's Catalina and Jugurtha.[2] The reviser was the totally unknown 30-year-old James George Frazer. In the preface to this second edition (dated 5 June 1884) he writes that he was approached by Bell and asked to produce a new and expanded version of the recension by the well-known classical scholar George Long (1800–79), which had first appeared in 1860. Bell understandably wished to use as much as he could of Long's text, and thus Frazer says that he was told to produce neither a new text nor a new commentary but instead to edit (that is, include, explain, and defend) some of Long's manuscript notes that had not appeared in the first edition. Aside from this, Frazer's contribution consists of the final section

53

of the volume (pages 287 to 349), containing a new selection of extracts from Sallust's histories ("Orationes et Epistulae ex Historiis Excerptae"), complete with introduction and notes.

The preface is notable for the first taste it gives of Frazer's scholarly diligence. Although he was not presenting a new text, he informs the classics master reading his preface that he has consulted no fewer than five recent (German) editions, and he cites the work of still another two German scholars on the difficult question of Sallust's chronology.[3] The main debt acknowledged, however, is to his friend and contemporary at Trinity College, the Latinist J. P. Postgate (1853–1926), to whom he turned for help on knotty points and who read and revised the proofs.[4] We may suppose that Postgate suggested Frazer to Bell when the publisher came looking for someone to revise Long's text.

Frazer was occupied with several projects simultaneously at this time. We know from the preface that Frazer completed Sallust on 5 June, but we do not know when he began it. Given the amount of work he put in, in order to make his debut in print as auspicious as possible, Sallust probably occupied him for much of the first five months of 1884. In July of that year he contracted with George Macmillan to prepare a translation of Pausanias; one would like to know when he began to work on it.

First, however, a few words about Pausanias, who is well known only to classicists, archaeologists, and ancient historians. Pausanias the Periegete (Traveler) was a geographer and antiquary of the second century A.D. who traveled widely in Greece and wrote a guidebook to what he saw. His *Description of Greece* is invaluable today because, although he omits much that we would gladly have, he was generally thorough and comprehensive. Happily for us he was content to describe what he saw faithfully and without rhetorical elaboration; inasmuch as nearly the whole of the architectural "glory that was Greece" was still standing and in good order, his account of it is by far the best that has come down to us. It has served as the principal documentary guide to archaeologists digging in Greece over the last hundred years, as well as to modern travelers interested in making sense of the ruins and excavations. Pausanias had as well a special and abiding interest in religion, myth, and folklore. When out in the countryside, he often noticed rites and customs that seemed odd and old-fashioned to him and had long since become extinct in Athens. Inquisitive by nature, he was always asking questions about the meaning of what he saw; as a result he has become an irreplaceable, and often a unique, witness to daily life and especially to religious practice in Roman Greece.

With our hindsight knowledge of the monument of scholarship that Frazer finally produced, it is tempting to ascribe its *raison d'être* to the obvious congruence of Pausanias' and Frazer's ethnographic and antiquarian interests. There can be no doubt that both of them were deeply taken with unusual religious beliefs and behavior, and both were more than usually inquisitive. No intellectual project, however, is undertaken for purely intellectual reasons, although *post facto* justifications are frequently offered to make it all seem a selfless struggle for Truth. It is hard to imagine anyone spending so long on something as recondite as Pausanias unless there is basic sympathy between himself and his subject. There was in addition the literary challenge presented in the problem of turning Pausanias' contorted and clumsy Greek into graceful English. We should not, however, assume that Frazer knew and intended from the start that his edition would take on the characteristics and the proportions that it finally did. His ethnographic orientation certainly grew over the course of the long project. Fortunately, the documents exist to permit us to understand to some extent how the work evolved.

Until Frazer came to the task, editions of Pausanias had run to two or at most three octavo volumes of text and notes.[5] After more than thirteen years of work, however, Frazer produced in 1898 no fewer than six thick quarto volumes, running to more than three thousand pages, consisting of an English translation (one volume); a huge commentary, unexampled in size before or since (four volumes); and maps, plans, and indexes (one volume) – but no Greek text. Frazer undoubtedly is the greatest commentator that Pausanias has ever had, in that he gave more time, effort, and attention to that author than has anyone else, and because he explained more about Pausanias than anyone else had ever done. Obviously, before he could translate the text he had first to construe it, so in that special sense he did edit it. But aside from fifty-two pages of critical notes there is no text, so that his Pausanias is therefore not properly an edition as classicists understand the term.

The entire project began, however, as a translation. This we know from the correspondence between Frazer and his publisher and friend for fifty years, George A. Macmillan (1855–1936).[6] The letters show that Frazer was already working on Pausanias by mid-1884, for on 6 July 1884 (that is, a month after Frazer finished Sallust) Dr James Gow (1854–1923), classical scholar and later headmaster of Westminster School, wrote as follows to his friend Macmillan:

A particular friend of mine, J. G. Frazer (Fellow of Trin: Second Classic in 1878), is very keen on translating Pausanias and wants to find a publisher. He has spoken to Bell about it (for whom he has edited a Sallust) but Bell wanted him to tinker an old translation, which he wouldn't do. I think a moderately cheap translation of Paus [*sic*] would pay very well just now and I am sure that Frazer would execute it extremely well. He is an excellent scholar, of prodigious learning and industry, and he wouldn't put his name to a book which wasn't as good as it could be made. He is also a reasonable person of methodical habits and would be inclined to meet any practical suggestions in a proper way. I should be glad if you could assist him.[7]

With this introduction Macmillan, who was himself a man of intellectual parts,[8] having been one of the founders in 1879 of the Society for the Promotion of Hellenic Studies, wrote to Frazer immediately upon receipt of

Gow's letter. He said (on 7 July) that he would indeed be interested in a one-volume Pausanias containing "a thoroughly scholarly yet readable translation" and "some notes," the whole to serve the needs of serious tourists unable to read Greek.[9] Such travelers were then becoming more numerous in Greece in the wake of the publicity received by the spectacular finds of Schliemann in the 1870s (which is probably why Gow thought that a translation of Pausanias might be a paying proposition). In that first letter Macmillan said that he thought the venture faced an uncertain commercial future and therefore proposed to publish it on a "half-profits" basis – that is, the publisher to pay all production costs and share equally with the author any profits that might accrue. (Frazer would go on to publish most of his books with Macmillan on a half-profits arrangement.)

On 12 July Frazer replied, in the first letter of a correspondence that would last fifty-five years, accepting Macmillan's offer but stating that "With regard to the size of the book I do not think it would be possible to include a translation and notes (at all adequate) within one volume." He pointed out that the Greek text alone, in the Teubner edition, ran to 850 pages. Instead he proposed "to issue the translation separately, to be followed by a volume of notes or perhaps a regular edition." If Macmillan was unwilling to do this, then Frazer would proceed with the translation and the commentary, which might be appended or else published later separately.

On 1 August, having had no response, Frazer wrote again to ask whether he might regard Macmillan's silence as implying assent to his suggestions regarding the size and scope of the work. For the first time he spoke of the possibility of "two volumes (Prof. Colvin[10] in conversation even spoke of three, but I hope two would be sufficient)," and raised as well the question of maps and plans, which would be "almost indispensable."

His letter alarmed Macmillan, who replied on 8 August that Frazer's idea of a translation and commentary running to several volumes entailed a greater risk than he cared to assume. He suggested that Frazer continue with the translation and continue as well to collect the materials for a commentary, "of which if space allowed a summary or selection might be given in the same volume with the translation."[11] Frazer's next letter to Macmillan (11 October) passed on a suggestion of Colvin's

that it might be desirable to issue the translation in separate parts, following Pausanias' own division into Attica, Corinthiaca, i.e., so that they might be employed as handbooks by travellers in Greece, each part with its notes and plans forming a handy and portable volume. If this plan meets with your approval I would hope to be able to bring out the first part (Athens and Attica) with commentary in the spring. . . . I may add that I have consulted Prof. Robertson Smith and that he entirely approves of Prof. Colvin's suggestion.

Macmillan at this point firmly called a halt to the imaginings of Frazer, abetted by Colvin and Robertson Smith. On 22 October he replied that publication in parts was out of the question because Pausanias' description of

Greece contains no fewer than ten parts, which made it a commercial nightmare.[12] However, he now accepted that the work should consist of "two handy volumes, answering perhaps to the Teubner division, each containing at the end the commentary which concerned that moiety of the text." There the matter rested – Frazer was to complete the translation and confine himself to such notes as were absolutely necessary for the traveler with volumes in hand. Thus at the outset Frazer and Macmillan agreed that what was needed was something portable and usable on the spot.

How and why the work took the form that it did when it appeared at long last are questions that require attention because the Pausanias, for better and for worse, is the prototypical Frazerian opus in its history of modest origins followed by riotous growth. This pattern of uncontrollable swelling became the rule in all his best-known works: *The Golden Bough*, originally a three-page essay on "Taboo" in the *Encyclopaedia Britannica*, grew to two volumes in its first edition (1890), went to three in the second edition (1900), and then expanded to no fewer than twelve (including index) in the third edition (1911–15), with the fourth edition appearing embryonically as a thirteenth volume, *Aftermath*, in 1936; an *Encyclopaedia* article in 1885 on "Totemism" became an 87-page book in 1887, and in 1910 turned into *Totemism and Exogamy*, four stout volumes comprising more than two thousand pages; *Folk-Lore in the Old Testament* started life as a long series of notes contributed to the Tylor *Festschrift* in 1907 and ended, eleven years later, as three bulky volumes.

In 1884, however, Frazer then was given his orders to translate Pausanias, and translate he did. His next letter to Macmillan about Pausanias comes nearly four years later, on 7 June 1888, and begins: "My translation of Pausanias was finished (but not revised) more than two years ago, namely in the spring of 1886." For the commentary (he says) he has gone through most of the foreign archaeological journals, noting anything important regarding his author. Finally, he has amassed "a considerable quantity of ethnological parallels illustrative of the Greek myths and customs described or referred to by Pausanias." He adds that much of the annotation on the "Attica" (that is, Pausanias' first book) was written out in the form of lectures that he delivered in the May term of 1886 – the earliest of his sporadic efforts as a college lecturer – but that these would form only "a foundation for the more exact and elaborate commentary which I propose to publish."

By 1886, then, Frazer had decided that he was going to prepare a full commentary, whether or not Macmillan would publish it. He also said that he discontinued working on Pausanias at the close of 1886 and had yet to return to him. The reason is that he had been collecting, and continued to collect, materials for a "work on comparative mythology," "my usual plan being to have gathered and arranged all my materials before I begin to write. The writing then takes comparatively little time." The work he had begun was, of course, *The Golden Bough*.

The Golden Bough therefore grew directly out of, and indeed marked an intermission in, the preparation of Pausanias, which explains to some extent why the latter took so long to appear. In addition the £100 advance that he received from Macmillan upon completion of *The Golden Bough* paid in large measure for his first trip to Greece (in 1890) to see for himself how the work of the archaeologists, then proceeding briskly, might be incorporated in order to enrich and clarify the text of Pausanias. But the two works are more closely related even than that. For it was precisely his effort to make sense of the religious, mythological, and folkloric element so prominent in Pausanias that made him see how similar the beliefs of second-century Greeks seemed to those of the primitives he had read about in Tylor and talked about continually with Robertson Smith. As a result his old ideas concerning the nature and quantity of data appropriate for annotating Pausanias must virtually have "exploded." At the same time he saw the possibility of explaining the "curious rite" in the Arician grove by analogy with the workings of the "savage mind" as exemplified in innumerable instances of religious belief and behavior gathered from around the world. Thus, although for purposes of discussion I shall separate Pausanias from the first edition of *The Golden Bough*, they must be seen as intimately connected.

Although we do not know exactly when Frazer began work on Pausanias, it is safe to say that not only had he decided to prepare the translation but he had already started working on it before he permitted James Gow to write to George Macmillan in July 1884. But in the winter of 1883–4, only a few months earlier, another event occurred that altered everything for him. For it was then that he met William Robertson Smith, the man who would introduce him to anthropology, become his best friend and mentor, and completely change his life. There can be no doubt that it was the intervention of Smith, and the consequences that flowed from it, that changed Frazer's ideas about Pausanias and the world of classical antiquity and led to *The Golden Bough*.

William Robertson Smith (1846–94) was the brilliant Scottish biblical scholar, Semiticist, and anthropologist who, more than any other single person, succeeded in interpreting for Britain a century of German "higher criticism."[13] For his pains Smith was prosecuted in the last great heresy trials in the British Isles; although he was exonerated, the protracted strain of that ordeal, together with his demonic energy that led to chronic overwork, undoubtedly shortened his life and prevented him from completing what would have been his masterpiece, *The Religion of the Semites*.[14]

Smith was the first person in Britain to apply the comparative evolutionary anthropological approach to the study of an entire family of religions, the Semitic. At home both in all the appropriate languages and in the methods of the German critics – he had studied with Lotze, Lagarde, Ritschl, and Wellhausen – and most unusually a man who had actually spent time in the Near East, he was, remarkably, the product of the same denomination as Frazer, the Free Church of Scotland. Smith, a philological prodigy who was already Professor of Hebrew and Old Testament at the church's theological college in Aberdeen at the age of twenty-three, was light-years ahead of his coreligionists; it was, therefore, only a matter of time before his views became an occasion for scandal to some of them. In the event, the *casus belli* was the articles "Angel" and "Bible" that he had written in 1875 for the *Encyclopaedia Britannica*, of which he was then coeditor. In them he had attempted to consider the biblical texts naturalistically, as written by men rather than dictated by God and therefore as reflecting the attitudes of the times and places in which they were composed; times which were substantially different from his own.

In short he treated them as difficult texts that would yield up their meanings only after the same sort of patient historical and philological study that had transformed the nineteenth century's understanding of Greece and Rome. Specifically, he asserted in the offending articles that the Old Testament, far from being monolithic and therefore homogeneous and unified, was in fact an anthology of books written, edited, and re-edited over many centuries that therefore did not necessarily harmonize with one another; that not every part of the Bible was, or could be, literally true, and that much of the text was intended and should be construed figuratively; that the typological citation in the New Testament of passages from the Old Testament did not prove that the earlier passages were prophecies that had been fulfilled; and that the existence of angels was not a biblical article of faith but had to be inferred from the text – in short, he offered an epitome of contemporary German higher criticism.

Predictably, a few of his fundamentally inclined fellow churchmen felt that Smith had launched a root-and-branch assault on the very basis of Protestant Christianity in general and of the Free Church in particular, and reacted by preferring charges of heresy against him before a series of church tribunals. Smith, of a combative temperament himself, would neither withdraw his statements nor promise to muffle his voice in the future. A protracted series of acrimonious hearings and trials concluded in his vindication, but by then he was too notorious to hold a position anywhere in Scotland. It was thus "providential" that William Wright, Adams Professor of Arabic at Cambridge, whom Smith had met when they were both members of the committee working on the Revised Version of the Bible, was able to secure his appointment as Lord Almoner's Reader in Arabic at Cambridge.

Smith was made a member of Trinity College in October 1883, and came to Cambridge at Christmas of that year. Happily, we have a remarkably full and detailed account by Frazer of his meeting with Smith. The account exists because in 1897, three years after Smith's death, a friend, John F. White, wished to write an appreciation of Smith. He wrote to Frazer, along with others of Smith's friends, for information and reminiscences; most unusually, because Frazer was neither a very expressive man nor one given to writing emotional letters, on 15 December 1897 he responded at extraordinary length (this is by far the longest letter of the many hundreds extant). The following extracts all come from this unique source.[15]

When he came to Cambridge he joined Trinity and had a very small set of rooms allotted to him in Whewell's Court. . . . I used to see him at dinner in the college hall and in the street for some time before I made his acquaintance. But one evening, I think in January 1884, when I had gone, contrary to my custom, to combination room after dinner he came and sat beside me and entered into conversation.

I think that one subject of our talk that evening was the Arabs in Spain and that, though I knew next to nothing about the subject, I attempted some sort of argument with him, but was immediately beaten down, in the kindest and gentlest way, by his learning, and yielded myself captive at once. I never afterwards, so far as I can remember, attempted to dispute the mastership which he thenceforward exercised over me by his extraordinary union of genius and learning. From that time we went walks together sometimes in the afternoons, and sometimes he asked me to his rooms. . . . Afterwards he moved to larger and better rooms. Here he staid [sic] till he left Trinity for Christ's College, where he was elected to a Fellowship [in 1885]. On selfish grounds I regretted his migration to Christ's, as it prevented me from seeing him so easily and so often as before.

Smith may have been glad to hear a Scottish voice (Frazer later remarks that Smith "once introduced me as 'one of the Scotch contingent' to a great friend of his, the late professor of Arabic, William Wright, himself a Scotchman"); in any event they soon became friends. Smith quickly saw that his compatriot was clever and that Pausanias and Sallust did not occupy all his waking hours. As editor of the *Encyclopaedia Britannica* he was always on the lookout for likely contributors and immediately pressed Frazer into service.

In those days volumes of the *Britannica* were published one or two at a time, as completed. By 1884 the first seventeen volumes, covering the letters A through O, had already appeared; thus it was that Frazer's contributions are all on subjects that begin with P and subsequent letters. Frazer continues:

While he was still living in Whewell's Court [in 1884] he gratified me very much by asking me to contribute some of the smaller classical articles to the *Encyclopaedia Britannica*, of which he was then joint editor. My little articles pleased him and he afterwards entrusted me with a more important one, that on Pericles. I was flattered by the trust, but when I came to write I could not satisfy myself and made great efforts to get him to transfer the work to someone else. He did his best to relieve me, even telegraphing (if I remember aright) to a man at a distance to ask him to undertake it, and when all proved fruitless he actually came to my rooms and began writing with his own hand at my dictation or from my notes to oblige me to make a start with it. This may serve to give some faint notion of the endless trouble he had to endure as editor of the Encyclopaedia.[16]

Again and again in his life, whenever Frazer was put under pressure or confronted by a *sudden* personal challenge – one that required him to make up or change his mind quickly, to show flexibility, to meet new people, to take an active role in public life – his characteristic and immediate response was either ambivalent (that is, self-doubt, leading to anxiety and vacillation) or else straightforwardly negative. His brilliant record notwithstanding, he seems always to have lacked self-confidence and to have had a settled conviction of his own inadequacy.

It is not excessive to describe this as an account of a courtship – in an intellectual relationship to be sure, but a courtship for all that. It is a testimony to the temper of our times that one is compelled to add that this does not mean that either man was homosexual. It does mean that same-sex friendships, then as now, and however intellectual their setting or *raison d'être*, obviously have deep emotional components, and that likening this one to a courtship does not do violence to Frazer's narrative, especially because the suggestive language – "yielding oneself captive," "mastership" – is his own.

This same long letter (written, it should be recalled, to a stranger) continues as he summons up, in an outpouring of emotion, some of the exceptional experiences that he and Smith enjoyed. They went on a walking tour in Scotland in September of that happy first year, 1884:

He loved the mountains, and one of my most vivid recollections of him is his sitting on a hillside looking over the mountains and chanting or rather crooning some of the Hebrew psalms in a sort of rapt ecstatic way. I did not understand them, but I suppose they were some of the verses in which the psalmist speaks of lifting up his eyes to the hills. He liked the absolutely bare mountains, with nothing on them but the grass and the heather, better than wooded mountains, which I was then inclined to prefer. We made an expedition in a boat down the loch and spent a night in a shepherd's cottage. He remarked what a noble life a shepherd's is. I think he meant that the shepherd lives so much with nature, away from the squalor and vice of cities, and has to endure much hardship in caring for his flock. After returning from our long rambles on the hills we used to have tea (and an exceedingly confortable tea) at the little inn and then we read light literature (I read French novels, I forget what he read), stretched at ease one of us on the sofa, the other in an easy chair. These were amongst the happiest days I ever spent, and I looked forward to spending similar days with him again. But they never came.

Frazer had never met anyone with whom he had such complete rapport; "But they never came" was the epitaph on one of the golden moments in his life.

Smith was brilliant, and unlike other clever men at Trinity he never used his learning oppressively.

As a companion he was perfect, always considerate and kind, always buoyant and cheerful, always in conversation pouring out a seemingly inexhaustible stream of the most interesting talk on a great range of subjects. Yet he did not monopolise the conversation. He talked in such a way as to bring out the best talk of others. He was the best listener as well as the best talker I ever knew. I mean that he paid close attention to what was said, and took it in with electric rapidity. I used to feel as if it were almost needless to complete a sentence in speaking with him. He seemed intuitively to anticipate all one meant to say on hearing the first few words. I used to think of him as a fine musical instrument, sensitive in every fibre and responding instantaneously to every touch. . . . One thing that gave one a special confidence in speaking to him was a feeling that he knew one inside and outside better than one knew oneself, and that though he must have discerned all one's blemishes and weaknesses he still chose to be a friend. He was almost, if not quite, the only one of my friends with whom I have had this feeling of being known through and through by him. This gave one an assurance that his regard would be unalterable, because there was no depth in one's nature which he had not explored and knew. With almost all other friends I have felt as if they knew only little bits of my nature and were liable at any moment wholly to misunderstand my words and acts because they did not know the rest of me.

No word other than "love" adequately describes what he felt for Smith, and in the early days he was completely taken with his new friend. In his understandable eagerness to please Smith, his reflex-like doubt about being good enough to write the "Pericles" must have produced a dreadful conflict within him. It is fortunate for both of them that Frazer somehow managed to produce the piece.

Later he relates a charming vignette that, *mutatis mutandis*, could once again be a lover's memory. One day after Smith had departed for Christ's, the two of them decided to watch a college boat race. Smith on the bank

in his eager enthusiastic way determined to run . . . beside the Christ's boat, his college boat. He started bravely but by the time we got opposite Ditton corner he was out of breath and stopped to rest. As there was some danger of his being knocked down and trampled on by the mob of undergraduates who were rushing along cheering their college boats in the usual vociferous way, I interposed my pretty robust form between his slight figure and the crowd, and I have a vivid recollection of his standing on the bank looking gratefully at me and panting while the roaring multitude swept past us.

It was on such a tide of emotion, then, that Frazer's introduction – perhaps "conversion" is a better word – to anthropology took place. That he wanted to know about Smith's special subject, in order to be a better friend to him, was undoubtedly part of the attraction of the new field. But there were other ways in which an ambitious young man might have found it attractive as well. One was that anthropology was then nearly "empty" as an area of study, at any rate in comparison with the well-plowed field of classics, and was as yet unorganized and unprofessionalized. Everything remained to be done. This became clear quickly, for as soon as Frazer overcame his hesitations about "Pericles," Smith immediately assigned him his first nonclassical essays, on "Taboo" and "Totemism." These assignments had profound consequences: from the former sprang, five years later, *The Golden Bough*; from the latter, twenty-five years later, the four massive volumes on *Totemism and Exogamy* (1910), which in turn was the direct inspiration for Freud's *Totem und Tabu* (1913), the title of which obviously chimes on Frazer's.

At that time Frazer did not know enough to write on either subject with the assurance appropriate for the *Encyclopaedia*; he could have been induced to take on these commissions only on the condition that Smith work with him closely. This is in fact what happened, as Smith wrote to their mutual friend J.S. Black in 1886:

I hope that Messrs. Black [publishers of the *Britannica*] understand that Totemism is a subject of growing importance, daily mentioned in magazines and papers, but of which there is no good account anywhere – precisely one of those cases where we have an opportunity of being ahead of every one and getting some reputation. There is no article in the volume for which I am more solicitous. I have taken much personal pains with it, guiding Frazer carefully in his treatment; and he has put about seven months hard work on it to make it the standard article on the subject. We must make room for it, whatever else goes. "Torture," though a nice paper, is not at all necessary, for people can learn about torture elsewhere, and the subject is one of decaying and not of rising interest.[17]

No editor, however, even the most sympathetic, could dispose of the space needed to encompass the astonishing fruits of seven months of Frazerian industry, and only an abridgment of the whole appears in the encyclopaedia. The entire essay became Frazer's first small book, *Totemism*, in 1887; it was the most considerable monograph on the subject that had ever been done, bringing together data from all over the world and, as Smith predicted, it immediately became the standard authority in the then sparsely populated field. Frazer soon became dissatisfied with both its data and its conclusions, but he nevertheless republished it unaltered, nearly twenty-five years later in 1910, where it appears at the beginning of the first volume of *Totemism and Exogamy*.

By 1885, then, Frazer had found his subject – the comparative anthropological study of the "primitive" mind and "primitive" religion, with special attention to mythology. Others, most notably Tylor and Andrew Lang, had anticipated him here. Frazer's special contribution lay in the use he made of his deep and wide knowledge of classical antiquity, which permitted him to extend greatly the field of comparison. No one had ever before focused so intensively on the "primitive" elements of the religions of Greece, Rome, and the eastern Mediterranean and had juxtaposed these on so large a scale with the religious activity of "savages" (as Frazer and his contemporaries often called preliterate peoples). Frazer seems to have understood early on – in the mid-eighties, while working on Pausanias – that he had lighted upon something unusual and important, and once he did, he never looked back. He never ceased purely classical work, but it was always carried out from an anthropological point of view. Whatever one's evaluation of Frazer's overall achievement, there can be no doubt that his work constitutes another sizable step in the century-long process, which began at the end of the seventeenth century and gathered force throughout the Enlightenment, to dethrone the cultures of classical antiquity from the privileged position they had enjoyed since the Renaissance. Plainly his concentration on those aspects of antiquity that resembled the behavior of the lesser breeds without the Law acted to deprive

Greece and Rome of their specialness, and to show them in a light in which they had hitherto rarely been presented.

But this is to gaze rather far into the future. In 1885 Frazer had a more immediate problem. He may have found a subject, but he now had to find a position, for that year the term of his fellowship ran out. He applied to the College Council for a renewal, but he cannot have been confident. The virtually untried new statutes, the product of the reforms of 1882, were now in force. But even under the old rules few extensions were ever granted. The reason was obvious: for Trinity, or any college, to continue to be able to invigorate itself through the award of fellowships, it could not afford to renew many because such prizemen ordinarily had no instructional duties.

Frazer may have tried for a vacant university classical post; if he did, no evidence of that effort remains. We do know that he applied to become the librarian of the Royal Geographical Society because the testimonials he gathered at the time have been preserved. Like those he collected when he sought the position at Aberdeen four years earlier, they are of interest for the light they shed on how he was perceived by his friends and colleagues.

Four letters exist: from W. H. Thompson (the Master of Trinity), Henry Jackson, James Ward, and J. Shield Nicholson, his old friend and traveling companion and now Professor of Political Economy in the University of Edinburgh.[18] Naturally all four touch on certain of Frazer's obvious qualifications for the post: his brilliant academic record, his erudition, his linguistic attainments, his industry, energy, and conscientiousness. Beyond that they diverge in interesting ways. Of the four Thompson knew him least well and thus confined himself to a recital of the objective record. Jackson and Ward both mention his deep interest in anthropology, which of course was directly relevant to the work of the Geographical Society, for it regularly sponsored expeditions to little-known parts of the world. Nicholson's letter, only three sentences long and thus much the briefest, is notable for its statement that he has known Frazer "intimately for many years"; he too remarks that Frazer is "painfully conscientious in performing his duties and is a courteous, obliging gentleman, whom everyone likes."

Ward's letter is perhaps the most illuminating in the detail he uses in illustrating Frazer's interests and talents. He places the latter's interest in anthropology in the context of a wider interest in "modern science" and goes so far as to say that he believes that Frazer "has probably a more thorough knowledge [of modern science and more especially of anthropology] than any other man in this University." Ward also testifies, on the basis of the ten years that he has known him, that

Mr Frazer is physically a very strong man: in studying and writing he is proverbial in Trinity for his continuous industry and enduring "power of work." He is a man free from every taint of affectation or conceit; warm-hearted, gentle, and without reproach; one who has many attached friends, and no enemies or detractors.

He concludes that Frazer would carry out the duties of librarian flawlessly: "If there *is* a risk it is that he might some day become an explorer himself, and so deprive [the Society] of services they would soon learn to value highly." From this last it is reasonable to suppose that Frazer, at least informally, had already broached the idea of a field trip. Indeed, ten years later Frazer was seriously thinking of joining Haddon in a trip to New Guinea. Although for us he is the type of the armchair anthropologist, he had other ideas himself.

Needless to say, like the Aberdeen professorship, the librarianship never happened, for the College Council on 22 May 1885 saw fit to renew Frazer's fellowship for a further six years.[19] Their decision was based mainly on Frazer's potential, for he had not yet many accomplishments: a revision of a school edition of Sallust, a few sizable articles for the *Encyclopaedia* (although no doubt Jackson testified about their merit), and a start on a translation and commentary on Pausanias. The decision to renew was also to some extent a social judgment: having had him in their midst for six years, the senior men judged Frazer to be the sort who fitted in with the spirit of the college.

Aside from Jackson, he had at least two influential friends, for both Francis Galton and Robertson Smith spoke strongly on his behalf.[20] It is probably not coincidental that he also then made his public scholarly debut, for he read a paper, his first on an anthropological subject, to a meeting of the Anthropological Institute in London on 10 March 1885. It bore the characteristic title, "On Certain Burial Customs as Illustrative of the Primitive Theory of the Soul."[21]

The title is characteristic because he assumes here and subsequently that the primitives perceive the world as a series of intellectual problems, much as a modern rationalistically inclined person would, and accordingly produce solutions to (or "theories" about) these problems – in this case, about the nature of the soul. The primary difference between their theories and ours is that theirs are false and ours are true, or at least ours are not false in the laughable fashion that theirs are. It is also characteristic in that Frazer feels easy about working backward from the behavior to the motives (that is, the "theory") that impel such benighted people to act as they do.

We have some sense of the delivery of the paper as a social occasion because the published text preserves a précis of the discussion that followed. Francis Galton (another of Frazer's mentors) was in the chair, and in the audience were, along with the travelers and explorers who made up the membership of the Society, Herbert Spencer and E. B. Tylor. Given his inveterate industry and his understandable eagerness to impress his auditors, in his talk Frazer produced a worldwide encyclopaedic survey of "primitive" ideas of death and the afterlife, and of funerary belief and ritual. The essay in its final form contains no fewer than 277 footnotes, most of which cite more than one source; aside from classical parallels he adduces works in English, German, French, and Italian; a number of his notes are miniature essays, running to more than a page of small type. Of course the footnotes were not read aloud, but the text from which they depend is equally formidable, often moving with dazzling speed from China to Peru in a single sentence.[22]

For such a sophisticated audience Frazer was at pains to strike the appropriate rhetorical note. His erudition and scholarship would speak for themselves but he did not wish to appear to be merely another pedantic don. Accordingly, the voice he adopts, in this his first public foray, is urbane and ironic. In conversation Frazer was certainly not noted for wit or brilliance; in print, however, it was otherwise. The entire canon of his work may be regarded as broadly ironic, as it charts the confused and often halting efforts of mankind to free itself from the errors of magic and religion and breathe the pure air of science and reason. Here, in his first essay on religion, the ironic, or sardonic, note is heard. In the very first footnote, which is important enough that he may have read it aloud, Frazer takes pains to distance himself from his sources:

It is to be observed that the explanations which I give of many of the following customs are not the explanations offered by the people who practise these customs. Sometimes people give no explanation of their customs, sometimes (much oftener than not) a wrong one. The reader is therefore to understand that the authorities referred to are quoted for the fact of the customs, not for their explanation. (p. 3)

That is, not only does Frazer use the customs as so many occasions for ironic commentary, but he stands in adversarial relationship to their very existence in the texts he annotates. He has no doubt that he can and does discern the intentions and motives of the ancients and primitives whose customs he surveys more clearly than they did (his audience had no doubts on this score either). This question – whether an anthropologist can ever understand the behavior of the natives better than they do or can – is a vexed one even today, with scholars to be found on both sides. In Frazer's day, however, such hermeneutical sophistication was unknown: quite simply, he (that is, a modern educated Westerner) knew better.

Having begun by denying the authoritativeness of his authorities, he proceeds to enforce his ironic position through a number of rhetorical devices. One of his favorites is the strategically placed modifier. An example: he is discussing the perilous consequences for the sick of the widespread belief that the soul of the sleeper leaves his body. For such a person sleep is dangerous because one cannot be sure that the soul, having wandered off, will ever return. Thus the invalid's friends must prevent him from sleeping.

With this intention the Circassians will dance, sing, play, and tell stories to a sick man by the hour. Fifteen to twenty young fellows, *naturally* selected for the strength of their lungs, will seat themselves around his bed, and make night hideous by singing in a chorus at the top of their voices, while from time to time one of them will create an *agreeable* variety by banging with a hammer on a ploughshare which has been *thoughtfully* placed by the sick man's bed. (p. 24; emphasis added)

Frazer clearly assumes his conviction of superiority to the natives and is therefore spared the need to prove it. He conveys and enforces that superiority only through such touches, which is inherently risky because some of the audience might misunderstand. In that sense the total confidence on which the tone of the essay is based marks it very much as a performance to a group of initiates, all of whom share the important relevant assumptions.

In keeping with what would become Frazer's practice, he begins in medias res, without any introduction whatever, by asking what to make of a curious funeral practice recorded in Plutarch. By dispensing with a "dry" analytic prologue he gains in interest, but he must maintain constant rhetorical control to assure that his point of view comes across. To this end Frazer employs an armory of devices. Along with artful adverbs, he likes brief asides. An example of the latter is to be found at the end of a note to a discussion of burial practices that attempt to mollify ghosts. He has just said that "when a death took place the Jews used to empty all the water in the house into the street, lest the ghost should fall in and be drowned." In the note here Frazer gives his sources and then remarks:

The reason assigned for this custom by the most learned Talmudists is that the water is unclean because the Angel of Death has washed his dripping sword in it. Contrast the vivid spiritualism of this explanation with the vapid rationalism of the view that the emptying of the water is a means of announcing the death. Truly it is vain to bottle the new wine of reason in old customs. (p. 32)

The talk was received well. From the record of the ensuing discussion we learn that Tylor himself "remarked that Mr Frazer's original and ingenious treatment of the evidence must materially advance the study of animistic funeral customs" (p. 48). On his side Frazer "expressed his deep gratification at the interest which Mr Tylor had expressed in his paper. It was the writings of Mr Tylor which had first interested him in anthropology, and the perusal of them had marked an epoch in his life" (p. 49). Although the minutes of the College Council at Trinity at this time consist mainly of a record of decisions taken, without offering explanation or context, one may safely assume that the success of Frazer's talk materially aided his application for the renewal of his fellowship.

In 1884 and 1885, then, Frazer's life changed dramatically. He made new friends, pre-eminently Robertson Smith, and he began to publish and embarked upon a translation of Pausanias, his first large-scale project. But this was not all, for his intellectual energy seems to have been boundless. At the same time that he was carrying on his classical and anthropological work, he continued to pursue his literary interests. On 18 July 1886, two years after their first exchange and while still working on Pausanias, Frazer wrote once again to George Macmillan, proposing this time to put together a selection, in German, of the poetry of Heinrich Heine. The volume would contain a sketch of Heine's life along with some notes, both linguistic and literary. "If you decide to publish such a volume, it would give me great pleasure to make and arrange the selection. As I am fairly familiar with his best poems (he being one of my favourite authors) I could very shortly furnish you with a list of the poems and the printing could proceed rapidly."

Heine was, as Frazer notes in this letter, "much read and admired in this country." Matthew Arnold, although not wholehearted in his admiration, had written an influential and generally positive essay twenty years earlier that had helped secure the poet's reputation in Britain.[23] For his part Frazer, as we know, had been an admirer of Heine's since he had gone to Germany in 1878 to perfect his German. He bought Heine's collected works while in Hamburg, and his devotion had never flagged.

Frazer's favorite poets were Heine and William Cowper, a distinctly odd couple. Cowper, whose letters he edited in 1912, was one of a number of eighteenth-century English poets whose lives were made wretched by recurrent mental breakdowns. His many affecting poems and letters render both his incipient madness and the hard-won calm he attained, once all passion was spent. During the last years of his life he lived quietly in the country, a devout communicant of the Church of England, writing no poetry and passing his days in religious meditation.

It is not easy to think of a poet more antithetical to Cowper in terms of the way he spent his life or the kind of poetry he composed than Heine. Heine, a German Jew, in his youth was intensely political; he was forced to leave Germany for what became his beloved Paris as a result of his left-wing opinions, which were expressed in a great deal of forceful political journalism. His extraordinary lyric gift, by which he managed mainly in simple ballad forms to express memorably the "naive" emotion surrounding and imbuing young love, was combined with a wit and mockery that, in the name of reason, attacked virtually all institutions and causes, even the liberal shibboleths of his erstwhile friends. He died alone and in misery, a syphilitic. As a result of what Victorian society saw as his "moral excesses," despite the approbation of Arnold and other critics his name was surrounded by scandal; he was like Shelley in that during their lifetimes and for several generations afterward, both were seen as dangerous and subversive voices.

Although we do not know what Frazer specially liked in Heine at first, the poetry seems soon to have become what might be called, in Eliot's phrase, the "objective correlative" of a range of keenly felt emotions that found little other expression in Frazer's life. Given his deep affection for Robertson Smith, it is not surprising that their friendship offers an excellent example. In the same long letter of reminiscences to J. F. White, consider this passage, in which Frazer has been describing Smith's Aeolian-harp-like quality:

If the conversation touched on any subject above the common, if any hint of the poetic or heroic were dropped in passing, it seemed as if you could almost feel the chords vibrating in him. And this one felt sometimes more by a sudden and unusual silence on his part than by anything he said at the moment. Two little instances that happen to stick in my memory will illustrate this. I used at one time to underline words and passages in some of my books in red ink, and chancing to come across some of these marks in a book at which we were looking together I spoke of them as "the thin red line." He said nothing, but I felt by his momentary silence that he thrilled at the words. The other instance was once when his friend the late Donald McLennan (brother of the well known anthropologist and himself a distinguished anthropologist) was spending the day with him in Cambridge. At Robertson Smith's wish I rowed them up the river, he sitting in the bow behind me and McLennan in the stern facing me. As we neared Granchester [sic] we heard a rumbling sound. McLennan asked "Is that a train?" I said, "No, it is the mill-wheel, *Ich höre sein fernes Gesumm.*" Robertson Smith, as I have said, was behind me so that I could not see him, but I knew perfectly, by the sudden silence that fell on him and that lasted for a minute or so, that the rest of Heine's beautiful verses were passing through his mind.

Macmillan felt that Heine might be appropriate for the Foreign Classics series, which would have appealed to university students in the event that Cambridge instituted a German Tripos. But Frazer was interested in a volume directed to a larger general audience, and they agreed to drop the project. Undaunted by this refusal, Frazer continued to suggest belletristic projects throughout his long relationship with the house of Macmillan.

The years 1884–6 were the breakthrough years, the period when all the preparation and all the reading came to fruition, all the indecision and all the false starts were forgotten. Once launched, it was as if Frazer had decided to make up for lost time and a late start. Henceforth his life was to be packed with work, usually with several major projects going on simultaneously. After the mid-eighties, Frazer would never look back.

5 · MYTHOGRAPHY AND AMBIVALENCE

Summarizing recent developments in mythography, the French classical anthropologist Salomon Reinach (1858–1932) remarked in 1911 that a sufficient epitaph for Robertson Smith might be "*genuit Frazerum.*"[1] Smith did indeed beget Frazer as an anthropologist. As long as Smith lived they remained the closest of friends, seeing one another often and going for long walks and talks. When Smith's health broke down early in 1890 under the onslaught of the tuberculosis that killed him four years later, Frazer visited him frequently, assisted him in every way he could, and after his death helped J. S. Black see the revised edition of *The Religion of the Semites* through the press. Nevertheless Reinach's epigram drastically simplifies and therefore distorts the true relationship between the two men. Both resident in Cambridge, they had little need to write to one another; therefore the few extant letters between them may represent most of those that ever existed. The letters from Frazer – to Smith and to others – permit us both to get a sense of their deep and abiding friendship and yet to state unequivocally that the period of Frazer's "childhood" at the feet of his intellectual father lasted practically no time at all. Or, to change the metaphor to one more in keeping with the language of courtship Frazer used in the reminiscences of the early days with Smith, this honeymoon, like all others, was a brief one.

From the start Frazer and Smith found themselves at odds regarding the meaning, value, and future of religion. They must have become aware of it immediately, and it must have taken them only a little while to resolve the matter – to resolve, that is, that their disagreement should never be allowed to undermine their friendship.

The differences are already apparent in Frazer's earliest foray into anthropology, "Taboo" in the *Encyclopaedia Britannica*. Frazer explains taboo as a system of religious prohibitions based on "negative *mana*," and presents numerous examples. Having demonstrated the ubiquity of taboo or something like it throughout the primitive world, he concludes that "some of the most characteristic features of taboo . . . have been found more or less amongst all primitive races."[2] He then goes on to discern "traces" of this primitive system in the religious observance of ancient Israel, Greece, and Rome.

However, in his most interesting paragraph, which in the *Encyclopaedia* bears the heading "Use in sociological evolution," Frazer lifts his eyes from his examples and ventures a speculative interpretation of the social function of taboo. Despite the fact that taboo is undeniably based on a primitive confusion of cause and effect and an ignorance of natural law, he unexpectedly argues that over the millennia it has nevertheless been of great evolutionary utility.

He distinguishes between those primitives (like the educated modern descendants of the Greeks, Romans, and Hebrews) who participated in, and therefore profited from, the slow but inexorable march from the kind of aboriginal mental confusion represented by taboo to the rational clarity of modern life, and the unfortunate others, who are banished to the sociological equivalent of outer darkness. This is not what we might label a racist judgment, for today's uneducated peasant descendants of the ancients are mentally exactly the same as those peoples who never took part in the upward march of rationality. Stylistically we recognize the mature Frazer: the speculative transitions ("we shall scarcely err in believing"), the eye-catching metaphors conveying a dislike and mistrust of religion that might have flowed easily from the pen of a *philosophe*.

The original character of the taboo must be looked for not in its civil but in its religious element. It was not the creation of a legislator but the gradual outgrowth of animistic beliefs, to which the ambition and avarice of chiefs and priests afterwards gave an artificial extension. But in serving the cause of avarice and ambition it subserved the progress of civilization, by fostering conceptions of the rights of property and the sanctity of the marriage tie, – conceptions which in time grew strong enough to stand by themselves and to fling away the crutch of superstition which in earlier days had been their sole support. For we shall scarcely err in believing that even in advanced societies the moral sentiments, in so far as they are merely sentiments and are not based on an induction from experience, derive much of their force from an original system of taboo. Thus on the taboo were grafted the golden fruits of law and morality, while the parent stem dwindled slowly into the sour crabs and empty husks of popular superstitions on which the swine of modern society are still content to feed.[3]

From the very outset of their collaboration, then, when Smith truly was his intellectual "father" in Reinach's terms, Frazer approached the study of early religion in the best Enlightenment manner. Whatever his ostensible subject, he was always ready to launch an attack on religion in general and Christianity in particular. In this article Frazer offers a list of incidents in the Old Testament that in his view are vestiges of (primitive) taboo in ancient Judaism. Inasmuch as Smith was also an evolutionist and comparativist too, he would have been the last to dispute such a description. But for Frazer, with his Comtean predisposition, to demonstrate that the Bible incorporated primitive elements was effectively to dismiss any religion founded on it from further serious consideration, whereas for Smith a recognition of the primitive element in Judaism, or Christianity for that matter, was in no sense a fatal indictment. Although the ninth edition of the *Encyclopaedia Britannica* has generally been seen as a high-water mark of Victorian rationalism,[4] which is to say that the tone of Frazer's contributions was of a piece with the work as a whole, it remains an indication of Smith's breadth of mind as well as his friendship that he did not suggest that Frazer tone down his tendentious remarks on his area of special knowledge. Having himself been persecuted for expressing his ideas, he would never have rewritten Frazer's work unless it were incompetent, which it plainly was not.

One assumes from the start the solidest sort of friendship as the bedrock. On this they created a somewhat ambivalent working relationship (or at least so it was from Frazer's side) that was marked by frequent intellectual disagreements. They worked side by side on many of the same subjects, throwing ideas out to one another for comment, knocking them down and having them knocked down and coming back for more. Smith probably knocked down more of Frazer's ideas than vice versa – for the first few years at least Smith was undoubtedly the more expert of the two – which is what was meant by the ambivalence being more on Frazer's side than Smith's.

For all the good feeling that prevailed between them, they were not equals in the relationship. Insofar as one can judge these things, the conclusion seems inescapable that Smith was the cleverer of the two.[5] Furthermore, Smith was better equipped temperamentally as well as intellectually for the study of religion, in that he had a deeper and broader sense than Frazer of the role that religion could and did play in people's lives. By comparison Frazer, although a man of great intellectual gifts and extraordinary industry, in his relentless reduction of religion to intellectual speculation seems often to have played the part of a color-blind art critic. In addition Smith was socially gifted, with a great sense of fun, a cosmopolitan person at ease with many kinds of people, from Bedouins to Cambridge dons and German professors.[6] Frazer, although certainly capable of friendship, was not endowed with social finesse. My sense is that Smith counted for far more in Frazer's social and psychic economy than vice versa. Smith was Frazer's best friend; I doubt that Frazer was Smith's.

To appreciate fully the relationship between them, one must have a sense of the intellectual landscape into which Frazer was led by Smith. The study of primitive religion, which in the days before field research was carried on largely through the study of mythology, has a long and complex history. No outline, however, can succeed in imparting the sense of *odium scholasticum* that since the seventeenth century has swirled around and generally obscured the questions relating to the origin, history, and meaning of primitive religion and mythology. This was true before Frazer's time and has continued to the present. Smith initiated him into what was then an extremely "hot" and sensitive subject.

It originated in the West with the ethnographic observations of Herodotus, became an organized enterprise in Alexandria before the Christian era in the Hellenistic commentaries on Homer, and then gained a second life in the

Renaissance.[7] Once the ancient classical manuscripts had been recovered and their contents edited and published, the scholarship on mythology divided into two streams. The first, and always the more considerable, was what might by analogy be called the "lower criticism" – the establishment by steady increments of better texts as the result of new data and improved techniques (for example, epigraphical and archaeological) and the steady effort and occasional brilliance of a long series of editors, all working by an accepted set of scholarly canons. The second or exegetical sort, the "higher" mythological criticism, was in the Enlightenment essentially the vehicle for a thinly disguised attack on Christianity. Because the *philosophes* and deists in eighteenth-century France and Britain courted severe penalties if they attacked Christianity directly, they took advantage of the large quantity of ethnographic information then coming into imperial capitals to discuss in a seemingly dispassionate and scholarly manner the striking similarities between the myths and beliefs of the ancients and those of some of the "primitives," especially the American Indians.[8]

For the first time, then, religion was examined not for its doctrinal value as the Word of God, to be accepted or rejected in terms of personal salvation, but as a social institution with a history rooted in human needs and actions, and with its own distinctive laws of development. This led naturally to the question of the origin of the religious ideas of the heathens, but only the most literal-minded of readers could fail to understand that Christianity was excluded from the discussion only for reasons of prudence. As a result, the speculative reconstruction of the motives of primitive men that led to the foundation of religion – in effect an "origins myth" itself for human (that is, Western Christian) culture – became a favorite subject for learned disquisitions in the eighteenth century. The reader was asked to imagine the thoughts and emotions of small bands of primitive people engaged in hauling themselves out of what German scholars later called *Urdummheit* (primeval stupidity) and trying to make sense of the horrifying, dangerous, and thrilling world in which they found themselves.

Given the absence of any real information, those who understood religion essentially as a great "error" (to invoke a favorite word of the Enlightenment) were free to conceive of these early people as in the grip of one overmastering feeling – fear. Terrified by uncontrollable natural forces, they personified the objects of their dread and thus created gods, whom they then strove to propitiate. Next, groups of wily priests, claiming special knowledge of these fictitious beings and eager to gain power and importance for themselves, quickly capitalized on this situation to impose a huge parasitical institution on society. The mythology recalling that earliest period is therefore a record of confusion compounded by fraud, now best forgotten by a humanity that happily has become increasingly rational and therefore less needful of the bogus consolations of religion. For writers of this persuasion mythology is discussed in order to be dismissed, or rather to be used as a stalking horse by means of which the real enemy, Christianity, may be attacked.

According to the other principal version of this origins myth, our earliest ancestors, far from being terrorized by nature and imposed upon by priestcraft, were closer to the Divine Source than we are. For that reason their cults were impelled by, and therefore organized around, the love and not the fear of God. It followed that mythology, recording as it does the religious intuitions of that earliest time, preserves, as if in a kind of linguistic amber, the closest collective approach that humanity has made to Godhead. From this point of view, mythology is seen as an intimation of the Truth, represented symbolically or allegorically, and therefore to be decoded in order to yield its precious evidence of the minds and hearts of the race when it was appreciably closer to the Golden Age. It is plain that just as the *philosophes'* account was one of progress, this is one of degeneration. Both agree in the assumption of a golden age: for the materialist and secularist critics of religion that age is to be found in an increasingly rational future; for the conservative and romantic mythologists it has already occurred, and the best we can do now is to recover its shards and be inspired by the gleams of divinity that continue to suffuse them.

Both tendencies had eminent expositors, with the philosophers of the French and Scottish Enlightenments (Bayle and Hume in particular) most prominent among the advocates of fear in the eighteenth century, whereas the German romantics from about 1770 to 1820 (Herder, Tieck, and the Schlegels) were mainly responsible for developing the transcendental view of mythology. In addition, there were the pioneering biblical critics in eighteenth-century France and Germany who distinguished different narrative and editorial hands in the composition and text of the Hebrew Bible, and the momentous posing of "the Homeric question" in 1795 by F. A. Wolf: were the Homeric epics the product of one bard, working alone as traditionally supposed, or were they the composite product of several hands working over several generations? The techniques of documentary analysis developed in the subsequent discussion of Homer and the Bible were soon turned to the many questions surrounding classical mythology, and historians of classical antiquity gradually realized that mythology offered the possibility of an invaluable glimpse behind the earliest historical records.

From about 1770 to 1830 German historians such as Niebuhr, and classical scholars such as Heyne and Otfried Mueller, demonstrated that patient linguistic analysis of individual myths often permitted one to thresh a significant kernel of history from the hull of imaginative fancy or syncretic confusion, and that in addition to their historical content myths were valuable as an irreplaceable insight into the *mentalité* of the ancient world. On the Continent, at any rate, some went so far as to envisage the study of mythology as the "master science" of the nineteenth century, potentially relevant to all the "human sciences." Indeed it is a striking fact that most of these fields of study, as they aspired to and arrived at conceptual and institutional autonomy in the course of the nineteenth century, engaged themselves somehow with mythology: the connections with linguistics, classics, the history of (classical) art, ancient history, archaeology, folklore, anthropology, theology, and the history of religion are clear enough.

Finally one must add to this potent intellectual mixture the fact that the comparative method, as such, had produced a number of triumphs. The paramount achievement was in philology. Two generations of (mainly German) grammarians and folklorists established the existence and unity of the Indo-European "speech family" and the widespread vernacular inheritance, in the form of folktales, of the peoples of Aryan descent. But the outstanding work of the anatomists, zoologists, and embryologists of the period also added to the esteem in which the comparative method was held. By the middle of the nineteenth century, and before the advent of university research laboratories in natural science, the comparative method was unrivaled as the procedure of choice for approaching scientific problems of any kind, and its adoption by the historical sciences is thus unsurprising.[9]

In Britain, it is a remarkable and as-yet-unexplained fact that the romantic view of mythology was not part of the cultural freight imported by Carlyle and Coleridge from Germany in the early part of the century. Further, many conservative scholars in Britain stoutly resisted German comparative philology, history, and especially biblical criticism, which were among the important scholarly vehicles for work on mythology.[10] This resistance was epitomized by the scandal that erupted upon publication of *Essays and Reviews*, an innocuous collection of articles written by a group of timid liberal churchmen and Oxford dons in 1860. Bishop Samuel Wilberforce, a clever man who is better known as Huxley's hapless opponent in the debates about evolution, clearly saw the tendentious uses to which the critical methods of the philologists could and would be placed. In an attack on one of the essayists, who had done no more than summarize the results of German biblical criticism, Wilberforce wrote that no one who "with Niebuhr has tasted blood in the slaughter of Livy can be prevailed upon to abstain from falling next upon the Bible."[11] Until well past mid-century, then, no single explanation of the origin or meaning of mythology held the field in Britain, and most writers on the subject who did not dismiss it on religious grounds as heathenish nonsense assumed either that it was merely a collection of pretty but meaningless tales or else, reflecting the prevailing utilitarianism, consigned it to the category of "superstition" and foolishness characteristic of the childhood of the race.[12]

Probably because of this theoretical vacuum, the ideas advanced in 1856 by F. Max Müller (1823–1900) in a long essay called "Comparative Mythology" quickly prevailed.[13] In it Müller, Professor of Sanskrit at Oxford, applied the techniques and results of triumphant comparative Indo-European philology to the origin and meaning of myth. After exhaustive analysis Müller, himself the son of a German poet and something of a nature mystic, concluded that the ancient Aryans were trying in the stories that we call myths to express their longings for the Absolute. (As a Sanskritist and comparative Indo-European philologist Müller confined himself to his own speech area.) Because, however, of what Müller alleged was an inherent limitation of primitive Aryan – namely, its oversupply of verbs but singular lack of abstract nouns – these proto-Wordsworthian yearnings for union with the Godhead could not be presented in straightforward philosophical discourse but instead were forced to assume the form of little narratives. The plethora of action words and absence of abstract nouns was due to the inveterate tendency of the primitive mind to animate the world: "the creation of every word was originally a poem, embodying a bold metaphor or a bright conception."[14] With the passage of time and the inexorable operation of the laws of linguistic change, the original meaning of these figurative mystical homilies could no longer be understood by the speakers of the languages that succeeded Primitive Indo-European, in which they had nonetheless been preserved. Myths, therefore, represent a linguistic breakdown or, in Müller's famous phrase, a "disease of language." And because, it emerged, so many of these misunderstood stories really concerned heavenly phenomena in general and the sun in particular, his theory also became known as "solarism." For Müller and his followers, myth was an artifact resulting from purely linguistic processes and therefore its meaning could be recovered exclusively by comparative linguistic analysis; any other approach was doomed to failure from the outset as unscientific.

The anthropological approach to myth established itself only after a prolonged controversy with the solarists. Müller and a considerable company on the one side versus a smaller but growing group of anthropologists and folklorists, led by the Scottish classical scholar, poet, journalist, folklorist, and man of letters Andrew Lang (1844–1912) on the other, conducted an intellectual battle that went on throughout the last quarter of the nineteenth century and ended only with Müller's death.[15] Lang, a brilliant wit, had a field day each of the many times that the solarists, employing an allegedly scientific method, disagreed among themselves about the meaning of a particular myth. Furthermore, if the myths of the Indo-European speech area were the inevitable products of several millennia of linguistic "disease," and entirely the results of the operation of ineluctable linguistic laws, he asked how it happened that many of the same narrative patterns, characters, and situations were to be found in mythologies created by peoples who spoke non-Indo-European languages. Instead, he asked, was it not more reasonable to understand myths as responses to the material, social, and psychological conditions in which the whole of early mankind, and not only the Aryans, lived?[16] This would certainly explain the undeniable similarities in the mythologies of peoples who could not have had any contact, linguistic or cultural, with one another, a fact that was baffling to the solarists.

The anthropologists of course were evolutionists. In the antepenultimate paragraph of *The Origin of Species* Darwin had called for the application of evolutionary principles to the study of mankind ("Much light will be thrown on the origin of man and his history"). Spencer had been advancing evolutionary arguments for social phenomena in the 1850s, so that although it is tempting, it is not accurate to understand the burst of evolutionary philosophizing in the third quarter of the century as directly and exclusively inspired by Darwin. John Burrow has put it neatly: "In this context, Darwin was undoubtedly important, but it is a type of importance impossible to estimate at all precisely. He was certainly not the father of evolutionary anthropology, but possibly he was its wealthy uncle."[17] Certainly the most important example of evolutionary anthropology was Tylor's *Primitive Culture* (1871), which is regarded with justice as the founding document in modern British anthropology.[18]

Edward Burnett Tylor was born in 1832, the son of a wealthy London Quaker family; like Spencer, he did not attend university. In feeble health as a young man (he died at the age of eighty-five in 1917), he was advised to travel. Instead of doing the Grand Tour of Europe, however, he went to Cuba and Mexico. The result was his first book, *Anahuac* (1861), written before its author had read Darwin. In it already appear, in a rather scrappy way, many of the ideas and issues to which he would return later: the notion and meaning of survivals, the assumption of the uniformity of human nature, and the question whether culture evolved independently in several places or diffused from a single center. Moreover, as might be expected of a Quaker, the author of *Anahuac* is staunchly anti-Catholic, and especially antipathetic to what he regarded as empty display in religious observance. Like nearly all students of primitive religion at this time, he was an agnostic. Lacking religious convictions himself, and prejudiced against ritual observance, his influence on the subsequent study of primitive religion acted to overvalue the intellectual and speculative component of religion (beliefs and intentions) at the expense of the physical and affective (rites and ceremonies). He cared more about creed than consolation.

Tylor's is an anthropology of origins. His self-assigned task was to recover the prehistory of mankind. He starts from the Enlightenment premise that a fundamental unity exists among humankind, and that the similarities among cultures far outweigh the dissimilarities. His work is thus a reflection of the tide of liberal democracy rising all over Europe among the educated middle classes, for comparative evolutionary anthropology may be thought of as a scientific, "objective" demonstration of the unity of mankind that both the deists on the one hand and the romantics on the other had been proclaiming in their different ways since the American and French Revolutions.

Tylor postulated the existence of an organic law of development and progress operative in the growth of human institutions. This meant that change was gradual and orderly, much the same the world over, and that human institutions, once simple and confused, had become complex and highly coordinated over the passage of time. (Spencer had been saying this for nearly twenty years.) Although this sounded reasonable enough, it was by no means obviously true and it was not easy to demonstrate. His problem was one of evidence. Writing before the archaeological data produced by the later excavations in Greece and the eastern Mediterranean became available, how was Tylor to substantiate his statement that human society had evolved, along with everything else in the natural world? How to secure anything firm on which to base developmental sequences charting the growth from savagery to complex, advanced (European) societies? The solution lay in the comparative method and the doctrine of survivals.

Tylor (and the many who followed him for forty years, including Frazer) simply asserted that, human nature and development being relatively homogeneous, one might legitimately discover, in the behavior of contemporary primitive peoples, living links in the evolutionary chain. Despite the absence of any evidence that their histories were any less lengthy than those of their European observers, these "savages" were postulated to be living fossils, to show man as he was thousands of years ago, before some or all of the great intellectual and cultural advances occurred that had (inevitably) led to the societies of the modern West. Once this giant step was taken, it was not much further to the next: to obtain the needed dynamic view of prehistoric development, one might string together items of culture taken from the most diverse primitive societies if in their totality they illustrated the steady upward movement of human development. The burgeoning ethnography of the time, made possible by the fact that traders and missionaries generally preceded the flag into the farthest corners of the world and through their extended residence *in partibus infidelibus* were able to observe and report on the native societies over long periods of time, was thus levied upon to provide examples of all the various "stages" of human behavioral and social development.

To be persuasive, any developmental argument based on artifacts and behavioral observations must demonstrate that in fact each of its elements grew out of the preceding one – that the series was indeed evolutionary. To this end Tylor came up with the notion of "survivals."[19] These were objects or traits or attitudes with a *raison d'être* in one stage that had become obsolete or misunderstood because they had, through social or religious conservatism, "survived" into a new, higher stage in which they were no longer functional.

Thus the magician's rattle and the warrior's bow and arrow had become children's toys. More to the point in this context, among his innumerable examples Tylor offered many religious beliefs and rituals based on primitive confusion or misunderstanding that exist today, in Christianity as well as in other religions. This device of survivals made it possible, Tylor and other evolutionists thought, to fill in the cultural blanks and reconstruct the life of bygone eras. The similarity of this argument to that of the Scottish conjectural historians is obvious.

All this was not enough. One might provide masses of evidence that material objects evolved in, and survived from, savage society, and not satisfy Tylor's readers. For in the late nineteenth century the most absorbing subjects, humanly speaking, were the origins and development not of agriculture or smelting but of religion and morality. With so many educated people in religious confusion and even crisis, any evidence that could be construed as either undermining or buttressing religion was sure to gain a deeply interested audience. Thus Tylor had important chapters in *Primitive Culture*, and later in his survey volume *Anthropology* (1881), on the origins and development of those sensitive social and "spiritual" institutions – art, language, mythology, and religion.

He begins with a minimal definition of religion as the belief in spiritual beings. For him religion and myth arise from the same source, although "error" is closer than "source" to what he intended. This source is exclusively mental, inherent in the functioning of the savage mind, which is postulated to be qualitatively different from our own. This mentality is radically subjective; its chief trait is an inveterate habit of animating nature, which survives in the vivid fancy of children.[20] The savage animates nature, or as Tylor puts it, "transfigures into myths the facts of daily experience," as the result of his application of a "broad philosophy of nature, early and crude indeed, but thoughtful, consistent, and quite really and seriously meant."[21] Like Frazer after him, Tylor is an individualist, for whom the significant actors in the mental advance of early society are solitary speculative thinkers intent on solving abstract philosophical problems. The "savage philosopher" (memorable phrase)[22] founds his theory on the notion of the *anima*, or soul – whence Tylor's theory is known as "animism." Souls exist because it is well known that the (spirits of the) dead appear in dreams and visions to the living; ergo, some part of them must continue to live. And from this the primitive savant proceeds to expand the scope of the doctrine, attributing souls of some kind to nonhuman objects – animals, plants, and even stones.

For Tylor the question to ask of religion or mythology was whether or not it was true. This followed from his premises, for myth (like its vehicle religion) was a product of primitive ratiocination, and therefore to be judged like any other mental effort for its truth value. Although most of it was patent nonsense by this standard, Tylor adjures his reader to take it seriously notwithstanding, for it can help us to understand much, especially concerning that dim prehistoric period about which we otherwise can know so little. As he wrote in 1881, "Myth is not to be looked on as mere error and folly, but as an interesting product of the human mind. It is sham history, the fictitious narrative of events that never happened."[23] It is both reasonable and useful, however, to inspect myths and other religious statements and extract from them whatever factual content they may have, discarding the quantities of rubbish that remain. The study of myth permits us, he says, to lay bare prehistoric connections between peoples that have been totally effaced in memory and of which we have no material evidence.

Another important contributor to the stock of anthropological ideas current in the eighties was John Ferguson McLennan (1827–81). McLennan, yet another Scot, and a good friend of Robertson Smith's from the Aberdeen days, was, as Frazer wrote, a pioneer in the use of the comparative method in the study of ancient and primitive religion.[24] In essays as early as 1869 and 1870, and then in *Primitive Marriage* (1875) and *Studies in Ancient History* (1876), he singlehandedly promoted to the center of the intellectual stage two topics that would pervade (and distort) the study of religion through the 1920s: exogamy and totemism. Like Smith, and unlike Tylor and Frazer, he was a sociological thinker. That is, he understood mythology and religion primarily in terms of the interaction of groups and institutions, not the thoughts and actions of remarkable individuals. In that sense, although his theories have subsequently been dismissed as completely as Frazer's, he is honored by anthropologists today for having at least understood the correct way of approaching the questions before him.[25]

Totemism and exogamy as subjects for analysis developed from his speculations about the primitive family and primitive marriage. In a suggestive throwaway remark, E. E. Evans-Pritchard wrote that the fixation of McLennan and those who followed him with these two topics comes from deep-lying Victorian obsessions with sexuality, private property, and social class.[26] The primitive world, and particularly its family, was postulated by nineteenth-century theorists to be the diametrical opposite of their own society, and its alleged social and sexual arrangements embodied everything that the Victorian male feared most. The results of this massive act of psychological projection were endless discussions of whether all or only most primitive marriage was carried on by capture, whether the primitive horde (for by definition the earliest people could not have known the family) was sexually promiscuous, what exactly a totem was and whether all or only some primitive people were totemists, and especially whether or to what extent primitive men were exogamous (that is, married outside the clan or tribal group).[27]

McLennan's main interest was in the family and marriage and not mythology, so that as far as Frazer was concerned, his effect on *The Golden*

Bough was indirect, mediated as it was through Smith, who was much more deeply immersed in McLennanite ideas. On the other hand McLennan may be said to be the ultimate intellectual begetter of Frazer's later encyclopaedic survey *Totemism and Exogamy*.

One other writer, like McLennan more interested in primitive behavior than in mythology, who strongly influenced Frazer, especially at the outset, was the German folklorist Wilhelm Mannhardt (1831–80). In the preface to the first edition of *The Golden Bough* Frazer says, "I have made great use of the works of the late W. Mannhardt, without which, indeed, my book could scarcely have been written."[28] Mannhardt had begun his study of primitive folklore as a Müllerian solarist but became disillusioned by the sharp disagreements he found among practitioners of an allegedly scientific method, so he turned from philology to fieldwork.

His great contribution lay in the way in which he forcefully broke the endless chain of theorizing by thinkers who were willing to pontificate forever about the nature of the primitive mind. Instead of engaging in a priori reasoning, Mannhardt opted for the then novel alternative of gathering empirical folkloric evidence – specifically, by going out and patiently collecting and classifying hundreds of examples of the behavior of contemporary European peasants. Frazer extols Mannhardt's work for providing "the fullest and most trustworthy evidence we possess as to the primitive religion of the Aryans."[29] Although the relation between the religious beliefs of a shadowy people who lived in Asia four thousand years earlier and the agricultural rituals of the European peasantry of the 1860s (when Mannhardt did his fieldwork) may seem tenuous to us, to Frazer and his readers it was not.

As his words about Mannhardt show, for Frazer in 1890 the question – the question that is the real subject of *The Golden Bough* – was still the same as it had been for Max Müller in 1856: the nature of "the primitive religion of the Aryans." Müller's essentially literary or textual method of analyzing ancient myths was defective because, for Frazer, "the primitive Aryan, in all that regards his mental fibre and texture, is not extinct. He is amongst us today."[30] Most of the descendants of the Aryans, who are the illiterate peasantry of late-nineteenth-century Europe, have essentially been untouched by modern (self-) consciousness and thus still participate in a mental universe that is unchanged from that of prehistoric mankind. Therefore philological scrutiny of mythological tasks must give way to folkloric inspection of what these contemporary primitives actually do.

Mannhardt had concluded that most of these modern peasant rituals were of a magical character, primarily intended to assure fertility of woman, beast, and field. Frazer understood this to mean that, their Christianity notwithstanding, the peasants also were unknowing continuators of an earlier pre-Christian faith, one that coexisted with and underlay the official cult of classical antiquity, one that was rooted in and grew out of the cycle of birth and

81

death in the agricultural year and was thus potentially as old as the Neolithic age. To Mannhardt Frazer owes the key concept of the "vegetation spirit" or "corn demon," that is, the divinity believed to be indwelling in growing things whom the magical rite is supposed to placate or gratify.

Mannhardt was also the source of one of Frazer's cardinal methodological tenets, "the law of similarity": when customs are similar in different societies, we may then safely infer that the motives of the people performing them are also similar. This suits perfectly with the Tylorian assumption of uniformity of mental functioning and is wholly consonant with Frazer's penchant for psychological explanations. For Frazer the main value of any rite or ceremony is that it lays bare and exhibits some otherwise inaccessible mental state *in action*. For him, likewise, these items of behavior were of interest because he believed that when (in his opinion) they resembled one another, that resemblance bespoke and emanated from similar or identical states of mind. The customs and rituals were thus invaluable for the folklorist or anthropologist interested in charting the overall course of the mental or spiritual evolution of humanity. Archaeology could yield only artifacts that were, if sometimes beautiful, nevertheless lifeless; at best they offered suggestive but finally ambiguous testimony about what Europe really wanted to know – the motives and emotions of the primitives and the ancients and thus the origins of religion.

If one assumed the law of similarity, however, and if one also assumed that the peoples who were backward at the end of the nineteenth century essentially had not changed in their mental makeup over thousands of years, then these two far-reaching postulates taken together amounted, conceptually speaking, to a time machine. For examples of "primitive" behavior one was now no longer limited to the few and in any case unconfirmable reports from classical historian-ethnographers like Herodotus, Pausanias, or Tacitus. Now, moving effortlessly through time and space, one could interweave classical and contemporary ethnography to produce, as it were, both an anatomy and an atlas of the unchanging primitive mind.

Tylor, Robertson Smith, McLennan, and Mannhardt were the most important presences for Frazer in the mid- and late eighties, as he immersed himself in the anthropological study of primitive religion and mythology. Of the four Smith was the most important because he was a cherished friend as well as a powerful intellect, but their affection notwithstanding, their virtually total theoretical disagreement led on Frazer's part to a tension that was never wholly resolved.

Some of Frazer's ambivalence emerges by implication in the obituary essay he wrote soon after Smith's death in 1894.[31] In it he praised Smith as the man who, following the lead of McLennan, had conclusively made the case in Britain for the comparative method in the study of ancient and primitive religion. Such study, says Frazer, has demonstrated beyond doubt that the evolution of religious ideas and institutions has been generally similar among all the peoples of the world, at least in early times, and that modern (Western) religions are built on a common primitive and ancient base. From which it follows that it is impossible to gain a complete understanding of any single religion – primitive, ancient, or contemporary – without seeing it in the context of others.

Frazer then argues that although such a historical and thematic analysis, carried out in what we should today call neutral scientific terms, is ultimately incompetent to pronounce on the truth of the claims made by any religion (including, by implication, Christianity), yet it can be of real assistance for ordinary educated persons in making up their minds on this most important question. The comparative method, in his view,

proves that many religious doctrines and practices are based on primitive conceptions which most civilized and educated men have long agreed in abandoning as mistaken. From this it is a natural and often a probable inference that doctrines so based are false, and that practices so based are foolish. . . . And as the rules of conduct which have guided and still guide men in the affairs of life are in large measure deduced from religious or theological premises, it follows that the comparative study of religion, in so far as it invalidates these premises, calls for a reconsideration of the speculative basis of ethics as well as theology.[32]

That Frazer was able to turn the occasion of the death of his best friend to polemic purposes is, in emotional terms, extraordinary; the most astonishing thing about the obituary is that it neglects to mention that Smith was a Christian throughout his life. Perhaps he passed over this because he could never understand it himself. Without any doubt, however, Smith, the ordained son of a Free Church minister, would never have endorsed Frazer's conclusions about the inevitable tendency of the comparative method to undermine religion.[33]

If they differed about the fundamental value and truth of religion, it will come as no surprise that they disagreed about what religion was and how it evolved. Frazer was at one with Tylor (and Comte) in taking religion to be essentially a philosophical system that incorporated supernatural sanctions. For him religion could be reduced without loss to theology, in the sense that from a set of propositions about the origin, nature, and governance of the universe and man's place in it all else – morality, ethics, ritual – flowed. As such it was essentially an intellectual construction, devised by individual thinkers in prehistoric times as a response, in its time sensible and even progressive, to the profound riddle of the world; as such it could and should be superseded by another intellectual system that might be shown to be more accurate and comprehensive, with greater explanatory power. That better system – science – was now at hand, which meant that it was time for religion to yield.

Smith, on the other hand, never accepted that primitive religion was the product of individual theorists devising answers to intellectual problems. For him the significant actors were not individuals but groups – tribes or clans related by blood or totem – and religious evolution occurred in response to changes within social institutions. For him the paradigmatic religious action was the sacrifice, in which the community of worshiping brethren came together more to achieve union with the god than to propitiate him out of fear. The sacrificial victim, he believed, was the totem animal of the community, ordinarily taboo and, like totems everywhere, never eaten except under extraordinary conditions. He theorized that at the moment of such a totem sacrifice the ancient Semites believed that the god had entered the animal, and that in eating the animal the god entered into them and they into him.[34] As a Christian Smith believed that primitive religion was, like all else, a gift from God, and therefore should be approached sympathetically, not dismissed out of hand as foolishness. For him it had value in itself, as well as because it had inevitably prepared the way for Christianity. Thus on intellectual as well as personal grounds Smith would never have agreed that modern religion was fatally undermined because it evolved from an earlier stage based on faulty speculation nor that it was therefore due to be replaced by science.

Further, although both were comparativists, they used the method in different ways and with different ends in mind. Smith was primarily a Semiticist, which is to say that although he certainly saw the Semitic group as participating in the overall evolutionary movement that affected all religions, yet his background in biblical criticism tended to give him a much more historical outlook than Frazer. Although the introduction to *The Religion of the Semites* is a notable exception to this statement, Smith was generally unwilling to elide stages in the evolution of Semitic religions in order to make Semitic developments conform to an ideal type, or to make sweeping comparisons between the Semitic and non-Semitic. Although he had no a priori objections to making such comparisons, Smith in *The Religion of the Semites* saw so many problems within Semitic religion that he had no need to give additional hostages by going outside that sufficiently large and controversial subject. (It may also be that when in 1892, already fatally ill, he turned to revising the first edition of that book, he lacked the time and the energy to enlarge his focus.) As Robert Alun Jones remarks, as a biblical scholar and a Christian Smith's goal "had less to do with the evolution of human thought than the discovery of the general and permanent features of ancient religion with which the revelations of the later [Old Testament] prophets might be effectively compared."[35]

Frazer, on the other hand, from the start, felt under no such constraint. His special subject, the religion of Greece and Rome, permitted him to widen the field in inquiry and comparison – both Spencer and Tylor lacked classical educations – but he never believed that classical religion was in any sense privileged, as Smith did of the ancient Semites. Although in the first edition of *The Golden Bough* he says that his general subject is "the primitive religion of the Aryans," in the second and third editions his subject is nothing less than the religious evolution of the whole of humanity. Because he was always confident about understanding the mental constitution of primitive humanity, he saw no reason not to reason backward, from the most varied behavior to the simple (that is, unmixed) motives that he saw behind it, which were by definition everywhere the same. As a result Frazer was never made uneasy by his use of data drawn without geographical or historical distinction from primitive and historical religions and communities. In his view the material differences between them, sometimes wide indeed, were insignificant in comparison to the mental elements they shared with all ancient and primitive peoples.

Their theoretical disagreements were plainly substantial, and probably caused Frazer some awkwardness because he was unable to be forthright about them. One result of all that remained unsaid by Frazer was that, unwilling to admit to the world – and maybe to himself as well – the extent of their differences, he proceeded over the twenty years after Smith's death to disavow Smith seemingly without knowing that he was doing so. Several times he would attribute to his mentor views that the latter never held in order to create a Smith who agreed with him in death as he never did in life. That the process began early is apparent in the obituary of Smith, in which he silently associated his friend with the antireligious conclusions that he himself drew from the use of the comparative method.

To this point the comparisons between Smith and Frazer have been drawn retrospectively and in the light of the work of both men considered *in toto*. Fortunately there exists a quartet of vigorous letters by Frazer (two previously unpublished) that present the gap *as it was widening* between him and Smith. Three date from the late eighties and in the other Frazer is looking back at that time from nearly twenty-five years later. Together they make clear how completely he had distanced himself as early as 1888 from the intellectual guidance of Smith (the latter's personal magnetism notwithstanding), that was so strong during the initial period of the *Britannica* articles of 1884–6. As these letters indicate, 1888 and 1889, when he was thinking out and writing *The Golden Bough*, were years during which he was actively questioning his own ideas and those of others, and when, from time to time, he found himself, within his Cambridge anthropological circle, in a minority of one.

Two of the letters are about Smith directly; the other two, to Henry Jackson, whom Frazer used as a sounding board for his ideas, concern Smith as well, although the connection is somewhat roundabout. In all but the last of the four

Frazer discusses the same important question – Is it appropriate to judge the behavior of "primitives" by the standards of modern rationality? – and answers it in the negative.

However emotional Frazer may have been as a teen-ager, he was never a true romantic. He loved Heine and like many intellectuals the world over was a Germanophile until the First World War, but he never believed that to understand the primitives he had to "feel his way into" their consciousness in the Herderian sense, much less that primitive consciousness, in its integrality, preserves something of inestimable value that has been lost and is now (except for myth) inaccessible to us. Nevertheless, although his argument in the letters to Jackson is entirely drawn from the language and habit of mind of utilitarianism – a central unexamined term in his discussion is "superstition," which obviously implies a criterion of modern rationality – his final position is not far from the romantic one.

The burden of the letters lies in Frazer's rejection of the assumption, which in his view was being made silently by everyone else writing at the time on mythology and "primitive" thought, that the world "really is" as it appears to the average educated Westerner. Instead he argues that consciousness itself is the product of lengthy evolution, like artifacts and institutions, and must be understood as such. Primitive mentality thus represents one point low down on the developmental line; modern consciousness marks only another point higher on the same line, rather than a position somewhere off the line from which we may see the primitives as they "truly" are. It follows, then, that anyone who either explicitly or implicitly imputes modern rationality to the primitives in evaluating their beliefs or institutions, or else berates them for not possessing our version of "common sense," makes a fundamental epistemological error and therefore cannot discover anything worth knowing.

This attitude represents a striking change of heart and mind on his part. For in both content and tone the paper that he had delivered to the Anthropological Institute only three years earlier had expressed complete confidence that modern rationality was both appropriate and effective in getting to the bottom of whatever foolish (because irrational) behavior the ancients and primitives were up to. It follows from this second letter that, if we today really wish to know why the natives act as they do, and are not content merely to deride them, then we must take them seriously and systematically try to inhabit the very different mental world in which the native lives.

From our point of view, of course, it is unfortunate that Frazer did not then conclude that such an effort of the historical imagination might be better carried out in the field rather than the library. Inasmuch as he considered accompanying Haddon to New Guinea in 1895, Frazer the fieldworker is not an absurdity. But, aside from the mundane reasons that prevented him from going – his marriage the next year, the need to complete Pausanias – there was a theoretical one as well. His commitment to comparison as the best method for uncovering the stages in human mental and spiritual development clearly implied to him that the worker in the field should present the facts as he found them and not risk distorting those facts by attempting to interpret them as well. Instead, such contextualization was the task of the library worker, who had the view that is available only to one who sees the ethnographic world steadily and sees it whole. In 1888, when fieldwork as we understand it had not yet been invented, and when comparison was accepted as the best method of obtaining worthwhile results, the argument made sense. And certainly if one grants the premise that fieldwork should be strictly separated from library work, then the indefatigable Frazer was supremely fitted for the latter.

Because this is the position that he would maintain for the rest of his life, and because he is usually held to have been a doctrinaire rationalist, these letters are especially important. Judging from the intellectual passion of the first two, and one's sense that Frazer is virtually thinking on the page, writing without the usual second and third thoughts, it is unfortunate that we have no more from this time. Given the air of urgency about the discussion between them, there is every reason to suppose that it continued, either in person or in letters that have not survived.

The first letter (22 August 1888) is a reply to Jackson, whose letter is not extant; Frazer's answer is so comprehensive, however, that the questions at issue between them are crystalline.

My dear Jackson,

Many thanks for your suggestive letter which I will try to answer. I did not mean to compare metaphysics and superstition in the sense you seem to suppose. As usual your horse seems to be my cart and vice versa. You speak of superstitition as a conjectural explanation of recognised institutions, and add that superstitions are similar all over the world because in the same state of society there are similar utilities and therefore similar institutions. At least you say that this seems to follow from a comparison of metaphysics and superstition and you seem to accept this view. According to you, then, men start institutions on a strictly utilitarian basis but afterwards invent absurd (superstititious) reasons to account for a sensible practice. Why should they do so? If they were rational at first, why should they ever be irrational afterwards? You suppose that the world suggested simple and correct ideas of utility to the earliest men, who shaped their practice according to these correct ideas. Afterwards, retaining the correct practice, they abandoned the correct ideas with which they had started and on which their social structure was reared, and gratuitously and (so far as I can see) causelessly exchanged the gold of primitive truth for the base metal of superstition. Why? Your position in regard to savage *practice* (institutions) seems to me exactly that of the "disease of language" people towards savage *theory* (mythology). The "disease of language" people say that the first men described natural phenomena in simple and correct language, because these phenomena presented themselves to primitive man in a simple and correct fashion, being seen through the clear light of natural reason instead of the blinding haze of superstition. But afterwards, their descendants, misunderstanding their language, were led to entertain absurd and phantastic ideas about those natural events which primitive man had regarded as simply and rationally as an average decently educated man in the nineteenth century.

87

Both you and they (Max Müller & Co.) make what seems to me the fundamental mistake of supposing that the world must always appear to any unprejudiced man, at any stage of human history, exactly in the way in which it appears to us in the year 1888. You do not see what I think is the case, that our way of looking at the world is not the simple direct reflection of the facts that it seems to us to be. It is a vast complex, slowly elaborated through countless generations, in the course of which many philosophies (explanations of the world) have been tried and rejected, wholly or in part, our present way of regarding the world being the net result of this endless process of flux of opinion. If we are to judge the future by the past, our present way of looking at the world, natural and correct as it seems to us, is probably only transitional and will perhaps one day appear as remote, absurd, and unnatural to our descendants as the worst extravagance of savage opinion now appears to us. [πάντα ῥεῖ καὶ οὐδέν] is as true of man (and therefore of his mind, for the mind is the man) as it is of nature. You seem to think that man stands for ever on the same spot in the river and sees it speeding past him. It is not so, he is borne along on the current. There is no *absolute* way of looking at the world. The whole course of opinion (savage, philosophical, scientific) is only a perpetual approximation ever nearer and nearer to what we call the facts, but never by any possibility to reach them, for

"All experience is an arch wherethro'
Gleams that untravell'd world, whose marge fades
For ever and for ever when we move."

However this is a question rather for a psychologist – not of course one of the old school, with his mental faculties and capacities all labelled and docketed. But I feel pretty sure that any one who has studied psychology from the physiological side would agree with me that the further we go back, the more unlike ours was the attitude of man to the world; and further that the more we could project ourselves into the future, the more we should find that the view of the world taken by men in the future will differ from that taken by us at present.

My view then is, not that superstition is invented to account for an institution, but conversely that the superstition gives rise to the institution. I hold not, as you seem to do, that superstitions are similar all over the world because institutions are similar, but on the contrary – that institutions are similar because superstitions are so. With you, superstition is a parasitic growth on the tree of custom; with me, it is the root from which custom springs. The world, I take it, suggested certain ideas to the primitive man; on these ideas he acted and could not help acting. But his actions were different from ours because the ideas which he received from the world were different from those which we receive. You ask me how I account for the *prevalence* of similar institutions. Because the facts of nature are everywhere pretty much alike and the savage mind is everywhere pretty much alike. The impression made by the former on the latter is therefore everywhere pretty much alike, i.e. savage ideas are everywhere pretty much alike, from which it follows that savage practice or custom is everywhere pretty much alike, the practice being necessarily based on the ideas. That is how I look at it. But how do you explain the existence of superstition at all, after postulating a primitive nineteenth century rationalism? This I should like explained. And how do you explain mythology? Was primitive man rational in his practice but irrational in his theory? Or do you think, like the "disease of language" people, that he was at first rational in his theory (philosophy of nature) as well as in his practice and that mythology, like superstition, was a parasitic aftergrowth? On my view there is no divorce between theory and practice as the first of these suppositions involves, and no such relapse from reason to unreason as is entailed by the second. Myths are only ideas of the same type as those which gave rise to superstitious practices and savage institutions; but dealing with things beyond human reach they (the myths) could not have the practical consequences which were produced by the similar ideas about things within reach of man. If we use mythology in the sense of primitive man's ideas in general, then superstition is only applied mythology – superstition is primitive ideas plus practice, mythology is primitive ideas minus practice. On this view, human progress or development has been steady and continuous. The first incorrect ideas suggested by the world and the institutions based on them have been gradually corrected by the rise of truer ideas and hence of better institutions. Man has risen, not fallen. On your view, *intellectual* progress at least has not been continuous. Man began with reason, lapsed into unreason, and then struggled out of the quagmire back into reason. This is the Fall of Man. Really I think you might throw Adam and the apples into the bargain, and swallow the whole. Between one theory of degradation and another there is very little to choose.

Might I ask you to keep this letter and show it to R. Smith if you think it worth while? I am always having little tiffs with him on these same lines but have never had a pitched battle. For my attitude to the philosophy of history is just the opposite of that of De Quincey to murder. "So far I will go – general principles I will suggest. But as to any particular case, once for all I will have nothing to do with it." I on the contrary care chiefly for particular cases and am apt to regard discussion of general principles as nearly a waste of time.[36]

If only this letter had survived, it would constitute *prima facie* evidence for the existence of a Cambridge anthropological circle, made up of at least Frazer, Jackson, Robertson Smith, the classicist W. H. D. Rouse of Christ's,[37] and probably James Ward as well – note the reference to the new kind of physiological psychologist just after the quotation from "Ulysses" – who met to talk out the important theoretical implications of their speculations about primitive mentality and religion.

This letter reads as if it had been written in a single impulse under some stress and then posted without having been reread and revised. He says at the start of the second letter that he wrote the first one while depressed; he therefore begins with something of an apology. It is dated only two days later; in that interval Jackson had had the time to read and digest the first letter and write one in return (an eloquent demonstration of the superiority of the Victorian postal service, with its six to eight daily deliveries, to ours), which has not survived.

My dear Jackson,

Your kind letter has quite relieved me of the fear which I confess I began to entertain that my first letter might perhaps have offended you. I am very glad it is not so. Please forgive me for having entertained the fear. I wrote under a certain amount of depression caused by an incident which annoyed me and this I daresay helped to give a gloomier colour to the recollection of my first letter. I shall always value very highly the privilege of discussing our views together. The conversations we have had this week have benefited me not only by the general stimulus they have given me but also by directly helping me to clear up points which were obscure before. There is hardly any one to whom I can speak on these subjects. Even R. Smith is so stern a utilitarian that to talk to him of ghosts and spirits is to venture on delicate ground. So if you will allow me now and then to open out my ideas to you I shall be grateful. I know the danger of pushing an hypothesis too far and shall be glad to have any tendency in this direction corrected by your criticism. We both believe, I think, that all institutions were suggested by external facts; our only difference is as to the way in which we suppose that this suggestion took place. It could only take place of course through the mind of the savage, and my position is that the mental attitude of the savage to the external world is so unlike ours that it is only by perpetually soaking oneself in descriptions of savage life and thought that one can to some extent realise that attitude. But when, having thus soaked oneself, one propounds explanations of life drawn from what one conceives to be savage ideas, these explanations sound so totally absurd to people of the present day that they are apt to think that no human beings ever could have believed in them and to fancy them mere cobwebs spun in a student's brain. With the awful example of the "comparative mythologists" before one, one ought not to be too sure that this condemnation is not just.[38]

The second letter also makes clear the importance of the others as sounding boards for Frazer, and from it we get a better sense of Jackson's role, as opposed to Smith's. Although Smith was the anthropological authority whereas Jackson was only the amateur, the last paragraph of the first letter implies that Frazer could speak more easily with Jackson and could entertain statements and attitudes that he could not indulge with Smith. His affection for Smith along with his dislike of confrontation may have made it awkward or impossible for him to speak his mind fully with his friend.

The third letter was written fifteen months later, on 27 November 1889 (that is, when *The Golden Bough* was virtually completed), to J.S. Black, long a friend of Smith's, and later his biographer, and by this time a friend of Frazer's as well. It concerns *The Religion of the Semites*, which had just been published.

It is beyond doubt a striking and powerful book, full of original thought and abounding in fruitful views. Still, I am inclined to doubt whether simplification has not been carried too far, whether the elements out of which the history of religion is reconstructed are not too few in number, and too simple and obvious. The latter objection you may think a strange one. What I mean is that primitive man looks at the world from such a totally different point of view from us, that what seems simple and obvious to us almost certainly did not appear so to him; and, *vice versa*, what seems simple and obvious to him is almost always so entirely remote from our ways of thought that we should never have dreamed of it. Accordingly, any explanations of the origin of religion or society which commend themselves at once to us as entirely agreeable to reason and probability ought always, in my opinion, to be regarded with the greatest distrust. Their inherent probability (from our point of view) is a strong presumption against them. Rousseau's views (to take an extreme example) on the origin of society commended themselves to the most reasonable people last century, just because, if *they* had to reconstruct society from the foundations, they would have proceeded much as Rousseau supposes that primitive man did. But from primitive man to a French

Encyclopaedist is a very long interval. I do not say that Smith has fallen into the mistake of making the early Semites reason like nineteenth-century people; all I would say is that the very simplicity and obviousness of the deductions inspire me with a somewhat vague and perhaps unjustifiable distrust.[39]

Finally, when in 1911 Black was writing his life of Smith, he sent Frazer's 1889 letter back to him and asked permission to publish it, as part of an evaluation of Smith's contribution to scholarship. But then the gap between himself and Smith had widened considerably. On 15 July 1911 Frazer replied:

I had quite forgotten the letter I wrote to you about *The Religion of the Semites*. But with the extracts which you give from it I still quite agree, and have nothing to modify or withdraw in them. I may add that it had long seemed to me that Smith, influenced probably by his deeply religious nature, under-estimated the influence of fear, and over-estimated the influence of the benevolent emotions (love, confidence, and gratitude), in moulding early religion. Hence his view of sacrifice as mainly a form of communion with the deity instead of a mode of propitiating him and averting his anger. The latter is the ordinary view of sacrifice, and I believe it on the whole to be substantially correct. Not, of course, that I would deny sacrifice sometimes to involve a form of communion with the deity, but I believe it to be far oftener purely propitiatory, that is, intended to soothe and please a dreaded being by giving him something that he likes. In short, I believe the old gift theory of sacrifice to hold good in the majority of cases. . . . I incline to agree with you in thinking that, with all its great qualities, Robertson Smith's most mature and important work was probably to some extent provisional and written against time. Had life and strength been prolonged to him, he would probably have modified a good deal in the volume. For example, I hardly think that the hypothesis of a totem sacrament would have occupied the important place it does in his theory, if he had been aware of the extremely scanty evidence for the actual practice of a totem sacrament, at least in a religious, as distinguished from a magical, sense, among totemic peoples.[40]

In these letters, and especially in the last one, Frazer enrolls under the banner of those who regarded ancient and primitive people as motivated primarily by fear of their surroundings, and religion as a response to their fear. He also is a convinced evolutionist and comparativist. Frazer changed his mind often and candidly admitted as much in print, but he never wavered on the value of comparison as the best method for illuminating large-scale movements in the development of Mind. Throughout these letters, but especially in the first one, he assumes (with Tylor) the existence of a discrete, homogeneous "savage mind, pretty much everywhere the same," and that humanity has made steady progress in understanding the world and therefore in controlling it.

These four letters to Jackson and Black, important though they are, do not exhaust the complexities of the relationship between Frazer and Smith in the late eighties, the years that saw the composition of *The Religion of the Semites* and *The Golden Bough*. There is more to be told regarding his connection to Smith – undoubtedly the central intellectual relationship in his life – as it affected *The Golden Bough*.

In *The Golden Bough* Frazer purports to guide us through a labyrinth of strange behavior and intentions in Nemi; as he does so he also produces a series of mysteries of his own, some of which have hitherto escaped notice. The first of these has to do with how the book came to be written. Recall that in 1888 Frazer wrote to George Macmillan to tell him that, although by 1886 he had completed the translation of Pausanias and made a start on the commentary, he had suddenly discontinued that project in favor of another. The new book was of course *The Golden Bough*. From our perspective it may be hard to imagine, but in the 1880s the priesthood at Nemi was an obscure and not specially important affair among classical scholars and historians of ancient religion. What had distracted him?

The extensive reading he had done for the *Britannica* essay on "Taboo" is an obvious source. After all, much of the literature on taboo deals with the innumerable prohibitions surrounding the lives of kings. When he recalled the dramatic and picturesque story of (in Macaulay's well-known words) "the priest who slew the slayer, and shall himself be slain," the fact that the "ghastly priest" was a "king of the wood" may well have been the jumping-off point for Frazer's fertile imagination.

Unfortunately Frazer's letters give no hint of what caused him to turn his attention to the strange goings-on in the grove; for an explanation we must turn to the preface (dated 8 March 1890) to *The Golden Bough*. It begins:

For some time I have been preparing a general work on primitive superstition and religion. Among the problems which had attracted my attention was the hitherto unexplained rule of the Arician priesthood; and last spring it happened that in the course of my reading I came across some facts which, combined with others I had noted before, suggested an explanation of the rule in question. As the explanation, if correct, promised to throw light on some obscure features of primitive religion, I resolved to develop it fully, and, detaching it from my general work, to issue it as a separate study. This book is the result.

This straightforward account becomes decidedly problematic, however, as soon as one asks what was the "general work on primitive superstition and religion" on which he had been working for some time. Frazer published nothing subsequently that could be so described, and the extant letters are likewise totally silent.[41] The correspondence with Macmillan, both sides of which have been preserved in their entirety, contains not a word on this major work, which, presumably, would have been occupying him in 1888 (if not earlier) if he discontinued it "last spring" (that is, in 1889).

In any event, on 8 November 1889, after sixteen months of silence, Frazer suddenly informed his publisher that he had nearly completed a study of primitive religion, to be called *The Golden Bough*, which offered an explanation of the events in the grove at Nemi. Needless to say, Macmillan expressed interest in seeing the manuscript; after he received an enthusiastic reader's report he quickly agreed to publish it. The argument from silence can never be conclusive, but the absence of evidence makes me believe that this phantom "general work" may never have existed. If I am right, then Frazer must have had a reason to invent it. I should like here to suggest an explanation that is plausible on the face of it.

Frazer does not name it but a work does exist that may have diverted him from Pausanias to Nemi. In 1885 the French Orientalist, historian, and man of letters Ernest Renan (1823–92) published *Le prêtre de Némi: drame philosophique*, a "drama of ideas" set in Nemi, in ancient Alba Longa.[42] The play, one of a series of Renan's closet dramas, is a moral apologue that illustrates humanity's abiding frailty and confusion. Renan sets forth his premise in its preface: an "enlightened" (*éclairé*) priest of Nemi wishes to introduce some rationality into the "absurd" cult of which he is the chief minister. Needless to say, this well-intentioned action produces calamity: the ignorant mob, demanding infallibility from its oracles, installs a criminal in place of this *philosophe avant la lettre*, and as a result his nation is betrayed and succumbs to Rome.

We know that Frazer was a great admirer of Renan for many years: in 1923 he published a small volume called *Sur Ernest Renan*, made up of two addresses that he gave to the Ernest Renan Society, that amply documents that admiration. There he goes so far as to say that he feels closer to Renan, as man and thinker, than to any other French writer or scholar.[43] In *Sur Ernest Renan* Frazer does not mention *Le prêtre de Némi*, but he does name Renan as the source of the image of the "eternal bells of Rome," whose tolling symbolizes the persistence of the religious impulse in mankind, with which *The Golden Bough* ends.[44]

In addition, Frazer's library catalogue lists no fewer than ten titles by Renan, several in editions of the 1860s and 1870s – testimony to a lengthy devotion – of which one is *Le prêtre de Némi*.[45] Significantly, Frazer owned a copy of the ninth edition, dated 1886 – that is, of the play as originally published, before it was combined with several other of Renan's plays to form the volume of 1888 entitled *Drames philosophiques*. Now recall Frazer's statement, in his letter to Macmillan of 7 June 1888, that "From working on Pausanias I was diverted at the close of 1886 by other work." I suggest that he read the play in late 1886, that it immediately appealed to him, and that it gave him the idea for a work that, although perforce speculative, would seek to explain in a new and scientific way what Renan had portrayed fancifully.

If I am right, then why did Frazer, the soul of Calvinist rectitude and a man whose scholarly identity was founded on the practice of acknowledging the work of others in innumerable footnotes, suppress any mention of Renan and *Le prêtre de Némi*? A reason is at hand: Robertson Smith had a particular dislike for Renan, regarding him as little more than a charlatan. He thought Renan so willing to subordinate critical rigor to his own hyperactive imagination that his work became little more than rationalist polemic masquerading as history. For Smith, Renan was an intellectual counterfeiter, passing off his opinions as scholarship.[46]

Frazer may have invented a nonexistent "general work on primitive superstition and religion," of which *The Golden Bough* was an alleged offshoot, in order to extricate himself from an awkward personal situation. He wished to (and did) dedicate *The Golden Bough* to his friend Robertson Smith and may have had reason to believe that if he explicitly acknowledged its Renanian inspiration, Smith might not be willing to be associated with the book. Certainly many people have uttered more serious "white lies" to avoid less embarrassment. If I am right, then not only did he and Smith disagree on important theoretical questions during the time he was writing *The Golden Bough*, but even the dedication of the volume to Smith was not without its difficulties.

6 · THE GOLDEN BOUGH

On 8 November 1889 Frazer wrote to George Macmillan to inform him that he had nearly completed a "study in the history of primitive religion." After noting that its ostensible purpose was an explanation, using the comparative method, of the priesthood in the grove in Nemi (or Aricia), he concluded:

By an application of the comparative method I believe that I can make it probable that the priest represented in his person the god of the grove – Virbius – and that his slaughter was regarded as the death of the god. This raises the question of the meaning of a widespread custom of killing men and animals regarded as divine. . . . The Golden Bough, I believe I can show, was the mistletoe, and the whole legend can, I think, be brought into connexion, on the one hand, with the Druidical reverence for the mistletoe and the human sacrifices which accompanied their worship, and, on the other hand, with the Norse legend of the death of Balder. . . . [W]hatever may be thought of [the book's] theories it will be found, I believe, to contain a large store of very curious customs, many of which may be new even to professed anthropologists. The resemblance of many of the savage customs and ideas to the fundamental doctrines of Christianity is striking. But I make no reference to this parallelism, leaving my readers to draw their own conclusions, one way or the other.

Although the three editions of *The Golden Bough* were to take twenty-five years to complete, and the distance from the Arician grove and Diana via sacrificial kings and totemism to the Norse forest and Balder was to grow from two volumes in the first edition to eleven in the third, this summary of 1889 would continue to serve as what Frazer called the work's "plot." Considerable additions were made over time, partly in response to criticism, and partly from discoveries made by others in the field and by Frazer in the library. Such expansions applied great pressure to what was a thin narrative structure in the first place; as a result the argument became harder and harder to follow as *The Golden Bough* became more and more capacious. Some things, however, did not change: the resemblances of the savage behavior and ideas to those of Christianity would continue to remain "striking," and his readers would continue to draw their own conclusions.

Frazer asked Macmillan the favor of a speedy decision regarding publication. Needless to say, Macmillan asked him to submit the manuscript directly, even before it was complete. Macmillan sent it on immediately to his friend and literary advisor, the Liberal politician, editor, and rationalist man of letters John Morley (1838–1923), who in a few days returned an enthusiastic report.

I have no claim to be an expert in the later work of the comparative anthropologists, but I feel sure that the present MS is an important contribution. In the first place it is clear that the author has both the scientific and the philosophic spirit. That is, he knows how to make great inductions of fact, and he is able to suggest probable and connected explanations. Second, the industry shown by the wide scope and range of his reading, is most remarkable: no German could be more thorough, precise, or definite in his research. Third, the book shows true ingenuity of mind, which rescues the enormous collection of primitive customs and notions from chaos. I am as confident as a man can be who is not an expert, that this is a work of the first rank in its own field, and that it extends that field. . . .

The explanation of [the rule of the grove at Nemi] leads the author into the whole question of the true significance of the widespread custom all over the primitive world of killing men or animals who were partaking of divinity. The development of a number of profound principles of interpretation of primitive religion is as wide and unexpected as Lessing's development of aesthetic science from the Laokoon. Whatever may be the stability of the writer's hypotheses, he has collected a vast store of curious customs, that will, I think, both astonish and delight everybody who is capable of taking an interest in this subject. He has (very wisely) been very careful to keep clear of any direct reference to the Christian mysteries of Atonement, Sacrifice, the Sacrament of Bread and Wine – but any reader with his eyes open will often be startled – almost painfully startled – by seeing before him the origins of these sacred things laid bare. Undoubtedly, then, this is a work that ought to find a publisher. . . .

The style is lucid, unpretentious, and proper to the nature of the subject. No reader would have any trouble in following its pages. The author hopes that he has written a book which may interest, and may be read by "all intelligent persons, and not merely professed students of anthropology and mythology." There is certainly no reason why it should not, except the indolence of even intelligent persons. To the ordinary reader the appearance of so immense a mass of detail, will undoubtedly be repellent. Maine, Spencer, and others, have rather taught a taste for full-grown generalisations in these subjects, without a sight of the materials from which they have sprung. On the other hand, the immense mass of savage customs which the author has gathered together from every age and society, contains much that is lively and entertaining. In one sense the field is narrower than that covered by Tylor's "Primitive Culture." Mr Frazer deals with one special group of primitive customs, and the theory of them. But undoubtedly it is a very important group – perhaps the most important – in the history of human religion.[1]

The manuscript was rapidly completed, and on 16 December, little more than a month after Frazer had submitted the first large installment, Macmillan offered to publish it. Frazer stipulated several conditions, in which Macmillan easily acquiesced: that the frontispiece consist of an engraving of Turner's painting "The Golden Bough" and that the cover be green and carry a stylized mistletoe ornament;[2] that the edition consist of fifteen hundred copies; that he and not the publisher own the copyright; and that he be advanced £100 against his share of the profits (like Pausanias, *The Golden Bough* was published on a half-profits basis).[3]

Only when all had been agreed did he explain to Macmillan his reason for pressing for a quick decision: he needed the advance to pay for a trip to Greece he was planning for the spring of 1890. Eager to return to his commentary on Pausanias, he had decided that only by going in person to the numerous archaeological sites then being excavated all over Greece and seeing for himself what was happening could he gain a full, accurate, and up-to-date idea of the remarkable discoveries being made. If he did not do so, he faced equally unacceptable alternatives: to wait many years while the results dribbled out piecemeal, dependent on the excavators finding time to write up and see their work through the press, or to publish soon and face the just criticism that his work was out of date even before it appeared. Given the amount of time and energy he had already invested, and the wish to make his the definitive commentary on Pausanias, he had to go to Greece.

With the manuscript accepted, Frazer then proceeded to make numerous requests and suggestions about the format and design of the book. Ordinarily of trifling interest, they are worthy of note here because they illustrate Frazer's keen visual sense, so important in the descriptions of scenery in Pausanias and throughout *The Golden Bough*.

All authors want their books to look good, but few have as many and as detailed ideas as did Frazer. Thus, along with the Turner engraving and the mistletoe ornament, he had definite preferences about type size and face, quality of paper, number of lines per page, and the printer to be used. This was not mere fussiness; rather, he wished every element of his book to contribute to a calculated overall effect, and he knew that a handsome volume would sell more copies than a drab one. The special effects were not confined to the external get-up of the book either, for he composed (for browsers in bookshops, and perhaps reviewers too?) elaborate opening and closing set-pieces as well. With only slight alterations he would retain both the opening – the wary priest, sword in hand, circling the grove, waiting for his assailant – and the closing – the Roman bells ringing out over the *campagna* in a blazing sunset – in the second and third editions.

The same worldly spirit of artistic-cum-commercial calculation, which one does not immediately associate with an ivory-tower scholar like Frazer, imbues his letter to Macmillan of 15 March 1890, in which he explained the problem he was having in composing the customary author's notice of the book for the columns of the literary periodicals *The Academy* and *The Athenaeum*:

I find it rather difficult to state summarily the gist of the book without disclosing what I may call the plot. The final result is one which may be rather startling to those who have accepted some long received views as to the early Aryan religion. Hence I do not wish to announce the result before hand, and for the same reason I have refrained from giving a full table of contents. To have done so would have been a mistake, it seemed to me, like the mistake of a novelist who should prefix a summary of the plot to his novel.

In other words, like many intellectuals who write on subjects of general interest, Frazer wanted it both ways: *The Golden Bough* was to be a work of sober scholarship and "science," which implied an expert audience, yet in making design suggestions and in eschewing jargon he hoped to reach the general educated reader as well.

Through the winter of 1889–90 the printing proceeded apace, and Frazer achieved his goal of seeing the book through the press by March (the preface is dated 8 March). By the end of that month he was in Greece, where he would remain for nearly three months. Meanwhile Macmillan obviously decided that *The Golden Bough* might be an important title on his spring list, and he was generous in sending out review copies. As a result the book, published in June 1890, received at least twenty-five reviews, which, for a first work of nonfiction by an unknown academic author, is notable in itself.[4] Virtually every major newspaper and periodical in Britain gave the book a substantial notice. Even more remarkable was the reviewers' unanimity: none was hostile, and the tone of most ranged from favorable to glowing. Then in late 1890 and early 1891 the serious journals weighed in with long, generally favorable review-essays. All in all, an astonishingly successful debut.

Generally speaking, the reviewers made the same points that Morley had: they were all impressed by both the quality and especially the quantity of Frazer's reading (in the view of a number of them, here at last was a Briton who could equal the Germans for industry), the absence of the partisan spirit in handling the sensitive questions that necessarily arose in any discussion of the origins of religion, and the engaging and most un-Teutonic style that helped the reader through what might have been veritable saharas of the driest of little-known facts. Without specialist knowledge few reviewers could go further, and they devoted most of their space to summaries of the book's argument.

Although the reaction was definitely positive, some even comparing it with the epoch-making work of Tylor and/or McLennan,[5] a few had reservations. Of these the best informed was Joseph Jacobs, who reviewed it along with *The Religion of the Semites* in *Folk-Lore*. Long as *The Golden Bough* was, Jacobs thought it in fact not long enough to deal adequately with the profound questions that had been raised; extensive as Frazer's evidence was, Jacobs pointed to the many speculations that perforce linked crucial points in the argument; although impressed by the erudition and the style he was finally not persuaded by the logic and decided that *The Religion of the Semites* was decidedly the more important work.

The first edition of *The Golden Bough* was a significant publication in that its timing was right and its style felicitous, but its advent was not earth-shaking. It may indeed be that for a few readers the book was a landmark.[6] Its importance, however, was as much literary as scholarly, in that it showed that the controversial subject of the history of religion could be made accessible in a nonpolemical way to a general audience by a writer endowed with grace and tact. Its true importance may have been as an indicator of what was to come in the study of primitive religion, both from Frazer and from others, in the quarter century that remained of the Edwardian sunset.

Since the 1920s the leading ideas of *The Golden Bough* have been so widely diffused through academic, literary, and journalistic channels that they are known to many educated people today who have never read the work or any of its abridgments, and are unable consciously to connect the ideas with Frazer. Furthermore, the great majority of those who have read any of *The Golden Bough* have done so in either of the abridgments of the third edition: Frazer's own, which appeared in 1922 and has been often reprinted, or *The New Golden Bough* (1959), an "updated" epitome by T.H. Gaster. Therefore, although all three editions are organically related, it is necessary to do a certain amount of exfoliation even to get sight of the first edition, much less see it as it was in 1890.

Any summary of the argument, however, gives little idea of how it feels to read *The Golden Bough*, in any of its editions. A modern is struck by the deployment of great (and in the third edition even numbing) masses of "evidence" – I use the quotation marks because the relation of the facts to the matter being argued is frequently anything but evident. Such a profusion of data is a consequence of the oceanic subject, in which virtually any topic, as in a dream, may turn into any other. This labyrinthine quality is the result of Frazer's unbridled willingness to digress. It is, therefore, not easy to keep in mind exactly where one is in the argument of the entire work. Further, although in the great mosaic to which the book may be compared the tesserae are facts drawn from all over the world and throughout history, all too often they are held in place by a mortar of speculative inferences and suppositions. This mixture of "hard" and "soft" elements acts to weaken the whole, so that the reader finishes by being unsure of the evidential value of any of it. Most serious of all is that Frazer lacks any idea of culture as the matrix of social, intellectual, and behavioral facts, relationships, and institutions – as the material and symbolic arena in which behavior takes place and gains its significance – and so he selects data from all times and places without any attempt at, or indeed interest in, placing those data in the context that gives them meaning.

Having said that, one must note that this is a *modern* reaction, founded on ideas of culture developed since the 1920s. One is entitled to ask what the readers of 1890 so admired. Frazer himself, in the preface, had disarmingly admitted that he might have pressed some of his speculations too far; a number of his earliest readers agreed that he had. But so impressed were they by the work's intellectual sweep and power, by the way it made coherent the vast range of savage behavior (and by the way that it allusively illuminated

99

Christianity as well) that none felt that this conjectural element was excessive or disfiguring to the book, nor did those who noted the digressions find them fatal either.

Most importantly, none of the reviewers indicted Frazer for taking items of behavior or belief out of context, nor did they find inappropriate the work's focus on belief to the virtual neglect of the material side in primitive life. The reason is not hard to find. Both Frazer and his reviewers had taken their leading ideas on primitive religion from the founders of the ethnographic school – McLennan and Tylor and Robertson Smith – who had defined the subject matter and proposed a method and sounded a tone appropriate for its discussion. But nothing in their work made Frazer seem old-fashioned or crotchety in 1890. Rather, he was hailed as having brought a welcome literary grace to a field not known for that attribute.

Further, by comparison with the elaborate philological fantasies offered by the solarists, Frazer and the entire ethnographic school had the great advantage of seeming to be rooted in observable reality. By 1890, after a generation of controversy between Andrew Lang and Max Müller, most readers were weary of arguments about changes that may or may not have occurred millennia ago in the reconstructed languages that scholars asserted had once been spoken by the Indo-Europeans. On the other hand, everyone knew or recognized the lore of everyday life, whether in the exotic colonies or at home in Britain among the lower classes; everyone could understand the importance of the fertility of the natural world and the anxieties that primitive humanity might have entertained about it.

The primacy of culture is a legacy of the structural–functional revolution worked by Malinowski and Radcliffe-Brown. But their theoretical innovations, far-reaching as they have been, do not in themselves explain the breadth of the gulf between our day and Frazer's regarding the study of religion. In that hundred years – and especially in the decades since the Second World War – we have undergone what Gilbert Murray, referring to the spiritual crisis in late antiquity, called "a failure of nerve." After two world wars, and the collapse of the European colonial empires, we no longer possess the cultural self-confidence that underlay the entire enterprise of anthropology during the half century from the publication of the first edition of *The Golden Bough* until the Second World War. To Europeans at the end of the nineteenth century – to the British perhaps most of all – it seemed self-evident that their political, military, and technological superiority was the result of their occupying a higher rung on the ladder of social and mental evolution. We no longer believe that any more than we accept that the divisions between social classes are natural, God-given, or eternal. Because these are such truisms today, it requires an effort of the imagination to feel the psychic reality of that self-assurance, so completely has it vanished.

At the end of the last century – and well into this one too – educated Europe believed in its "civilizing mission"; respect for the cultures of others barely existed. Frazer (and his fellow folklorists and anthropologists) repeatedly urged that the culture of backward peoples be studied immediately, before their inevitable and impending disappearance, for the resulting information might be material to our effort to understand the history of mankind on the planet.[7] But the knowledge produced in this effort was the intellectual equivalent of the political and economic control exercised directly by the colonial powers. Neither Frazer nor any of his contemporaries, convinced as they were that progress in the European mode was the law of life, was particulary interested in preserving for its own sake what they saw as savagery; an ecological regard for the conservation of exotic cultural varieties as a good in itself was as yet unknown. On this question a century is a long time, and the psychological distance between them and us is great. Frazer was ethnocentric because nearly all Europeans then believed in their superiority to nonwhites and non-Europeans.

Nor is this reading an anachronistic imposition of our modern categories on scholars of another time. Here, to take an apposite example, is Charlotte S. Burne, a leading folklorist and contemporary of Frazer's, writing in December 1886. All the more tellingly for its unself-consciousness, this passage comes from a brief "in-house" article addressed to serious folklorists in the *Folk-Lore* journal. Burne takes up the bread-and-butter question of how to gain for folklore in general and for the Folk-Lore Society in particular the publicity and membership that spiritualism and the Society for Psychical Research had attracted. She considers but rejects an informational campaign based on the inherent interest of the subject; instead, she proposes one based on folklore's *real* utility, which she says has not yet been fully appreciated by its students and therefore not been communicated to the world at large. Although she refers to folklore rather than anthropology, in the late 1880s the line between the two fields was not clear, and the same people were active in both; in this passage "anthropology" may legitimately be substituted for "folklore" without doing violence to the author's intention.

But apart from interested motives, the promotion of the study of folk-lore is a desirable object in itself. It has a practical bearing on the affairs of human life. Captain Temple has pointed out . . . the value of the study to all Englishmen who are called upon (as so many are called upon) to exercise authority over savage and uncivilized tribes. But there are barbarians nearer home than in India or New Zealand, and surely anyone who is placed in a position of authority over uneducated folk must gain in largeness of judgement and breadth of view, and must, therefore, be better fitted for his post, when he has arrived at a perception of the cardinal fact that widely separated stages of progress may coexist in the same country at the same time, and has learnt that the ideas of the folk are not necessarily to be ridiculed or despised when they differ from those which his education has instilled into him. When people understand the prejudices of uneducated folk they must know better how to deal with them, and how to set about trying to reconcile them with the principles of modern culture and civilization.[8]

It is such words and sentiments, and the unquestioned *authority* behind them, that underlay Frazer's assertion in his paper to the Anthropological Institute that he knew better than the primitives the real reasons for their often outlandish behavior. "Trying to reconcile them with the principles of modern culture and civilization" is thus the task for all those who have been called to positions of leadership and control, the magistrate in the counties no less than in the colonies. The white man's burden is just as heavy and as inescapable when those lesser breeds without the Law are white as when they are of a dusky hue.

The Golden Bough opens with a piece of word painting that can stand comparison with anything of the kind in the nineteenth century. This of course is equivocal praise, for painting in words is usually done only in shades of purple. Although some of this is "fine writing" – archaisms, tired Miltonic echoes, and the like – the passage is not merely moonshine.

In the first six pages Frazer not only informs the reader about the priest in ancient Nemi and the bloody rule of the grove to which he must submit, but also intentionally heightens the strangeness and otherworldliness of what took place there. Rhetorically, the plausibility of a recherché explanation such as the one he will offer is increased if he can make a mundane explanation seem unlikely; although he must make that case logically, atmospheric effects render subliminal assistance. Ideologically, it is an important part of Frazer's program that if moderns are to understand the world of the primitives, they must first discard their intellectual assumptions or prejudices. From this standpoint these pages not only orient the reader to the specific scene in which the events took place, but more importantly reorient him to the different world-view that animated those events. In the light of these two considerations, the language of the first paragraph, in which Frazer invokes Turner's picture of the golden bough (which serves as the frontispiece), merits a closer look.

Who does not know Turner's picture of the Golden Bough? The scene, suffused with the golden glow of imagination in which the divine mind of Turner steeped and transfigured even the fairest natural landscape, is a dream-like vision of the little woodland lake of Nemi, "Diana's Mirror," as it was called by the ancients. No one who has seen that calm water, lapped in a green hollow of the Alban hills, can ever forget it. The two characteristic Italian villages which slumber on its banks, and the equally Italian palazzo whose terraced gardens descend steeply to the lake, hardly break the stillness and even the solitariness of the scene. Dian herself might still linger by this lonely shore, still haunt these woodlands wild.

The Golden Bough is essentially a speculative historical reconstruction of a distant period in human mental evolution, which means that its author must offer as much factual evidence as possible to act as ballast for the inevitable conjectures. All the more remarkably, then, he begins by claiming the license of the imaginative artist, typified by "the divine Turner." Turner was anything but a realistic painter, in the common acceptance of that term, and his picture of Aeneas holding the golden bough that confronts the reader in the frontispiece can only be described as a visionary landscape. Originally Frazer may have decided to use Turner's well-known picture simply because of its Virgilian subject. As the editions succeeded one another and *The Golden Bough* grew to epic size, however, the Turnerian or visionary analogy grew increasingly apt.

The figure of Turner and his landscape, acting as a frame to a work of "historical science," nicely represents the inner tension in *The Golden Bough*. Its highly literary author was torn between the attractions, regarded by him as opposites, of science and art, and wished to produce a book that would possess some of the excellences of each. This enchanted landscape and the explicit celebration of the power of imagination stand as the introduction to a brief piece of prose that presents, in highly charged language, the mystery of the Nemian grove that is to be solved; that preamble in turn introduces a work, filled with facts and theories, that claims to contain the solution. Frazer asks for the suspension of the reader's disbelief as we travel to the dreamland of ancient Rome, to a scene possessing the heightened, unearthly stillness of a work of art.

The next paragraph throws a nightmarish cast over this idyllic picture: "In antiquity this sylvan landscape was the scene of a strange and recurring tragedy." Here, quickly, the reader is told, in emotional language, of the priest, ceaselessly on his guard, circling the tree, waiting for the attacker, who like himself is an escaped slave, and who is sure to come. "A candidate for the priesthood could only succeed to office by slaying the priest, and having slain him he held office till he was himself slain by a stronger or a craftier."

Having presented this stark account, Frazer now states the question that he will attempt to answer:

This strange rule has no parallel in classical antiquity, and cannot be explained from it. To find an explanation we must go farther afield. No one will probably deny that such a custom savours of a barbarous age and, surviving into imperial times, stands out in striking isolation from the polished Italian society of the day, like a primeval rock rising from a smooth-shaven lawn. It is the very rudeness and barbarity of the custom which allow us the hope of explaining it. For recent researches into the early history of man have revealed the essential similarity with which, under many superficial differences, the human mind has elaborated its first crude philosophy of life. Accordingly if we can show that a barbarous custom, like that of the priesthood of Nemi, has existed elsewhere; if we can detect the motives which led to its institution; if we can prove that these motives have operated widely, perhaps universally, in human society, producing in varied circumstances a variety of institutions specifically different but generically alike; if we can show, lastly, that these very motives, with some of their derivative institutions, were actually at work in classical antiquity; then we may fairly infer that in a remoter age the same motives gave birth to the priesthood of Nemi.

This is a preliminary paragraph of assertions, with the proof to come later; nevertheless one may already question some of the logic and the language. Assuming that it is true that no parallel to the priesthood exists in antiquity, it does not follow that its explanation is therefore not to be found in antiquity, which is plainly the most likely place to look. The ritual in the grove is alleged to "savour of barbarity" – barbarity supposedly being self-explanatory – and it is said to stand out against the background of the polished manners of imperial Rome like a solitary boulder jutting out of a smooth lawn. Further, it is the very "rudeness and barbarity," qualities that "no one will probably deny," that make us hopeful that an explanation may be forthcoming. Putting to one side the unexpected characterization of imperial Rome as uniformly cultivated, one still might have expected exactly the opposite – that the priesthood's uniqueness would make it difficult and not easy to establish its *raison d'être*. The confusion is mirrored in the metaphor, for it is also more likely that a geologist could explain the origin of a large outcrop than a single "primeval rock." Finally, the word "primeval" is tendentious in that it implies that the rock (or priesthood) is of immemorial antiquity, when that is what is to be demonstrated.

Frazer in the third paragraph then offers a series of conditions which, if he can but satisfy them, will mean that he has made his case. All of them flow from intellectualist assumptions, particularly the focus on the "crude philosophy of life" and the "motives" of savages who, though superficially different, are all really similar; as such there is nothing here that would have been problematic to the knowledgeable reader of 1890. The paragraph ends with a frank admission of the speculative character of the inquiry; in view of the inevitable gaps in our knowledge and the inherently conjectural nature of the comparative method, the best that the book can do is "to offer a fairly probable explanation of the priesthood of Nemi."

If one were sufficiently interested and sufficiently patient, one might go on at virtually endless length with such a running adversarial *explication de texte*, scoring points off Frazer at will. The resulting commentary would be longer than *The Golden Bough*, and would be both easy and pointless to compose. But such an exercise carried out on only the first three paragraphs is instructive.

First, it indicates the "literariness" of the work, which his early readers appreciated. When Frazer is not stating facts but is striving for effect, his is often an artful and mellifluous prose, usually latinate, based on the "best" classical and neoclassical models. Today some may find his manner a stale compound of airs and graces, but the cultivation and finish of his writing commended it to educated people who may have thought that writing about the lower races tended to be somewhat barbarous itself.

His literary finesse certainly succeeded in promoting anthropology as a field of humanistic discourse.[9] As anthropology became more explicitly scientific in the twentieth century, it developed its own vocabulary, which always accompanies the coming of age of a profession. But partly because of the humanistic legacy of Frazer and the other late-nineteenth-century founding fathers (and a few founding mothers as well) who believed that works of anthropology, as the science of humankind, should be directed to all educated readers, each succeeding generation has produced some work that is directed to a general audience.

Second, that none of the 1890 reviewers noted any of the logical difficulties in Frazer's third paragraph means not that we are keener dialecticians than they were but that the holes in the argument were invisible to them because they accepted his assumptions, whereas we do not. It is not that anthropologists today are uninterested in beliefs, nor that comparison is a useless method; what has been rejected is his way of collating items culled from literally everywhere and every age to produce sweeping synthetic results. The method declared inadmissible, we find an argument based on it to be largely beside the point. It seems safe to say that today literally no student of Roman religion in particular nor of primitive religion in general is sympathetic to the basic contention or method of *The Golden Bough*.[10]

Further close reading of the text, which would necessarily involve an endless and increasingly irritable questioning of the logic of the narrative, is an unprofitable way of proceeding. What seems appropriate, then, is a summary–discussion of the work's contents, so as to permit a comparison later with the second and third editions.

The two volumes of the first edition of *The Golden Bough* comprise 800 pages. The work is divided into four chapters, of very unequal lengths. The first, "The King of the Wood," begins with Frazer's usual minimum of theoretical introduction; it deals mainly with the sacred kingship, incarnate gods, and tree worship, introducing the concepts and adducing much evidence for their prevalence in the primitive and ancient worlds. The second, "The Perils of the Soul," like its predecessor about a hundred pages long, presents the idea of taboo, and especially royal and priestly taboos. The third chapter, "Killing the God," at more than 400 pages, is by far the longest. After an explanation of the idea of killing the divine king, most of the pages are given over to innumerable illustrations from two sources: contemporary peasant customs (Mannhardt) and the religions of the ancient world (Attis, Adonis, Osiris, Dionysus). There follow relatively brief sections on the idea of sacrifice ("eating the god") as a totemic communion sacrament and on the idea of the scapegoat. In the final chapter, "The Golden Bough," Frazer in 150 pages explains and illustrates the idea of the external soul, a common motif in folktales, and then by its light explains the Norse myth of Balder.

Of those themes, none is more important than the one that would become the heart of the matter for T. S. Eliot and many other readers: the dying god. Frazer has argued that the priest–king at Nemi was an incarnation of the tree-spirit, a group of beings widely worshiped in a more superstitious age, and hence a member of the large class of men who claimed to be the embodiments of gods. Such sacred rulers were venerated because they were believed to control the natural forces, such as sunshine, rainfall, and especially fertility, that determined whether their people would live or die. Because their powers are so awesome, they themselves are surrounded by a myriad of taboos to keep them from all harm. Moreover, any sign of age or physical infirmity is intolerable because it would imply that the vital indwelling force was waning, with dire consequences for the nation. The king must always be at the height of his powers. If he is or seems not to be perfect, then he must be put to death.

We then learn about killing the king (1) when he is infirm or (2) after he has ruled for a certain set term. The kings, understandably made unhappy by this drastic view of their efficacy, responded over the years by various shifts, such as creating contemporary kings and mock kings – even kings for a day – to permit merely an intermission rather than a true termination of their reigns. This leads to a discussion of the many folkloric performances still extant in 1890 in which royal surrogates, personifications of the life force, are killed.

For us one of the unintentioned results of the numerous surveys of peasant behavior in *The Golden Bough* is pathos. If only as a result of the passage of time, this world of innocent-seeming rural popular amusement is, for a modern reader, heavy with unconscious emotion. Not only has the Europe in which these arcadian events took place been transformed by industrialization and then savaged by war, but the unself-consciousness that (Frazer believed) informed them is gone as well. Implicitly, the world of Frazer's peasants is whole and functioning, unlike that of his acquaintance Thomas Hardy.

Here are two short examples, one from Silesia and the other from Sardinia. They look and sound like the peasant festivities that make up the background to the aristocratic foreground in *Giselle*. Indeed, its ubiquity and availability may suggest why such folklore (duly prettified, to be sure) was so attractive to nineteenth-century choreographers.

Thus at Braller [in Silesia] on Ash Wednesday or Shrove Tuesday two white and two chestnut horses draw a sledge on which is placed a straw-man swathed in white cloth; beside him is a cart-wheel which is kept turning round. Two lads disguised as old men follow the sledge lamenting. The rest of the village lads, mounted on horseback and decked with ribbons, accompany the procession, which is headed by two girls crowned with evergreen and drawn in a waggon or sledge.[11]

In Sardinia the gardens of Adonis are still planted in connection with the great midsummer festival which bears the name of St John. At the end of March or on the 1st of April a young man of the village presents himself to a girl and asks her to be his *comare* (gossip or sweetheart), offering to be her *compare*. The invitation is considered an honour by the girl's family, and is gladly accepted. At the end of May the girl makes a pot of the bark of the cork-tree, fills it with earth, and sows a handful of wheat and barley in it. . . . On St John's Day the young man and the girl, dressed in their best, accompanied by a long retinue and preceded by children gambolling and frolicking, move in procession to a church outside the village. Here they break the pot by throwing it against the door of the church. Then they sit down in a ring on the grass and eat eggs and herbs to the music of flutes. Wine is mixed in a cup and passed round, each one drinking as it passes. Then they join hands and sing "Sweethearts of St John" . . . over and over again, the flutes playing the while. When they tire of singing, they stand up and dance gaily in a ring until evening.[12]

From his coverage of European peasant life he then turns to the religions of antiquity. Here the first edition differs greatly from its successors. In later years Frazer rewrote the entire work, but no section as completely as this one. In the third edition an entire volume was dedicated to *The Dying God* and two to *Adonis Attis Osiris*, and the three occupy the literal as well as the symbolic center of *The Golden Bough*. In the first edition, however, the entire discussion of Attis, Adonis, Thammuz, Osiris, Dionysus, and Demeter and Proserpine – all the vegetation cults of the ancient eastern Mediterranean – occupy barely fifty pages, which for Frazer amounts to little more than a clearing of the throat. The transition to the religions of the ancient Levant is managed by a single sentence, linking them in a tenuous and mechanical way to the preceding copious analysis of the European peasant vegetation rituals: "But it is in Egypt and Western Asia that the death and resurrection of vegetation appear to have been most widely celebrated with ceremonies like those of modern Europe."[13] That is to say, the religions of classical antiquity are little more than an antique pendant to the modern European peasant rites. They offer Frazer an opportunity to use his classical learning, thus diluting somewhat the massive indebtedness to Mannhardt.

The last important section of this chapter on the dying god deals with the widespread primitive custom of killing and eating divine animals or men in order to acquire the powers and attributes of the god they incarnate. After an exhaustive summary of the ways in which agricultural peoples kill and eat the god (mainly in springtime and harvest ceremonies), Frazer describes the analogous ceremonies for pastoral and hunting peoples. He then passes to the idea and ritual of the scapegoat, which he derives in a utilitarian way from the insight of the ancients that the god as he dies can be used to bear away the load of evil and sin that has accumulated in the tribe over a year. A survey of such rites leads him to observe that the discharge of evil energy takes place at specific times of year, when the seasons are changing, and is preceded or followed by period of license or misrule. This observation foreshadows the development in succeeding editions of the presentation of what might be called the overall rhythms, based on vegetation or fertility cult, of the ancient and primitive world. Unfortunately such analytic passages tend to be rare in comparison with the assemblage of disparate facts that swamp the discussion, and these rhythmic patterns must be inferred by the reader without much help from the author.

The last section of the book deals with the myth of Balder. Frazer isolates two features of the myth – the plucking of the mistletoe by Loki and the death of Balder by burning – which he asserts are central to the story. He then offers the expectable surveys of the primitive worship of mistletoe and the oak on which it grows, and of the widespread practice of midsummer bonfires. In tracing the occurrence of both customs, he is indifferent to the facts that many of the peoples who observe one do not observe the other, and that even among those who have both, there is no special connection between them. It is enough for him that their prevalence be demonstrated.

A discussion of the common folkloric motif of the external soul, familiar to the reader of folk- and fairy tales, introduces the idea of totemism. In totemistic societies the external soul is said to explain the relation between people and their totem: "The totem, if I am right, is simply the receptacle in which a man keeps his life."[14] Frazer admits that he is speculating here, on the basis of extremely fragmentary evidence, and this explanation would be scrapped when he came to rewrite a decade later.

We are, at long last, at the conclusion, and he moves to tie up all the threads. Balder's life was lodged in the mistletoe, which was why he could be killed only by that plant. Analogously, to the mind of primitive man, the life of the oak itself was deposited in the mistletoe. Next, despite the fact that Virgil does not identify the Golden Bough with the mistletoe but only compares the two, Frazer claims that the Golden Bough was the mistletoe nevertheless: "The inference is almost inevitable that the Golden Bough was nothing but the mistletoe seen through the haze of poetry or of popular superstition."[15]

By this time Frazer seems impatient to finish, perhaps somewhat winded from the effort involved in having started so many intellectual hares. One result of this mental fatigue is that he has forgotten completely the same "haze" of imagination that he himself invoked at the beginning, with Turner and the idyllic landscape. Had he recalled it, perhaps he might not have been so quick to yoke poetry and superstition as equals in their power to create illusions. Perhaps in this dismissal of the imagination we have yet another example of that persistent inability or unwillingness in Britain to acknowledge that fiction (or poetry) is neither a lie nor the truth but something else, a *tertium quid*. Had Turner been less of a figurehead, and had his influence pervaded more of *The Golden Bough*, Frazer might have been less insistently utilitarian and accordingly might have given more weight to the symbolic dimension of religion.

In the best tradition of the nineteenth-century three-decker novel, the conclusion ties together the main elements in the obscure drama in the Nemian grove. The conclusion is, like the rest of the argument, entirely speculative. Unlike the detective who solves the mystery by means of fresh evidence that makes us see everything in a new light, Frazer's wind-up is completely deductive. The priest – the king of the wood – personified the tree on which the Golden Bough grew. If that tree was the oak, then the king must have been an incarnation of the oak spirit. Before he could be killed, therefore, the Bough had to be broken off.

As an oak-spirit, his life or death was in the mistletoe on the oak, and so long as the mistletoe remained intact, he, like Balder, could not die. To slay him, therefore, it was necessary to break the mistletoe, and probably, as in the case of Balder, to throw it at him. And to complete the parallel, it is only necessary to suppose that the King of the Wood was formerly burned, dead or alive, at the midsummer fire festival which, as we have seen, was annually celebrated in the Arician grove. . . . The rite was probably an essential feature in the primitive Aryan worship of the oak. . . . The result, then, of our inquiry is to make it probable that, down to the time of the Roman Empire and the beginning of our era, the primitive worship of the Aryans was maintained nearly in its original form in the sacred grove at Nemi, as in the oak woods of Gaul, of Prussia, and of Scandinavia; and that the King of the Wood lived and died as an incarnation of the Supreme Aryan god, whose life was in the mistletoe or Golden Bough.[16]

But this is only the penultimate paragraph. The last, completing the frame that Turner began, returns to the idyllic lake in the Alban hills. The landscape is said to be "not much changed from what [it was] when Diana and Virbius still received the homage of their worshippers in the sacred grove." Although the temple is no longer there, and "the King of the Wood no longer stands sentinel over the Golden Bough," yet, "if the air be still," one may still hear the Renanian bells of Rome ringing the Angelus. The timelessness of the scene, and by implication the timelessness of the round of death and resurrection that has just been presented, are summed up in the final sentence: *"Le roi est mort, vive le roi!"*

It is fitting to conclude by remarking the absence of something that might have been expected. The progression of magic, religion, and science as the universal and inevitable stages in the mental evolution of humanity – probably the thesis for which Frazer is best known – is nowhere to be found. Instead, it constitutes the main theoretical novelty of the second edition. Here, however, the crucial distinction between magic and religion has not yet arisen, as is clearly to be seen when, having described dozens of peasant springtime and harvest customs, he moves easily from behavior to belief:

Plainly, therefore, these spring and harvest customs are based on the same ancient modes of thought, and form parts of the same primitive heathendom, which was doubtless practised by our forefathers long before the dawn of history, as it is practised to this day by many of their descendants.[17]

This, in turn, acts as a springboard for him to describe the leading features of what might be termed the theology and liturgy of this universal "primitive heathendom." In his list of the "marks of a primitive religion," the fourth and

109

last is "The rites are magical rather than propitiatory."[18] Magic here is merely a subheading to be found under the rubric of religion that describes the style and intention behind certain religious performances. Only in the late 1890s, with the emergence of remarkable new data concerning the Australian aborigines, did he turn to the overall movement of human mental and spiritual development, with momentous consequences for his work.

7 · SMITH DIES; FRAZER MARRIES

Vɪʀᴛᴜᴀʟʟʏ ᴀs sᴏᴏɴ as he had read the last proof of *The Golden Bough* Frazer left for Greece. He kept an *aide-mémoire* pocket diary of this trip (and of the one he made in 1895 as well); although the entire series of volumes for 1895 has survived, for 1890 unfortunately only the first volume, given over mostly to preliminaries, is extant.[1] In it Frazer copied out a good deal of information on Greek sculpture supplied by his friend Middleton, along with many pages of detailed descriptions of objects seen in the National Museum in Athens and numerous inscriptions from the Acropolis. Only after he had been in Athens for nearly a month did he set off (with a dragoman), on 21 April, to tour the sites in central Greece and the Peloponnese mentioned in Pausanias. Until he left Greece eight weeks later on 15 June he was constantly and tirelessly on the move, talking with the directors of excavations, visiting their sites and taking copious notes, and scrambling over rocks and copying the many inscriptions he came across by chance.

In short, he became a second Pausanias, strenuously following his author's itineraries on horseback and on foot. (Railroads were only then being built in Greece, and many of the archaeological sites were in remote locations, to which access was possible only on horseback or in a bone-jarring horse and cart.) The diary contains notes on his visits to Sparta and Olympia and ends on 9 May in Olympia; in addition we know (from retrospective remarks in the 1895 diary) that in 1890 he went to (at least) Epidaurus, Mantinea, Plataea, Thespiae, Nauplia, Argos, Tiryns, Mycenae, Piraeus, Munychia, Kephisia, Marathon, and Rhamnus.[2]

Most noticeable in this otherwise unexceptional volume is Frazer's sensitivity to, and appreciation of, scenery; however, he seems virtually incapable of presenting anything he sees without embellishing it. Although he takes pains throughout to present a temple, village, or ruin in its natural setting, nearly everything is heightened and dramatized. In the following example the invocation of Doré lies at the heart of the matter:

After passing the village of Trypi we entered the Langada gorge. Words would quite fail to convey an idea of the grandeur and beauty of the scenery. Huge pinnacles of rock shot up into the sky, their faraway summits fringed with pines, that stood out against the sky. In some places beetling crags, such as Doré might have imagined, hung over the path, and in others precipices yawned beside the narrow path.[3]

Such scene-setting is gratuitous. It has nothing to do with Pausanias; Frazer

111

never attempts to connect the scenery with his author, nor is he writing a travel guide to Greece. Rather, he had a reflex impulse always to frame the observer or the thing observed in its natural setting, usually in a dramatic fashion. It occurs in virtually everything that he composed.

While in Athens at Easter Frazer had an "adventure." Its context is supplied in his discussion ten years later, in the second edition of *The Golden Bough*, of "new fires" – the widespread custom of extinguishing all fires at certain critical points in the year and then rekindling them.[4] He witnessed this ritual in the cathedral in Athens at midnight on Holy Saturday, 13 April 1890. After describing how the church is totally darkened, "at the presumed moment of the resurrection the bells ring out and the whole square bursts as by magic into a blaze of light." This gives him a chance to get off one of his better anticlerical wisecracks: "Theoretically all the candles are lit from the sacred new fire in the cathedral, but practically it may be suspected that the matches which bear the name of Lucifer have some share in the sudden illumination."

The Greeks have a custom of shooting at effigies of Judas on Easter Saturday and Easter Sunday, but the shots sometimes go astray and hit people, "and the cartridges used on this occasion are not always blank." The excitement, which took only a few minutes, occurred when he was caught in just such a crossfire, with live ammunition whistling over his head. The long account, which he decided finally not to publish, is to be found in the margins of his interleaved copy of the second edition of *The Golden Bough*, when he was revising for the third edition.[5] The bullets sang around his ears until he managed to get round a corner "with great celerity. While executing this strategic movement to the rear I was kept in countenance by a Greek soldier in uniform. When we had the corner between us and the next discharge we smiled in each other's faces and parted ... Whether he or I was mistaken for Judas I did not stop to enquire." The rarity of that smile makes it precious; Frazer excluded such personal moments from his work because they did not comport with his idea of the gravity befitting a work of science.

Aside from the diary, the only mementoes of the journey are a few books that he took along with him. Of these the most important is his inscribed and annotated copy of the then newly published *Mythology and Monuments of Ancient Athens* (Macmillan, 1890), by Jane Ellen Harrison and Margaret Verrall.[6] It is easy to see why he should have taken it. In a sense it is the book that Macmillan wanted Frazer to produce back in 1884 – a single volume containing both a translation (by Verrall) of Pausanias' description of the art and architecture of Athens and commentaries (by Harrison) on the ruins then visible as well as on the many myths that Pausanias discusses (Harrison's special interest).[7] In that it does not offer even a complete translation of Pausanias, much less a full-scale commentary, it is no rival to Frazer; its compact format and its focus on Athens, however, made it ideal for tourists and it continued to sell well for many years – indeed, long after Harrison herself had changed her mind about many of the topographic and mythographic issues.

Frazer, back in Cambridge in mid-July 1890, was understandably gratified by the favorable initial reception of *The Golden Bough*, and immediately plunged back into Pausanias. The first letter to Macmillan after his return (15 August 1890) raised the question once again of the text. Turning Pausanias' clumsy Greek into graceful English had been challenging, and of course his heart was really in the commentary – but what of the text? Frazer was aware that virtually ignoring the text at the same time that he offered many pages of anthropology was not a formula calculated to ingratiate him with traditional classical scholars. On the other hand, given his current interests he was unwilling in 1890 to start from scratch and expend the considerable time and energy involved in a fresh collation of the manuscripts. Instead, he suggested a shortcut: to publish a text that would incorporate the best of the many corrections that had been advanced by *other* scholars to Schubart's standard edition (then more than thirty years old), thereby producing with a minimum of his effort a far better text than any then in existence. This text, with notes, he suggested, might be brought out as a separate volume. "I do not however feel strongly about it and only write to make the suggestion and to learn your views on the subject."

Macmillan's own classical background informed his publisher's sense of the market to produce an interesting reply. One can easily imagine him, after six years, wondering whether he would ever see Pausanias and, if it did finally appear, whether it would be even halfway viable, commercially speaking. One might, therefore, expect him to embrace Frazer's offer to cobble together a secondhand text or else decide not to have one at all. Instead he advised Frazer (19 August) to prepare a proper text, with a full *apparatus criticus* (that is, with manuscript variants and other textual information in Latin footnotes), and – equally important – to trim the entire edition drastically so as to make it fit into three octavo volumes: the first to contain the text and the second and third to present translation and commentary together. He already saw the danger: runaway expansion of the commentary without a text meant an expensive hybrid that would find an audience among neither scholars nor travelers.

Macmillan's motive is to be found in his last paragraph, which appears as an afterthought but is anything but tacked-on:

I am sorry to say that the sales of "The Golden Bough" have been rather disappointing. So far [about two months after publication] we have sold about 220 copies in England and sent 100 to America. I am afraid that a good many readers have been frightened by the size of the book, and the rather bewildering abundance of detail. My own feeling is that it might have been considerably compressed without loss either to general interest or scientific value. We must hope however that its almost universal recognition as an important contribution to the study of primitive religion will produce a steady, though not rapid demand that will in time exhaust the edition.[8]

This was the first time that Macmillan had uttered a critical word about any aspect of *The Golden Bough*, much less the profusion of detail that is its chief feature. Frazer must have felt that the time to have mentioned it was before and not after publication, and he must have been alarmed at this procrustean solution to the question of size, but he made no reply. Instead he decided the matter himself five months later, on 17 January 1891:

I am now hard at work on Pausanias and mean to undertake no work of importance till Pausanias is finished. The notes promise or rather threaten to expand to a great length. I fear they will extend to two volumes by themselves, without the translation. I have rather abandoned the idea of publishing a text to range with the translation. It would not only add to the bulk and expense of the book but would compel me to devote a good deal of time to the not very congenial task of minute verbal criticism. I am desirous of getting back to my comparative religion as soon as I can. . . . I hope to go out again to Greece, for the sake of Pausanias, in February or March.

This was what Macmillan had been fearing, and it put him in a decidedly awkward position. He believed in Frazer as a promising author and wished to encourage him, and he himself was interested in Frazer's subject, but as an editor and publisher he had to speak his mind bluntly – so bluntly, indeed, as to run the risk of seeming ungentlemanly, which went much against the grain. Yet he had to make his misgivings as clear as possible. Once again he began his reply, on 21 January, with a sales report on *The Golden Bough*: since 1 July 1890 only about 130 copies had been sold. (This is impossible to reconcile with the figure of 220 he had already mentioned on 19 August; it might be a slip. Whatever the exact figure, the point is clear – sales were anything but robust.) He followed this by expressing his "alarm" at Frazer's latest estimate of the size of the edition.

We do not doubt the value of your material but the public is not a large one and it would be a pity to have to make the price prohibitive. I would certainly urge you to compress as much as possible . . . I have always felt that "The Golden Bough" would have gained by compression. . . . I think you are right to give up the idea of a Pausanias text.[9]

His change of heart in accepting the absence of a text may well have been based on two facts: publication would thereby be accelerated by at least a year or two, and the firm would be spared a very expensive job of Greek and Latin composition.

Frazer's hope for a speedy return to Greece would remain only a hope for four more years; in 1891, however, he believed that the commentary could be contained in two volumes, and that another quick trip to Greece would suffice to give him the information on the excavations in Attica he had been unable to secure in 1890. Neither would prove correct.

About this time Frazer's concentration on Pausanias was broken by a communication from one of his early readers and reviewers. Frazer's letter of 6 November 1891 to the Master of Trinity, H. Montagu Butler, explains what happened.

Two days ago I received from [the historian of Roman religion] Mr W. Warde Fowler of Lincoln College, Oxford, a letter in which he points out that in my book *The Golden Bough* I have mistranslated a passage in Pliny (xvi. 250) which, as I interpreted it, was of great importance for my main argument. Properly interpreted, as I now see, the passage not only does not support my argument but is positively opposed to it and consequently my argument, so far, falls to the ground. I have asked Mr Warde Fowler to write to the *Athenaeum* pointing out my mistake and I have suggested that I should at the same time send a note to the *Athenaeum* acknowledging my mistake and pointing out how seriously it invalidates my main argument. I have not yet received an answer from Mr Warde Fowler, but if he prefers not to publish his correction, I shall consider it an imperative duty to do so myself.

As the Council in deciding to renew my Fellowship last year had regard, I believe, in part to my book *The Golden Bough* and as the mistake in question not only seriously impairs the value of the book, but may also naturally beget a doubt as to the accuracy of my work in general, I think it right that the Council should have an opportunity of reconsidering their decision. I therefore beg leave to intimate that they have my full consent to re-open the question from the beginning and that I will accept as just any decision at which they may arrive. If the Council think that it would facilitate their decision, I will submit to them the manuscript of the book I am now engaged on and any other of my manuscripts that they may wish to examine.[10]

The same day Frazer sent a letter to the *Athenaeum*, which was duly printed as "A Correction," in the issue of 21 November 1891. This sets forth the facts and their implications as stated to Butler but does not mention Fowler by name. The passage in question relates to Frazer's discussion of Midsummer Eve festivals, and the plants gathered for them. An important testimony here is Pliny's description of the Druids, who plucked the sacred mistletoe on the infrequent occasions when they found it, and Frazer therefore translated Pliny's account at some length, as follows: "'This they [the Druids] do especially in the sixth month (the beginnings of their months and years are determined by the moon) and after the tree has passed the thirtieth year of its age.'"[11] Fowler pointed out that Pliny's phrase *sexta luna* meant the "sixth day of the month" (that is, the time when the moon was crescent), not the "sixth month," which of course (as Frazer notes to Butler) completely undercut at least this section of the argument. Whatever the Druids were up to, in looking for the mistletoe they were not preparing a midsummer rite, as Frazer had supposed.

The matter ended there, at least so far as the outside world was concerned. Butler and the College Council did nothing, and Frazer did not resign his fellowship. Psychologically, however, the aftershocks must have rumbled on for a much longer time. Frazer had a high idea of the calling of scholarship and of himself as a scholar. Like all scholars he hoped that his ideas would prevail in the proverbially crowded intellectual marketplace. From time to time he could expect the consensus of qualified judges to decide against him on the grounds that his ideas were unpersuasive or that another's ideas were superior to his. Such a grave scenario of high-minded combat, however, definitely did not include being shown up as a bumbler who misconstrues in print the meaning of a passage.

The event has become part of the folklore of Trinity College and is now known and told by the Fellows as part of the corpus of Frazeriana. Downie gives a slightly different version, which he credits to Lady Frazer, whose memory (at least at the end of her life) was not particularly accurate and who was in any case not above embroidering the truth. In Downie's account Frazer wrote this letter after first having gone to see the Master in some agitation and offering to resign his fellowship. When Butler, who was famous for the Jamesian refinement of his feelings, finally understood why Frazer was so wrought up, Downie (per Lady Frazer) has Butler saying, in most unlikely dog-Latin, *"Pecca fortiore"* ("Commit a more serious transgression").[12]

This shock having passed, he soldiered on with Pausanias. As the commentary grew the schedule inevitably slipped, and with it the return to Greece receded as well. From time to time he would send a status report to Macmillan. On 4 June 1892 he wrote:

The commentary on books II–IX is now finished, with the exception of a few gaps to be filled in before the MS goes to press. The commentary on book X is in progress and should be finished by about the end of July. It will then only remain to write the commentary on Attica, which I should hope to finish by the end of the year. I have left Athens to the last in order to include the latest discoveries. This will prevent my going to press till the MS is practically complete. Otherwise the printing might have begun before now.... As to the translation, my version of books II–IX and part of X is ready for the press. The rest of the translation is finished but not revised for the press.

At Macmillan's canny suggestion they then agreed to set in type those large sections of the work that were complete; for Macmillan at least, along with accelerating the publication (whenever that might actually happen), such a *fait accompli* had the great merit of acting as a deterrent, on the real enough grounds of added expense, to the second and third thoughts that Frazer was sure to have. They therefore agreed on the basic design specifications, and the typesetting began. Starting in late 1891 their letters for the next several years are filled with the details concerning the preparation of the hundreds of illustrations, figures, maps, and excavation site plans that make the work so comprehensive and valuable. An added complication arose concerning the maps and site plans: most of them either did not exist or, because the best maps were military, were not publicly available and therefore had to be specially drawn. In addition, once the printing actually began in 1894, there were the proofs, which contain thousands of words, phrases, and passages in Greek and Latin and probably the same number of bibliographic citations of titles in foreign languages. It is a tribute to Frazer's stupendous capacity for taking pains and the outstanding competence of the printers (R. & R. Clark, of Edinburgh) that typographical errors are rare in Pausanias or, indeed, in any of Frazer's books.

Predictably, the longer Frazer worked, the larger Pausanias became. Nine and a half years – the length of the siege of Troy – after Macmillan's first letter to Frazer in July 1884, a letter to Macmillan on 22 February 1894 began on a mildly exultant note: "I have the pleasure of informing you that my translation of Pausanias, revised and corrected, is now ready for the press." But he had then to beat an immediate and embarrassing retreat, for he was forced to acknowledge that he could not even estimate the number of pages the commentary would take. He could say only that, "I fear that by itself, without the translation, it may possibly occupy three volumes." Having for the first time admitted aloud that the project had now expanded to four volumes, he continued hurriedly: "But considering that no adequate commentary on Pausanias exists and that the mass of illustrative matter which has been accumulated in the course of this century is enormous, I trust that you will not think this excessive." Macmillan did not reply. Having already spoken his mind as clearly as he knew how about the need for compression, to no effect whatever, he could now only hope for the best – that the sale would be reasonably good and that profits from *The Golden Bough* and any later books would offset the likely losses that Pausanias would produce.

Meanwhile, although Frazer wished only to put his head down and work on Pausanias, this laudable desire was frustrated by several interruptions. At this time the only distraction that Frazer willingly allowed from his concentration was the many hours he devoted to visiting Robertson Smith, whose decline was becoming more obvious, and to reading the proofs of the revised second edition of *The Religion of the Semites* (1894). Smith died on 31 March 1894, and Frazer immediately wrote an obituary, which appeared in the *Fortnightly Review* for June 1894.

He had returned to Pausanias for only three months, however, when, in July 1894, out of the blue, he received news of the kind that every scholar dreads, and none more than one in his situation, in what he hoped were the penultimate stages of a large project. A hurried conversation with an American scholar met by chance had revealed the hitherto-unknown existence and impending publication of an elaborate German edition of Pausanias, to run to no fewer than ten volumes, edited by the well-known scholars Hermann Hitzig and Hugo Bluemner. This mighty scholarly engine had obviously been gaining speed for some time, for (he was told) the first volume might be expected shortly. His informant therefore advised him to pre-empt the field by bringing out at least his first volume as quickly as he could.

Frazer agreed; he could hardly remain passive in the face of this threat. For threat it certainly was, financial to Macmillan and academic to Frazer.

Although his edition was not to be anywhere as large as the German one, both were grandiose enough that only university libraries and wealthy classical amateurs could be expected to afford them. How many of this relatively small group of buyers might be expected to acquire both? (The news also meant that he and Macmillan had lost part of their potential market, for the Germans would of course publish a properly edited text, and German scholars would naturally prefer a commentary in their own language.) He broke this dramatic news to Macmillan on 15 July and suggested the following:

I think it would be well to ascertain when exactly the first volume of the German work will appear, and if necessary to anticipate it by publishing the first two volumes of my Pausanias (including the translation and the commentary on Attica) as soon as they are ready, without waiting for the other two volumes.

This expedient created problems, however. From Frazer's point of view the difficulty lay in the fact that whereas the commentary on Attica was at last nearly ready for the printer, that on some of the other books now inevitably needed to be brought up to date in the light of the most recent research and scholarship. If he stopped to do this, however, then his commentary on Attica, which for most readers is the heart of the matter in that it contains the most important archaeological and architectural material, might be anticipated by the Germans. Would Macmillan be prepared, therefore, to bring out the first two volumes – the translation and the commentary on Attica – even without a general introduction to the edition, in order to be first? From Macmillan's point of view, on the other hand, although competitors had not been foreseen, it was precisely to forestall just such an endless vain attempt on Frazer's part to keep the entire commentary current that books II–XI had been set in type.

Remarkably, the Macmillan letter books contain no response to Frazer's cry of alarm. George Macmillan was away from the office when the letter was received, and no one else in authority (that is, Frederick or Maurice Macmillan) answered in his stead. More remarkably, when George Macmillan did return he still did not reply (at least in writing; perhaps they judged the situation grave enough to warrant a meeting in London). Whatever took place between them, the important facts are that publication was not brought forward nor was Frazer permitted to alter the sections already set in type. His fears about being beaten to the post gradually subsided. Further, it emerged that even German efficiency had its limits, and the first volume of Hitzig and Bluemner did not appear until 1896, which allowed Frazer in his preface (dated December 1897) to say in truth that it had come to hand too late to use; in fact he was able to incorporate a few of its readings in his addenda.[13] The six volumes of Frazer's *Pausanias's Description of Greece* were published in February 1898, fully three and a half years after the German competition made itself known.

The strangest event in the protracted history of the Pausanias took place on 18 August 1894. With his anxiety about the German competition at its height,

Frazer decided to break away from Pausanias and embark on something entirely new: He suggested to Macmillan the preparation of an anthology of biblical passages "chosen for their literary beauty and interest." Equally surprisingly, Macmillan did not simply tell Frazer to get on with Pausanias; instead he considered the idea for a long while before rejecting it.[14]

I suggest that the anthology, which comes from nowhere and lacks all connection with Frazer's previous interests, and even more its odd timing, were delayed products of his grief at the death of Smith some four months earlier. Perhaps Frazer had been numbed by pain at the time; whatever the reason, in the obituary he had chosen to discuss Smith entirely in terms of his intellectual contributions. For this reason it cannot have been emotionally cathartic. It may not therefore be excessively fanciful to see the anthology as an oblique memorial, a way of expressing what he had been unable or unwilling to say in the *Fortnightly*. The biblical subject matter is thus to be read as a symbolic equivalent of Smith, and Frazer's own ambivalent relation to both Smith and Christianity is embodied in the unconventional principle of selection on literary grounds.

What makes such a reading even possible is the importance the idea had for Frazer at a time when self-interest required relentless concentration on Pausanias. When Macmillan turned it down, Frazer, undeterred, approached A. & C. Black, publishers of the *Britannica* and of his *Totemism*. Black accepted it, and it duly appeared in June 1895. (Although at least in North America virtually every college and university English department offers a course on "the Bible as literature," and for this reason numerous anthologies of this kind now exist, Frazer's may have been the first ever published.)

A volume compiled by an unbeliever of extracts from the Scriptures to be read for their aesthetic interest is likely to be an example of the right hand not knowing what the left is doing, and one's expectations are not disappointed here. The note of sadness and ambivalence is struck in the preface:

Apart from all questions of its religious and historical import, which do not here concern us, the Bible is an epic, if not a history, of the world; or, to change the metaphor, it unrolls a vast panorama in which the ages of the world move before us in a long train of solemn imagery, from the creation of the earth and the heavens onward to the final passing away of all this material universe and the coming of a new heaven and a new earth wherein shall dwell righteousness. Against this gorgeous background, this ever shifting scenery, now bright with the hues of heaven, now lurid with the glare of hell, we see mankind strutting and playing their little part on the stage of history. We see them taken from the dust and returning to the dust: we see the rise and fall of empires: we see great cities, now the hive of busy multitudes, now silent and desolate, a den of wild beasts. All life's fever is there – its loves and hopes and joys, its high endeavours, its suffering and sin and sorrow. And then, last scene of all, we see the great white throne and the endless multitude gathered before it; we hear the final doom pronounced; and as the curtain falls we catch a glimpse of the fires of hell and the glories of heaven – a vision of a world (how different from this!) where care and sin and sorrow shall be no more, where the saints shall rest from their labours, and where God himself shall wipe away all tears from their eyes. This may not be science and history, but it is at least an impressive pageant, a stately drama: without metaphor, it is noble literature; and like all noble literature it is fitted to delight, to elevate, and to console.[15]

This grand piece of brocaded prose is redolent with the writer's resignation at the melancholy spectacle of modern man clinging to the spars of the great ark now foundered, for such literary debris is all that remains afloat. Especially notable is the last sentence, which implies that the Bible, as the vehicle for an affecting vision of life, attains grandeur and nobility even though it finally is inferior in truth-value to either history or science, seen as the embodiments of things as they really are.

Even if one chooses not to read the passage as a displaced personal allegory, then the metaphor of shipwreck remains appropriate to describe Frazer's bereavement. I see the personal dimension as reinforcing the ideological, which is why the passage is affecting rather than merely sonorous. As one might expect, the plangent quality died down as the passage of time slowly effaced Smith's loss. But the same vein of sentiment recurs in subsequent years, albeit perhaps without the same sad urgency as here.

The publication of *The Golden Bough* immediately propelled Frazer to the first rank of British students of mythology and comparative religion. Or rather, it would have done so if the numbers of people active in the overlapping fields of folklore, anthropology, and mythography were large enough to make two distinct ranks. It is not as if Frazer had been on the outside, with his nose pressed against the glass of the scholarly establishment, and now at last he was invited in. He was already known to his friends and colleagues as an extraordinarily erudite man. Now that he had written an important book addressed to a mixed scholarly and general audience, one result was a considerable broadening of the circle of his friends and correspondents. Among those to whom a first letter appears among the extant correspondence at this period are the classicist Gilbert Murray (1866–1957), the folklorist and rationalist propagandist Edward Clodd (1840–1930), and the novelist and rationalist propagandist Grant Allen (1848–99).

This expansion of his world notwithstanding, the most important (from the professional point of view) of Frazer's new friends and acquaintances from this time was A. C. Haddon. Fortunately a group of six letters from 1889–92 has survived that permits us to trace the development of their friendship.[16]

The speed with which their friendship grew is corroborated by Haddon. In the introduction to his essay on "The Ethnography of the Western Tribe of Torres Straits" (1890), Haddon, then an anthropological novice, acknowledged his indebtedness to various scholars, including the questionnaire "drawn up by my friend J. G. Frazer."[17] It was precisely at this point in his life that Haddon, then Professor of Zoology at the Royal College of Science in Dublin and a notable marine biologist, had made the decision to abandon natural science and chance the financial uncertainties attendant upon a career in anthropology in Cambridge.

In 1888 Haddon had gone with Edward Beardmore to Torres Straits, near New Guinea, to study coral reefs and their associated fauna; to defray the costs of the expedition, he also proposed to collect native "curios" to sell to museums back home.[18] But when he arrived he found that the

natives of the islands had of late years been greatly reduced in number, and that, with the exception of one or two individuals, none of the white residents knew anything about the customs of the natives, and not a single person cared about them personally.[19]

He felt (he tells us) that it was his "duty" to salvage what he could of a rapidly vanishing way of life; if he did not, the record of an entire society and way of life would be irretrievably lost. Beardmore helped, and together they set down an important description of the culture they had found. Haddon concluded that the coral reefs could wait, but that "man's life history was changing more rapidly" and could not.[20] Because Haddon had gone to Torres Straits (rather than to Ascension Island or the West Indies, the other possible sites for his research), the islands in those straits became the site, a decade later, of the first explicitly anthropological field trip, which he organized.

Haddon's biographer writes that "In 1887 J. G. Frazer, hearing that a zoologist, then unknown to him, was going out to Torres Straits, wrote to ask him to collect information about totemism, but Haddon would make no promises."[21] With his letter Frazer enclosed several copies of the 1887 questionnaire.[22] Upon his return Haddon wrote to Frazer, but only Frazer's half of the correspondence has been preserved. Even in the first extant letter (of 11 January 1889) one can see that he is pleased indeed that a reputable scientist like Haddon had sought to get answers for at least some of his questions, and especially in an area so poorly known as New Guinea.

In the next two letters we find Frazer thanking Haddon for his work and that of Beardmore, whose notes he will transmit to the Anthropological Institute for publication.[23] (He frequently acted as a conduit, receiving and sending on for publication the anthropological writings of fieldworkers.) He remarks (on 22 July 1889) that it is his

rule to publish all first-hand observations exactly as I receive them, except where the rules of grammar require some slight changes (one's correspondents are not always educated men), but even there I touch the MS as sparingly as possible. One cannot be too careful in dealing with descriptions of manners or customs; an apparently insignificant alteration or omission might efface an important piece of evidence.

The remark about grammar was the literal truth; he did not want "refined" readers to dismiss, as well they might, the contribution of an unlettered informant. And he was certainly right in thinking that even the most trivial-seeming emendation might be of interest to future readers. He continues, asking Haddon for

a list of all the totems you know, with any special rules (even the minutest) observed in respect of particular totems. At present we are absolutely ignorant of the reasons for selecting any particular animal as a totem. But perhaps if we had a sufficiently large list of totems before us, we might arrive by induction at some conclusions on this point.

Frazer was an excellent linguist, at home in the classical languages (later adding Hebrew to Greek and Latin), French, German, Spanish, Italian, and Dutch (he was the first British anthropologist to understand the importance of the ethnographic material about the East Indies written in Dutch). Significantly, however, he made no effort to learn the language of a primitive people. Although it was more difficult to study such languages then than now, lack of opportunity was not the reason; this omission was intentional. Knowledge of such a language would (or might) imply a specialization that he explicitly rejected. The role he assumed from the start was that of the generalist, one with the entire ethnographic world spread before him.

Thus, when Haddon offered him the word-lists he had compiled in the islands, he demurred ("I have made no study of savage language") and suggested instead that they be sent to Dr R. H. Codrington, the foremost authority on the Melanesians and the scholar who had introduced the term *mana* into anthropological discourse. Codrington, too busy with other work, suggested that they be sent to Sidney Ray. Ray, self-taught, was the foremost expert on Melanesian linguistics in Britain, although his scholarly work was carried out in his spare time, for he gained his livelihood as an arithmetic master in an East London primary school. (Ray was to be a member of the Torres Straits expedition.)

Haddon, at that time uncertain about the value of his work, needed encouragement, which Frazer, always generous in his praise for anyone whom he believed to be competent and honest, was glad to offer. In urging him to write up his findings, he put forward the claims of the generalist who will sift the detailed evidence later: Haddon must be sure to distinguish his own observations from those he had read in the works of others.

This is probably a superfluous caution to give; but as an anthropologist one finds that a man mixes up what he has seen and heard with what he has read, with the result that he loses credit for what he has himself ascertained at first-hand, since one can never know whether he is speaking from personal knowledge or only dishing up observations which were perhaps made hundreds of years before and which in the meantime may have lost all truth.[24]

Twenty years later, in 1910, when Haddon was at last established in Cambridge and justifiably confident about the value of his work, he wrote a *History of Anthropology*. In it he notes the then-accepted division between those who worked in the field and those who worked in the library. The former produce the data that the latter then "weld into coherent hypotheses." But to his mind "the most valuable generalisations are made, however, when the observer is at the same time a generaliser."[25]

After the First World War Frazer was the subject of numerous attacks. But here, before the war, the absolute division between field and library work was rejected by a man who was a personal friend and a professional ally. Haddon had come to see that the two aspects of anthropology were mutually interdependent, and that it was likely that the best work would come from people who were able practitioners of both.

Frazer's next letter (18 July 1890) congratulates Haddon on the publication of his essays on the islands. It is noteworthy for the first expression of an attitude that would be reiterated in later years: "Work like yours will be remembered with gratitude long after the theories of the present day (mine included) are forgotten or remembered only to be despised as obsolete and inadequate." A. H. Quiggin, Haddon's biographer, plainly likes Frazer, and quotes this sentence, reading it as having been written "with characteristic generosity and modesty."[26]

Today Frazer's words have come true, and his theories are indeed "despised as obsolete and inadequate." But in 1890 Frazer was not yet what he would be thirty years later – the most famous anthropologist in the world, the king of the grove who had to be supplanted. On the contrary, he was only minimally better known than the then completely obscure Haddon. Although in retrospect one may describe his statement as "generous and modest," it was intended in literal earnest. Frazer was genuinely humble before his facts and those who supplied them, and Haddon was respected as one of those who went out and discovered the facts and brought them back.

Believing as he did that time was running out for research in the islands he had seen, Haddon was keen to return, and during the nineties he worked tirelessly at two objectives: to secure a permanent position at Cambridge where he could support himself and his family teaching anthropology, and to return to Torres Straits. He managed the first, barely, in 1893; he succeeded much more handsomely in the second, organizing an expedition in 1898–9.

The most interesting point in Frazer's next letter (29 January 1891) comes when he asks whether Haddon will attend the upcoming Folklore Congress. "They have put me down as president of the mythology section, but I think I shall back out of it. To preside at public meetings is not in my way and the prospect of doing so is 'far, far from gay.'" This is an early example of Frazer's temperamental aversion to putting himself forward in public, which increased markedly in the later nineties.

The last letter in this series (27 July 1892) expresses pleasure that Haddon has decided to settle, as of September 1893, in Cambridge. This requires some explanation. Once Haddon had decided to become an anthropologist, he bent every effort to return to Cambridge, where he had been an undergraduate and where he had many friends. Those friends campaigned to induce the university to establish a lectureship in anthropology, which he would occupy. Most unusually, Frazer, who generally avoided university politics, was active in this effort. His hopes for his friend combined with his hopes for the establishment of anthropology as a proper subject at Cambridge, and he worked hard on Haddon's behalf. Haddon and his friends, who included no fewer than seven professors, in the end prevailed, but their victory was pyrrhic. He was indeed appointed lecturer in ethnology, but at the derisory salary of £50 a year. He accepted nonetheless; if he was to starve, at least it would be as an anthropologist.

In terms of their consequences, the most significant of Frazer's non-Macmillan letters from the mid-nineties are an innocuous pair addressed to his friend Baron Anatole von Hügel.[27] In the first (1 December 1894) he writes to introduce "a French lady, Mrs Grove, who is at work on a history of dancing," and who had come to Cambridge seeking information for the first chapter, inevitably on "Primitive Dance." She is studying the subject "in a comprehensive and philosophic way, taking in savage dances in connexion with war, death, hunting, initiation, etc." Frazer, knowing virtually nothing about the subject, asked von Hügel to afford her any assistance within his power. What help von Hügel may have given Mrs Grove is unknown, but a year and a half later, on 22 April 1896, Frazer married her.

E. O. James (1888–1972), probably the last of the true-believing Frazerians, wrote the notice on Frazer in the *Dictionary of National Biography*. He describes Elizabeth (Lilly) Grove Frazer as a Frenchwoman, *née* Adelsdorfer, of an Alsatian family; however, Downie, who had many talks with her, states flatly, though without evidence, that she was a French Jew.[28] To this last assertion, although based on Downie's personal knowledge, I must demur. I put the question directly to two elderly Fellows of Trinity,[29] who remembered her well and who both heartily disliked her: had they heard that she was Jewish? Each said that he had not and that had this been true it would have been common knowledge.

In any case it is fair to say that she had had a full life before meeting Frazer. According to Downie, she had married Charles Baylee Grove, a British master mariner, and with him had traveled widely, spending considerable time in South America, where she learned Spanish. (Indeed, in the second note of introduction he gave Mrs Grove in sending her to call upon von Hügel, he mentions that not only is she interested in savages, but "she has travelled among them" as well.) Upon her husband's sudden death she found herself in Britain with not much money and the pressing need to support herself and her two teen-aged children, Lilly Mary and Charles Grenville.[30] Like many other quick-witted women before and since who have found themselves so situated, she turned to writing. Although she seems to have had no special knowledge of the subject when she began, and although her written English was fluent but not completely idiomatic, she nevertheless managed to obtain a commission from the Badminton Library to do an encyclopaedic survey of dancing.[31] By then eight months had passed since Robertson Smith's death, during which time Frazer presumably had gone through the first, most intense, stage of mourning for his friend.

To this point we know of no women (aside from his mother and sisters) in Frazer's life at all. His life in Cambridge seems to have been totally given over to scholarship or intellectual recreation, and it all took place in what was still the overwhelmingly bachelor and clerical society of Trinity College. In the summers he was in the habit of returning to Scotland, where he spent time with his family, but there is no report of a female friend there either. Although since 1882 Fellows had been permitted to marry without forfeiting their fellowships, he must have seemed the very type of the Cambridge bachelor don, content to live and die in the bosom of his college. The news of his marriage – and to a foreigner with two children at that – must therefore have stunned his many friends.

There is no reason to believe that he married Lilly Grove for any other reason than that he cared deeply for her, and there is much testimony that they were devoted to one another throughout their lives.[32] It will contradict nothing already said to add that she was likely to have been more interested in marriage than he. For her, marriage to a don conferred much-needed status and greatly eased the anxieties she must have had about bringing up her children; for him it meant nothing short of a revolution in his settled domestic life. There can be no doubt that she was definitely more strong-willed than he, and probably her dominating personality as well as her social needs contributed importantly to their decision to wed.

Inasmuch as she will figure in the rest of this narrative, some general remarks about her are in order. The first is that to those who knew her, whether in her middle years or old age, her image is incomparably clearer and more vivid than her husband's; moreover, the witnesses, who range from dons to personal secretaries, are unanimous in their description of her. They agree that her behavior ran the gamut from the difficult to the unbearable; in a word she was a dragon.

But one must ask: "difficult" or "unbearable" for whom? It is worth noting that even though she had few friends in Britain, she had numbers of them in France and Italy.[33] Even her detractors agree that she was hard-working, intelligent, and forceful, and that virtually everything she did, however high-handed it may have been, was done to further her husband's welfare and interests, as she understood them.[34] She was French, she was not academic, and she was not in awe of the august, often stuffy, and sometimes intimidating world of Cambridge that she entered upon her marriage. She was often impatient with accepted ideas about what was and was not done, and was willing to say straightforwardly what she wanted. To her, being married to a man she saw as too mild-mannered to look after himself meant that she had to fight his battles for him. By well-bred British standards – and especially those of Cambridge, where so much is achieved by indirection – such behavior was guaranteed to be judged rude and inconsiderate.

Because she has had no defenders at all, I offer the above to show that it is possible to place a favorable construction on some of her behavior. Having said that, I must fill out the portrait with a catalogue of the behavior that her contemporaries found so objectionable. She was rude, overbearing, and peremptory with people who worked for her, as the memoirs of Frazer's amanuenses in old age demonstrate; she was devious and manipulative with those whom she could not order about; she was given to endless self-aggrandizement and self-dramatization, as extracts from her letters will illustrate. She was a quick but often inaccurate judge of character and motives, and frequently assumed that others were out to snub her and ignore her husband. The effect of these shortcomings was greatly exacerbated by the fact that shortly after their marriage her hearing began to fail, and by about 1910 she was profoundly deaf in both ears and forced to depend for the rest of her life upon ineffective hearing aids.

Unquestionably the deafness aggravated her unpleasant side, and as she got older she brooded disagreement less and less well. There is no doubt that she was not easy to live with. Nevertheless, in my view this indictment, lengthy and harsh as it is, does not list her main faults. By all accounts, she not only ran the Frazer household but her husband as well. This affected his work adversely because her presence was enough to deter some people from coming to see him, and in addition she tried to keep some people out (Haddon, for example) because she decided that they only wasted his time. Worse, she mothered him. Now it may well be that the only woman Frazer would have married would have been one ready to take care of him. Whatever the reasons, the effect on him was to exaggerate his helplessness and unworldliness. In view of the fact that his entire life was devoted to speculations about the psychology and motives of others, it cannot have helped that he came to know fewer and fewer people as he grew older. In any case, for better and for worse, this, then, was Mrs Frazer, the woman whom Malinowski called Frazer's "redoubtable" companion.

1. J.G. Frazer (right), his brother Samuel, and his sister Christine

2. J.G. Frazer (left) with his brother and his mother, Mrs Katherine Frazer, in the family home in Garelochhead

3. The "intense" teenager

4. *En famille:* with his mother, father, sister Isabella, and an unidentified family friend

5. Playful: with Christine and Isabella and a Mr Edwards

6. With an unidentified scientific friend at Cambridge, 1880s

7. As a young Fellow of Trinity College, 1880s

8. Receiving an honorary degree: Frazer (left) with M. Paul-Emile Appell (Rector of the Sorbonne) and Rudyard Kipling, 1921

9 and 10. Sir James and Lady Frazer, annual dinner of the Royal Literary Fund, London, 1930

11. The blind old man, mid-1930s

8 · PAUSANIAS'S DESCRIPTION OF GREECE

Pausanias and frazer were made for one another. Both are erudite, both tend to the encyclopaedic, the curious and out-of-the-way, and the digressive. Both have an abiding and complex interest in religion. Both are essentially commentators, whose talent requires for its fullest expression a large body of material to describe and a large canvas on which to work; both tend to be impressive in the mass as well as in the detail. In addition, because Pausanias' guidebook gave Frazer a ready-made armature for his commentary, the latter's tendency to expand and let his learning run riot at the expense of forward movement was kept generally under control.

There had been other guidebooks, and even other guidebooks to Greece, in the ancient world, but Pausanias' had several inestimable advantages over all others. The first is the critical one: his work has survived nearly intact whereas those of the others did not. Aside from that, he had the great good luck of being in the right place at the right time: had he come to Greece (and in particular to Athens) a century earlier, many of the finest Roman buildings would not yet have been built; had he come a century later, much of the classical inheritance would already have been destroyed by earthquake or through neglect. Greece in the second century – or at least its southern half, for Pausanias refers to the north only a few times – for all its size, and despite the fact that Pausanias did not complete its description, has a natural geographical, historical, and cultural unity. Frazer, who lived in a considerably more self-conscious age and in any case had more staying power than Pausanias (although he too tired toward the end), appropriately enough has a complex subject, namely, Pausanias' Greece in the light of the vast mass of historical and anthropological knowledge that had accumulated in the intervening seventeen centuries.

Just as Pausanias was fortunate in the moment of his advent, so for different reasons was Frazer. His two trips to Greece to see for himself the classical sites and the excavations have already been noted. However, if he had not been diverted into anthropology by falling under the spell of Robertson Smith in 1884 – precisely when he was about to set to work on Pausanias in earnest – and had therefore turned to Pausanias in the middle eighties rather than the early nineties, he would have started (and presumably finished) a decade too soon.

Although there had been earlier digs and earlier finds, the course of archaeology in Greece had been conclusively determined by the immense sensation created by Schliemann in the 1870s. Schliemann, however, had been obsessed with Homer and Troy, so that the sites he sought out and dug were all preclassical. It was not until the 1880s and especially the 1890s that classical sites, and especially Athens, became the focus of large-scale scholarly attention. During the eighties, in the intervals between Schliemann's campaigns, Wilhelm Doerpfeld, his chief assistant at Hissarlik, had moved to Athens and taken over direction of the extensive German effort there. The French had established themselves as early as the 1830s, and they had been followed by the Germans, the British, the Americans, and the Austrians. Each nation founded a school of classical studies in Athens, and each staked out significant field sites as well. During the decade 1885–95 important excavations were carried out at Delphi, Corinth, Epidaurus, Sparta, Mantinea, Thebes, and Plataea. Of course the digging continued long after Frazer's edition, but he was able to incorporate the finds made at most of these major sites. It is impossible to feel it now, but at its publication in 1898 Frazer's Pausanias had an almost journalistic, up-to-the-minute quality. A good deal of his material had not been published anywhere, in any language, and he is at pains to thank a number of scholars for cooperation and their willingness to permit him describe their work in progress.[1]

Not only was his conversion to anthropology fortunately timed in that it inadvertently kept him from full-time work on Pausanias for about six years, thereby permitting him to include later information, but it also introduced a totally new dimension into a commentary on a classical text. In the 1880s Pausanias' claim on our attention was the same as it is now: his guidebook offers by far the single most important – because most accurate and most detailed – topographical and architectural description of ancient Greece that has come down to us. But once Frazer had seen the anthropological light he was able to amplify an aspect of the text that had, in comparison to the architecture and topography, hitherto received relatively little attention – that of Pausanias as historian of ancient religion.

To be sure Pausanias had often been cited by earlier writers on Greek religion and mythology. But as a result of having written *The Golden Bough* Frazer now saw Pausanias in a new context, that of the ethnography of the entire primitive world, of which in his view classical antiquity, properly understood, was but one small part. For Frazer, Pausanias, like his predecessor Herodotus, was a proto-anthropologist, and his book a mine of ethnographic information about the classical world, comparable to the best accounts of Africa and Oceania by contemporary researchers, and comprehensible only in relation to other anthropology. Having interrupted his classical work in order to write *The Golden Bough*, he returned to Pausanias with primitive religion uppermost in his mind. The result was that when Pausanias discussed a religious custom or narrated a myth, this regularly evoked from Frazer a small essay, and/or an exhaustive bibliography, in which he collected all the relevant evidence. And because the writing of *The Golden Bough* had made him aware of evolutionary analogies from every time and place and had given him a global perspective, his idea of what was relevant was extremely generous.

Frazer's theoretical contribution to classical scholarship was thus the introduction of a new category of information – anthropology – as potentially relevant to the text. Sometimes the anthropology is used in a fashion that most readers would regard as appropriate, as when Frazer elaborates on one of Pausanias' own frequent observations about a myth or ritual practice. Other times it is introduced in a seemingly automatic fashion and appears gratuitously, as a kind of King Charles' head.[2]

Today, of course, anthropology, along with other, newer perspectives drawn from the social sciences and politics like Marxism, psychoanalysis, feminism, and semiotics, has been incorporated into the armory of classical studies. But even now there are substantial numbers of classical scholars who are temperamentally and/or theoretically opposed to the expansion of the nonlinguistic element beyond the now-traditional core of history (including numismatics and epigraphy) and archaeology. If this remains true today, when classical studies have become dramatically more permeable to outside influences, how much truer was it at the turn of the century in Britain, when classics had only begun to budge off its philological base. The ethnographic discussion and references in Frazer's Pausanias must have irritated a large part of his traditionally minded audience. It was, after all, only in the 1860s – well within the memory of then-living men – that British classicists had grudgingly accepted that *archaeology* might have something important to contribute to understanding. And was the entire scholarly world now to be obliged to absorb vast amounts of bizarre information about savages before they could claim to have made sense of a passage that had been clear enough heretofore?[3]

To those who have never had occasion to consult a classical edition, it may be worth noting that, considered as a literary genre, it is a relatively "open" form. An edition must contain the text and critical apparatus, including a survey of the manuscript tradition; it usually offers as well an introductory essay that sets author and work in historical and literary context. The largest, grandest editions also contain an extended commentary, in which the problematic elements in the text, both linguistic and otherwise, are discussed. (Frazer's Pausanias would obviously be a member of this dreadnought class except that it lacks a text and therefore, strictly speaking, is not an edition at all.) Because literally anything in the text can be an occasion for comment, a "complete" commentary is theoretically impossible, which is one reason why texts require and engender repeated scholarly consideration. Each generation inevitably supplies different contexts and makes different connections from the text to the world. And given the presence of a suitably educated scholar for whom the text resonates in multiple ways, then a new edition-cum-commentary may result.

For the purposes of discussion, one may distinguish two tendencies within classical commentaries: the philological and the historical. Depending on the nature of the text and their own background and temperament, editors have tended to focus either on the language of the text or the objects or events to which the language refers. The philological emphasis might be called "centripetal," in that it focuses on the text as linguistic artifact, a construction *in language* to be seen and understood in a context made up finally and essentially of other texts. Philologists create and use such necessary instruments as dictionaries and concordances, which bring together examples of usage to create a linguistic universe that, through a complex process of historical and semantic triangulation, finally delimits the meaning of the word or phrase under discussion. Even when the philological editor aspires to wider, comparative horizons, the centripetal impetus persists, so that, say, Sanskrit or Semitic examples might be adduced to gloss an obscure Greek expression. Always, however, nonlinguistic materials are employed to return one to the *language* of the text.

On the other hand, commentaries of a historical tendency are essentially "centrifugal," in that the editor tends to direct the reader off the page, away from the text and into the world. Thus archaeology, architecture, epigraphy, numismatics, papyrology, and topography, to name only some, are ancillary bodies of knowledge levied upon by historical critics, the principal goal being the use of the text to improve our understanding of those disciplines. In fact, good editors shuttle back and forth between the language and the world, using each to clarify the other, but the analytic distinction between the two still seems worth making. Needless to say, although Frazer does comment upon Pausanias' language when it is unclear or otherwise noteworthy, as that term is used here he is virtually the pure type of the historical critic, as he himself acknowledged. For him the text of Pausanias is interesting mainly for the light it sheds on history, topography, architecture, etc., rather than the other way round. All the classical work he ever did bespeaks this attitude and motivation; it is safe to say that he would never have undertaken any classical project that did not permit him somehow to employ anthropology.

If we put aside its effect on classical studies at the time, biographically the Pausanias is perhaps most important for its revelation for the first time of Frazer's tone of *authority*, the result of his complete mastery of an immense range of materials. As the critics were unanimous in noting, on every question he brings all the evidence together, sifts it, and comes down on the side of one or another (or none) of the competing theories, in a magisterially impartial manner.[4]

It is instructive to compare the Pausanias with *The Golden Bough* on this point. For all its obvious and undeniable erudition, *The Golden Bough* did not, and probably could not, demonstrate such control. That work was essentially a concatenation of speculations, supported by analogies, about a subject that was in the end inaccessible – the mental functioning and religious temperament of primitive and prehistoric mankind.

However interesting the individual links in the argumentative chain may be, we cannot escape the feeling that *The Golden Bough* – even in the two volumes of 1890 – goes on too long. One reason is that, because of the very novelty of its thesis, its argument has no natural shape. Although vast amounts had been written about classical religion, until *The Golden Bough* the world of antiquity had never before been discussed *primarily* as a repository of primitive religious attitudes. For this reason Frazer had virtually no need to tailor his argument to meet objections; further, the very novelty of his thesis meant that more evidence rather than less was called for, which acted as a license for his copiousness and discursiveness.

In the Pausanias, on the other hand, he was obliged to discuss, incisively and decisively, literally thousands of detailed points of art history and architecture with the art historians, topography with the geographers, inscriptions with the epigraphers, and so on through the entire vast range of information covered by Pausanias in his lengthy text, and as debated in a voluminous secondary literature. In anthropology, the primary task of gathering information was then only beginning, and theorizing was accordingly in its infancy; *The Golden Bough* is a first – indeed, as Frazer admits, probably a premature – synthesis based on admittedly incomplete data. For Pausanias the intellectual situation was quite the opposite. Although archaeology was each year revealing much that was new, ancient Greece had been studied systematically, and from various points of view, for centuries.

The result was that most of the questions had long ago been framed and the issues joined. As it were, Frazer was coming on stage at the end of a play that had been running since the Renaissance, in a role that many others had enacted before him. Only when Pausanias ventured, as he often did, into ethnography or religion could Frazer bring a special flourish to the part with his anthropological expertise, but even then only in moderation, for he was always constrained by the need to return to the text if he was ever to finish. If, as occasionally happened, he did permit himself to enlarge on an anthropological topic in which he was specially interested, he knew full well that at the end of such a pleasant digression the same very large number of lines of text still remained to be discussed. It was this chastening fact, and not pressure from George Macmillan, that constituted the discipline that finally got him through.

The size of the task must often have discouraged Frazer from pursuing questions even more fully than he did. Huge as the commentary is, the main reason for its size is not massive self-indulgence (as it was in *Folk-Lore in the Old Testament*, twenty years later) but simply the size of the text, the thoroughness of the coverage of all questions, and the vast amount that needed to be said. Scholars who have lived for years with Pausanias have remarked that Frazer's commentary might with advantage have been even longer.[5]

In addition to the total mastery and control – which was highly appreciated by all the reviewers – the Pausanias also sounds another new note. For in it we see the quiet, retiring Frazer for the first time entering into sharp and sustained struggle against the most eminent of his intellectual contemporaries. To the extent that scholarship was then a male competitive activity, it was the Pausanias and not *The Golden Bough* that represents his coming of age, in the sense of participating in an intellectual rite of passage.

So far as one can tell from the earliest correspondence with Macmillan, Frazer chose to work on Pausanias for a combination of reasons: if he succeeded in creating a clear and readable version of a clumsy original and in producing usefully annotated portable volumes, he would certainly have rendered a service to both scholars and travelers. By early 1884, when Frazer first actively and publicly committed himself to Pausanias, and when presumably he had not an anthropological thought in his head, Schubart's edition had already been emended by other scholars in scores of places on philological as well as historical grounds. As the pace of archaeological activity increased over the next decade, Pausanias became increasingly important. Regardless of Macmillan's sense of the commercial possibilities represented by the growing numbers of tourists who needed a guidebook as they peered at the ruins, a reconsideration of the text was needed on purely scholarly grounds; the existence of the competing German edition of Hitzig and Bluemner testifies to that.

Let us assume, then, that Frazer's initial aims were modest: to bring out a translation accompanied by a minimum of notes, thereby both enlightening the traveler and contributing toward a resolution of the many difficulties in a difficult text. Such a formulation is certainly consistent with the received picture of meek-and-mild Frazer, content to beaver away in the dim light of his study in Cambridge on a rather obscure Greek author. But the same facts permit another interpretation as well. In 1884 he was sufficiently lively to attract the attention of the charismatic Robertson Smith and sufficiently flexible and enterprising to be able to move quickly into anthropology. Frazer in 1884 was unlikely to sentence himself to a long-term classical project of great worthiness but numbing boredom if there were not other gratifications to be hoped for as well.

Although we need not go so far as to envisage young Frazer as a hothead spoiling for a fight, we must assume that in entering upon a subject he knew to be embattled he also recognized that, his personal wish for peace and quiet notwithstanding, he could not and would not remain above the fray. Even at the outset, when all he had in mind was a translation with notes, the potential for "trouble" was clear, and we ought not to dismiss the possibility that one reason he chose Pausanias may have been precisely the excitement that comes with being on the intellectual front line. Certainly the letters already quoted from the late 1880s to Jackson and Robertson Smith are not those of a mouse afraid to squeak. He was then thirty years old, brilliant but unknown; we need not impute overweening ambition to him, only energy and enterprise. That modest assumption made, it is easy to imagine him thinking, with reason, that if he were to bring out a well-received translation of an author that was at the center of so much contention, he would have established himself in classical studies.

It is therefore necessary to understand at least the outlines of the controversy then swirling around Pausanias to appreciate fully Frazer's decision to embark on the work, much less his achievement – at least from a biographical point of view. *The Golden Bough*, after all, dealing pointedly if allusively as it did with the origins of Christianity, was not the work of a cloistered scholar, content to write on technical, recondite questions for a tiny academic audience. So Frazer in his mid-thirties, even as he was protesting to Haddon that he intensely disliked public gatherings, scholarly politics, and "fuss," was already used to a measure of controversy surrounding his work and did not necessarily find it distasteful.

This is not the only time his actions illustrate the wish to have things both ways. The Pausanias, however, unlike *The Golden Bough*, was not going to give sleepless nights to readers agonizing over their faith. Its battles were caviar to the general; needless to say, their arcane nature did not at all mean that they were any the less hard fought. Anyone who has written for a small group of academic specialists knows how gory such encounters can be.

Without a doubt the two dark, looming figures in Frazer's Pausanian carpet were those of his eminent German contemporaries, Ulrich von Wilamowitz-Moellendorff, acknowledged by all (but Frazer) to be the greatest Hellenist of at least the last hundred years, and Wilhelm Doerpfeld, the leading classical archaeologist of the day. Of the two, the animus against Wilamowitz was much the sharper because it was he who was the source and prime mover of the controversy surrounding Pausanias, and therefore Frazer's lifelong *bête noire*.

When Frazer's edition appeared in 1898 Wilamowitz's (and his students') vendetta against Pausanias had been going on for no less than twenty years.[6] Given the importance of Pausanias' book, their charges were as serious and as sweeping as they could be: essentially, that he was either a lying knave or a confused fool. His honesty was impugned; he was said not to have seen most of what he purported to describe, but instead to have invented or else borrowed wholesale from a number of other writers, from Herodotus onward. This essential dishonesty was tempered by an out-and-out lack of intelligence, the result being a totally unreliable pastiche of plagiarism and fantasy. As if this were not enough, it was further alleged that because his main source was supposed to be the travel writer Polemo of Ilium, who lived in the second century B.C., fully three hundred years before Pausanias' time, his description was three centuries out of date.

Although in time extreme denigration usually produces its own reaction, in this case it is not difficult to see why the pendulum swung quickly back in Pausanias' favor. As the pace of excavation quickened in Greece in the eighties and nineties, again and again either Pausanias was shown unequivocally to be right, or else when he was mistaken the reasons for his mistakes usually became clear as well. By the turn of the century his good name was largely vindicated, and nowadays he is recognized as the most trustworthy and therefore the most important witness we have to the glory that was Greece. Any writer working on Pausanias at the end of the nineteenth century would therefore have had to take sides. Frazer was a stout partisan of his author, and in fact was the main conduit through which this new appreciation of the hitherto much-maligned Pausanias reached the English-speaking world.[7]

Great scholar that he was, Wilamowitz's disparagement of Pausanias had originated in an all-too-human combination of anger and pique.[8] In Greece in the spring of 1873 he joined and offered to lead a party of aristocratic German travelers from Olympia to Heraea. Reasonably enough, he tried to use Pausanias as his guide, but the attempt was a total failure. The reason was that he and his party were traveling from the north, whereas (although Wilamowitz did not know this) Pausanias' itinerary assumes a traveler coming from the south. Needless to say, nothing was where it was supposed to be, and Wilamowitz, the great expert, was publicly humiliated. As if that were not enough, in the same year Schliemann, using Pausanias as his guide, found "Priam's treasure" at Troy (Hissarlik). Wilamowitz's first reaction was mockery at the expense of this middle-class upstart, this businessman playing at archaeology, which turned to anger when Schliemann was proved right. Then Schliemann, again using Pausanias to provide a crucial clue, in 1876 found the royal tombs at Mycenae. In 1877 Wilamowitz launched the first salvo in what became a war on Pausanias.

In view of the length and depth of Frazer's immersion in Pausanias, his polemic against Wilamowitz and his followers, although sharp, is measured and not all-pervasive, as it might have been in the hands of a lesser man. The decision to stand his ground against Wilamowitz but not to become shrill flowed from his temperate manner and was probably not the result of conscious restraint. Whatever its origin, it was effective.

The appropriateness of his tone is necessary but not sufficient, however; Frazer also had the crucial advantage of being right. Wilamowitz's undoubted brilliance notwithstanding, his immutable and long-lasting prejudice against Pausanias meant that everything he wrote about that author was shoddy, and his students did no better. There must have been many times when all Frazer wanted was to secure a hearing for his author on his merits, only to find irrational Wilamowitzian antipathy repeatedly standing in his path. Unlike some scholars, who would use an edition of such an embattled author to carry on a no-holds-barred war against all enemies, Frazer permitted his animosity to appear only when the facts warranted it.[9]

Here is one example that will stand for all; it also gives a taste of the extraordinarily fine-grained texture of the commentary. The passage occurs in the gloss on Pausanias ii.17, where Frazer discusses "the Water of Freedom." According to Athenaeus, there was a fountain or conduit called Cynadra, the water of which was drunk by manumitted slaves as a token of their new freedom. The minor point at issue here is whether the fountain of Cynadra is the same as the "Water of Freedom" that Pausanias mentions as being on the way from Mycenae to the Heraeum. After a lengthy survey of the archaeological evidence Frazer recapitulates the arguments of one of the excavators, Captain Steffen, who had concluded that the Water of Freedom was not to be located in a certain ravine but elsewhere, nearby on the road to Mycenae. Frazer then turns to Wilamowitz:

Prof. von Wilamowitz-Moellendorff agrees with Captain Steffen in identifying the Cynadra and the Water of Freedom with this spring on the road from Mycenae to the Heraeum. Yet though he assumes on the authority of Pausanias the Water of Freedom was here, and not at Argos, he charges Pausanias with having taken his information from the book from which Eustathius and Hesychius derived their information – that is, from a book which stated that the water in question was at Argos. It would thus appear, on Prof. von Wilamowitz-Moellendorff's own showing, that the book from which Pausanias copied made a mistake, which fortunately cancelled the original error of his authority, with the net result that he finally blundered into placing the water quite correctly where Captain Steffen found it. It requires less credulity to suppose that Pausanias saw the water for himself.[10]

Frazer's scathing comment is accurate. That Pausanias was always wrong had become so much an *idée fixe* with Wilamowitz that he was prepared to assert, without any evidence whatever, a theory involving two successive blunders, the second undoing the first, with Pausanias emerging from the confusion as right for the wrong reasons. Although the entire controversy is inconsequential by any standard, this is the sort of uncharacteristically poor work that led Frazer to think ill of Wilamowitz.

There are several larger points here that do not emerge from this squabble over minutiae. First, Wilamowitz, throughout his career, was mainly interested in that which had been completed and achieved. Unlike Frazer he had no interest in or temperamental affinity for the autochthonous or the primitive, nor in awkward first attempts for their own sake. As he showed in his epochal 1889 edition of Euripides' *Herakles*, the proper business of a classical philologist was the establishment of a text and then the elucidation of its meaning through the use of the most rigorous scientific methods. The *Herakles* set a new standard in the thoroughness with which every textual element was tested, every potentially relevant historical fact was sifted for the light it might shed on the meaning of the play. Equipped with a near-total knowledge of Greek language, history, and culture, Wilamowitz believed himself able to resolve virtually any question while sitting at home, in his library. In view of his success with Euripides and the general brilliance of his work, his confidence in himself and his methods can hardly be thought of as misplaced. If ever there was a scholar who could resolve any classical question from his library, it was Wilamowitz.

Frazer, on the other hand, never cared about texts as such but instead was mainly interested in (primitive) behavior and psychology, and therefore in *pretextual* and *nontextual* actions and motives, both archaeological and anthropological. In this case, then, when Wilamowitz attempted to settle by literary means what Frazer saw was entirely an archaeological question, it is not hard to see why the latter might have bridled. (For us the irony lies in the fact that this experience did not temper Frazer's own confidence when the positions were reversed, when Frazer the library scholar boldly ventured to interpret what the anthropological fieldworker had observed and reported.)

Second, Pausanias was not, by any standard, a "good" or "fine" writer, nor has anyone ever claimed that he was. Indeed, Frazer and Wilamowitz are in rare agreement in their low estimate of Pausanias' prose style.[11] But for Wilamowitz, to notice this rhetorical ineptitude was to pass a sufficient judgment on the mind and achievement of the plodding Periegete, whereas Frazer regarded Pausanias' maladroitness as a kind of guarantee of his accuracy, sincerity, and trustworthiness.[12] Thus Wilamowitz's suggestion that Pausanias had clumsily tried to pass off a literary reference as a personal observation went much further with Frazer than the trivial matter of the true location of the Water of Freedom. This attack, and the many others of the same kind launched by Wilamowitz and company, in undermining and finally in denying Pausanias' reliability, subliminally carried the fearful suggestion that Frazer's own efforts to edit the text on such a grand scale were misplaced and overdone and therefore ultimately foolish. It is not hard to imagine how determined this made him to show that Wilamowitz was wrong.[13]

By comparison, Frazer's quarrel with Doerpfeld, although sufficiently sustained to warrant comparison with the running battle with Wilamowitz, lacked personal animosity.[14] Nevertheless it does seem fair to say that Doerpfeld, like Wilamowitz, seems to have inspired profound, even visceral, distrust in Frazer; one has the feeling that Frazer was predisposed to disagree with virtually anything that either man said. Here is one example of many; unlike some, such as those concerning the Enneacrunus fountain or the Dionysiac theater, whose length and detail defy summary, this one is not only brief but has the added advantage that Frazer includes Wilamowitz as a joint target for his obloquy. It relates to Frazer's discussion of the battle of Marathon. The way he effortlessly turns an admission of his own error into an assault on his opponents is scholarly gamesmanship of a high order and demonstrates the existence of a real taste for polemic that one would not have expected in Frazer.

Here, too, I desire to correct a mistake of my own. In the text (vol. 2 p. 442) I have spoken of Athens as if it were an unwalled town at the time of the battle of Marathon. I did this, not in reliance on the opinion of Professor von Wilamowitz-Moellendorff (*Aus Kydathen*, p. 97 *sqq.*) and Dr Doerpfeld (in Miss Harrison's *Ancient Athens*, p. 21) that it was so, but merely because I overlooked the testimony of Herodotus (ix.13) and Thucydides (i.89) that it was not. On the question of the state of Athens in the fifth century B.C. I decidedly prefer the evidence of Herodotus and Thucydides to that of Dr Doerpfeld and Professor von Wilamowitz-Moellendorff.[15]

The Pausanias, like all of Frazer's writing, is full of vivid visual imagery, especially in the form of descriptions of scenery.[16] Frazer was always sensitive to natural setting, and the wilderness and majesty of the Greek countryside moved him deeply. The result – dozens of passages, some only a few sentences long, others running to several pages – represents a typically Frazerian enrichment of the original. *The Golden Bough* begins with a visionary scene that forms the backdrop to the nominal action, but when Frazer wrote it he had never been to Italy. It therefore cannot be surprising that he insists on detailed depictions of the places that he has in fact seen. For this reason, along with the ancient monuments, virtually every description of a Pausanian site is framed by a careful rendering of the natural surroundings.

Before the age of easy air travel, with its weight limits on baggage, there doubtless were some travelers to Greece serious enough and hardy enough to carry Frazer's six volumes with them to Greece. But as the edition grew and assumed its final proportions, Frazer could hardly have imagined their number ever to be substantial. In the preface he says that "The readers for whom this book is especially designed are students at the universities." Having said that, and knowing that the volumes would rarely be opened anywhere except on a table in a university library, he nevertheless continues: "but in order to render it intelligible to all who interest themselves in ancient Greece," he will give quotations from foreign languages in English.[17] So, once again having it both ways, he describes how everything looked on the day he was there (and gives the date of his visit), and includes the distances from other places and whether they conform with Pausanias' measurements, and other such information that is of use only to someone walking the site who is using the work as a literal guidebook. It may be that these details are a remnant of the earliest phase of the project, the two portable volumes that were encapsulated in and then buried by the commentary. In view of his compulsion to verisimilitude, once he had begun with the descriptions, perhaps he could not or would not discontinue them even when the work was destined for the reference shelf. It is as if he could not help but frame his discussion of a site by a description.

In what follows on the township of Icaria (i.33.8) the most interesting thing about it is that the place is *not* mentioned by Pausanias. But if Pausanias did not go there, Frazer did, and in such instances, which are not infrequent, he includes it nevertheless. Did Frazer think he was commenting on second-century Greece or on Pausanias' Greece as it was in the 1890s? If the former, then he was writing a commentary on a classical text; if the latter, then he was writing a guidebook on ancient antiquities for the modern traveler. The answer seems to be both; his focus is Pausanias' Greece, but he gives the reader the modern overlay as well.

The situation of Icaria, the earliest home of Dionysus in Attica, is solitary but pleasing. It lies in a wooded dell at the foot of the northern forest-clad slopes of Mt. Pentelicus. A reminiscence of the Dionysiac worship for which Icaria was famous in antiquity survives in the name *Dionysos*, by which the place is still known to the people of the neighbourhood. There is no village here, only a long straggling house occasionally inhabited by the peasants who come hither to gather resin in the surrounding pine woods. Eastward the ground slopes in terraces, intersected by runnels and shaded by plane-trees, to a wooded glen where, not far from a cave in the side of the ravine, a stream tumbles over rocks in a picturesque cascade. Similar glens, their sides clothed with luxuriant vegetation, divide *Dionysos* from the deserted village of *Rapentosa* situated only about a mile to the east, the inhabitants of which were forced to flee before the bands of robbers who, not many years ago, infested this wild and secluded district. A pleasant excursion can be made from Athens to Icaria and back in a day by taking a morning train to Cephisia on the south side of Mt. Pentelicus, then walking or riding round the north-west shoulder of the mountain, and so through the beautiful woods and dingles at its northern foot to Icaria. (I understand that these woods have suffered greatly by fire since I walked through them on a summer day in 1890.) The distance from Icaria to Cephisia is about seven miles.[18]

These scenic passages were sufficiently numerous and sufficiently admired to be noticeable. After the publication of the six-volume edition he proposed, and George Macmillan agreed, to collect them in a separate volume in the hope of appealing to a nonscholarly audience that eschewed erudition but enjoyed scenery and word painting. Of course both author and publisher were hoping for some income that might offset the massive production expenses of the Pausanias. To no fewer than ninety-two passages was added the long life-and-times essay on Pausanias that stands as general introduction, and the whole was issued in May 1900 as *Pausanias and Other Greek Sketches*. It sold well enough to warrant reprinting in 1917, under the catchier title *Studies in Greek Scenery, Legend and History*, and under the new title was reprinted twice more, in 1919 and 1931.

As for the unabridged Pausanias, although it bore the very high price of six guineas and sales at first were slow, it sold steadily. In the light of the price and the limited market for so specialized a work, it is extraordinary that by

1913 the thousand sets of the original edition were exhausted, and Macmillan then printed a second thousand (which inevitably included some corrections by Frazer).[19] So in all respects the saga of Pausanias ended happily. Although the work that Macmillan published in 1898 bore no resemblance to the work he had commissioned in 1884, his faith in Frazer, which never (or hardly ever) wavered, had been borne out financially as well as intellectually, and both author and publisher in the end actually made money as well as kudos from this monument of scholarship.

The other literary feature of the edition that must be noticed is the translation, partly for its own qualities and partly because it prefigures Frazer's later efforts of this kind: Apollodorus' *Library* and Ovid's *Fasti*. Then as now, an inherent tension exists among translators of literary texts. On the one side are those who feel that accuracy (usually construed as literal fidelity to the text) must take precedence over any other consideration, resulting awkwardnesses notwithstanding; on the other are those who ask that the translator find words in English that give the reader as much as possible of the complex of meanings the text contains, even if this means "taking liberties" with the text. To this perennial debate must be added the strength at the time of the idea of decorum, which dictated that classical texts be translated in a "high" style. The task, then, for Frazer, who had begun with the educated traveler rather than the academic specialist as his intended audience and who was always sensitive to literary values, was a formidable one. The strict claims of scholarship could not always be reconciled with liveliness and readability, mainly because of Pausanias' own inadequacies as a writer. How could one be true to a text – whatever that meant – when the author wrote in so crabbed a fashion that the literal meaning was often unclear?

Given this problem, it was the judgment of those reviewers who remarked on the translation that he was generally successful. Considering the size of Pausanias' text and the propensity of academic reviewers to concentrate on pointing out errors, it is not surprising that the praise was mixed with criticism. Here, for instance, is the anonymous writer of the generally glowing notice in the *Cambridge Review*: he calls the translation "masterly" and says that it succeeds because it at once "satisf[ies] the requirements of the critic, and appeal[s] to the appreciation of the ordinary reader."[20] Here are examples of the vigorous language that makes this version of Pausanias so good: "that King Archidamus himself had a finger in the sacred pie" (iii.10.4); "being flown with wine" (iv.16.5); "he would always be a thorn in the side of Sparta" (iv.23.2); "The poisoned cup was child's play" (vii.7.3). On the other hand he demurs at some expressions as "having a somewhat falsely modern ring": "crack troops," "pic-nic," "plainly showed his hand." The examples make one wonder: "a finger in the sacred pie" is good, but "a thorn in the side" was then as tired as "showed his hand," which for us at any rate is no modernism at all.

But without worrying the matter overmuch, it is clear that Frazer was striving to produce a version that would be as fast-moving and energetic as the "loose, clumsy, ill-compacted, rickety, ramshackle style" of his author would allow.

In his enthusiastic review the Oxford archaeologist Percy Gardner says that it marks a great improvement over A. R. Shilleto's inept version of 1886, but he criticizes Frazer for occasionally overtranslating, as when he calls the Greek underworld "Hell" and when he calls lampstands "chandeliers." He likes Frazer's willingness to translate rather than offer mere transliterations of technical terms. However, while it is good not to employ "nekropoleis" and "stamnoi" as if they were English, Frazer strikes a provincial note when he refers throughout to "Athena Serve-them-right" and "Dionysus of the Black Goatskin." "It is to be hoped that Mr Frazer's book will be used in many countries, and this over-Englishing is scarcely suitable to an international work."[21]

Inasmuch as the critics themselves silently subscribed to the idea of decorum, only its breach (as above in the *Cambridge Review* notice) is mentioned, as when Frazer strives too hard for up-to-date diction. But to a modern ear the repeated note of the false-antique (to take examples randomly) in words like "fain" and "despoiled" (4.16.5) or phrases like "Piraeus was a township *from of old*" (1.1.2) and "the Messenians began to find themselves *in evil case*" (4.9.1) sounds wooden and labored. Pausanias was certainly lumbering and awkward, but never in the pseudo-medieval manner of the disciples of William Morris or the Pre-Raphaelites. From the vantage point of a century later, Frazer's translation, though creditable, creaks. In his later efforts to create an English equivalent for Ovid's mannered style in the *Fasti*, this vein of conscious elaboration and archaic diction becomes so prominent as to become a problem in itself.

In retrospect it is clear that 1884 was the year of decision. He could have elected either classical studies, in the form of Pausanias and archaeology, or anthropology, in the form of the articles in the *Britannica*. Frazer's brilliant solution, probably arrived at unconsciously, was not to choose – to exclude neither but instead to point himself simultaneously toward both anthropology and Pausanias. He had no idea where that would take him, but he was both fortunate and courageous in accepting this ambiguity about his future. Whatever worries he may have had seem not to have been grave, perhaps because at that time he had no money worries and was without domestic or emotional ties or responsibilities. Once he met and was overpowered by Robertson Smith, he wrote *The Golden Bough* (I suspect) partly to express his admiration for Smith, partly to free himself from the very power of Smith's domination.

The effects of Smith's death must have been devastating because he found no outlet for his feelings. Only after he had assimilated that event was he ready to admit another person into his life. In 1894 he met Lilly Grove and in 1896 he married her. It is excessive to say that he began his scholarly career as a boy and ended as a man, for in 1884 he was already thirty years old, but he certainly was both intellectually and emotionally immature at the start of this period in his life; when it ended he was a complete scholar who had established himself in both classical studies and anthropology and a man who was ready, willing, and able to take on the responsibility of a wife and children.

In December 1897, thirteen and a half years after he received from George Macmillan a first intimation of interest in publishing a one-volume translation of Pausanias, Frazer composed the four pages that stand as preface to the work's six volumes. The preface contains the inevitable expressions of gratitude: to his publisher, who never stood in his way as the edition grew larger than anyone would have dreamed; to the group of scholars who have been specially helpful. He wishes that his two friends, William Robertson Smith and J. H. Middleton, had lived to see the book, and closes with an elegiac paragraph that sounds the same note of elaborate melancholy first heard in his 1895 anthology of biblical extracts, and still audible less than three years later in the preface to the second edition of *The Golden Bough*.

One reason the three passages sound alike is that in the preface to a scholarly book the author is permitted to express personal feelings; inasmuch as prefaces are always written last, and Frazer's books are long, and writers are frequently tired when they finish books, it is not surprising that he sounds weary. But there is something else here that cannot be explained entirely or merely as authorial fatigue, for in the preface to the first edition of *The Golden Bough* he does not sound played out, as he does after 1895. I suggest that this weary sadness may be a sign of something, perhaps unexpressed emotion arising from the death of Smith. This note is first heard in 1895 and lasts for about five years; it is absent from the prefaces to the works of the next decade.

The paragraph in question is an expression of thanks to Trinity College, which in renewing his fellowship three times has freed him from "sordid care" and permitted him to pass his days in the atmosphere best suited to the pursuit of pure scholarship. In its "high" diction, full of archaisms and Miltonic echoes, and its confessional tone, the passage seems to be intended as a kind of lament, or at least a marker of an epoch that has come to an end. In this regard the last sentences are especially important.

The windows of my study look on the tranquil court of an ancient college, where the sundial marks the passage of the hours and in the long summer days the fountain plashes drowsily amid flowers and grass; where, as the evening shadows deepen, the lights come out in the blazoned windows of the Elizabethan hall and from the chapel the sweet voices of the choir, blent with the pealing music of the organ, float on the peaceful air, telling of man's eternal aspirations after truth and goodness and immortality. Here, if anywhere, remote from the tumult and bustle of the world with

141

its pomps and vanities and ambitions, the student may hope to hear the still small voice of truth, to penetrate through the little transitory questions of the hour to the realities which abide, or rather which we fondly think must abide, while the generations come and go. I cannot be too thankful that I have been allowed to spend so many quiet and happy years in such a scene, and when I quit my old college rooms, as I soon shall do, for another home in Cambridge, I shall hope to carry forward to new work in a new scene the love of study and labour which has been, not indeed implanted, but fostered and cherished in this ancient home of learning and peace.[22]

Throughout his life Frazer was a deeply loyal son of his college – he left a life interest in his estate to his wife, the whole to revert to Trinity after her death – but this expression of love for his Alma Mater is compounded of apprehension as well as loyalty. For now, nearly a quarter-century after he had come up as a freshman, he was at last departing, moving out of college at the age of forty-four into his very first house and leaving an institution and a setting that had been the only home he had known throughout his adult life. He was exchanging the comfortable bachelor existence of Trinity for the unknown trials of life as a husband and stepfather. He was leaving behind the ghosts of those he had loved, and the setting in which that love had unfolded itself, for a new and uncertain future.

9 · BALDWIN SPENCER, ANDREW LANG, AND EDMUND GOSSE

Frazer's main emotion upon completing the Pausanias must have been immense relief. At last the labor, which often seemed Sisyphean, was behind him. But, as the preface to Pausanias intimates, there were other, nonacademic questions on his mind. Although from the outset of their married life his wife was the manager in the Frazer household, the new residential and family arrangements must also have occupied him as well, if only because they involved the profound disruption attendant upon moving house. For a man so focused on his work and so settled in his ways as Frazer, it cannot have been easy. There must have been great problems in organizing his new life.

No doubt the first question was whether to buy or rent a house or else build one of his own. Inasmuch as Trinity lacked any provision for married Fellows, Frazer had had to find quarters for his new family. The first letter after the wedding is written by Lilly Frazer, to Macmillan, and is dated 30 May 1896. She writes from 4 Market Hill (her address on the marriage license) to say that "We are now settled in Cambridge again and have both resumed work." There is nothing further from this address. As the accommodation must have been small, and the location inherently noisy because it was situated above one of the shops that ring the market, it must have been temporary lodging. Indeed, it may well have been her rooms only, and they may never have lived there together. The first post-Trinity letter from Frazer, dated 24 November 1898, bears the address 13 Guest Road, a modest terrace house to which they repaired (with the children) and rented until they decided where they would live permanently. On 7 June 1899 Frazer writes from "our new house," called Inch-ma-home, on Adams Road, a quiet street of a few large houses. There he and his family would live for about five years.

We have some information on the domestic arrangements that prevailed during the Frazers' early married life. A dozen years later, on 25 June 1910, Lilly Frazer wrote a long and frank letter to Edmund Gosse; it was occasioned by the possibility that Gosse might, through his good offices, secure a grant in aid for her husband from the Royal Literary Fund. To be able to make an effective presentation to the Council of the Fund he needed full knowledge of Frazer's circumstances. Frazer had already supplied some information, but she thought it wise to supplement his letter with one of her own, in which she could be more forthright about the family finances that she suspected her husband had been. In explaining why they are experiencing financial hardship she tells Gosse that although J. G. (as she regularly calls him in her letters) wants nothing for himself, he is not the easiest man to live with, for he does have special requirements that are difficult to satisfy.

Yet he has some needs and his books could not be produced without those being satisfied. The first is absolute quiet – both in and out of the house; the slightest noise disturbs him and my experience has been that it is the most difficult condition to procure. Long before our marriage J. G. had Fellow's rooms in Nevile's Court and had to give them [up] and to take rather undergraduate's rooms as his neighbours in Nevile's Court poked the fire inconveniently. I give you this one example, but the need of total silence is growing on him with growing work and growing age. In a small house such as *I* personally dearly like, silence either domestic or other is an impossibility. We have tried it twice and failed.

The second of J. G.'s needs is space for his library – another very serious condition – so serious that while in Trinity (Great Court) writing the first edition of the G. Bough – also before our marriage – he was asked *not* to put any more weight of books on the floors – I myself saw the ceiling below him looking like an inflated sail. . . .

The next need is that his working library should all be in one room; his methods of work necessitate to *him* instant reference to *any* book. He has worked that way all his life and is too old to change. Perhaps had he begun earlier he might have adopted a system of *"fiches"* in the French style; as it is it is too late and he has his own method. It however necessitates size and loftiness of study.

After giving the details of Frazer's heroic stamina – "J. G. works from 7.30 a.m.–1.30, again from 4–8 p.m. and again from 9 p.m. to midnight or *later!*" – she goes on to offer more about Frazer's crotchets regarding his library:

dealing as he does with mankind in all places and at all time[s], he needs his books – *all* of them – at any one moment. He is not able for ex: to take up a certain period as an historian might and do with a few books at a time. This leads to the fact that he cannot now (his library and his need having increased) go, as before, between College and home without serious loss of time and a certain amount of irritation at missing perhaps the very book he needs. In order that he might complete his Pausanias, G. Bough II, etc. in serenity I have spent the first 12–13 years of our married life *in* college with him – usually being there from 8 a.m. to midnight!

Although she is given to overstatement, I think we must take this portrait at face value; by 1910 Gosse was an old friend and would recognize exaggeration. It is therefore an open question whether Frazer in this account can properly be described as merely "crotchety," or whether a stronger word like "neurotic" is in order. We have no record of how Frazer got on with his new stepchildren, but that too is a relationship that usually does not settle down quickly. For a "confirmed old bachelor" who is virtually phobic about noise of any kind, a man for whom his neighbor's loud poking of the fire was so "inconvenient" as to become intolerable, it requires little imagination to conceive the potential "inconvenience" represented by Lilly Frazer's children. Grenville was eighteen in 1896. Lilly Mary's age is unknown, but from the fact that her doctoral thesis was published in 1908, she must then have been in her middle or late teens as well.[1] They may of course have been away at school. But if either or both lived at home (and Downie says that Lilly Frazer disapproved of sending children away to school),[2] and even assuming that they were excessively well behaved, adolescents sometimes make noise. Then as now, they need to move about, their voices are not always perfectly modulated, etc. It is an understatement to say that they must have taken some getting used to. On their side the children, too, had an adjustment to make, for although we know nothing about their father Mr Grove, ships' masters and Cambridge classical dons tend not to resemble one another.

Finally, that Lilly Frazer was in college all day every day (for Frazer worked seven days a week, and about fifty weeks a year) in the early years of their marriage became one of the main reasons for her unhappiness in Cambridge. She was faced with a difficult choice: if she wished to see her husband, it would have to be on his terms, in his college rooms; otherwise she would virtually never see him, for he was unwilling or unable to change his lifetime addiction to work for a more domestic regime. They doubtless discussed the new arrangements before they were married, but she cannot have had any idea how much she would come to resent it. In any case, her presence at J. G.'s side is now part of Trinity College folklore; two elderly dons who recalled her vividly, but who of course did not themselves go back as far as the 1890s, nevertheless knew about her presence in college in those days.[3] Both gave what might be termed the "official" Trinity version – that Frazer had been a reasonably sociable and companionable man until he married. His impossible wife, however, took him totally out of college life, for whether or not he was working, she was always there. On account of her, his decision to move out of college was not regretted.

However, there is, as usual, another side to the story. His married state meant much more than new library arrangements and getting used to the patter of not-so-tiny feet. Consider this paragraph of a letter to Macmillan from this period, 14 July 1898:

My dear Macmillan,

You see I have adopted your suggestion that we should drop the formal "Mr" in writing to each other. I am glad to do so and to think of the friendly relations established between us. I trust that they will long continue, and that for many years to come we may work together each in his own way and to good purpose. I cannot but feel that I owe this happy result, like so much else that is good, in large measure to my wife, but for whom you and I would probably not have met to this day. Before my marriage I was growing almost morbidly averse to meeting strange faces, even when the faces were connected with hands whose writing was familiar to me.

Our first reaction may be to smile – that it should have taken *fourteen years* for Frazer and Macmillan to unbend sufficiently to drop the "Mr" is mildly comical. But the last two sentences sound very much like the voice of a man who knows he has passed through something of a crisis and has some idea of its cause. We lack conclusive evidence but have a suggestive chronology. The anxiety or depression occurred after Robertson Smith's death. Although Frazer wrote an obituary of Smith and continued with Pausanias, it does look as if he was greatly cast down in and after 1894, and that his growing affection for Lilly Grove helped pull him through. It may well be that he forfeited the friendship of many at Trinity as a result of the very actions that in his view nearly saved him from breakdown. Both may well be true.

There is more than the letter to Macmillan. A quarter of a century later, in 1924, after a year of living in hotels in London and Paris, the Frazers returned to Cambridge. Edward Clodd had written to Lilly Frazer expressing regret that they had moved about so much, and especially about the effects of those moves on J. G. (who was then seventy years old). Lilly, as she did so frequently, projected her own personality onto her husband's and responded that there was no need to pity J. G., as many people seemed to do. He was a man who needed diversion (at any rate she always did); he loved being in the metropolis (hard to credit given his aversion to noise, but she loved London), and he certainly preferred it to poky Cambridge (which she always disliked). The interesting moment comes at the end, when she recalls the old days, when they met and married:

J. G., of all people whom I know, and I know a great many, is the happiest man on earth – yet his friends *keep* saying "Poor Frazer"! Like people without history he is happy – a move or two or even twenty!! are mere earth tremors, and dont shake anything and only serve usefully, even if unintentionally so. But, what could form a deeper anchor cast in a fathomless shore than the library (and what a library now!!) put up at Trinity . .?? – You say distractions are not for him any more . .! you mistake, and that mistake which might have been *a fatal one* (question *him*) has been made all along by all his friends with the single exception of Robertson Smith whose last service to J. G. was: "Bad company is better than none." Smith died – I never knew him – and by a miracle I turned up, the bad penny to form the "bad company" – but my heart is wrung, even now, in remembering the *total isolation* I found my dearest one in 28 years ago. – Think what since he has produced! and how he *enjoys* life, how gregarious he is and how vivid is his work.

Even allowing for her tendencies to exaggeration, the image that remains is of J. G. in "total isolation." Robertson Smith, who knew his friend best of all, had counseled him at the end to be among people, but when Smith died Frazer became withdrawn and depressed. The depression was not so total as to be immobilizing, and it is easy to believe that Frazer thought that by immersing himself in work he could bring himself out of it and at the same time finish the endless Pausanias, which had by that time been blocking the sunlight for a decade. This might have been a reasonable course of action had his loss not been so severe, but as it was, he only became more inward and isolated. One imagines him shutting himself in, seeing no one, and doing nothing but work. This may be overstating it somewhat, but probably not much. Perhaps it took someone like Lilly Frazer, with her masterful personality and her unwillingness to take no for an answer, to reach him through his depression.

Two years earlier he had had the idea of accompanying Haddon to New Guinea. If Frazer was depressed in 1895, then it is quite conceivable that Haddon, who had been keen to return to Melanesia for some years, asked him to come along for several reasons, among which might have been a hope that the trip would "take him out of himself." The two of them may have reasoned that by the time the expedition actually set forth, Frazer would have completed Pausanias and be ready to travel. Obviously neither imagined that he might marry. After the usual delays the expedition did finally set out in 1898; by that time, however, he was married and once again working hard at his own kind of library anthropology.

That episode surely must rank among the great "what-might-have-beens" in anthropology, for it is difficult to believe that Frazer could have lived for long in the field without his overly clear ideas taking a beating from the waywardness of reality. (Indeed, what one misses amid all the exotica in his books is any sense of the inherent strangeness of things; the primitives' behavior is *outré* to be sure but Frazer's categories permit him to *understand* it all so well.) There is no regret in his letter to Galton in 1897 mentioning the possibility now foregone; either his pangs (if any) had passed or perhaps he had never believed that the project had much chance of ever coming to fruition.

We should not imagine him, then, as continuously depressed about Robertson Smith in the mid-nineties. He no doubt did have such moments, which may at times have extended into hours or even days, but if he had allowed these feelings full expression he might never have finished Pausanias. Although Frazer may have been neurotic and was certainly capable of anxiety, we shall probably get the balance right if we keep in mind that he was generally able to maintain his forward motion, and that these years contained other moments, with other tonalities, as well.

For example, in the letter below, from 7 June 1895, to his friend the folklorist Sidney Hartland, we hear once again the toughminded mockery of the letters of 1888 to Smith and Jackson. It probably represents the truth of those years just as much as the amazing letter of reminiscences about Smith to J. F. White. One now appreciates the significance of the date of that letter to White: 15 December 1897. Inasmuch as the preface to Pausanias is dated December 1897, the eruption of long-pent emotion in that letter may plausibly be attributed to Frazer's having nailed shut the mental door behind which he kept the memories of Smith until he completed the book that had consumed his life for so many years. Only then could he allow himself to relive such deeply felt and long-suppressed experiences. I suspect that he wrote that letter within a day of the time that he sent off the last proof to the printer.

Dear Mr Hartland,

It is one of my rules never to review any book. I certainly should not be tempted to depart from this particular rule in favour of any book by such a notoriously incompetent scholar as Thomas Taylor. It is a pity that any of his work should be reprinted.

As for stirring up Cambridge to appoint a professor of anthropology, I fear that I must confess to never stirring up anybody to do anything. The character of an agitator is not one to which I aspire. Besides, the University and colleges are miserably poor, and their scanty incomes are necessarily devoted to far more more important objects, such as giving feasts, keeping up gardens and chapel services, and maintaining hundreds of Fellows and Masters of Colleges in idleness. Or rather I should say that these are the prime objects to which the Colleges devote their energies, and that the small surplus which is left over when these essentials have been provided for is handed over to the University to be by it applied to the subordinate object of promoting science and learning. This small surplus is not sufficient to endow a professorship of anthropology.[4]

Nor was Hartland, a solicitor whom he probably met through the Folk-Lore Society, his only new acquaintance. Unquestionably his most important friendship (measured in terms of consequences) was with the eminent man of letters (Sir) Edmund Gosse (1849–1928).[5]

Frazer was among the least celebrated of Gosse's glittering acquaintance; in worldly terms, Gosse was probably the most powerful man whom Frazer knew well. They met in Trinity in 1885, introduced by J. H. Middleton, when Gosse came to Cambridge to give his ill-fated Clark Lectures.[6] Frazer admired Gosse extravagantly, seeing him as a man of brilliant intellect who mixed in a glittering world of celebrities and at the same time remained completely dedicated to Higher Things. For Frazer, Gosse represented the literary and aesthetic life as he imagined it really was lived in London; in his company, both actual and epistolary, Frazer felt that he could indulge his own sensibility, which he felt had been smothered by the all-consuming demands of dusty scholarship.

His first letter to Gosse (10 May 1895) is given over to a diatribe about authorship. As a result of having joined the Society of Authors in 1890 when he signed his first contract with Macmillan, he received its monthly magazine, *The Author*. That "filthy publication" "disgusted" him because it treated the profession of authorship not as the high calling it was, but simply as a way to make money.

[*The Author*] is nothing but a roar for money and a vituperation of publishers. The only article in it which I read with pleasure was one on yourself in which (so far as I remember) you protested against the treating of literature as if it were as much a business as stock-broking. It is not. A man takes up stock-broking or any other trade purely for the sake of making money, and if the trade ceased to bring him in money he would drop it. But the man of letters is what he is for the love of letters, because it is his greatest pleasure to do so, and he would do it if he did not make a half-penny by it.

This is the voice of one who has never (yet) had to worry about where the money would come from to pay his bookseller's bill, much less his next meal. Frazer simply could not imagine that there were any publishers less gentlemanly than George Macmillan, nor that there were any authors who, subsisting solely on their earnings from writing, were sweated nearly as much as the tailors in the East End. Privation for Frazer meant the possibility that he might be forced to sell his shares in Frazer & Green, the family business. Otherwise he was completely unworldly, a baby so far as money was concerned, and a man who (properly) left the running of the household entirely to his astute wife. Soon, however, his new domestic responsibilities would help bring him financial anxieties hitherto unknown.

Upon the completion of Pausanias Frazer allowed himself only a few weeks off to visit family and friends in Scotland, and then immediately set about revising *The Golden Bough*. A new edition had been his intention for a number of years. In a letter to Macmillan of 4 October 1896, he remarks in a postscript: "I am pleased to see that the sale of *The Golden Bough* continues steady or rather has slightly improved. I suppose the question of a new edition will have to be considered before very long." A "new edition," not a new printing. For some time he had had it in his mind to rework the book, but he probably did not then know how thoroughgoing the revision would be.

Throughout the Pausanias years he never lost touch totally with anthropology, although he was unable to keep up with the growing scholarly literature. The publication of *Totemism* and *The Golden Bough* had made him an important member of the small international anthropological–folkloric network and as such he was constantly receiving books, articles, and letters from other scholars. In thanking them for their publications, he often regrets the amount of time he has had to spend on Pausanias, which is delaying his return to his real love, anthropology.

But his keenness to return to anthropology does not in itself explain why he wanted to revise *The Golden Bough* rather than start something new. He had at least two reasons, both related to developments in the study of primitive religion and mythology. The first was a number of articles and books by the ubiquitous and prolific Andrew Lang that together represented a direct challenge to some of the ideas advanced in *The Golden Bough*. The other was a new, opportunely timed, and most important epistolary friendship, dating from early 1897, with the Australian anthropologist W. Baldwin Spencer (1860–1929).

First, Lang: since the 1870s Lang had been the chief champion of the anthropologists in their running battle with the solarists concerning the origin and meaning of ancient and primitive mythology. This controversy was in fact the latest version of a philosophical quarrel about the nature of primitive religion that had been going on since the Enlightenment.[7] Defenders of orthodoxy had long been arguing that the primitive heathens had shared, if only obliquely, in the original divine revelation made to the Hebrews and therefore that their religions too had begun as monotheism, only to be degraded later into the farrago of superstition now found among savages. The solarists may have employed the modern methods of comparative philology, but their notion of mythology as the end product of a "disease of language" was really only another form of degenerationism.

On the other hand the *philosophes*, who were progressivists and evolutionists, had argued that primitive religion originated in the universal psychological facts of dreams and visions and the fear that these produced. This fear was assuaged through propitiatory ancestor worship; the ancestors over time evolved into gods, responsible for different departments of nature; in the course of many more centuries in some places the gods coalesced and finally became God. The inescapable conclusion was that religion of all kinds, Christianity definitely included, was the product of primitive confusion or error. Tylor and Spencer had been the continuators and propagators of this argument in Britain, which was embraced by most anthropologically oriented writers on primitive religion in the half century before the First World War (and indeed by some for years thereafter).

Lang, as an early follower of Tylor and Spencer, had at the outset taken this evolutionist line.[8] In the seventies and early eighties, while he was leading the charge against the solarists, Lang accepted animism as both an accurate and a sufficient description of the earliest religious intimations of humanity. Of course he eschewed any hint of degenerationism, which he and his likeminded colleagues saw, probably correctly, as crypto-Christianity. But he was always a man of independent mind – sometimes extravagantly so – and he began to become less certain as he examined more closely his opponents' case that some primitive peoples indeed possessed a "high monotheism" of their own (that is, a belief in a single ethical Supreme Being that was not attributable to their contact with others) when they were first encountered by Europeans.

Starting with *Myth, Ritual and Religion* (1887), Lang began to consider the implications of new, more comprehensive, and more reliable information that was becoming available about Australian aboriginal religious belief and behavior.[9] These accounts, from observers who had gained the confidence of the natives and in some cases had been initiated into their mysteries, contained evidence that the aborigines, who were universally regarded as the most backward people in the world, nevertheless knew a high god (the "All-Father"), one who had created the world and had instituted human morality. But having done all this, the high god either removed himself or somehow was shunted off to one side, with little to do in the day-to-day supervision or operation of the world. One reason was that his worship had been supplanted or corrupted by mistaken beliefs and foolish "superstitions" about spirits and ghosts. Now spirits and ghosts conformed exactly with what, based on their position in the evolutionary sequence, such primitive people "should" believe. Lang, who was still locked in controversy with Max Müller, was not then willing to explore this new material fully, but equally was he unwilling to ignore it. He contented himself with distinguishing two elements in the primitive faith: the monotheism was "religious" whereas the superstitions were "mythical."[10] That is, unlike his ideological allies, he did not rule out absolutely the possibility of backsliding having taken place, from a "religious" phase to a "mythical" phase.

In the mid-1890s, with the solarists on the run, Lang returned to this question of primitive monotheism among the Australians, and it preoccupied him until his death in 1912. His work was one reason why Australian aboriginal religion remained a subject of intense international scholarly controversy (for the French and Germans entered into it too) until the First World War. Inasmuch as he did not succeed in bringing anyone round to his views, he had many occasions to play the gadfly and to exercise his formidable wit on what he regarded as the mistakes of others. Lang was as prolific as he was brilliant, and with access to a number of serious London journals he scourged his opponents tirelessly with the strength of ten men. And, for reasons that are not altogether clear, the polemical energy he had earlier expended in confuting Max Müller was now redirected against a new enemy-in-chief – J. G. Frazer. From 1900 until Lang died in 1912, Frazer could count on at least one hostile review of virtually anything he published.

From the point of view of his erstwhile friends in the evolutionary anthropological camp, what happened was little short of an intellectual scandal. In a word, Lang defected; in a series of books and articles written during the nineties he resurrected and lent new respectability to the degenerationist hypothesis that they thought had been finished off in the rout of the solarists, but this time the theory was much more securely founded because he employed their own anthropological evidence against them. On the personal level, after Frazer had been on the receiving end of no fewer than four scathing reviews by Lang of the second edition of *The Golden Bough*, relations between the two men came to an end. Frazer, wounded by Lang's allegations that he had played fast and loose with the evidence, and perhaps even more by the playfulness that was always part of Lang's seriousness, refused ever to see or speak with him again.

It is clear that for this entire post-Darwinian generation of mythographers dispassionate intellectual interests and passionate personal opinions about religion were inextricably mingled. It is unclear, however, exactly what impelled Lang to change his position. A man of a thousand jokes, he always turned away inquiries about his private life and especially about his religious position. Whatever his motives, however, the change in his views is clear enough. By 1894, in *Cock Lane and Common-Sense*, he began with an inquest into spiritualism, then much in the news as a result of well-publicized investigations into the claims of several famous mediums by the Society for

Psychical Research (SPR). This he proceeded to combine with a discussion of primitive religion. Perhaps, he suggested, the ideas of gods and of immortality had indeed been a mistaken development from the primitive notion of the *anima*, as evolutionist orthodoxy asserted. But, he asked, what if the natives in elaborating their ideas also used, along with "normal facts" like ghosts and dreams, "abnormal facts" like hallucinations and clairvoyance – concepts drawn from the vocabulary of spiritualism?[11] Lang asserted, with justice, that although most of his (rationalist) colleagues – men like Hartland, Clodd, and Grant Allen, although Tylor was an honorable exception[12] – claimed to be objective in their study of religious origins, they were really furthering their own ideological presuppositions. Accordingly they rejected a priori spiritualism and all its manifestations, for to them it could be understood only as an inexplicable and regrettable modern survival or recrudescence of the ghost worship of savagery. But in Lang's eyes this refusal even to investigate amounted to nothing less than an admission of prejudice and vitiated their professions to be advocates of a scientific discipline.

Clodd used his presidential address to the Folk-Lore Society in 1895 to protest and to counterattack: any serious attention paid by scientists to psychic phenomena, which were by definition delusions and frauds catering to all-too-understandable hopes and fears, only gave them a status they did not deserve. There were enough real questions, both ancient and modern, for serious students of religion to investigate without being drawn into nonsense and charlatanry.[13] But Lang pressed on. In the first part of *The Making of Religion* (1898) he defended the work of the SPR and again asserted that evolutionists were obliged to take spiritualism seriously if only because of the possibility that primitive religion may have been based on such phenomena. If they refused to do so, they could not claim logically that theism was *necessarily* a confused outgrowth of animism. He argued not that spiritualism was correct but that it could not be dismissed out of hand by the anthropologically enlightened, who imagined that their researches had effectively consigned all such beliefs to the refuse heap of error.

The second half of the book proposed a new explanation of the existence of high gods among low savages. A generation earlier, in *Primitive Culture*, Tylor had noted such deities but had argued that they had begun, like all others of their kind, as spirits who had somehow been promoted over their fellows to become kings of heaven.[14] Lang denied this account of their origin. Instead, he said, these gods were found in societies that lacked the idea of natural death, which was assumed in the notion of an afterlife, and lacked as well the hierarchical institutions which, the evolutionists claimed, served as a conceptual model for the high god himself. To him this implied the strong possibility that the primitives had begun with some form of true monotheism, which had later been corrupted by beliefs centered on ghosts and souls. Therefore the presence of animism, far from constituting theological bedrock as had been claimed, might be no such thing at all. If he was right, then it marked a falling away from the older belief in an ethical high god who could not be bribed or propitiated by sacrifice or prayer.

In one place, however, animism had not supplanted theism: ancient Israel. As he wrote to a friend, "The idea of the *soul* very nearly ruined the idea of *God*, and would have done so altogether, except for the Jews."[15]

The Old Testament is the story of the prolonged effort to keep Jehovah in His supreme place. To make and succeed in that effort was the *differentia* of Israel. Other peoples, even the lowest, had, as we prove, the germinal conception of a God . . . "But their foolish heart was darkened."[16]

The prophets were the heroes who tore away the strangling ivy of animism that threatened to choke the religion of Jehovah and restored the belief in one high God. "The long, intricate and mysterious theological education of humanity" culminated when Christianity combined a philosophy of the soul from the Greeks with the fierce monotheism of prophetic Israel.[17]

From this it was only a small step to the conclusion, where Lang at last dropped his reserve. The evolutionists had asserted that ghosts or spirits were the sole origin of religion; he declared that religion had two chief sources:

(1) the belief, how attained we know not, in a powerful, moral, eternal, omniscient Father and Judge of men; (2) the belief (probably developed out of experiences normal and supernormal) in somewhat of man which may survive the grave.[18]

The cat exited from the bag completely in the form of a strained footnote from "how attained we know not": "The hypothesis of St Paul seems not the most unsatisfactory." The secret was out: Lang was (had always been?) a Christian.[19]

The result for the next decade was the spectacle of Lang *contra mundum*, which predictably produced much more heat than light. No doubt Lang had hoped that his arguments would force the more honest among the evolutionists at least to do as he had done and re-examine the facts, and perhaps cause some of them to recognize (if only in private) that their conclusions followed from unspoken assumptions rather than from the preponderance of the evidence. Nothing like this happened. Aside from some expectably hostile reviews, he was henceforth largely ignored by his one-time friends and allies.[20] As might be imagined, this silence irritated him more than outright hostility could have done, and lent an extra sting to his lash, which he plied freely. It landed on no one more than on Frazer.

Meanwhile, Frazer was already back into anthropology in early 1897. For him this meant catching up on all that had appeared since 1890, which he proceeded to do with his characterstic industry and comprehensiveness. But nothing he read in the journals had the impact of a letter he received in early 1897 from his friend, the well-known Australian anthropologist, Revd Lorimer Fison (1832–1907).[21] The bombshell was contained in a letter Fison enclosed that he had just received from the Australian anthropologist, Baldwin Spencer.

Like Haddon, Spencer had started as a zoologist but had switched to anthropology when, on a collecting expedition in the Central Australian outback, he saw with his own eyes the pressing need for scientifically trained people to describe the aboriginal cultures before they were extinguished. Then he met and befriended F. J. Gillen (1856–1912), who, as Sub-Protector of the Aborigines, probably knew the natives of Central Australia better than any other white man. For a number of years they had both been working heroically to create while it was still possible a record of those tribes in the remote center of the continent that had been relatively untouched by contact with Europeans. What had greatly piqued Frazer's interest was a postscript in which Spencer said that he had noted that some of the Arunta men "ate their own totems."[22]

Robertson Smith had claimed (or guessed) in *The Religion of the Semites* that in primitive times the totemic tribes occasionally ate the otherwise taboo totem animal as a sacrament in order to achieve communion with their god. Smith's problem had been in finding evidence; virtually his sole exhibit had been St Nilus' account of pre-Islamic Semitic nomads sacrificing and consuming a camel. When no further examples came to light, Frazer had become increasingly skeptical. Hence his excitement at Spencer's casual mention of the consumption of the totem animal by the Arunta tribesmen. Best of all, theoretically speaking, was that the observation was made among the Arunta because of all the aborigines they had probably been least affected by outside influence.

Frazer immediately wrote to Spencer with questions and requests for information. Spencer's lengthy response (dated 12 July 1897), the first letter in their long correspondence, is significant. In it he told how he and Gillen had worked together, and he tried to answer some of Frazer's questions about Arunta belief and behavior. Spencer (like Gillen) was a great admirer of *The Golden Bough* – and especially of Frazer's style – and was therefore flattered by its author's interest in his work.[23] As a zoologist lately come to anthropology, and therefore a novice in his new field, he immediately assumed the role of disciple to Frazer the master and put himself and Gillen at Frazer's service. Any question he was unable to answer himself he would refer to Gillen, who remained in the bush and was therefore able to do research on the spot. From Frazer's point of view it could not have been better.

The importance of Spencer and Gillen's research and information over the next several years for Frazer's subsequent work cannot be overstated. They enabled Frazer to propose not one but two new theories of the origin of totemism; they gave him the empirical basis for his distinction between magic and religion and for the idea that the former everywhere preceded the latter;

and they promoted to center stage the question of exogamy and its possible relation with totemism. These themes would engross Frazer for the first decade of the new century.

In his pioneering survey of 1887, *Totemism*, Frazer had brought together all the extant evidence on that then-little-known institution, concluding tentatively that it had originated in primitive man's idea that the totem creature was the repository of his external soul. He had arrived at this theory from a canvass of the ethnographic materials at his disposal, many of which were confused or imprecise in the way they understood the phenomena loosely labeled as totemic. Now, with two first-class ethnographers ready to do his bidding, and ideally situated to investigate totemism among truly primitive people at first hand, his collaboration with them quickly produced a new explanation.

It grew directly out of Frazer's offer in 1897 to help Spencer and Gillen find a publisher for their work. They gratefully accepted, and of course he went first to Macmillan, who agreed to bring out their book, *The Native Tribes of Central Australia*. Frazer also offered to read the proofs, which (given the time the mails took to Australia) appreciably brought forward the date of publication; again they were pleased to accept. This of course gave Frazer first sight of everything, and for him the whole book was filled with amazing material. Frazer's first attempt at a hypothesis, predictably utilitarian, was expressed in a letter to Spencer of 15 September 1898:

In going through the second proofs of your book, I have been more than ever struck by your account of the intichiuma ceremonies. Such ceremonies for the multiplication of the totem plant or animal have not been (so far as I know) reported from any other part of the world, and taken in conjunction with other facts that you mention, seem to set totemism in an entirely new light, at least so far as the Central Australian tribes are concerned. It almost looks as if among these tribes totemism was a system expressly devised for the purpose of procuring a plentiful supply of food, water, sunshine, wood, etc.[24]

According to Frazer, in the old days the aborigine felt free to kill and eat his totem animal. But somehow a feeling against such behavior arose. Frazer's hypothetical aborigine then thinks to himself:

"I am, e.g., a Kangaroo man, and I want to make as many kangaroos come and be eaten as I can. Now if I kill and eat them myself, the kangaroos will regard me with fear and distrust as a dangerous creature, not as a genuine kangaroo at all. I must therefore be very kind and gentle to my brothers and sisters the kangaroos. I must never injure them myself, and then I shall be able to induce them to come quietly and confidently to be injured (in fact to be killed and eaten) by my fellow tribesmen. It is a pity certainly that I am debarred from eating roast kangaroo while my fellows are feasting on it; but then, they make it up to me in other ways. The Grub men bring me grubs to eat which they may not touch themselves; the Emu men bring me emus, etc., etc."

By means of this just-so story Frazer develops what is essentially an economic theory of the origin of totemism based on a rational aborigine calculating how best to assure and enlarge the food supply. Although Spencer's descriptions of the *intichiuma* embed its premeditated element in a dense ritual context, Frazer characteristically ignores this in his reconstruction of the mental life of this *homo economicus aboriginalis*. Although he writes to Jackson about how much the mental life of the primitives differs from that of modern people, and how difficult a modern European would find it to understand the thought process of the savage, one would never guess it here. With his propensity for economic planning and for taking the long view, this Kangaroo man would have been at home in the Fabian Society in 1898. Both earlier and later writers, such as Robertson Smith, Lang, and R. R. Marett, are much more sensitive to the potentially numinous quality of the religious event, the sense (or at least the possibility) of awe in the presence of the more-than-natural.

In response Spencer (20 October 1898) put forward a far-reaching suggestion of his own.[25] He remarked that although practices vary from tribe to tribe, totemism taken overall is really best seen as a cultural system with two quite different aspects, one religious and the other social. The religious side is Frazer's totem sacrament, consisting of magical performances designed to produce and guarantee a bountiful food supply. The social has nothing to do with the food supply but everything to do with the regulation of marriage, for in many tribes men may not marry women from their own totem clan but must instead marry outside it. The religious aspect seems older than the social, which has the air of having been added later. Noting the geographical distribution of the religious and the social factors for all the tribes about which information is available, he concludes that in the center of the continent, where physical conditions are hardest, the religious side predominates (that is, the need for a stable food supply is paramount). Among the coastal tribes, however, where more favorable conditions mean that the struggle for survival is not so unrelenting, social totemism is present in varying degrees – sometimes alongside and sometimes even supplanting the religious side.

He then turns to Frazer's theory. He sees no evidence that the taboo on killing and eating the animals arises from the wish to conciliate them, the better to catch and kill them.

The two fundamental points seem to be (1), and much the most important, that a man has the power of increasing his totem and (2), though it must be remembered that as yet we have only one bit of evidence of this, a man has some special power in regard to catching his own totem.[26]

Gently he rejects Frazer's scenario of the primitive Kangaroo economist reasoning that although he must forgo eating his delicious namesake, yet he is consoled in the knowledge that he will receive other tasty morsels from clansmen of other totems who in turn may not eat their animals. In its place he proposes that eating too much of the totem might estrange the animal from the clansman, "the result of which will be that I no longer possess the influence over them by means of which I can secure their increase."[27] Although this argument also assumes what might be called an economic psychology – which is reasonable enough given the harsh physical surroundings in which the Arunta live – it is less crudely one of direct and unremitting self-interest than Frazer's.

This letter had a profound effect on Frazer. So impressed was he by Spencer's hypothesis that he was willing to say that it was not merely plausible but probable. To ensure that Spencer should go down in history as the man who had solved what Andrew Lang would later call "the secret of the totem," Frazer suggested that Spencer immediately write a letter to either *Nature* or the *Athenaeum* outlining his ideas or, better still, read a paper before the Anthropological Institute. This last was possible because Spencer was coming to England for a brief stay, and Frazer offered to (and did) arrange a special meeting of the Institute for him.[28] He added that he himself had already independently worked out a theory of the totemic origins of exogamy identical to the one Spencer had sketched, basing himself on the comparative evidence supplied by the existence of exogamously bisected communities in Melanesia and North America, as well as in Australia.

All this points to totemism having existed at first as a purely religious (or as I should now prefer to say magical) system, and exogamy having been afterwards, as you say, tacked on to it more or less accidentally. . . . In short, totemism and exogamy are two entirely distinct things that may and have existed quite independently of each other.[29]

The parenthesis shows that by late 1898 Frazer had already hit upon his distinction between magic and religion. Later in this long, important theoretical letter Frazer makes clear that this dichotomy is not just an inspiration of the moment but something he has been thinking about for some time. This sequence of the major stages in mental evolution seems to have arisen directly from the new Australian context supplied by Spencer rather than from his undergraduate exposure to Comte, the resemblances to the latter's scheme notwithstanding.

In fact I am coming more and more to the conclusion that if we define religion as the propitiation of natural and supernatural powers, and magic as the coercion of them, magic has everywhere preceded religion. It is only when men find by experience that they cannot *compel* the higher powers to comply with their wishes, that they condescend to *entreat* them. In time, after long ages, they begin to realize that entreaty is also vain, and then they try compulsion again; but this time the compulsion is applied within narrower limits and in a different way from the old magical method. In short, religion is replaced by science. The order of evolution, then, of human thought is, magic – religion – science. We in this generation live in a transition epoch between religion and science, an epoch which will last, of course, many generations to come. It is for those who care for progress to aid the final triumph of science as much as they can in their day.[30]

Even though it marked a seemingly inevitable phase in human mental and spiritual evolution, Frazer regarded the intermediate religious stage as a backsliding from the more objective view of the natural world embodied in magic. Magic is admittedly crude and primitive, but it bears important resemblances to science nevertheless. The medicine man or magician, despite the foolishness he undoubtedly perpetrates, is basically like the scientist in that both believe that mastery of the natural world is possible and both strive to attain it. The magician, convinced that nature is unvarying, uniform, and controllable, seeks techniques for working his will upon it. Unfortunately his reach exceeds his grasp, for he misunderstands the natural laws that govern how things really happen, and this misunderstanding gives rise to a false psychology and epistemology. That is, the confusion in magic, and the ultimate reason why it does not work, is that it is based on "mistaken applications of one or other of two great fundamental laws of thought, namely, the association of ideas by similarity and the association of ideas by contiguity in space or time."[31] The magician correctly sees the importance of the association of ideas; however, he misunderstands how ideas and events are in fact associated and therefore produces nonsense.

Legitimately applied they [the principles of association] yield science; illegitimately applied they yield magic, the bastard sister of science. It is therefore a truism, almost a tautology, to say that all magic is necessarily false and barren; for were it ever to become true and fruitful, it would no longer be magic but science.[32]

Unable, therefore, to devise an effective magic, he retires, defeated, and is replaced by those who lead society into the servility and obfuscation implied by religion. Implicitly, the medicine man is morally superior to the priest in that the former at least stands upright whereas the latter is on his knees or perhaps even prostrate in the dust. The former believes in man's power to determine his own destiny whereas the latter abdicates before what he sees as the all-powerful gods. Humanity having caved in under its loss of confidence and the weight of its fear of the unknown, religion has held sway for millennia, thereby denying the world during that time all the philosophical clarity and technical advantage that science brings with it. But finally the objective temperament and world-view that characterizes magic is somehow reborn in more effective form as science, and all is (or ultimately will be) well.

When this three-stage developmental scheme was advanced in the second edition of *The Golden Bough*, it elicited several different kinds of objections. Some critics pointed out contrary examples, where religious behavior preceded magical, or where the magical stage seems never to have occurred.[33] Others argued that Frazer's clear and distinct phases are entirely a product of his inadequate and tendentious definitions of magic and religion, which are framed exclusively in terms of the responses of terrified humans cowering before overwhelming power and recognize no human need or wish to love, or at least to move toward, the deity.[34] Today we might remark that his explanation, which is typically psychological and individualistic, offers no social context or process by which these transformations are supposed to have occurred, and certainly in historical times his description of the alleged change from religious to scientific modes of thinking does not fit the facts.

Peter G. Baker believes that Frazer had developed this theory of the priority of magic in direct response to Lang's new insistence on high gods among the primitives.[35] This implies that the theoretical differences between Frazer and Lang were by this time (late 1898) already substantial and were then heightened by personal animosity to the extent that Frazer was provoked into a controversy with Lang. Although the argument is attractive, the evidence does not support it. On the personal level, it is certain that there was no bad blood between them at this time. On 25 October 1898, only a month before the momentous letter to Spencer, Frazer writes to Macmillan to say that Lang has written to ask whether he might see proofs of *The Native Tribes of Central Australia* because he is in the process of revising *Myth, Ritual and Religion* and wishes to incorporate the latest information. Frazer is unsure whether Macmillan should agree because he does not want anyone to steal Spencer and Gillen's thunder. But when Macmillan points out that the Australians' book will certainly appear before Lang's, and moreover that Lang's discussion is likely to attract attention to their work, Frazer agrees. He writes, on 27 October 1898, "So it is all right. I quite share your wish to oblige Lang, who is a friend of mine."

Plainly, then, relations between Frazer and Lang were still unclouded late in 1898. Further, *The Making of Religion*, which contains the explicit endorsement of Pauline theology, has a preface dated 3 April 1898, and the book appeared several months afterward. Assuming that he read Lang's book (or at least reviews of it) on publication, Frazer may have been surprised or even saddened by what he found there, but he was not sufficiently moved to write anything in response, and certainly was not impelled to break off their friendship. In the light of all this, the only plausible possibility remaining is that it was Spencer's new information, not Lang's falling away or a personal feud, that inspired Frazer's new theories.

Meanwhile, Frazer's acting as agent for Spencer and Gillen during the production of their book created, as an unintended by-product, a dispute between him and Tylor. When Macmillan accepted the book for publication, Frazer suggested that Tylor be sent a set of proofs, more as a courtesy than anything else, which was done. Tylor, however, had only recently (in May 1898) proposed to the Anthropological Institute a quite different theory of totemism of his own, one that grew out of his own animistic assumptions, namely (in Frazer's summary), that "the souls of ancestors animate the totem animals or plants, and therefore these animals or plants are sacred to their descendants."[36] Perhaps because Spencer and Gillen's evidence did not support his theory, when the book was already in page proof Tylor proposed to

Macmillan that the chapter giving a minute description of the crucial *intichiuma* ceremonies be drastically compressed, in order to elide many "tedious and disagreeable details." In a letter to Macmillan of 13 September 1898 Frazer disagreed most forcefully.

The part to which Tylor takes exception as containing "tedious and disagreeable details" . . . appears to me the most interesting and important in the whole book. It sets the system of totemism, at least as it exists among those tribes, in an entirely new and wholly unexpected light, and it furnishes the first well-attested case of what appears to be a real totem sacrament – a thing which hitherto had only been inferred from a few very uncertain examples. The whole chapter is, in my opinion, of the highest importance for the history of religion, and opens up lines of enquiry which it will now be most desirable to prosecute in many parts of the world. I am about to write to Spencer to see if he cannot obtain more of the details which Tylor finds so "tedious and disagreeable" that he would like to omit them.

After a brief exchange Tylor backed down, and the book was published intact.[37]

In late 1898 Frazer, having caught up with his reading and powerfully stimulated by his exchanges with Spencer, began to compose the new *Golden Bough*. True to form, because he wrote quickly and easily, or perhaps because the writing of the first edition had been straightforward, he thought the new edition would not take long to complete. Macmillan may have experienced something of a sinking feeling, or at least one of Pausanian *déjà vu*, for no sooner had Frazer predicted smooth sailing than he immediately began to report delays. On 24 November 1898 he apologizes for not sending copy to the printer because illness in the family had obliged him to go to Scotland; the patient was his mother, who had entered a terminal decline and died in February of the next year. He is, however, reassuring: "But I am working steadily at the subject, and the book is only gaining the longer time I give it." Then nothing more until March 1899, when he asks Macmillan to have the printers run off a special interleaved copy of the first edition, with blank sheets between the pages. This, he says, will obviate the need for cutting and pasting, for much old copy is to be picked up intact and incorporated in the new book, albeit with more and updated references in the footnotes.[38] He now estimates that the new material will make about 150 additional printed pages. He suggests, therefore, that the new edition be printed in smaller type, in order to stay within two volumes. On 7 June he writes to say that he has lost several weeks' work because he just undergone the trauma of moving house; it has taken that long to reinstall self and books in the new surroundings. In the interim, however, the goal has once again receded.

I see that the additions will be considerable. The type will have to be reduced and perhaps a thinner paper adopted if the volumes are to be kept of about the same size as before. But we must try to make the second edition as attractive outwardly as the first was. As to the inside I think I shall manage to increase the interest and value considerably. If you have no objection I should like to be allowed to keep the whole book in slip [galley proof] till it is ready for the final revision. This would enable me to introduce new matter and perhaps recast certain parts up to the last, though I should not expect to make many changes after the first proof.

Publishers and editors must work with their authors as they find them. By now Macmillan must have realized that Frazer was past changing, and that he would continue to alter the text until the last moment in any case, so he agreed to allow Frazer to keep the whole book beside him in galleys. A month later (8 July) the first two chapters are ready to send to the printer, and Frazer finds that "the additions to the first chapter are very considerable." Accordingly he asks whether the printers might run off some sample pages, showing how the text would look in various small sizes of type. Then, in a postscript, as if in an afterthought, comes his real idea: "I don't know whether you would think it worth while to consider the possibility of bringing out *The Golden Bough* in three small volumes." With only the first two long chapters completed, Frazer must already have realized that retention of the two-volume format would mean a type size so small and a page so packed as to approach illegibility. Macmillan did not resist, and the work, when it finally did appear the next year, was in three volumes.

The letters to Macmillan from about this date also begin to contain Frazer's recommendations about anthropological books that he thinks ought (and ought not) to be published. He became Macmillan's regular anthropological consultant, and was largely responsible for making the firm's list in that subject second to none, the university presses included, over the first quarter of the century. Thus, in 1898 he wrote on behalf of W. W. Skeat, on the basis of an incomplete manuscript that would be published as *Malay Magic* (1900). Many others would follow – the most important by far being Malinowski – and at the start Macmillan usually accepted Frazer's suggestions. Not surprisingly, the qualities the latter especially esteemed were an abundance of facts; if possible a willingness on the part of the author to forgo generalizations or comparisons or, if the author insisted on theorizing, then at least a clear separation between facts and theories; and an agreeable, which is to say limpid and nontechnical, style.[39]

Another new element in the Macmillan correspondence from about this time is the appearance of what would become a steady stream of letters from Lilly Frazer. As she already was a professional writer before they married, after 1896 Frazer suggested, and Macmillan accepted, that the Frazers henceforth become a one-publisher family. (This meant that Macmillan had first refusal of her books; those he declined were brought out by others.) It was this arrangement that enabled her to bring husband and publisher face to face for the first time. Such a happy result notwithstanding, there would be many days when Macmillan regretted that decision, because Lilly Frazer was not easy to deal with. In any event, along with taking care of her household, her children, and her husband, she continued to write – mostly playlets in French

161

for classroom performance and books of stories and poems for children.[40] In addition, starting with the second edition of *The Golden Bough*, she took charge of the important task of finding and supervising French translators for each of J. G.'s major works, as they were published, which meant that by the 1920s he was nearly as well known in France as he was in Britain.

In 1899 Frazer unexpectedly received the first of what would become over the next thirty years a long series of honors. In June of that year he was awarded an honorary Doctorate of Civil Laws from Oxford, essentially on the strength of the Pausanias (and probably at the urging of Percy Gardner). The irony implicit in the recognition coming from "the other place" angered Lilly Frazer, and confirmed her in her settled belief that he would always be overlooked by Cambridge because he would not and did not put himself forward and cultivate the people who mattered when it came to such considerations. No doubt the Oxford degree came up in domestic discussions when in 1907 he received an offer to move to the University of Liverpool and become professor of social anthropology there. By that time he was much better known than he had been in 1899, but Cambridge still had conferred no honor upon him.

The publication of the second edition of *The Golden Bough* was a major intellectual event, which made Frazer's name well known among the readers of the serious magazines as well as the ranks of professional scholars. This period in Frazer's life, however, ends as it began, rather more quietly, with another letter to Edmund Gosse about money. This time the revelatory letter (dated 2 December 1899) comes not from Lilly but from Frazer himself. Gosse learned that the Frazer exchequer was in poor condition and had sounded his fellow members of the Council of the Royal Literary Fund about the prospects of an award; these soundings had proved positive. He then prudently wrote to Frazer to be sure that the help if offered would be accepted. (Frazer's refusal to mention the Fund by name is a mark of his gentility, not a primitive avoidance taboo.)

Thank you for your most kind letter. I cannot but be deeply gratified by the mark of appreciation of my work which the Council of the public body you speak of propose to bestow on me. The Council is right in believing that my writings do not yield me a livelihood. The "Golden Bough" brought me in annually about £30 for several years (the last year it brought in over £46), but for a year or more it has been out of print, and some little time must elapse before the new and enlarged edition, on which I am at work, can be published and begin to yield a return. From Pausanias I have as yet had nothing, though there is a fair prospect that in another year it will begin to bring in something annually. At the same time it is to be remembered that for many years my College has allowed me to hold a research Fellowship, so that I am in a sense repaid for my work even if my writings brought me in nothing. Owing, however, to the depression from which my College, like many others, is now suffering, the dividend has now fallen to an extent which makes a serious difference in my income. In these circumstances I accept most gratefully the help you so gracefully and delicately offered me by the public body on whose behalf you write. It will be a very real and welcome help towards enabling me to carry on my work without those pecuniary anxieties and distractions which might otherwise press upon me in the near future.

The help amounted to £250, which more than doubled Frazer's income for the year, as the Trinity dividend, derived as it then was from agricultural rents, was throughout the depressed nineties closer to £200 than the £250 it had been in the eighties. Frazer, too, had the substantial additional expenses represented by his family. His wife's writing brought in a little but, as everyone knows, children cost money. Although Frazer "was singularly free from especial needs and wants," as Lilly wrote in 1910, one of the few things he did require was having virtually every book he required at hand. His unwillingness to use the library meant buying all his books, an expensive need that had to be satisfied. And if Lilly was in college helping J. G. all day long, someone had to oversee the Frazer home. They had no cook, but at least one maid was a necessity in even the most straitened middle-class household. And so it went, one thing after another; in 1899 Frazer must have felt that Gosse was indeed a bright ministering angel, for he certainly ministered to the Frazer family when they needed help most.

10 · THE SECOND EDITION

Despite the wisdom summed up in the phrase that "no one reads prefaces," like so many other authors Frazer found irresistible the opportunity to drop the pose of scholarly objectivity and speak in his own voice. As a result many of his prefaces became the repositories for hopes, wishes, and other forms of special pleading that had no other place in the books; they are therefore invaluable for the biographer. Perhaps of no other book is this more true than the second edition of *The Golden Bough*.

Its most notable passage, both because of its rhetorical flourish and because of its intimations of his divided consciousness, is its conclusion, where in an extended military metaphor Frazer exposes the subversive nature and aims of the comparative study of religion as he understands them.

Well handled, it [the comparative method] may become a powerful instrument to expedite progress if it lays bare certain weak spots in the foundations on which modern society is built – it shows that much that we are wont to regard as solid rests on the sands of superstition rather than on the rock of nature. It is indeed melancholy and in some respects thankless task to strike at the foundations of beliefs in which, as in a strong tower, the hopes and aspirations of humanity through long ages have sought a refuge from the storm and stress of life. Yet sooner or later it is inevitable that the battery of the comparative method should breach these venerable walls, mantled over with the ivy and mosses and wild flowers of a thousand tender and sacred associations. At present we are only dragging the guns into position: they have hardly yet begun to speak.... Yet this uncertainty [about what will replace religion] ought not to induce us, from any consideration of expediency or regard for antiquity, to spare the ancient moulds, however beautiful, when these are proved to be out-worn. Whatever comes of it, wherever it leads us, we must follow truth alone. It is our only guiding star: *hoc signo vinces*.[1]

He acknowledges the tension between his position as artilleryman in the army of reason and his sentiments. He does not seem to understand, however, that his highminded obligation as a historian to follow the facts wherever they may lead is not merely in conflict with what he learned in his pious home but also with his partisanship as a determined enemy of religion.

But although the preface ends with the siege guns of the comparative method ready to open up on the venerable fortress of religion, it begins slowly and conservatively. So far as Frazer is concerned, on the main points nothing has changed; everything that has come to light since 1890 has only strengthened his position, and he sees no reason to modify, much less abandon, it. In fact the publication in 1897 by the Belgian historian Franz Cumont of the medieval *Martyrdom of St. Dasius* goes far to confirm his theory that the King of the Wood was an embodiment of a tree-spirit and that long ago one of these priest-kings, taken to embody the god dwelling within the green natural world, was annually put to death to ensure continued fertility.

Moreover, this corroboration, though unexpected, was not unique. From the other side of the world the much more startling researches of Spencer and Gillen among the Australian aborigines had powerfully reinforced the work of Mannhardt on the agricultural practices of the Central European peasant. The Australians "regularly perform magical ceremonies for the express purpose of bringing down rain and multiplying the plants and animals on which they subsist," which, *mutatis mutandis*, correspond to the European spring and midsummer rites that occupied so prominent a place in the first edition. The aborigines, not being agriculturalists, have no harvest customs, but this lacuna is filled by the somewhat more highly developed Malays, thanks to the work of W. W. Skeat. "Occupying a lower plane of culture than ourselves, the Malays have retained a keen sense of the significance of rites which in Europe have sunk to the level of more or less meaningless survivals."[2] Thus, as it evolves ever upward, is the whole world shown to be kin.

On one point, however, he does admit to having changed his mind: the relation of magic to religion. In 1890 he had not thought out the essential nature of each and thus had classified magic as a low form of religion. Now he sees that not only does the one precede the other but that they are essentially in opposition to one another. Foreseeing disputes, he cautions those who would disagree to note the special definitions he gives to "magic" and "religion."

Although Frazer continues to embrace Mannhardt, he takes the opportunity to emphasize the distance between himself and Robertson Smith. In 1897 the French sociologists Henri Hubert and Marcel Mauss had stated that Frazer's theory of the dying god had arisen from Smith's derivation of animal sacrifice from a totem sacrament.[3] Frazer uses this occasion to deny the connection: each man arrived at his own idea independently, and in fact he never accepted Smith's theory. His reason for demurring then was the paucity of evidence, which even now, despite the amazing confirmation from Australia, remains insufficient as a base for asserting the existence of totem sacraments as a universal feature of an early stage in human development. It may well be that the facts will lead him to accept that such was the general case, but he is not yet ready to say so. But, lead where they will, he will follow the facts: *hoc signo vinces*.

One point remains to be made before the guns of anthropology can begin to speak, namely, that the reader appreciate the context in which his work should be understood. His book is "a contribution to that still youthful science which seeks to trace the growth of human thought and institutions in those dark ages which lie beyond the range of history."[4] This science, though young, is about to open up extraordinary vistas by means of which our view into the prehistoric past will be greatly extended. Anthropologists in 1900 find themselves in the same position as that of the humanists at the beginning of the Renaissance, who were vouchsafed a brilliant vision of the achievement of classical antiquity. The anthropology of human origins promises even more, for the prospect – or retrospect – it gives is more extensive still. It is in that atmosphere and against that background of intellectual excitement that the bittersweet polemical conclusion comes, in which the fortress of religion is invested and the siege begun by the unwilling cannoneers. The pathos of its conclusion – "we must follow truth alone" – arises not only from the complex emotional associations of the past that make the necessarily destructive work of the present a melancholy task, but also from a vision of the future that is perceived through the lens of hope. It is reminiscent of the heartbreaking conclusion of a contemporary work, *Uncle Vanya*, in which Vanya enjoins his niece to work hard to build the glorious future that unfortunately they will not live to see. Frazer, for all his undoubted belief in the ultimate moral as well as technological redemption that science will finally afford humanity, is conscious of living between two worlds, with the new one still only a gleam on the horizon.

Once out of the preface and into the book proper, we meet the ghastly priest circling the tree once again. Excepting the amplified notes, the first six pages are taken from the first edition verbatim. But immediately thereafter Frazer introduces the antithesis of magic to religion and the necessary priority of the former to the latter. This theory is important not only in itself but lies at the center of an effort to impose a new theoretical structure on the work.

The first edition of *The Golden Bough* consisted of four long chapters on the themes of vegetation, fertility, and kingship in primitive life that were only loosely and intermittently connected by the motif of the golden bough. Those readers who may have been made uneasy by the many conjectural links in the argument could at least enjoy the imaginative sweep and agreeable style of the work. The quickened tempo of anthropological research and the increase in empirical data in the nineties meant that in an enlarged, revised *Golden Bough* he could no longer afford such slackness (or geniality) of presentation; if the reader was to follow and appreciate the argument, stricter organization and a more clearly articulated structure were needed. To this end, and convinced by the new information from Australia, he decided that the progression of magic, religion, and science, seen as not only conceptually differentiated but historically sequential to one another, was to be the theoretical basis of the new book. Even the subtitle has been changed accordingly: the first edition, less doctrinaire, had been subtitled "A Study in

Comparative Religion"; the second and third are called "A Study in Magic and Religion."

Frazer offers much more about magic than merely an argument about its priority in mental evolution. He analyzes it as a phenomenon and isolates two simple principles that explain all its innumerable manifestations: sympathy (like produces like) and contagion (things that have once been in contact continue to influence one another after the contact has ceased). Although he presents a cornucopia of examples of both kinds, one of each will suffice: injuring enemies by sticking pins in an effigy or image illustrates the first, whereas using discarded hair or fingernail parings to cast a spell exemplifies the second. This analysis, although from a modern viewpoint incomplete because it ignores the social processes in which magic takes place and the psychological needs it fulfills for the practitioner and the community, is genuinely useful and remains Frazer's single most important contribution to the anthropology of religion.[5]

The other noteworthy features of the new edition were intentionally "provocative." In 1890 Frazer had taken pains to avoid the touchy subject of Christianity, circling round it geographically and doctrinally but never mentioning it explicitly. A reader would have been slow indeed not to take his antireligious point, but his tone in the first edition is distinctly unpolemical. In the second edition, however, in keeping with the artillery metaphor of the preface, he drops his caution and brings his rationalist and antireligious intentions into the open.

The vehicle for these aggressive intentions was an extended analysis of three ancient pagan festivals, about which relatively little information existed, thus permitting him a free field for conjecture: the Persian Sacaea, the Roman Saturnalia, and the Babylonian Zakmuk. (1) At the Sacaea (c. sixth century B.C.), celebrated in the summertime, a condemned criminal was dressed up as the king and afforded royal privileges (that is, access to the royal harem) for five days, after which he was stripped, scourged, and hanged. Frazer speculates that this mock-king was killed as a royal proxy; his death recalled an earlier time when the king, who was believed to incarnate the principle of vegetational growth, was put to death after reigning for only one year. His sacrifice was required to maintain fertility of woman and beast and field; sexual intercourse with the royal harlots therefore was mimetic or sympathetic fertility magic. (2) The Saturnalia, occurring around the winter solstice, was a Roman holiday of misrule. During its week-long carnival, ordinary authority was annulled and all customary relationships were turned topsy-turvy. In Frazer's reconstruction, however, the nonstop merrymaking originally also included a human sacrifice. The reason he thinks so is that, according to the medieval manuscript published by Cumont, in the province of Lower Moesia in A.D. 303 a Christian soldier in the Roman army named Dasius was chosen by lot to be the mock-king in his garrison's celebration; he was to impersonate the god Saturnus throughout a month of revelry and then, having enjoyed royal power and privileges, go to his death. He refused this dubious honor and therefore was killed (martyred). Frazer reads this to mean that the jolly mock-kings of Saturnalian misrule descended from a not-so-jolly original in which a mock-king assumed the god's role and then was killed. (3) Lastly, at the Babylonian Zakmuk, a much older (c. 3000 B.C.) springtime new-year festival, the fate of the kingdom and the king over the coming year was weighed in the heavenly council.

Unfortunately for Frazer, none of these festivals contains the entire ritual of the priest-king who is sacrificed to ensure the fertility of the land and the health of the kingdom, so he must arbitrarily amalgamate features from each to produce the ideal scenario that suits his purposes. This presents no theoretical problem because all three holidays are the products of the same stage of mental evolution, and therefore their local variations are unimportant in comparison to the underlying overall design.

All these festivals are described and analyzed at length as connected links in a conjectural chain. In themselves, however, they are nothing, for they exist only to serve as the platform from which to launch his two most controversial speculations. Purim, commemorating the Jews' miraculous deliverance from destruction in Persia, is a festival that they brought back when they returned from exile in Babylon. Frazer claims that Purim was yet another member of the family of Near Eastern holidays of misrule that were founded in agricultural magic and in their original form contained a human sacrifice. Like the Sacaea and the Zakmuk, its underlying idea was the ratification by the gods of the king's rule for another year, which originally required the shedding of blood. The human sacrifice was, over time, commuted to a ritual in which a mock-king was scourged. The plot of the Book of Esther and its principal characters – Haman, Mordecai, Esther, Vashti – therefore may be traced back to Babylonian originals.

Having offended the Jews he now turns to the Christians. On the basis of his reconstruction of Purim, the Passion narrative is now interpreted as follows: "we may suppose" that at Purim, and perhaps at Passover as well, the Jews were in the habit of drafting two prisoners to enact the central roles of Haman (the mock-king who is killed) and Mordecai (the true king who is enthroned) in the passion play that constituted the heart of the festival. Thus Jesus, who was "playing" Haman, was killed while Barabbas, as Mordecai, was spared. As evidence he points to the name Barabbas, meaning "son of the father," which sounds like a ritual title rather than a proper name, and which recalls the custom of the killing of the firstborn son throughout the Semitic world. He conjectures that the roles of Haman and Mordecai were really two aspects of the same god, one considered as victim and the other considered as risen.

The entire discussion constitutes a putative solution to a puzzle in the history of religion. It had always been tacitly assumed that the pattern of the dying and reviving god, common throughout the Near East, did not prevail in one place – Jewish Palestine. Frazer now asserts that this was only a seeming exception. Contrary to what had been believed, Judaism, and therefore Christianity, had *not* been immune from the widespread bloody worship of the procreative principle that peoples like the native Canaanites knew. The observances of the Jews and the Christians exemplified the same seasonal rhythmic pattern found among all the others, and therefore they were at bottom connected (at several removes, to be sure) with the fertility magic that was worked by the divine priest-king/tree-spirit prowling warily around the tree in faraway Aricia. Jesus was really (and therefore, in Frazer's reductionist analysis, only) a member of the group of dying and reviving gods that included (to invoke the title of one of his subsequent works) Attis, Adonis, and Osiris.

But Jesus' significance is not confined to the sphere of ritual, for Frazer places him in the long line of Hebrew prophets and reformers. His prophetic mission was transfigured, however, literally as well as figuratively, when because he had offended certain important personages he was given the Haman role of victim in this age-old ritual drama. For although the vexatious and popular preacher was thus put out of the way, the manner of his death seemed to give his

ethical mission the character of a divine revelation culminating in the passion and death of the incarnate Son of a heavenly Father. In this form the story of the life and death of Jesus exerted an influence which it could never have had if the great teacher had died, as is commonly supposed, the death of a vulgar malefactor.[6]

This is the rhetorical highwater mark of Frazer's provocative speculations; now he retreats. He notes that the Christian, faced with the resemblances between the death of Jesus and that of the myriad of other ritual martyrs in the Levant, will interpret the latter as merely so many forerunners of the former. God in his wisdom chose his son to redeem mankind, which had been made ready for redemption precisely by those other victims. The skeptic, on the other hand,

will reduce Jesus of Nazareth to the level of a multitude of other victims of a barbarous superstition, and will see in him no more than a moral teacher, whom the fortunate accident of his execution invested with the crown, not merely of a martyr, but of a god.[7]

Which of these views is correct? Which will prevail? Although the entire tendency of the argument leaves no doubt where Frazer stands, nevertheless at this last moment he recalls the objectivity appropriate to science by saying that only time will tell, and that the truth will finally overcome.

On 22 September 1900, Frazer had written to his Jewish friend Solomon Schechter about the second edition that he was on the point of completing: "I trust that you will approve of the book in its new and enlarged form. There are things in it which are likely to give offence both to Jews and Christians, but especially, I think, to Christians. You see I am neither the one nor the other, and don't mind knocking them impartially."[8] He was right: he did give offence, and just as he had knocked them, they returned the favor. The book received a great deal of attention, which must have helped sales; many learned of its existence from the chorus of disapproval it called forth, and some may have bought it for that reason.

If the reception among the popular reviewers was generally favorable – as in 1890, they were impressed by the erudition and the polished writing and were unable to criticize the content – that of his professional colleagues, even those who as ideological allies might have been expected to approve, was mixed and generally negative. The latter all too often objected to the piling of conjecture upon conjecture that is the essence of Frazer's argumentative strategy. Although Frazer was henceforth to be the favorite anthropologist of educated laymen on account of his scope and his style, a good number of those closest to him became and remained opponents from this point.

In 1890 *The Golden Bough* had been reviewed in *Folk-Lore* in tandem with Robertson Smith's *The Religion of the Semites*. By 1900 Frazer's standing within the scholarly world had risen dramatically.[9] His new status was best expressed by the fact that the second edition received no fewer than eight reviews in the spring 1901 number of *Folk-Lore* alone, by a battery of well-known anthropologists and folklorists, including Lang, Haddon, Alfred Nutt, Moses Gaster, and Charlotte Burne.[10] Placing to one side Lang's predictable antipathy, the reactions of all but one of the others ranged from a mild demurrer (from Haddon, distinctly embarrassed) to apoplexy (from Gaster, an eminent folklorist as well as a well-known Sephardic rabbi, about what he saw as Frazer's ridiculous Purim fantasy).

The exception was Nutt, a leading folklorist and later president of the Folk-Lore Society, whose remarks anticipated to some extent the direction of the work on Greek drama a decade later of the Cambridge Ritualists. For Nutt, regardless of the way historians of religion might criticize the accuracy of Frazer's reconstructions, folklorists would continue to embrace his ideas. They had accepted what he calls the Mannhardt–Frazer hypothesis because "it satisfies psychological requirements of which every student is conscious, although very few are at the trouble of formulating them." Its appeal lies in the fact that it is grounded in the universal human need for an adequate and assured food supply and the inherent uncertainties and anxieties people experience while cultivating the crops and waiting for the harvest. Any body of practices arising over time that purport to dispel injury to the harvest and make it succeed will automatically and necessarily be invested with general significance. "If any ritual, if any mythology, could count upon persistent survival after what may be called their social and economic justification has ceased to be operative, it would be these."

This is the economic heart of the matter, but secondarily "the animating spirit of the practices is influence exerted by imitation, mimetic magic," which in turn originates and develops the dramatic faculty. And if the craving for food be the most insistent physical demand of man, delight in dramatic representation is one of the most potent of his psychical emotions. Man lives by bread – man does not live by bread alone; these two statements contain in germ the Mannhardt–Frazer hypothesis, the one which I firmly hold to explain most adequately the largest body of those diverse and well-nigh innumerable practices, opinions, and fancyings designated folklore.[11]

To Nutt, whether Frazer is right about the goings-on in the African grove is immaterial to the question of the fundamental correctness of his general theory.

Inasmuch as Frazer thought of himself as a practitioner of a historical science, and believed that he was describing, or at least speculating about, human sentiments and mental processes as they (might have) evolved in history, these words may have struck him as excessively faint praise. But so far as the general reception of the book went, Nutt's approbation, and that of the popular press, was as nothing compared to one overpowering negative presence, that of Andrew Lang. It is not excessive to say that Lang was driven half-insane by the book, for he reviewed it no fewer than four times, of which the notice in *Folk-Lore* was the briefest and least consequential. He wrote a long criticism of the whole book in the *Fortnightly* in February 1901, then came back only two months later in the same journal with a second piece devoted entirely to shredding Frazer's theory of the Crucifixion. But even this was not enough, for on 15 September 1901 we find him writing to a friend about the work he had in hand at the moment:

my only joy is a book mainly against Mr Frazer's *Golden Bough* New Edition. It is not a dubious case, nor one in which two opinions are possible. That is the most learned and the most inconceivably silly book of recent times. To criticize it is really too like hitting a child. And the gifted author thinks he has exploded all of Christianity that Mrs [Humphry] Ward had left. . . . One laughs out loud in bed at the absurdity of it.[12]

The book was *Magic and Religion* (1901). It is a collection of his controversial pieces on religion, with chapters directed against his various adversaries, such as Tylor on the by-now-perennial subject of high gods among the savages. Of its 305 pages, however, nearly two-thirds are devoted to a sustained close reading, with an amplitude and on a level of detail impossible in even the longest magazine essay, of every major contention in the second edition of *The Golden Bough*. Absolutely nothing is overlooked, and absolutely nothing is found to be valid.

In *Magic and Religion* Lang has paid Frazer the ultimate compliment of taking him seriously enough to have checked the evidence offered for every one of his principal assertions. In view of the number and the exotic nature of the sources cited in *The Golden Bough*, and even allowing for the fact that he incorporated into his book the two *Fortnightly* articles in their entirety, this represents a considerable piece of research and writing. It was carried out at top speed, for the book had to appear while *The Golden Bough* was still fresh in the public mind or it was pointless. As a result no summary can provide any sense of the intensity with which the attack is waged. For *Magic and Religion* marks the culmination of Lang's gradual movement to theism through the nineties and one that was called forth by Frazer's aggressive attempt to undercut the historical basis of Christianity.

First, then, Lang's indictment. He finds Frazer's entire argument – ranging from the priest at Nemi to the priority of magic to the analysis of the pagan festivals and especially that of the biblical narratives – to be a concatenation of unsupported conjectures, self-contradictory statements, and confused and naive thinking. As if this were not enough, Frazer is also said to have engaged, on a grand scale, in tendentious reporting and suppression of evidence unfavorable to his views. The criticism at times comes uncomfortably close to being *ad hominem*, to which is added humor and even ridicule.[13]

According to Malinowski, after Frazer read *Magic and Religion* he was so "deeply upset and irritated" that he stopped working for "several months" and as a result "never read adverse criticisms or reviews of his books" thereafter.[14] If runners accustomed to training for 50 to 100 miles a week are suddenly unable to run, they experience serious physical and mental discomfort. Such a comparison is apt for by 1901 Frazer, that athlete of the study, had been habituated for at least twenty years to working twelve or more hours a day, seven days a week. For him to have stopped work for even a few days, much less for several months, is not only an index of the effectiveness of Lang's assault, but is tantamount to an admission of a total collapse. To use an old-fashioned phrase, it sounds as if Lang's book produced in Frazer a nervous breakdown.

Or *did* he have a breakdown? Although Malinowski says that Frazer himself said that he stopped work, there is much evidence to make that unlikely. The letters show that Frazer indisputably did *not* come to an intellectual halt during 1901, much less one of several months duration.

Here are the facts. Once the second edition had been seen through the press, the Frazers rented their house from 1 October 1900 and left for Italy. It was to be their first real holiday since their marriage, and they planned to stay away for about nine months. On 16 March 1901, however, he is back in Cambridge, for he writes on that date to the Master of Trinity, H. M. Butler, explaining that their tenant unexpectedly decided to leave at the end of the Lent term (in March) rather than as planned at the end of the Easter term (June).[15]

When would he have read *Magic and Religion*? Putting it that way begs the question, for I do not believe that he ever read it. The book appeared in July 1901, and Frazer, knowing what it contained, did not rush to get a copy. In a letter to Clodd of 21 July Frazer says, "I have not yet seen Lang's book (except the outside of it in a bookseller's window) or any reviews of it." However, he did see at least the second of Lang's two articles in the *Fortnightly*, for on 5 June 1901 he had written to Clodd:

I [had not] seen Lang's reference to Robertson Smith in the article in which he made one of his now customary assaults on me. I only glanced at the article, enough to see the tone in which it was written. I warmly sympathise with R's protest and with all he says about my dear and venerated friend Robertson Smith, but of course it will be easy for Lang to reply that the words he used implied no disrespect.

Let me thank you again for all your kindness and hospitality. My stay at Aldeburgh was very pleasant. My recollections of these days are very agreeable.

Thus Frazer dismisses Lang's assault as predictable. He may have been stung by what he read of Lang's article, but it certainly did not (then) crush him. As *Magic and Religion* incorporates this essay, and its earlier counterpart from the *Fortnightly*, it is unlikely that the reprint would crush him either. It was Clodd's annual custom to invite a number of his friends of the rationalist persuasion to his house at Aldeburgh at Whitsuntide. Clodd had asked Frazer to come several times in the preceding years, but the latter had always to beg off due to pressure of work. In the spring of 1901, however, he went and he enjoyed himself.

As it happens, Clodd himself kept a fragmentary diary in the form of virtually illegible (and therefore completely candid) telegraphic entries in his pocket diary.[16] On 17 April Clodd writes: "Haddon says that Lang's article on Frazer is giving the poor little man bad nights." Six days later he notes: "Haddon told me that Frazer is not proposing to answer Lang re *Fortnightly* article." And then, when Frazer finally visited Aldeburgh, Clodd notes (on 25 May): "Had some talk with Frazer re Lang's criticism of *Golden Bough*. He says that Lang never forgave the ignoring of *Making of Religion* by Tylor and himself." Whether or not this was rationalization on Frazer's part, any period of anguish was now behind him.

This is confirmed by a letter to Clodd (on 22 June) in distinctly good spirits in the face of the criticism from the massed band in *Folk-Lore*. In his next to Clodd three weeks later (11 July) he is troubled, not by Lang but by his eyes. His doctor has suggested that he consult the noted ophthalmologist and eye surgeon Pagenstecher, in Wiesbaden; he and Lilly are off to Germany in ten days time. The treatment was successful, but the (unnamed) complaint would recur often over the next twenty-five years and necessitate several operations.

There is a gap in the letters at this point of two months, but much of that time must have been spent in travel and at the clinic. There he would not have been allowed to read or write, so the break is not *ipso facto* suspicious. If he was then in low spirits, the cause is much more likely to have been his eyesight than Lang. The letters resume in September, in a spirited exchange on questions relating to *The Golden Bough* with Sidney Hartland. Hartland, on 20 September, writes:

While away I read Lang's ferocious onslaught. Of course it is clever. But it is overdone. He makes some points: but after all what the *Chronicle* said in reviewing the book is true: "No nagging at minor details can upset the cardinal theory of the *G.B.*" The attack will do it no harm in the long run. Those who read both (and that will include every serious student) will appreciate pretty accurately the force and the weakness of Lang's arguments; and they will not forget that much of his hammering is wasted on subjects quite aside from the main question and only put forward tentatively and as mere conjectures.[17]

To which Frazer replies two days later:

I have not read Lang's book yet, and I doubt whether I shall. Since the publication of *The Making of Religion* I have ceased to attach much importance to his utterances on these subjects, and his articles in the *Fortnightly* (out of which, I gather, his book is mainly made up) showed that he is capable of misapprehensions which indicate, to my thinking, an actual obtuseness of mind. I was struck by the same obtuseness when I was in correspondence with him about the new facts of Central Australian totemism revealed by Spencer and Gillen's book, and before the publication of my articles on the subject. It seemed to me that even a blind man might have perceived that the *intichiuma* ceremonies gave the key to the whole business; but he could make nothing out of it all, and confessed plainly that he could not.[18]

Frazer in 1901 sounds exactly like the Frazer of 1900 and 1902; there is no discontinuity. Nor are there distraught letters marked "private" from Lilly Frazer to Macmillan, to whom she sometimes confided when she was concerned about J.G. The inescapable conclusion is that no evidence whatever exists to support Malinowski's assertion that for a time in 1901 Frazer had been pushed to the brink of despair by Lang's criticism.

The Frazers arrived in Rome in December 1900. Certainly by comparison with their existence in Cambridge, Rome was exciting indeed. Lilly Frazer was exhilarated at being out of Cambridge, free at last of *The Golden Bough*, and among people whom she saw as like herself – worldly and sophisticated. Among the people they met in Rome were Wickham Steed, then the *Times* correspondent and later its editor; the archaeologist Giacomo Boni, in whose company Frazer visited Nemi, which at last became a physical and not a visionary locale; and their Cambridge friend Jane Harrison. Harrison has left a brief but telling vignette of their encounter in the postscript to a letter of February 1901 to Lady Mary Murray:

Mrs Frazer (your double!) has been sitting on my bed for two hours, telling me "who not to know," i.e. who has not paid Mr Frazer "proper attention"! This is the price I pay for a few shy radiant moments under the Golden Bough – Good conservative tho' I am I am ready for any reform in the Game Laws for the Preserving of Eminent Husbands.[19]

Yet another voice corroborates this portrait of the masterful Lilly Frazer and her meek husband. Among the guests staying at the same *pensione* as the Frazers happened to be William James. Here are his amusing and perceptive comments, in a letter of 25 December 1900. One would give much to have heard their discussions.

Our neighbors in rooms and *commensaux* at meals are the J.G. Frazers – he of the "Golden Bough," "Pausanias," and other three- and six-volume works of anthropological erudition, Fellow of Trinity College, Cambridge, and a sucking babe of humility, unworldliness and molelike sightlessness to everything but *print*; she a deaf and lebenslustig cosmopolitan Frenchwoman, clever in all sorts of directions, a widow with a motherly heart, who has adopted him and nurses him. She is actually making him sit up, smile and take notice. He, after Tylor, is the greatest authority now in England on the religious ideas and superstitions of primitive peoples, and he knows nothing of psychical research and thinks that trances, etc., of savage soothsayers, oracles and the like are all *feigned*! Verily science is amusing! But he is conscience incarnate, and I have been stirring him up so that I imagine he will now proceed to put in big loads of work in the morbid psychology direction.[20]

When Frazer returned to England he asked Macmillan to send a copy of *The Golden Bough* to James, but unfortunately he did *not* put in any work in the morbid psychology direction. Frazer's psychology in general, and his analysis of magic and religion in particular, were explicitly associationist. The savage tries this or that, a favorable or unfavorable outcome results, a positive or negative connection is thereby established and subsequently reinforced, and he continues his behavior accordingly. One suspects that, greatly impressed as Frazer must have been when they talked, he later found the irrationalist vistas, or abysses, that James opened up too potentially upsetting – which is easily converted into too time-consuming and distracting – to be investigated further.

Frazer regained his magnanimity as well as his equanimity, for when Lang died in 1912, he wrote to Marett (14 August 1912), saying that if a memorial volume was to be published, he would like to contribute "a short paper to it to mark my respect for his memory." He continued:

The obituary notice [in the *Athenaeum*] was not very generous or sympathetic. It hardly, I think, noticed his poetry, which always seems to me to possess the true poetical ring and a very musical cadence. I do not think it has been appreciated at its true value, and I am almost inclined to think that by it he will be chiefly remembered. I regret that he did not write more of it instead of the dreary controversial stuff about the Arunta &c. His light humorous prose was also exquisite in its way. He was essentially a man of letters rather than a man of science, though no doubt by his writings he did an immense deal to popularise and extend the study of primitive man. But it would have been better for his reputation and for the world if he had given us more of pure literature and less what I would call adulterated science. At least that is how I regard his real vocation. Peace to his memory![21]

Eleven years later there is still an echo here of hurt feelings, but his words were not merely a dismissal with faint praise, for many of Lang's contemporaries would have agreed in valuing his literary work more highly than his anthropological scholarship. If one substitutes classical scholarship for poetry, there are many today who would accept this as a fitting evaluation of Frazer himself.

As one might expect, many of the letters of 1900–2 are responses to congratulations and comments from various correspondents about *The Golden Bough*. A brief and unusual episode at this time, however, marked yet another road not taken. On 6 July 1900 Frazer writes to Macmillan to thank him for having sent him the German scholar August Mau's descriptive volume on Pompeii.[22] With the volume had come the suggestion that Frazer consider writing a companion volume on Athens. On the face of it this was reasonable: Frazer's knowledge of Athens was still fresh, and interest was great among the public. But Frazer, in declining, makes a statement about how he sees his future.

My main interest is in anthropology, especially the early history of religion and institutions; and my intention is, if health and leisure are continued to me, to devote myself to this line of work for at least a good many years to come. I have made large collections for a book or rather series of books on the subject, and I shall hope, granted the same conditions, to write them and to offer them to you as they are ready. To work at archaeology (which is not really my subject at all) would be to turn aside from this line which I have marked out for myself and which I am determined (if the circumstances of life allow me) to stick to till I have carried out the series of researches which I have planned. The work seems far more important than any mere archaeological investigation; since if properly accomplished it ought to influence the course of thought on some of the most important subjects, which a mere description of ruins, however beautiful and interesting, could never do. I regret the years I spent on Pausanias. I think they might have been better employed. But I am resolved not to commit the same sort of mistake again, if I can help it.

This is straightforward and thoughtful, the voice of a man who knows what he wants to do and will not deviate from it. He wishes to complete the work not so much for its own sake as to satisfy his larger ambition, which has been motivating him all along: "to influence the course of thought on some of the most important subjects." Given all this, his next letter (1 August) to Macmillan strikes an odd note. It concludes:

Do you think there would be room for a new translation of Augustine's *Confessions*? I have been turning over the leaves and have been struck by the extraordinary beauty of the thought and language. It would be a real pleasure to try and put the book into worthy English, and I might amuse some of my leisure hours with it next winter when we are abroad.

Although this does not fit in with his elaborate plans for the future enunciated only three weeks earlier, it is not necessarily an about-face either. The translation was more a *jeu d'esprit* than anything else. Throughout his life he engaged, for pleasure and relaxation, in literary *divertissements* from time to time. In July he was referring only to his scholarly work. Macmillan (7 August) needed time to think about the offer: "the only question is whether the demand would be sufficient to make it worth your while, and ours."[23] Nothing further is heard of it. Had he translated the *Confessions*, it would have been the only piece of classical work not undertaken essentially as an occasion for commentary.

Beyond that, he was abroad for about six weeks in the spring of 1902, most of that time at Pagenstecher's clinic for a checkup (letter to Clodd, 14 April 1902). When he and his wife returned to Cambridge, the task that awaited them was the old misery of moving into a new house. But all that is behind him when, on 29 July 1902, he writes to Macmillan after a long interval to say "I had hoped to begin printing the new edition of *The Golden Bough* before now, but as it is I hardly expect to go to press before September. When I once begin, I shall try to keep the printer busy."

What was this third edition that Frazer was sure he would finish soon? The print order for the second edition had been 1500 copies, 20 percent larger than that for the first edition. This was reasonable in commercial terms: Frazer was better known and the potentially explosive discussion of Christianity ensured that it would be widely reviewed. The notoriety generated by those reviews had exhausted the first printing quickly, perhaps as quickly as two years, thus alerting Frazer as early as 1902 to the possibility of returning to the pleasantly endless task of revising and expanding still further. Frazer is undoubtedly talking about a new (that is, a rewritten) edition of *The Golden Bough*, not a new printing.

Whatever it was, it came to nothing at that time, for it was immediately and oddly sidetracked. On 7 October he writes to Macmillan that he is pleased that the latter approves of

my scheme of a book on the American Indians, consisting of translations of early accounts by French and Spanish writers which are now accessible to very few students. The title would be "Early accounts of the American Indians by French and Spanish writers (Thevet, Arriaga, Simon, etc.), edited and translated with notes by JGF" – or something of that sort. It will interest me very much to put the book together, and the labour of the translation and annotation will not be very great. I feel sure that I can make it valuable and acceptable to anthropologists, whatever the public may think of it.

Aside from the signed contract (dated 17 December 1902) in the Macmillan corporate archives, the book is a phantom; it is never mentioned again. Frazer had long ago read these early accounts of the Indians, but only in the same way that he read everything. Because of the legacy of Mannhardt, the two *Golden Boughs* had been heavily Europocentric, with the religions of the ancient Near East and now the magic of the aborigines supplying a secondary focus. Until this moment he had never expressed any special interest in early North American ethnography. Indeed, given the feverish interest that anything relating to Australia was receiving at that time, it is surprising that Frazer could detach himself sufficiently to attend to old notices about American Indians.

Further, it is surprising that Macmillan agreed, for it would only delay the revision of the increasingly popular *Golden Bough*, and it sounds like something that would appeal only to the tiny audience of professional anthropologists. The only possibility is that Frazer intended to comb these narratives for accounts of totemism, thus opening a second front in America to complement the main campaign in Australia. I take it as self-evident that he was attracted to the project only because of the possibilities of the annotation, which would permit him to show in detail how the North American data resembled and differed from those from elsewhere. Indeed, it is exactly the likelihood that the annotation would swamp the translation, as occurred in the Pausanias, that makes one wonder why Macmillan went along. However, either Frazer's commitment to North America was never strong or else it quickly waned in the face of the evergreen attraction of returning to *The Golden Bough*. No doubt by mutual agreement, he and Macmillan decided to forget about it.

On 13 April 1903 Frazer wrote another of those letters to Macmillan that was guaranteed to raise a smile:

Certainly my book [the third edition] will go to press this summer. You may be quite easy about that.

As to the size I have never contemplated more than four volumes, and I am not sure that four will be necessary. By adopting a thinner paper it would be possible, I think, to add about 600 pages without exceeding three volumes, and such an addition ought to suffice or nearly so. . . .

I hope that this time you will print a really large edition, so as to leave me as free for other work for a good many years to come.

In making the additions I will try to study brevity, as far as that is consistent with scientific exactness and literary form. I believe I shall considerably increase the real value of the book, and I am sanguine enough to expect that the sale will not be diminished thereby. Remember how in the case of the second edition the great increase of the book was followed by a great increase of the sale. With me, oddly enough, it is always the little books that fail and the big ones that succeed.

The next, predictable letter (18 July) began: "I am very sorry that the preparation of the new edition has dragged out so much longer than I had expected. There has been a great deal to read, but my reading is almost complete, and the mere writing will take comparatively little time." Then, on 14 October: "I am hard at work at the new edition of my book and hope to send copy to the printers before long. Some of my critics have complained of the difficulty of following the thread of argument through the mass of facts. This difficulty would be lightened by a marginal summary." Macmillan agreed, and such summaries remained a feature of all his subsequent big books.

Frazer spent half his life on *The Golden Bough*. It served as a lodestar, always bringing him back to the path that seemingly was ordained for him. He never did finish it and he never could finish it. Whenever he completed anything else, he returned, as if by instinct, to yet another revision of The Book. It seems to have represented for him a great – even an infinite – quest.

Like a Grail knight, he may have known that he could never reach the goal but that its inachievability did not therefore release him from the task. As he went further with it, more and more branching paths opened out from the high road of the argument, and he followed each to its end before returning once again to the quest. Today, his classical scholarship continues to be esteemed; otherwise, everything that is not *The Golden Bough* constitutes distinctly the lesser half of his achievement and could be dispensed with painlessly. Not so the *Bough*: as it perennially engaged him, so it contains that part of his anthropological work that retains some power of engaging us.

11 · THE HEBREW WORLD

F RAZER HAD PROBABLY IMAGINED that as soon as the second edition was behind him and he returned from his holiday, he would settle back to work. Instead, 1901 and even 1902 were unsettled, filled with the tumult occasioned by Lang, by the worries about his eyesight, and by other events as well. Those two years were worse than the two preceding, for at least the strain of 1899–1900 had produced the new *Golden Bough*, whereas all the ensuing noise and polemic produced only exhaustion of spirit and a consciousness that time was wasting.

This edginess is the context for a striking letter of 10 July 1902 to Haddon that illustrates Frazer's prickliness about the sensitive matter of priority in intellectual property. If one accepts that being first with an idea is important and confers property rights, then anyone unwilling to acknowledge indebtedness is committing the equivalent of theft. Especially was this true to the scrupulous Frazer, whose work, standing as it does atop a mountain of footnotes, would be impossible without his predecessors. The letter was occasioned by Haddon's sending him an advance copy of the address on totemism he would be giving the next month as head of Section H (Anthropology) at the meeting of the British Association for the Advancement of Science.[1] Frazer is pleased that Haddon accepts his position on so many points: that totemism is essentially magical, intended to increase the totem animal or plant; that religion is entirely absent from such ceremonies, and the like.

But while I am pleased that you should have adopted so much of a view of totemism which, when it was first put forward three years ago, excited something like a storm of adverse criticism, I confess I am surprised that you should be entirely silent as to your agreement with me in some essential points, while you are careful on the the other hand, as it seems to me, to mention a number of other less important points (turning chiefly on words and definitions) on which you or others differ from me. To speak quite plainly, I consider that your view of totemism has been deeply influenced by mine, and that it would be proper that you should make some acknowledgement of your agreement with me, instead of absolutely ignoring that agreement and emphasising our differences. It is of course for you to decide whether you will make that acknowledgement or not. If you do not, I shall retain a very decided opinion of your treatment of me, and I shall not feel bound to keep it to myself.[2]

Haddon must have been stunned to receive such a rebuke, especially one concluding with the threat implied in the last sentence. But the incident was

180

smoothed over. Haddon evidently wrote to explain that he had not intended any slight, and Frazer was mollified. On 13 August he responds:

I do not for a moment think you capable of willfully doing injustice to me or to any one. The mere fact of your sending me your Address to criticise would be enough to show me (even if I did not know you) that you intended no such thing. But one may be unjust without intending it. I am afraid that happens to us all only too often in judging of each other. In this particular case I certainly think that you would do less than justice to Spencer and myself if you did not explicitly mention (among other views which you consider worthy of notice) the view which Spencer and I reached independently and with which your own agrees in some very important particulars. Subsequent researches (including your own) have confirmed our view; and I believe that, despite the uproar raised when it was first put forward, the adhesion of anthropologists in general to it is a mere matter of time. The facts (of which plenty will soon be coming from Australia and probably elsewhere) will speak for themselves. Of course a number of subordinate questions in connection with totemism will still await solution, for instance, the origin or mode of formation of the totem groups. But the meaning of totemism (in my opinion) we know already: it is a co-operative system of magic designed to provide the community with the necessaries of life, especially of food.

He concludes with a burst of sniping at Tylor:

By the way, what is Tylor's theory of totemism? He seems to have committed himself to at least three distinct and apparently inconsistent theories; (1) that the totems contain the souls of dead ancestors; (2) that the totem is merely the crest of an exogamous clan; and (3) that the Arunta totemism is the only clearly intelligible system, although it neither has exogamy of the totem clans nor (pace Tylor) the transmigration of souls. . . . The solemn warning which Tylor here gives to anthropologists, not to frame theories prematurely as to the origin of totems, is amusing, when one remembers that a few months before he had been propounding a theory of totemism in the same room, without waiting to read through Spencer & Gillen's book, of which he was actually receiving proofs at the time he propounded the theory, without the least regard for their facts. If this is not being premature or "previous," I can hardly imagine what would be so.[3]

This waspish passage is both revealing and amusing. In 1898, at the time of his falling-out with Tylor, with whom he seems never to have been fully reconciled, Tylor had accused him of exactly the same offense with which he now charged Haddon. Tylor had said that in his judgment Frazer had not given adequate credit to the Dutch scholar Wilken for the theory of totemism that had been advanced in *The Golden Bough*.[4] Needless to say, Frazer was incensed, for he was always careful to acknowledge the work of others. In an exchange of letters he and Tylor had built up a considerable head of steam on this question when Tylor's suggestion that deletions be made in Spencer and Gillen's book gave them something else to quarrel about. The amusement arises from the fact that by 1902 Frazer had already espoused two different theories of the origin and meaning of totemism – the respository of the external soul (1887) and the magical system for ensuring and controlling the food supply (1900) – and he would advance yet another in 1905.

The friendship with Haddon weathered this brief storm and continued lifelong. But Frazer suffered a great and irremediable loss when Solomon Schechter (1849–1915), probably his best friend at the turn of the century, left Cambridge permanently for New York in 1902.[5] The century that ended in 1914 was a golden age of scholarship in Europe, and the Jewish world has had an unbroken tradition of men, learned in the Law, that stretches back two thousand years. But in the latter half of the nineteenth century a new kind of Jewish scholar arose, brought into being by the emancipation of the Jews in post-Napoleonic Europe, one who had in his youth been immersed in the Bible and Talmud and had then been exposed to modern secular learning. The ensuing cross-fertilization and conflict of traditions created a new kind of modern Jewish self-consciousness. One thinks of polymath historians like Heinrich Graetz; the work of Gershom Scholem and Salo Baron indicates that the tradition continues in the twentieth century. In that company must be enrolled Schechter, who had come west from Romania via Vienna and Berlin to Britain, where he was tutor in rabbinics to Claude Montefiore and later Reader in Talmud at Jews' College in London in the 1880s. In 1890 he left London to become Lecturer in Talmud at Cambridge.

The achievement for which he gained scholarly immortality is that of retrieving from the "manuscript graveyard," or *geniza*, of the main synagogue in Cairo the masses of fragments that comprised (until the discovery of the Dead Sea Scrolls) most of the earliest extant biblical and extrabiblical texts as well as nearly all that was then known of the literature of the Essenes. His intellectual brilliance, combined with catholic interests and attractive personality, guaranteed him a remarkably wide circle of Cambridge friends, among whom were Charles Taylor, F.C. Burkitt, J. Rendel Harris, Mandell Creighton, A.C. Haddon, and Robertson Smith. Of these, according to his biographer, the most intimate of all was Frazer.[6]

There is no information about how or where they met, but since he was attached to Christ's College, it must have been Robertson Smith who brought them together. After Smith's death in 1894 Schechter seems to have become his closest friend. Frazer and Schechter were regular afternoon walking companions. According to Downie, Lilly Frazer, jealous of the time J. G. spent with Schechter, decided to break them up. She announced "that she too needed exercise, and though she hated cycling she bought two cycles, so that instead of walking with his friend, Frazer had to go cycling with his wife."[7] This, however, seems to be more of Downie's anti-Lilly bias, for the few surviving letters to Schechter make it clear that both Frazers and both Schechters were good friends. The letter of 22 December 1900 has already been quoted regarding the antireligious tone of the second edition. But those sentences about offending both Jews and Christians are in fact embedded in a long, news-filled, even gossipy letter that includes "My wife will soon write to Mrs Schechter and give her the Cambridge news much better than I can."[8]

Although his life in Cambridge was pleasant, Schechter was dissatisfied. He was a natural teacher but had virtually no students, so he felt frustrated at his inability either to pass on his knowledge or to make Cambridge a center for Jewish studies. And because Cambridge then contained only the small, transient group of Jewish students and virtually no indigenous families, he felt keenly his inability to live a complete Jewish life, which can take place only within a community. So after a number of invitations he finally accepted the call to become chancellor of the Jewish Theological Seminary, the first rabbinical seminary of the then-fledgling Conservative moment within Judaism, in New York.

Frazer was distinctly philo-Semitic, which was an uncommon sentiment in both British society at large and particularly within the universities.[9] Not only were "some of his best friends Jewish," and not only was Heine his favorite modern poet, but he does seem to have admired the Jews as a people. In 1913 he had a chance to give public testimony, for that year saw the resurrection by the Tsarist authorities of the ancient blood libel against the Jews. A Jew named Mendel Beilis was arrested in Kiev and accused of killing a Christian child in order to use its blood in making Passover *matzot*. To counter the chorus of liberal opinion throughout Europe that denounced the charge as lies and the trial as a frame-up, at the end of the trial a reactionary newspaper published a list of scholarly works that allegedly supported the charge of Jewish ritual murder in the past. Prominent on that list was a passage taken out of context, from *The Scapegoat* (Part VI of the third edition of *The Golden Bough*), published only that year. As soon as he learned of this, Frazer immediately wrote a letter to *The Times* (11 November 1913) denying that his works supported the libel and denouncing the "vile calumnies" of the Tsarist authorities. Beilis was acquitted on the day his letter was published, so his gesture had no effect. Nevertheless, he was undoubtedly and, indeed, passionately on the right side.[10]

This sentiment also emerges in a letter to A. E. Housman (24 October 1922) in response to the latter's having sent him his *Last Poems*. His praise takes the form of comparing Housman's work to that of Heine,

and I cannot say fairer than that, as I regard Heine as one of the most consummate geniuses who ever used human language to express human thought and emotion. His mastery of language seems to me to approach the magical and supernatural. So I hope that you will not take it ill that I compare you to – I was about to say a German poet; but I never forget that Heine was not a German, but a member of a far finer race, who handled the German language and drew music from the instrument in a way that no native of the coarser German race has ever, to my knowledge, approached.[11]

His friendship with Schechter and his interest in things Hebraic manifested itself directly in his work. In 1904 or 1905 the Revd Robert H. Kennett (1864–1932), Regius Professor of Hebrew in Cambridge, was prevailed upon to offer a small, private beginners' class in his subject. Its membership was select and perhaps even intimidating: Jane Ellen Harrison, F. M. Cornford, A. B. Cook, and J. G. Frazer. Their aim was to acquire enough knowledge to read the Old Testament in the original. The most diligent and assiduous of the four, and certainly the one who did the most with what he learned, was Frazer. The Wren Library holds his Hebrew Bible, from which one may chart his predictably steady progress.[12] At the end of the Book of Genesis Frazer has written "Finished reading Genesis in Hebrew, Wednesday, 18th April, 1906," and so on at the end of each book of his Hebrew–English edition. In fact he went through the entire Hebrew Bible several times, ranging from five times for Genesis (he began again as soon as he had finished) to four times for the Earlier Prophets to once only for the Minor Prophets. Reading the Old Testament became his main scholarly recreation during the first decade of the century. He traversed most of the text in 1906–7, 1909, 1910, and 1915, and the notices of completion in the later passages include "for the most part without a dictionary."

Through his long life Frazer studied many languages. Of these, Hebrew (undertaken at the age of fifty) was possibly the most difficult because of the considerable linguistic distance between it and the Indo-European languages. But Frazer, like his three classmates, was a trained philologist, and more important was possessed of immense powers of concentration and perseverance. It is not surprising that he made headway quickly. Because his Bible offered only the Authorized Version as the English translation, he soon was covering its margins with alternative readings from the Revised Version, and he quickly began proposing his own textual emendations and contextual footnotes.

So confident did he become that on 19 September 1906 he wrote to Macmillan:

For some time I have been reading Hebrew at odd times and am much fascinated by the Old Testament in the original. The study has suggested various books, which I should like to discuss with you sometime, e.g. a Hebrew Reader, to consist of the finest parts of the Old Testament in a revised and corrected text with a corresponding translation and perhaps some notes. I think it would be possible to produce a book which might come to be used generally by all learners of Hebrew. So far as I know there is no such work. But perhaps to print Hebrew texts is not in your way, and I could hardly take up that or any other heavy task till I have finished the G.B.

Nothing came of this. The letter dates from the same time, however, as the true first fruits of his new interest, the essay he contributed to the Tylor Festschrift of 1907. By the turn of the century it was apparent that Tylor was a spent force, intellectually speaking. In 1890–1 he had given two sets of Gifford Lectures on natural religion, and thereafter began to work on a book to be entitled, echoing Hume a century and a half earlier, *The Natural History of Religion*. This project, which was to sum up his thought, occupied him through the nineties. Although he got far enough to have the early chapters set in type, he never completed it.[13] By the turn of the century he was suffering from some form of senile dementia, for his memory had deteriorated and he was unable to concentrate. When it became clear that the long-awaited book would never appear, his friends decided to offer him a volume of essays as a homage on the occasion of his seventy-fifth birthday in 1907. Although he and Frazer had never been fully reconciled after their altercations of 1898, Frazer was nonetheless asked to contribute. He produced "Folk-Lore in the Old Testament."[14]

This long (73-page) essay consists of extended notes on eight unconnected biblical topics: "The Mark of Cain," "Sacred Oaks and Terebinths," "The Covenant on the Cairn," "Jacob at the Ford of the Jabbok," "The Bundle of Life," "Not to Seethe a Kid in Its Mother's Milk," "The Keepers of the Threshold," and "The Sin of a Census." Insofar as they have a common intellectual theme, they stand as extended illustrations of Frazer's contention that the Old Testament incorporates a body of folklore, one closely related to, or at least resembling, that of the various "lower races" on whom he had written so extensively. As Tylor was no biblical scholar, the tenuous connection of this essay to his work consists mainly in the noting of survivals; Festschriften being inherently miscellaneous and baggy affairs, however, that is no serious defect.

In practice each brief essay offered Frazer an opportunity for wide-ranging comparative anthropological commentary. As might be imagined, the disconnectedness of the subjects makes for a slack whole. Had this been a series of notes on the folklore to be found in, say, Genesis, that alone would have imposed a structure of sorts. As it is, there is no reason why the essay contains eight sections rather than seven or nine or any other number. Its size seems to have been more a result of the amount of time Frazer was willing to devote, and the point he had reached in his reading of the Old Testament, than anything else. Indeed, after the Festschrift appeared, Frazer suggested (31 October 1907) to Macmillan that he turn the essay into a book.

I am glad you like the idea of publishing "Folk-Lore in the Old Testament" as a book. I think it might be quite popular. Consisting as it does of detached notes, it could be indefinitely extended at any time. I mean that I could add a fresh note from time to time at the cost of a few days' work so as to make a volume.

In the best Frazerian manner, this essay became both the nucleus and trial run for the three large volumes, with the same title, that appeared eleven years later, in 1918.

The commentary format, which had served him brilliantly with Pausanias, works much less well here with the Bible. The reason is to be found in the nature of the text and Frazer's relation to it. Pausanias' guidebook is relatively long as classical texts go, and had been discussed intermittently since the Renaissance, with a new burst of interest as a result of recent archaeology. Having worked on Pausanias for years and then seen the excavations for himself, and having understood the text and the questions at issue deeply, he could speak with genuine authority. By comparison with Pausanias the Old Testament is not merely long but epic, and commentary on it is nothing less than oceanic. Further, not only was Frazer not a Hebrew scholar in 1906 when he wrote the piece, but, his confidence notwithstanding, he was in fact only a beginner. In Hebrew in particular and biblical studies in general he had not yet reached the stage of preparation that he had attained in classics in 1874, when he came up as a freshman to Trinity. By 1907 he had read the Bible in Hebrew exactly once, and of the critical literature as yet he knew nothing. Far from being steeped in the text or the history of its scholarship, he was only a first-time scholarly tourist in the vast landscape of biblical studies. His proposal to prepare an annotated textbook of Hebrew selections was simply presumptuous. It is good that the pressure to revise *The Golden Bough* continued, or he might actually have tried to bring off this Hebrew project and ended in disaster.

Frazer understood the essay of 1907 (and the expanded treatment that followed a decade later) as yet another step in the same process of demythologization that he had begun in *The Golden Bough*. In the direct, *in medias res* manner that marks most of his work, "Folk-Lore in the Old Testament" is supported by only the flimsiest intellectual structure (to be precise, the eight essays are introduced by a page and a half of preamble). He begins with the sketchiest syllogism: because the Hebrews participated in the same process of cultural evolution as every other nation, it cannot be surprising that their National Book contains material as primitive as any to be found elsewhere. This material is therefore best understood in the light of comparative parallels. Having said that, he launches himself into the biblical motifs and the allegedly relevant ethnographic parallels. So, for example, to understand the sacred oak of Abraham at Mamre, we receive a long survey of the differing ways that various species of trees have been deemed sacred or holy throughout the primitive world. This advances our understanding of the oak at Mamre not one whit because in fact Frazer says nothing about it, only about tree worship by other peoples in other places and times.

Although the existence of traditional lore in the Scriptures had not been explicitly recognized as such until the idea of folklore itself had been enunciated in Britain in the mid-nineteenth century, since that time much work had been done by liberal scholars, of whom the best known was Robertson Smith. Frazer had touched on the subject in his essay on taboo twenty years earlier, but then he had been dependent upon Smith for the Semitic examples. His contribution in 1907, and probably the source of his confidence in venturing into such an immense and novel intellectual world, was his willingness to link ancient Israel so completely to the rest of early heathendom and contemporary savagery, the literary records of which he knew better perhaps than any man living. Even Smith in *The Religion of the Semites*, although more for tactical than theoretical reasons, had not been so insistent in connecting the lore and mentality of the ancient Semites and that of "the nations." But Frazer, having persuaded himself of the ubiquity and universality of totem sacrifices while writing the *Lectures on the History of the Kingship* (1905), was not now about to make an exception for the Israelites.

In the first years of the new century, before he had become involved in Hebrew and Semitic folklore, Frazer got down to writing the new *Golden Bough*. Batches of copy began to flow to the printers. To no one's surprise but his own, the composition of the book followed the same pattern as that of Pausanias and the second *Golden Bough*: a promise of imminent delivery, followed by a silence of several months, followed by an apology for the delay and another promise, and the cycle starts again. A letter to Macmillan of 12 August 1904 begins:

I much regret the delay in *The Golden Bough*, but I have been adding a long new piece, which has cost me some months of work. It is the chief change and addition which I have to make to the book. After that the rest of the book will go by comparison easily and rapidly. Certainly I do not anticipate any delay such as there has been the last six months.

On 10 November 1904 he is making steady progress and is nearing the end of the first volume. "I hope to finish the book by next autumn, if not by the end of the summer, and to publish it by the end of 1905." Five days later he writes again:

In writing about the progress of my book I referred to the three volumes of the second edition, but I did not mean to imply that the third edition might not be in four. It will certainly be a good deal larger than the last, but how much larger I cannot say yet. By the use of thinner paper, it may perhaps be possible to keep it within three volumes. But I doubt it. I know your wishes in the matter. By far the most serious addition I had to make to the book is finished, but there are still many minor additions to make. My effort is simply to make it as good as I can, and I will do my best to publish it next year.

In 1895, while immersed in Pausanias, he had broken away to prepare his anthology of Bible passages. The letter of 10 November is somewhat analogous. Changing the subject from *The Golden Bough*, he mentions how highly he thinks of Macmillan's Library of English Classics series. Not only does he admire the series, but he wishes to propose six new titles for it. Predictably, all are from the eighteenth century: Dryden's poems, selections from Swift, the essays of Addison, selections from the *Spectator*, Cowper's poems, and Crabbe's poems. "If I could do anything to help actively the Library, it would give me real pleasure to do so, for example by making selections from Addison (or the *Spectator*), Cowper, or Crabbe, all of whom are great favourites of mine." This suggestion was not lightly made, for he later managed to make time to edit the *Letters of William Cowper* in 1912 and the *Essays of Joseph Addison* in 1915.

187

This time, however, his motive was nothing more pressing than a desire for belletristic recreation, a luxury he could not permit himself. His chronic financial problems, assuaged in 1899 by the grant secured by Gosse, had recurred. His royalty income had fallen off to practically nothing, for Pausanias had yet to produce a penny, the second edition of *The Golden Bough* had been virtually exhausted, and the third edition was taking much longer to write than he had imagined.

In addition, a troublesome distraction arose that gave him more than a month of mental turmoil, during which time he made no progress on *The Golden Bough*. He had become friendly with James Hope Moulton (1863–1917) in the mid-eighties, when they met as members of the Cambridge Philological Society.[15] Moulton was a progressive Methodist theologian, which, until he met Moulton, Frazer would doubtless have thought a contradiction in terms. Moulton, whose scholarly specialty was ancient Iranian religion, was a great admirer of *The Golden Bough*. A lengthy correspondence (which has not survived) led to close friendship that continued for many years. The distraction in question took the form of an invitation in 1904 from Moulton, then a Professor of Theology at Didsbury College, Manchester, a Methodist seminary, to lecture to the students there on comparative religion.

Frazer disliked lecturing and engaged in it only when he needed money. But he was now hard pressed, and in addition Moulton was a friend whom he wished to oblige. The problem as Frazer saw it, however, was neither one of overcoming his distaste for lecturing, nor of the bother involved in traveling to Manchester throughout term-time. Instead, he construed it in conscientious terms. Could he suppress his animosity to Christianity while lecturing? And even if he found himself able to do so, was it right in any case? Racked with anxiety, he turned to his close friends for counsel. Letters to and from two of them – Henry Jackson and J. S. Black – survive.[16]

On 18 April 1904 he set out the problem in a letter to Jackson:

Forgive me for troubling you again about the Manchester affair. . . . I had an interview with the Principal after I spoke to you, and I have got further information from J. H. Moulton. . . .

The appointments are to be for three years. The number of lectures wanted in Comparative Religion would be small (sixteen and thirty were mentioned by the Principal as possible limits) and the salary would vary from £150 to £300 according to the number of lectures. They might all be given in one term of ten weeks. There is no obligation of residence. Thus I should not have to leave Cambridge.

Thus far the proposal attracts me. (Please remember that the post has not been offered to me yet. The Principal only asked whether I should be disposed to take it, if it were offered. He is to write me fully at the beginning of term.) But I feel a serious difficulty about accepting, and it is on this point I particularly wish your advice. The lectureship forms part of a Theological faculty founded (as Moulton says) by Christians for the training of Christian ministers. I am not a Christian, on the contrary I reject the

Christian religion utterly as false. Yet if I accepted the post I should be expected (as the Principal insisted repeatedly) to say nothing that would offend the religious feeling of the students. That is, I should be implicitly bound to conceal my own firm belief of the falseness of Christianity, and, I suppose, not to put before the students facts which might tend to undermine their faith. Do you think that would be honest? Would you accept yourself if you were in my place? Before I saw the matter in this light, I wrote to the Principal that if appointed I would be scrupulously careful not to say anything that would hurt the feelings of any reasonable man. I do not remember the exact words, but that was the substance. Certainly I would not attack Christianity openly, even if I had given no pledge or implied promise to abstain from doing so. Such attacks are repugnant to my feeling and I regard them as bad policy besides. But the facts of comparative religion appear to me subversive of Christian theology; and in putting them before my students without any express reference to Christianity, I should still feel as if I were undermining their faith, contrary to my implied promise not to do so. This is how the matter strikes me at present. But perhaps I am wrong. I shall be very much obliged if you will turn it over in your mind and advise me when we meet.[17]

His belief that Christianity is false comes as no surprise. What is striking is that he feels unable to trust himself in the classroom not to stray from the subject and enter into controversy. He seems to be suppressing an overpowering anger in the face of the intolerable imposition represented by Christianity. Certainly in his hands comparative religion was a weapon to be employed in the war against religion or it was nothing. This letter implies that the military metaphor may go deeper than was at first imagined. To invoke Keats's phrase, Frazer totally lacked "negative capability" – the ability to see things as they are without being overpowered by the need to rush to judgment. On the other hand, however, partisan though he was, he was unable to maintain any one position for very long, and so found himself buffeted throughout his life by the play of opposing impulses.

Jackson, in his reply (19 April) had no doubt whatever that Frazer *should* take the position and gave his sensible reasons:

(1) It is for *them* to say whether they care to appoint a lecturer on Comparative Religion who is not a Christian, like themselves. (2) That you are not a Christian, is hardly a secret; and you have spoken openly to the Principal and to Moulton. (3) If in lecturing on Comparative Religion, any one were to begin discussing the validity of religious belief, he would, I think, be leaving his subject for another, which I should call theology. (4) In lecturing on Comparative Religion, you, I should imagine, would, in consequence of the direction of your previous studies, be concerned with primitive and savage religions, rather than with those which find favour with Europeans at the present day, and in consequence, you would be in no danger of diverging into theology. (5) Hitherto, you have with difficulty *indicated* your position in regard to Christianity; but you have not thought it necessary, in recording the little which can be known about primitive and savage religion, either to investigate the principles of religion now prevalent, or to inquire into their validity; and if you have not thought it necessary in books, a priori it would be unnecessary in lectures.

I see no reason why they should not appoint a non-Christian professor to teach the facts about religions, especially savage and primitive religions, trusting him not to desert his proper province; and I see no reason why the non-Christian should not accept the appointment, knowing that they trust him not so to diverge. It is true that there are some people who cannot control themselves; people who, if they were lecturing on logic or on Shakespeare, would import theological controversy by means of illustrations: but you are not thus intellectually incontinent.

[. . .] you may say that, in your opinion, the facts observed about primitive and savage religions point irresistibly to the falsity of Christianity. To this objection I should answer that there are others who do not think so. I myself, who regard myself as a Christian, hate nothing so much as the notion that Christianity has a monopoly of religion, and am prepared to recognize as religions the mythical speculations by which men at different stages of development complete what is wanting in their scheme of life, and to attach a value to such speculations however mythical their presentation.[18]

After two more weeks of wavering, on 2 May Frazer writes to Jackson to say that he has decided to decline Manchester. His reasons have now changed, and most of what he says sounds like rationalization; reading between the lines, we can overhear anguished discussions between him and Lilly.

First, with the views I have as to religion, I could not possibly reconcile myself to accepting a teaching post in what is practically a seminary for the training of Christian clergy. The feeling may be unreasonable, but I could not rid myself of it.

Second, I could not bring myself to give up, even for a time, research and literary work for teaching. I am perfectly happy in research and believe that it suits me far better than anything else I could put my hand to. Of teaching I have practically no experience and, so far as I know myself, no aptitude or inclination for it. Why should I desert work that I love and that I believe I can do fairly for work that I have never done, that I believe I should dislike, and that disliking I should probably do badly? I know you think I should gain in clearness of view and perhaps in other ways by the change. It is possible there might be some gain of this sort, but the gain, I fear, would be more than counterbalanced by my fretting at uncongenial work and chafing at the delay of my literary work. At present I am in the very thick of preparing a new edition of my book (*The Golden Bough*), adding some new chapters, which have cost me a good deal of thought and labour, and which are now going fairly well. It would be heartbreaking to me to lay all this aside and write elementary lectures on animism, totemism, and other anthropological commonplaces. I could only do it by putting an almost physical constraint on myself which could not be good for the lectures, and I am sure would have been very bad for me. I ought to have seen this clearly from the beginning and not to have troubled you and other friends with my indecision. But my wife's wishes weighed heavily with me, and the salary was certainly an attraction. I have put my reasons for declining before my wife very fully, and she entirely acquiesces in my decision.[19]

Two observations: (1) As a platonist and a teacher, Jackson might be expected to endorse the value of dialectic. Frazer's vague reference to Jackson's reasons – that Frazer might gain in "clearness of view and perhaps in other ways by the change" – may imply that it was not good for anyone to spend all his time in the study and that it might be desirable to try his ideas on a live audience. (2) Lilly Frazer had been growing increasingly restive in Cambridge, and may well have seized upon Manchester as a means of effecting a permanent move. She had several reasons to be unhappy. She thought the university treated her husband shamefully. But her unhappiness did not arise solely from a disinterested wish that intelligence – even if it was J. G.'s – be honored for its own sake. In hierarchical Cambridge, she, as the wife of a mere college Fellow, was socially invisible. In addition, she had a predisposition to respiratory infections and therefore disliked the climate. One suspects, however, that she might have learned to bear Cambridge and its weather if he had had a chair.

But if he turned down Manchester, he also turned down the income that would make the difference between a life of financial well-being and one that featured a large permanent overdraft at the bank. In such circumstances he did the only thing he knew to do – turn once again to Edmund Gosse and the Royal Literary Fund. On 9 September he writes to Gosse: Is there any chance for a second grant from the Fund? He explains that his embarrassment is only temporary, the result of the fact that the second edition of *The Golden Bough* is out of print, and the third is taking longer to write than planned. If the Fund cannot help, then he must invade his small available capital (£1500 in government bonds), which he is loath to do, as it represents the whole of his wife's security were he to die. Two days later he writes to Gosse again, with a scrupulous amendment to the first letter. In listing his resources he had forgotten to mention his shares in Frazer & Green, which produce between £200 and £300 annually. (That is, book royalties aside, his annual income at this time – allowing for variations in both fellowship and share dividends – came to between £400 and £550.)

You will see that this is an important correction, and I wish to put you in possession of it at once. You will of course make no use of my former letter without supplying this correction. But the fact remains that, apart from a grant, I may have either to borrow or to trench on my capital. Of the two I should much prefer the latter. Forgive me for troubling you with a second letter, but I feel that my former, through a serious oversight, misrepresented the state of my affairs, and naturally I could not rest under that idea without putting myself right with you at once.

On 5 October Lilly Frazer writes a long confidential letter to Gosse to give him the emotional context to her husband's request, a context that she is sure that he will not have supplied. Frazer has now gone off on a brief holiday with his sister, and in his absence she has taken charge of his correspondence, which means that she has written to him of Gosse's letter but has not sent it on. Her reason for not doing so concerns the form from the Royal Literary Fund that Gosse had enclosed. Must J. G. fill it out? After all, he had not had to do so last time. (This was true. Gosse had managed to put Frazer's case to the Council without any application from the latter.[20] As a result, Frazer – no doubt with the active concurrence of Lilly – had come to construe that grant as a "*reward* for his long and unremunerative work and not merely as an assistance in distress.") She knows that seeing it will make him anxious. "He would always be troubling himself about any farthing omitted etc. You may know how terribly he worries himself over trifles?" The second reason is that

you have touched a real sore in saying that Cambridge has shown strange neglect in not providing for him. The university has done absolutely nothing for Mr Frazer – they never even acknowledge him – never choose him as a representative of learning, nor otherwise honour his work. This is the great grievance which we feel, tho we rarely, if ever, speak of it and which I believe [is] due to the fact that Dons are people who run in grooves and have no imagination. They cannot realise that a man may be personally modest and retiring yet proud of his work and grateful for the recognition of patient labour unrewarded. This neglect of Mr Frazer was most marked when deputations were sent to Glasgow for the University Jubilee there, and Mr Frazer – of whom Glasgow is very proud – was not even invited to be among the *Cambridge* delegates who went to the ceremony. There are thousands of such instances – but we ignore them. I always tell my husband that such as he is, he is – and that suffices – but on his holiday away from me I did not wish him to brood over this subject. He is so wonderfully generous that he will probably write to you acknowledging enthusiastically the favour his College does him by giving him a Fellowship! What were Fellowships made for – if not for workers like him?

The plural pronoun in "There are thousands of such instances – but *we* ignore them" is splendid. J. G. probably never gave it a thought, but Lilly Frazer was acutely unhappy about her lack of status, and was probably irritated with J. G. for not resenting the university's neglect as much as she did.

Lilly Frazer knew her husband. When he returned and saw the form from the Fund, he promptly wrote to its secretary saying that he would not be applying, and in a letter to Gosse (9 October) explained why. The reason, as she had foreseen, is that the applicant is obliged to make a declaration of financial distress. "As my wife will have told you, it is impossible for me to make such a declaration for the simple reason that it would not be true." He also learned from Macmillan's royalty statement that, contrary to what he thought, *The Golden Bough* was nearly but not quite out of print – all of twenty copies remained. As to why the university did not provide for such as himself, the answer is simply put – there was no money. There was money for practical subjects, "but few people care to give their money for such a very unpractical subject as comparative religion, which puts nothing in anybody's pocket and only makes people uncomfortable by unsettling their beliefs." Furthermore, he wished to remain a research student and was not interested in lecturing.

But Gosse liked Frazer, and he was not one to give up easily. He must have told the Fund's governors that the appearance of a great work of learning (*The Golden Bough*) would be endangered because its author, though in straits, was too proud to describe the gravity of his financial situation. Would they, exceptionally, make a grant without the requisite declaration? Whatever he said was effective, for on 17 November Frazer again received £250. When he wrote to thank Gosse for once again having rescued him, he also said that he had not been inactive. He had written several magazine articles and was awaiting their publication, and although it was not to his liking he had agreed to lecture as well, using as his text parts of his new book.[21]

Which explains why in the Lent (winter) term 1905, for the first time since 1886, his name appeared on the lecture list at Trinity College, with a course of nine lectures under the collective title of "The Sacred Character and Magical Functions of Kings in Early Society." From these he quarried two that dealt with the question of the evolution of the kingship and gave them, in May 1905, to a larger, more general audience at the Royal Institution, London. Dedicated to Gosse "in gratitude and friendship," the full set of nine were published by Macmillan in October 1905 as *Lectures on the Early History of the Kingship*, the preface of which announces them to be part of the as-yet-incomplete third edition of *The Golden Bough*.

Bearing in mind the brisk sale of the second edition, Macmillan decided to print 2000 copies, which sold well. As a result of the controversy surrounding the second edition, Frazer had made the all-important leap in the popular mind from obscure don to public expert. (Part of the sale may also have been attributable to the fact that this was his first considerable book in a single volume.)

But this was not all, for when Frazer's luck turned, it did so completely. With the help once again of Gosse, on 17 January 1905 Frazer was granted a Civil List pension of £200 annually.[22] The Civil List is the name for the very large sums voted by Parliament for the support of the royal family. But this annual appropriation bill is also the convenient vehicle by which the Prime Minister may each year award small pensions, up to a total of £1200, to a handful of ordinary citizens (each, needless to say, provided with a powerful political sponsor). Most of those awarded Civil List pensions at this time were the impoverished spouses and/or children of deceased military or diplomatic officers. Usually the brief citation reads, "In recognition of her inadequate means of support (or straitened circumstances)." But along with the distressed gentlewomen occur the names of scholars and others who deserve the thanks of the nation, among them a number of anthropologists.[23] Frazer's citation reads, "In recognition of his literary merits and of his anthropological studies." The phrase, no doubt composed by Gosse, naturally says nothing of "distress."

Within a period of six months, then, through two interventions by Gosse, Frazer's income more than doubled (although of course the Royal Literary Fund grant was for one time only), and both the present and immediate future were secure. Now he would be undisturbed by mundane cares for at least the next two years, by which time (he believed) the third edition should be completed and producing income as well. Years earlier he had made a list of books he wished to write; now he was free to write them, and he breathed a deep sigh of relief. Of course those plans would not be realized completely, but in general his financial situation in the years to come would always be better than his intellectual reception.

In 1906, as part of a long-running feud with *The Times*, the press magnate Lord Northcliffe decided to strike a blow at *The Times Literary Supplement*, founded only four years earlier and thought to be vulnerable to competition.[24] He accordingly appointed Edmund Gosse to edit a small literary supplement, called *Books*, to appear each Saturday in the *Daily Mail*. Gosse was told to enlist the best literary and critical talent in Britain, which he promptly did. Among the participants were William Archer, G. K. Chesterton, Thomas Hardy, Andrew Lang, A. J. Symons – and J. G. Frazer. The supplement ran for only six months, and during that time Frazer contributed perhaps half a dozen reviews. How many exactly it is impossible to say because when Lady Frazer commissioned a bibliography of her husband's works, the entire episode seems to have been forgotten (perhaps because of the painful incident to be described below). As a result none of his reviews appears there. From references in the letters and from the single signed piece, one can make some safe attributions as well as pretty good guesses, all of which appear in Appendix 1.

In the light of his policy (as he remarked to Hartland in 1895) of never writing reviews, we should take at face value Frazer's plaintive statement, below, that he agreed to participate only out of friendship to Gosse. He reviewed only anthropological and classical books that he would have bought and read in any event, so the distraction to his work was minimal. Since it is a truism of intellectual life that no one makes (enough) money reviewing, the fees he received probably made no appreciable difference to the state of the family exchequer.

It is therefore ironic that a misunderstanding about his fees produced the most important event, biographically speaking, in the entire *Books* affair. It is described in the following letter from Frazer to Gosse of 16 January 1907, which, purely for the pitch of its emotionality, can be compared only to that of 1897 to J. F. White about Robertson Smith. In it Frazer whips himself into a fury of remorse over the pain he imagines that he may have caused Gosse.

My dear, dear Gosse, my life-long benefactor and honoured friend, how could you imagine that such a dreadful idea ever crossed my mind? It never did so for an instant. If I were to go mad, in the maddest nightmare of my disordered brain I could not conceive of such a thing. I am as incapable of such a thought as you are of such an act. It fills me with grief and horror to think that any time, for hours certainly and perhaps for days, your kind heart should have been wounded by such a cruel thought of a friend. Put it away from you once and for all.

How my letter to Mr Lingard could have been so misunderstood, I find it hard to imagine. I wrote to him rather than to you (as I first thought of doing) simply and solely to avoid troubling you in a matter with which I thought you had no concern. I supposed, and I still suppose, that you have only to do with the editorial department and have nothing to do with the payment. If this supposition is wrong, at least it is natural, since the payments come to me from a different person (Mr Lingard) in a different office in a different part of the city. Accordingly I thought that if a mistake had been made, it had been made at the pay office, not by you, and accordingly I wrote to the pay office to enquire. But I wrote under no impression whatever of being cheated (I hate even to write the word) by anybody. I had gathered from one of your early letters on the subject that articles were to be paid at two different rates, and that I was to be paid at the higher. It seemed to me, judging roughly by the length of my articles (I have never measured them exactly or counted the words), that I was not being paid at the higher rate mentioned by you, and I thought that through a mistake at the pay office I might be being paid at the lower instead of the higher rate. So I wrote to enquire mentioning to Mr Lingard that you had told me (what I thought he might not be aware of) that I was to be paid at the higher rate. I expected him to answer me and to tell me, what I do not yet know, whether any mistake has been made, or whether it is I, and not the office, that is in error. I may be wrong in my recollection of your letter, wrong in the estimate of the length of my articles, and wrong as to the scale of payment and as to deductions that may possibly have to be made for reasons with which I am unacquainted. I simply wrote for information to what I regarded as the proper quarter (the quarter from which I received the money), and instead of a simple answer from Mr Lingard correcting my mistake (if I had made one) or correcting his mistake or that of one of his subordinates, there comes this morning your letter like a thunderbolt out of the blue. I was surprised at not hearing from Mr Lingard, and if I had not heard from him in a day or two, I intended to mention the matter to you in my next letter (when I was going to ask you to let me have Farnell's *Cults of the Greek States* for review) and to ask you to look into the matter for me. But I did not wish to trouble you needlessly and so intended to let a few days pass in hopes of hearing from Mr Lingard. This is the whole of the matter. When I think of the pain you have suffered, I bitterly regret that I did not (as my first impulse was) write to you direct to enquire. If I could have thought that my writing to Mr Lingard could possibly have been so frightfully misinterpreted, I would never have written to him. But it was impossible that such an idea as you put into words could ever have crossed my mind. Forgive me, my dear friend, for having, with nothing but a kind intention, caused you such dreadful pain. Nothing like this has ever happened to me in my life before, and surely it will not happen again. You know that I write these articles to please you, my friend and benefactor, and not for the wretched pounds (I call them wretched because they have made you and me so wretched) that I receive for them. I would write them for nothing but the pleasure of pleasing you, though I willingly and gratefully accept payment for them besides. But I would far rather never have received a penny for them than that you should have suffered for them thus.

Of course I will write at once to Mr Lingard to correct the extraordinary misapprehension which my unfortunate letter seems to have created in his mind as well as in yours. I will take care never to write to him again.

Now my dear Gosse, we must meet and shake hands. Will you come to me or shall I come to you? My mind will not be at rest till I see you or hear from you at least that this dreadful cloud of mistake has quite passed away from your mind and that you forgive me for the pain I have unwittingly caused you. May I come to you and bring my dear Wife with me? She wishes so much to know you and to thank you for all you have done for us both. And when you know her, you will love and honour her, as her noble and beautiful nature deserves, and as my best friends do. Only let us know and we will come at once to you. I am grieved to hear that you have been ill. Do write or telegraph to me at once to say that all is well and that we are friends as ever. At all events I am and shall be to the end of my life.

It is unfortunate that we lack the letter Gosse wrote that provoked this amazing outpouring of anxiety and abjection. Perhaps it was a brisk business letter such as are written in their thousands every day in every metropolis, not least by editors who face dozens of importunings daily. If it was such a stiff letter (Gosse seems to have defended himself against an imagined accusation of cheating), then it was grotesquely misaddressed to a person so naive and defenseless as Frazer.

In the face of having his motives unjustly impugned by one whom he regarded as a dear friend and unrivaled benefactor, Frazer falls apart. He has absolutely no idea of what to do. It is not merely that he was not guilty of anything that could be thought of as self-seeking or hostile in thought or deed. Rather, one is reminded here of the panics and the torrents of emotion that prevail in friendships between children. Children have no masks or subterfuges behind which to hide. After an all-out fight with one's best schoolfriend that has ended in tears or blows, one is totally bereft, there seems no way out, and the misery is pure and unrestrained.

Frazer's letter is the adult equivalent of uncontrollable childish sobbing. He will do anything to explain and to regain Gosse's friendship, and his desperation is fueled by a consciousness that the whole thing is horribly, nightmarishly unfair, which again is the sensitive child's perennial indictment of the world. It is one thing to hear Bronislaw Malinowski or William James say that Frazer is unworldly, quite another to encounter this piece of naked, pathetic pleading for reconciliation from a man of fifty-three. At this point one wants a stronger word than "unworldliness."

This letter permits us to understand why Frazer, who could be hurt so easily, avoided controversy when he could. He had not the stomach for it and could not trust his reactions under pressure. One also discerns a possible source of his deep-lying tendency to ignore emotional factors in human relationships among primitive peoples. He may have been one of those people who never learn to deal adequately with the depth and power of their own feelings and those of others, and as a result cultivate the intellect as a defense against emotion.

It is only fitting to mention that the story ended happily. Gosse did see immediately that a misunderstanding had occurred, they were completely reconciled, and their friendship continued as before (Frazer to Gosse, 9 April 1907). Once Gosse left the *Daily Mail*, Frazer immediately stopped reviewing and did not return to it for fifteen years. In 1922 after a number of requests from the editor he agreed to write for *The Times Literary Supplement*, and reviewed anthropological books for that journal for four years.

12 · *LECTURES ON KINGSHIP* AND LIVERPOOL

THE *Lectures on the History of the Kingship* is an extremely important book, for in a number of ways it marks the point of furthest development in Frazer's thought. It goes largely unmentioned, however, even by those interested in his work.[1] The reason is that it was incorporated into, and in that sense effaced by, the third edition, which is massive enough to eclipse its two sizable predecessors, much less this sketch.

Whatever the reason, its obscurity is regrettable. Its considerable merits derive from two sources. The first is the lecture format, which forced Frazer to be direct and concise. Each lecture had to make one or two main points and each had to follow directly on what had gone before. In view of the salutary results of this discipline, one wishes that he had been more willing to present his ideas so clearly and modestly to the public, rather than burying them in increasingly large and unmanageable works. Although after 1911 Frazer lectured a good deal, which is to say that he read from the proofs of his books, *Kingship* had something that these later talks lacked. That is, the lecture format was necessary but not sufficient.

That missing ingredient, and the second source of the book's interest, is intellectual energy. *Kingship* is lively because it represents the results of Frazer's first collaboration with anyone since the death of Robertson Smith. In this case the coworker was his Cambridge friend and colleague, Arthur Bernard Cook (1868–1952).[2] A. B. Cook was among the few classical dons in Cambridge who rivaled Frazer in sheer erudition. Never more than a Fellow of Queens' College and a college lecturer until the end of his academic career, he was perhaps the most learned classical archaeologist in Cambridge. As Frazer spent half his life writing *The Golden Bough*, so Cook spent half of his writing *Zeus*.[3] Put simply, Cook attempted in *Zeus* to bring together the entire vast corpus of information – literary, anthropological, philological, epigraphical, archaeological, and cultic – available about the lord of Olympus. *Zeus* originated in Cook's collaboration with Frazer at this time.

Aside from their prodigious learning and modest positions within the university, Cook and Frazer resemble one another in the way in which both believed in, and dedicated themselves to, scholarship as an ideal. Inevitably there were differences too. Cook was a Christian throughout his life, and for that reason understood Greek religion as an imperfect forerunner of Christianity, whereas for Frazer it was finally only one branch of primitive

197

religion. For Frazer, a Nazarene-like consecration to scholarship did not rule out – indeed it positively enjoined – an activist approach to those questions upon which his specialist knowledge fitted him to pronounce, whereas Cook never allowed his own religious views to color his scholarly work in a polemic fashion. Unlike Frazer, Cook never sought an extra-academic audience, nor was he adept at presenting his theories readably; the result was that he remained unknown outside the university. For this reason, and because he was (like Frazer) the opposite of assertive, he had to wait for recognition until 1931, when shortly before his retirement he became the first Laurence Professor of Archaeology at Cambridge.[4]

In October 1902 Cook published a long, acute, and strongly critical review of the second edition of *The Golden Bough*.[5] Although he was primarily an archaeologist and philologist, he had long been interested in anthropology and folklore as well, and he and Frazer were friends of some years standing. For this reason Frazer knew Cook to be as modest and sincere as he was learned and, though a Christian, uninterested in engaging in pointless disputation. After the sustained ferocity of Lang and the massed hostility of the reviewers in *Folk-Lore*, Frazer thought that Cook, however much they disagreed, was a man from whom he might learn. Accordingly (*pace* Malinowski), not only did he read Cook's review but, having done so, neither withered nor withdrew in the face of its criticism. Instead he took the initiative and on 21 December 1902 invited Cook to talk about the questions raised in his review.[6] Cook, moved at Frazer's asking him to come despite his criticism, accepted immediately.[7]

The conversation proved stimulating to them both, and in the next few weeks they had a number of long, intense sessions, filled with something of the intellectual excitement that Frazer describes in his reminiscences of Robertson Smith. Although he never had the total rapport with Cook (or with anyone else) that he had with Smith, the working relationship may in fact have been better because this time he was the senior partner, in terms of both years and recognition, and was not constrained as he had been with Smith. The result of their conversations was immensely heartening to Frazer, for in the end he was able to persuade Cook to change his mind on a number of crucial points. By 6 February 1903 Cook was willing to defend many of the same statements he had attacked in print some months earlier.[8] He then proceeded to do exactly that, in a series of no fewer than seven long archaeological and philological articles embodying his new, evolving position in 1903–5.[9] These articles constituted the tiny acorn whence grew the mighty oak of *Zeus*.

In its length, detail, and thoughtfulness Cook's review of the second edition is one of the best pieces of criticism that Frazer ever received. Although Cook thinks the book gravely flawed, he takes it seriously and writes disinterestedly and unmaliciously. In view of the sensitive subjects that Frazer's major books address, it is not surprising that these qualities were rare enough, and it is easy to see why Frazer valued this review. Cook wished that Frazer had written a different book from the one he wrote, not merely to dismiss the book in the usual way of reviewers but because he believed that the great mass of useful material it contained would have profited from a different presentation, the outlines of which he suggested.

Cook's numerous difficulties with the text were of two different kinds. The first was formal: he thought it a serious mistake that Frazer's discussion of primitive religion was carried out within the framework of the analysis of the ritual at Nemi. Because it was, only those principles that entered into the explication of that strange rite are discussed. Frazer's canons of relevance were very wide, and as a result vast territories had been annexed to Nemi; nevertheless, only indirectly if at all was a general theory of religion expounded. Cook recognized that the priest and the golden bough were literary devices and nothing more, but thought that their artificiality acted as an unnecessary constraint.[10] Further, because *The Golden Bough* purported to be an explanation of the Arician cult, if a more persuasive explanation of that cult were offered, then its acceptance might well sweep away the entire work, which would be both unfortunate and unfair. Cook even recalled the "general work on primitive superstition and religion" that Frazer referred to in the preface of the first edition, from which he claimed to have been distracted in order to write *The Golden Bough*; he suggested that Frazer return to it in the future.

The second category of objections was substantive. Cook was not at all put off by the fact that *The Golden Bough* is a tissue of conjectures. For him there was nothing especially inadequate about a wholly speculative theory, particularly one explaining phenomena for which there is never going to be much evidence. Such a reconstruction of primitive mental processes has two built-in limitations, however: it must be internally consistent and it must not base conclusions on assumptions that are inherently improbable. Cook believed that Frazer was guilty on both counts, and the second half of his review documents this in detail. He objected specifically to Frazer's contention that the Arician priest was the surrogate for, and incarnation of, an oak-deity. Finally, he proposed a different explanation of the cult based not on exotic parallels with Balder but with the institution of the *rex sacrorum* in nearby Rome.

Cook concluded that if he was right – and on the face of it his explanation seemed more likely than Frazer's because more parsimonious – then the Arician framework of *The Golden Bough* must be dismantled. His verdict: "The real value of the book will be found to lie not in the particular Arician hypothesis – that is wrong – but in the generalisations with regard to magic and early religion, many of which are undoubtedly right."[11]

As a result of his conversations with Frazer, in which Frazer put before him information that he had accumulated since the completion of the second edition, Cook came round to the view that the god in the tree *was* Jupiter and that the tree *was* an oak. Probably no single datum caused him to change his mind, but once he dropped his scepticism suddenly it seemed that a large body of evidence of various sorts made the equation of Jupiter (Zeus) and the oak possible, then plausible, then likely. In his way Cook was as inclined to speculation as Frazer, and once he started to speculate, there was no stopping him either. Although Frazer never claimed to be more than a competent philologist, Cook had a real flair in this direction, and he produced numbers of etymologies that suggested prehistoric connections.

Exhilarated by the fruitful way they worked together, they decided not to allow themselves to be carried away until they heard a second, disinterested opinion. Frazer tried out some of Cook's ideas on his friend R. S. Conway (1864–1933), Professor of Latin at Manchester. Although Conway pricked a few of Cook's airier fancies, most encouragingly he confirmed others and even added some of his own.[12] The string of articles Cook published in the *Classical Review* and *Folk-Lore* in 1903, 1904, and 1905 kept the questions before the eyes of scholars and therefore acted as an ideal preparation for *Lectures on the History of the Kingship*.

The lectures advance a speculative theory concerning the evolution of the institution of the kingship. They begin and end with an analysis of the king of the wood at Nemi, but in terms quite different from those in *The Golden Bough*. There are two striking omissions: neither the golden bough itself nor Balder and the mistletoe is mentioned. That neither is needed to explain the ritual suggests that neither is integral to the argument. Their absence should be seen as a direct response to Cook's suggestion that the Arician framework be dismantled. Frazer here made his first and only effort to rethink the entire question afresh, dispensing with the Virgilian and Scandinavian references and employing many fewer savage parallels.

Nor does this exhaust the interest of the work by any means. Instead of the second edition's flat assertion of a monolithic movement from magic to religion – that is, of a movement taking place entirely within the minds of a few especially gifted thinkers – here Frazer tries to indicate what the social and political consequences might have been of such a radical epistemological shift. In doing so he advanced a paradox, the germ of which appeared first in his article on taboo as long ago as 1888. It is that many of the most useful advances in human life, such as the institutions of government, private property, and marriage, owe their origin and continuation to the action of "superstition." That is, although superstition is and always will be the enemy of reason, henceforth it will not suffice merely to name it as such and dismiss it. Frazer now recognized that although its truth value may be nil, it is nevertheless the source of much that is best and most important in our lives. This argument implies that religion, as a form of superstition, has had and continues to have beneficial effects. For the first time, that is, he discerned something other and more complex than a straightforward movement of the whole of humanity toward the shining light of reason.

Thus in discussing the proto-kings whom he calls "public" magicians, a group whose interest in the workings of physical nature shows that they are among the most intelligent members of the primitive community, he says that these men early on must have realized that their magic did not work. Once that realization had sunk in, two courses of action lay open. Some carried on knowing they were gulling the credulous community, whereas others continued to believe in magic and imagined only that their technique was faulty. Of these two groups, Frazer prefers the former.

> The general result is that at this stage of social evolution the supreme power tends to fall into the hands of men of the keenest intelligence and the most unscrupulous character. If we could balance the harm they do by their knavery against the benefits they confer by their superior sagacity, it might well be found that the good greatly outweighed the evil. For more mischief has probably been wrought in the world by honest fools than by intelligent rascals.[13]

Further, because the profession of magic tends to place public affairs in the hands of the most able, it acts to transform the mode of government from the democracy of the tribe to the autocracy of the exceptional individual, thereby introducing innovation into the life of the otherwise inert and conservative group. This in turn brings about economic, social, and intellectual progress. Although in an autocracy one is free to think one's own thoughts only in private, nevertheless the dynamism of the leader marks an improvement over the torpor of the democratic mass.[14]

For the intellectualist Frazer this was reasoning of a surprisingly sociological kind. He also discussed, in Spencerian fashion, how the transition from magic to religion took place within the context of the increasing differentiation of social function. This growing complexity is reflected in the movement from the civil to the sacred aspects of kingship and from democracy to despotism.[15] Finally, when he returned to the grove at Nemi, he concluded that what probably occurred there can be restated "by saying that the King of Rome was married to the oak-goddess Diana either in the sacred grove at Nemi or, according to others, in a grove outside the walls of Rome."[16] Although the second edition had discussed sacred marriage – a mimetic magical ritual consisting of a ceremony leading up to sexual intercourse between the priestly celebrants that was intended to imitate and thus induce fertility in humans, crops, and animals – that concept was made more important here. We are now far indeed from the solitary priest warily circling the tree, awaiting his fate.

Nor was Cook's the only criticism that Frazer received at this time. Cook had disagreed on historical grounds; in June 1904 the Oxford anthropologist R. R. Marett (1866–1943) demurred, but on psychological grounds.[17] Although its tone is just as friendly and courteous as was Cook's, Marett's long paper in *Folk-Lore*, "From Spell to Prayer," examines the associationist psychology implicit in Frazer's antithesis between magic and religion and finds it entirely wanting. The very absoluteness of the difference between these two world-views does not answer to anything known in nature, where gradual evolution is everywhere the rule. Instead Marett advanced a much more complicated, albeit equally a priori, description of the way in which the spell may gradually have become the prayer.

This essay is one of a series, written in the first decade of the century, in which Marett produced an important critique of associationist psychology as it applied to anthropology. He agreed that primitive humanity did indulge in some abstract problem-solving, but said that this represented a later phase of mental evolution. Earlier had been a stage that he called "pre-animism" (later renamed "animatism"), in which primitive people intuited rather than ratiocinated. They sensed the presence of a vague but nonetheless real impersonal force (called variously *mana* by the Melanesians, *wakanda* by the Iroquois), and their response was not terror but awe. Likewise, when the magician performs his rituals, Marett was interested in the subjective feelings of the performer while he acts rather than in deciding whether to classify him as either an objective proto-scientist or a shrewd charlatan.[18] It should be noted that Marett was no more a field researcher than was Frazer. He was not arguing against Frazer's theories on the basis of counter-examples drawn from experience but from his own subjective sense of the complexities of thought and feeling, of which associationism offers so poor a description.

Although a keen controversialist Marett was not interested in taking his opponent by surprise; accordingly he wrote to Frazer at the end of June 1904 to warn him of his forthcoming essay in *Folk-Lore*. In the first letter of what would be a correspondence and friendship of thirty-five years, Frazer responded immediately on 4 July to thank him for his courtesy.[19] His letter is cordial, and he welcomes Marett's criticism, which he is sure will be constructive. Frazer repeated here what he had said elsewhere, that anthropology is still in its infancy, that his own theories may be all wrong, and that he always stood ready to modify or discard any of them in the light of new evidence. "I sometimes fear that people may think me deaf to reason and wedded to my own opinions because I avoid controversy and seldom or never reply to criticism, unless it is to acknowledge a gross and palpable blunder which I have committed. But I really do try to profit by all sound criticism."

He went on to say that although he had not yet read Marett's piece, he would not be surprised if the differences between them turn out to be verbal rather than substantive. That is, he was keenly aware of the difficulty in finding the right language to express the epistemological gulf between savages and moderns in terms that are true to the very different mental reality of the savages and yet comprehensible to modern minds. As a result misunderstandings arose and probably would continue to do so. "The language of a civilised people has been slowly elaborated and refined to fit and express the complexities of civilised thought. It cannot fit and express the crude vague thought of the savage." He hopes that after he has read the paper they might discuss their differences either in person or by letter.

For the next twenty years he and Marett talked and wrote to one another often, without any perceptible effect on either, for Frazer was unable to make sense of Marett's psychological subtleties any more than he could fathom those of James Ward or William James. Although it is good that they agreed to disagree and that they remained friends, it is unfortunate that they could not work together, for Frazer's greatest shortcoming lies in his psychology, in the totally unrealistic simplifications that he projects into the primitive mind. The result was that Marett regularly reviewed Frazer's works and used them as a series of whetstones upon which to sharpen his own theory of the social psychology underlying primitive religion.[20]

The next letter to Marett (17 December 1904) reminds us that while Frazer was revising the discussion of the fertility gods that would become *Adonis Attis Osiris*, research on his other great subject, totemism, was proceeding apace. In 1904 Spencer and Gillen brought out *The Northern Tribes of Central Australia*, the companion piece to their earlier volume, with Frazer once again seeing the book through the press. Marett in his review criticized their conclusions regarding magic, religion, and totemism, which, given their relationship to Frazer, were unsurprisingly Frazerian.[21] Frazer could not have disagreed more, as he made clear in his semi-humorous response:

On every point on which you express an opinion you are, so far as I can judge, just as far from the truth as it is possible to be! I mean, that if your opinions were just exactly inverted, they would be the nearest approximation to the truth that we can get, or nearly so, at the present time. What I mean will, I hope, be clear from the article on the beginning of totemism which I shall publish shortly in the *Fortnightly Review*.

This article – which inevitably grew to become a pair of articles – contains Frazer's third and last theory of the origin of totemism. As might be expected, it is based on Spencer and Gillen's newest findings. It proposes that his theory of 1899 – that totemism was a large-scale system of cooperative magical performances instituted to increase the food supply – described only a relative refinement or secondary elaboration in the history of that strange institution. The earliest or bedrock stage, he now thinks, arises from the belief, widespread among the aborigines, that sexual intercourse has nothing to do with the production of children. Because of the relatively long interval that elapses between intercourse and the first quickening of the fetus, they deny any connection between these two events. Instead they believe that the child, who is really a reincarnation of an ancestor, enters the mother at the moment when she feels the first fetal movement.

This theory of conceptional totemism, as Frazer calls it, explains why in the northern tribes the children do not belong to the totem clan of either the mother or the father. To these tribes, who have not yet reached the stage of social development that is marked by exogamy, the natural environment is divided into what might be termed fields of totemic force in which various totems hold sway. The totem of the child is determined randomly, by whichever animal, plant, or object happens to be the *genius loci* where quickening was first observed. Only later, with the institution of exogamy – which is now seen as overlapping only somewhat with totemism and having no causal or logical connection with it – does the totemic descent of the child become regularized.

Although *Kingship* was atypical, undertaken out of financial necessity, intellectually it turned out to be worthwhile. In addition, the 1500 copies that Macmillan printed sold quickly. Meanwhile, however, he continued to beaver away at the third edition and, needless to say, it grew under his hand. In particular the discussion of the cults of the vegetation gods Adonis, Attis, and Osiris had become so large that, encouraged by the success of *Kingship*, Frazer proposed to Macmillan (8 March 1906) that it be brought out as a separate volume.

While the contents would not be so varied, and there would be nothing amusing in them [he seems to have thought *Kingship* humorous], the interest might to many people be greater. The subject is the death and resurrection of these Eastern gods, and I show grounds for thinking that their ritual has influenced that of the Christian Easter ceremonies, as these are observed by the Catholic and Greek churches. But there is nothing in my treatment of the subject which need offend any reasonable man. My hypothesis as to the Crucifixion would not enter into the volume. It belongs to a later part of the G.B.... As for the G.B. itself, at the present slow rate of progress it cannot be published before next year. Indeed I shall be satisfied if it appears any time in 1907.

The letter raises two points. That concerning the dying gods and Easter will be discussed in Chapter 14. Here it is worth remarking that in 1906 Frazer still had not decided either the ultimate dimensions or the contents of the third edition. He intended that both *Adonis Attis Osiris* and *Kingship* would be parts of it. At the same time he distinguished between them, for he knew that although *Kingship* would be incorporated into the third edition, it neither could nor would stand by itself. *Adonis*, however, as Frazer remarked to Macmillan (15 May), was "an extract from the G.B., but . . . complete and intelligible by itself"; for this reason he asked Macmillan (6 July) that the type be kept standing not merely in the event that a reprint was wanted but because "the book is part of the third edition of the G.B."

He then raised the question with Macmillan of acquiring the copyright from A. & C. Black of the two books that that firm had published earlier: *Taboo* (1887) and *Passages from the Bible* (1895). This presented some difficulty because in 1897 *The Times* had entered into an agreement with Black, owners of the *Encyclopaedia Britannica*, to market, at a steeply discounted price, the by-then-outdated ninth edition. That edition contained Frazer's original article on "Totemism," and by extension Black construed this to mean as well the book based on that article.

Black, reminded by Macmillan's approach that they owned *Totemism*, now wanted to reprint it. If *Totemism* was to be reprinted, whether by Black or Macmillan, then Frazer said he wished to add to it his two *Fortnightly* essays – from 1899 and 1905 – on the origins of totemism. He wrote to Macmillan (10 November), "As the two latter essays are intended to form part of the third edition of *The Golden Bough*, I cannot of course reprint them without the permission of your firm." Although the problem was resolved by Macmillan buying both copyrights from Black, and thus becoming the publisher of the whole of Frazer's work, the point is that in 1906 Frazer thought that the third edition would contain a full analysis of totemism. It did not. Instead when Frazer in 1907 finally decided the contents of the third edition, he excluded most of the material on totemism, including all three of his earlier discussions. Instead, they were reserved to stand as the theoretical introduction to *Totemism and Exogamy*, the writing of which was to occupy (or distract) Frazer between *Adonis Attis Osiris* and the rest of the third edition.

Frazer thought *Adonis* the best thing he had ever done, and he was pleased that the public liked it too.[22] The first printing of 1000 copies sold out quickly. When Macmillan decided to reprint (1500 copies this time), Frazer of course took the opportunity "to correct a few misprints, to improve a word or two here and there, and probably to make a few small additions which will add to the value and interest of the book. . . . Don't be alarmed about the additions. They are really very few and small, the snowball has not had time to roll far since the book was published" (3 February 1907). This time he was as good as his word, and the "second edition, revised and enlarged," appeared in November 1907.

In October 1907 both J. G. and Lilly came up to London for an important meeting with Macmillan to settle the question of the contents of the ever-enlarging third edition. At the meeting Lilly had an excellent idea. She saw that the confusion really arose from the fact that the third edition was not going to be merely an expanded version of its predecessor but was really more like a series of thematically connected monographs. That being the case, she thought, reasonably enough, that the third edition should be so understood and described publicly by both its author and publisher. Unfortunately J. G. prevented her from raising it then, as he admitted to Macmillan afterwards, "partly through a misapprehension, partly through a wish not to occupy your time with unnecessary discussion." But we may be sure that the Frazers subsequently discussed it, for Lilly Frazer was never one to fold her hands and agree meekly with her husband. J. G. then came round to seeing it her way, and he now raised it with Macmillan (18 October 1907). It would be simple to communicate the idea that the monographs were parts of a larger whole by means of a general title page to appear in all volumes. In addition, it might well increase sales of *Adonis* as well as subsequent volumes because buyers would understand that each was a part of a whole that was in the process of publication. Then, although this was to be kept secret, once the whole series was completed, he would produce a one-volume abridged edition.

Macmillan saw the merit of this plan and quickly agreed. He and Frazer also agreed that a start could be made at once by producing a new title page to be inserted into all existing copies of *Adonis*.[23] The only problem was that Frazer could not, at this early stage, and in the light of his books' tendency to balloon in size, assign a volume number to *Adonis*. He knew only that it would appear somewhere in the middle, but he was unwilling or unable to be more precise. He therefore sidestepped this difficulty by breaking up the series into parts rather than volumes. Although he could not predict the number of volumes, he could decide the number of parts; *Adonis Attis Osiris* would constitute Part IV of the third edition.

Once the canon of the third edition had been settled, Frazer did a surprising thing – he immediately put the entire project to one side and turned, or returned, to totemism. On 16 March 1908 he wrote to Macmillan that he was now

writing a new "Geographical Survey of Totemism," which is intended to include all the important and well-authenticated facts about Totemism which are at present known, arranged according to geographical and ethnical areas, to be followed by a general Summary and Conclusion. The whole will probably occupy two substantial octavo volumes and rank among my most important works. The mere reprints [*Totemism* and the two *Fortnightly* essays] will occupy only about 180 pages of the whole.

Allowing for the inevitable expansion that occurred whenever he got down to writing – four substantial volumes emerged rather than two – this is a good description of *Totemism and Exogamy* (1910).

Considering that he had just achieved his largest audience and greatest success with *Adonis*, why did he suspend work on *The Golden Bough* at that moment? The preface to *Totemism and Exogamy* does not explain. There he says only that he had originally planned to reprint the 1887 *Totemism* because it had long gone out of print but was still in demand. Then he decided that he could not reprint it without also including the two *Fortnightly* essays, containing his more recent statements on the matter. So far so good. Here, however, follows a strange, highly colored passage:

This was all that at first I proposed to do; for my intention had long been to defer writing a larger treatise on totemism until the whole totemic harvest should have been reaped and garnered; and moreover at the time, a little more than two years ago [i.e., 1908], I was deeply engaged in other work which I was unwilling to interrupt. To-day the totemic harvest still stands white to the sickle in many fields, but it may be left for others hereafter to see the sheaves brought home. My sun is westering, and the lengthening shadows remind me to work while it is day.

This self-dramatizing metaphor sounds a distinctly odd note for a man of fifty-six in good health, except for occasional eye trouble. Why, suddenly, had the sun begun westering? Why, if he really saw himself in the late autumn of his days and if he was engaged in other work (the third edition of *The Golden Bough*), did he persist with the survey of totemism? The answer is that he does not know. Having moved from a simple reprint of *Totemism* to something larger that would incorporate the results of the new Australian evidence, he somehow felt that he could not stop there but had to do the same for the rest of the world. "Thus, *insensibly* [emphasis added], I was led into writing the Ethnographical Survey of Totemism which now forms the great bulk of this book."[24] Nor do the letters to Macmillan clarify the matter. He simply announced, in the letter quoted above, that he was at work on the survey of totemism, without warning or explanation.

There can be no doubt, however, that the decision to drop the third edition in favor of totemism was taken at a sensitive moment in his life. For just then, when his work was going well and his reputation was at its height, Frazer embarked on perhaps the most important change (his marriage excepted) in his life. In April 1908, having spent nearly thirty-four years – his entire adult life – in Cambridge as undergraduate and Fellow, he left. He went to the University of Liverpool, there to become Professor of Social Anthropology – not only the first of that title at Liverpool, but anywhere in the world. Perhaps he felt that, in the light of the inevitable disruption that the move would cause, he might be able to work more easily on a work of compilation like *Totemism and Exogamy* than on something that required sustained original thought like the new *Golden Bough*.

A number of reasons contributed to the inevitably difficult and painful decision to leave Cambridge. On 9 April 1907, before he received the offer from Liverpool, Frazer wrote to Gosse, "My wife and I have serious thoughts of leaving Cambridge and coming to live in or near London. Indeed we are looking out for a house. If successful we shall hope really to see something of you." One must assume that the main impetus behind this house-hunting was Lilly Frazer's long dissatisfaction with Cambridge.[25] Because the Frazers were thinking seriously of leaving Cambridge, the overture from Liverpool, when it came, must have changed everything. Instead of vaguely "looking out" for something in or near London, they now had a new geographic, professional, and social focus. Suddenly it became sensible to make plans for a future in Liverpool, and both J. G. and Lilly were energized.

In Lilly's eyes, Cambridge ignored her husband; in Liverpool he would be a *professor* (and she a professor's wife).[26] In her eyes Cambridge was a small town suffocated by the university's ubiquitous and conservative presence, a place where nothing ever happened. Liverpool, by contrast, was a great city in its own right, where the university was neither ubiquitous nor conservative, as the very establishment of a chair in the new subject of social anthropology demonstrated. Liverpool, moreover, was a city of international character and sophistication, where one met all kinds and conditions of people, not merely the same small collection of dons, variously reshuffled, who were experts in one small field of knowledge and uninterested (many of them at any rate) in anything else. Furthermore, as Frazer says in a letter to Galton of 24 November 1907, she had lived in Liverpool for some years during her first marriage, and thus had a number of friends whom she was eager to see once again.

Assuming that something like this collection of reasons and complaints, variously combined and modulated, was a constant and long-running feature of Lilly's conversation with her husband, it remains to be asked what reasons Frazer himself may have had for leaving Cambridge. Although the least self-seeking of men, he must have been gratified that Liverpool had approached him and invited him, on the basis of the eminence of his work. The fact that he would be professor in itself indicated the high value that the university placed on anthropology, which made a pleasant contrast to Cambridge, where its furthest penetration – Haddon's readership – had been established only after a long and wearisome struggle. And, once he realized how much more widely and deeply his words would be attended to when pronounced from the eminence of a professorial chair, the prospect began to be genuinely attractive in its own right.

The offer from Liverpool must have come between April and July 1907, for the first written intimation came in a letter to Gosse of 26 July 1907.[27] In it he said that he had told the university that he would accept the position, which was "honorary" (that is, it carried no salary), but only on certain conditions. Chief among these was that he would be under no obligation to lecture on a regular basis if such activity would detract from his research and literary work. Although on the one hand he wanted his appointment to mean that Liverpool would become a center for anthropology, on the other hand this goal was not important enough for him to sacrifice time from his research. (The prospect of actually seeing a student or two seems never to have been mentioned by either the university or by Frazer; had that been one of the conditions of the post, it alone might have dissuaded him from coming.) Although quitting Cambridge would be painful after all these years, he had been told that the intellectual atmosphere of Liverpool was "exceedingly keen and the enthusiasm for the advancement of knowledge great."

From Liverpool's point of view, the appointment was a splendid coup: they were getting a world-famous figure as the first occupant of their new chair – which they named for him – in a new subject, and to top it off, he would cost the university nothing. Even in those days, when public relations counted for much less in academic life than they do now, such considerations did not go unremarked. The appointment plainly meant that the University of Liverpool was on the move, a place to be watched in the future.[28]

On 9 November Frazer informed Gosse that the offer had now been made officially by the Vice-Chancellor and that he had accepted. The university had acceded to his conditions, which meant that he could take what part he would in university life. He will be spared "any of the compulsory teaching or examining, which are such serious drawbacks to most professorships. I quite agree with our Vice-Master [Henry Jackson] who once was asked to examine for the Theological Tripos and answered that nothing but extreme hunger would induce him to do so." They would let their house in Cambridge, thus permitting them to return if Liverpool did not suit, but he fully expected the city to be a most agreeable place in which to live.

To Galton (24 November) he described the move somewhat differently. Here he wrote of his hopes that the chair would give him a pulpit from which his voice would be heard, as it had not been heard before. For he had a specific proposal to make:

I have a scheme, which I intend to advocate in my inaugural lecture, of establishing a fund for sending anthropological expeditions to collect information about savages before it is too late. Liverpool with its wealth and its connections with foreign lands is perhaps the best place in the country to launch such a scheme, but I would try to get the older Universities, the Royal Society, the Anthropological Institute, and the British Museum to join in the work and help in the management of the fund.

Here speaks the organizational novice, completely naive about how difficult it is to get a number of institutions, especially of such augustness, to cooperate in a venture they do not control.

Frazer had had the idea in mind of an expeditionary fund for some time. Five years earlier, in 1902, he had been selected, in the History and Archaeology section, as one of the seventy founding members of the British Academy.[29] The Academy was created to act as the counterpart for the "historical sciences" to the Royal Society, which spoke for the natural sciences. Although its primary function was to participate in international scholarly projects and to represent and advise on matters connected with its areas of expert knowledge, it also envisaged the sponsorship of independent research. It was under this latter rubric that Frazer, on 8 December 1903, submitted a proposal for the creation of a fund to underwrite anthropological field expeditions.[30] The proposal was wildly premature because the Academy was at the time without any government or other financial backing, and quite unable to involve itself in anything so ambitious; of course, nothing happened.

The chair in Liverpool therefore gave Frazer an opportunity to revive this cherished dream. He had decided that the first expedition to be financed by his fund would be Spencer and Gillen to Western Australia.[31] Novice though he may have been, he knew that the plan would never be realized unless he worked to make it happen. For this reason, although it went against the grain, he actually went out and raised some money. Even before he took up residence in Liverpool he went to Edinburgh and there laid the plan before the explorer Sir John Murray, the leader of the *Challenger* expedition, who pledged £200.[32] As the expedition would cost about £1500, Frazer required only seven more such contributions to make the plan a reality, and there certainly must be more than seven progressive, wealthy Liverpudlians whom one could approach. He then sent off an urgent letter to Spencer – if the money were forthcoming, could he go? He was to telegraph yes or no; if yes, Frazer would make the dramatic announcement at his inaugural lecture, on 14 May. Unfortunately the answer was no; Spencer's past expeditions had taken him away from his university so often and for so long that he could not get away again for at least two years. As a result Frazer altered his proposal from the establishment of an expeditionary fund to the creation of an institute, on the analogy of the Smithsonian Institution, to study the primitive peoples of the Empire before their behavior and beliefs were completely and forever changed by exposure to Europeans.

In fact he had another string to his expeditionary bow, but that too snapped. From the start he had in mind two candidates were his fund to become a reality: Spencer and Gillen were to go to Western Australia and John Roscoe was to go to Central Africa. Roscoe (1861–1932), one of Frazer's closest friends during the second half of his life, was a well-known missionary and African enthnographer. Frazer and Roscoe began to correspond in 1891, and they met in 1896 when Roscoe was on home leave.[33]

Some seventeen years' worth – that is, about half – of Roscoe's lengthy and extensive correspondence with Frazer has survived.[34] The most eye-catching thing about the first extant letter, from May 1907, comes at the end: Frazer signs himself "Yours affectionately," which remained his regular closing. Frazer never used this formula with anyone else, and he was not one to use such words without meaning them. Another mark of their intimacy is the fact that it was Roscoe who compiled the 1907 catalogue of Frazer's library. Frazer, who lived in and for his books, would never allow anyone whom he did not like to handle them.[35] (Finally, in view of the hard words that have been written about Lilly Frazer, it is only right to note that the close relationship with Roscoe seems to have included the wives on both sides.)

Roscoe, who trained as a civil engineer and then entered the Church Missionary Society in 1884, lived for twenty-five years in Uganda. He was interested in ethnography from early days, and during his time in Africa contributed to the *Journal of the Anthropological Institute* and *Man*.[36] As it happens, he spent about six months in England in 1907, before returning to Uganda for a final two years; it was during that interval that the extant correspondence with Frazer begins. On 15 December 1907, when Roscoe had just returned to Uganda, Frazer wrote to tell him about his impending move to Liverpool and his scheme for an anthropological fund. Was Roscoe absolutely bound, he asks, to the Church Missionary Society for the next two years? For if the fund idea received support in Liverpool, and if Roscoe could see his way clear to leaving the Society, then Frazer would like him to lead an expedition to Central Africa, at the time poorly known. Although Roscoe was eager to go, he nevertheless felt bound to serve out his last two years, which meant that Frazer was unable to name any prospective explorers when, the next year, he finally announced the plan in Liverpool.

Frazer actually lived in Liverpool (at 24 Abercromby Square) for only five months (from April through September 1908), and while there he accomplished little. His entire sojourn in the city was a time of immediate and great unhappiness. He may have worked on the survey of totemism, but because of the pains attendant upon moving in and setting up his library, he was able to complete only his inaugural lecture, *The Scope of Social Anthropology*.

Although brief, the lecture, which starts modestly as a sketch of his subject to an audience that knows nothing about it, contains much more than his proposal to found an ethnographic research body. Although Frazer believed in the potentially limitless benefits that flowed from the life of the reason, his current personal misery was so acute as quite to unsettle him, and it undoubtedly spilled over into his inaugural. The address offers an unrelievedly gloomy assessment of the long-term social and political implications of anthropology. His unhappiness obviously did not create this vein of melancholy sentiment but acted to bring it out. Plainly the ideas and tone of the inaugural represent an aspect of his thought that usually did not gain expression.

For Frazer, anthropology has two main departments – the "customs and beliefs of savages" and such "relics of these customs and beliefs as have survived in the thought and institutions of more cultured peoples" – of which the second is in some ways the more important because it touches more directly on the lives of educated people in the West.[37] The source of these survivals, which collectively are known as folklore, is to be found in "the natural, universal, and ineradicable inequality of men." In the preface to *The Golden Bough* of 1890 Frazer had spoken of the mentality of the modern European peasantry as being essentially that of the ancient Aryans, but such backwardness is the result of history, not inherent stupidity. Here, however, we face the inescapable brute fact that many, even most, people are "dull-witted." Because of this, "disguise it as we may, the government of mankind is always and everywhere essentially aristocratic. No juggling with political machinery can evade this law of nature." By aristocracy, however, Frazer intends not the hereditary political caste but the "keener-witted minority" of "thinkers who advance knowledge." The nominal rulers notwithstanding, it is these thinkers who in every age are its unacknowledged legislators and uncrowned kings.

Clearly, the foray into an alien sociological mode of thought represented by *Kingship* had been abandoned, and his true intellectualist and platonist colors are once again nailed to the mast.

The more we study the inward workings of society and the progress of civilization, the more clearly shall we perceive how both are governed by the influence of thoughts which, springing up at first we know not how or whence in a few superior minds, gradually spread till they have leavened the whole inert lump of a community or of mankind.

Perhaps these thoughts are the mental aspect of the interplay of physical variations that determines the evolution of the human species. The same fierce struggle for existence that prevails in the physical world between individuals and species is also the law of intellectual life. Ultimately, however, "the better ideas, which we call the truth, carry the day." Whenever a new idea first appears and threatens to upset old prejudices, however, the doltish mob, for whom prejudice takes the place of thought, resists it fiercely and does all it can to destroy the promulgator (its ultimate benefactor).

Picking up an idea of Renan's, Frazer says that humanity advances in *échelons*, or unevenly. At any one time within any nation, as between nations, a small minority is far ahead of the rest of the population. The reason for their success is that they have

thrown off the load of superstition which still burdens the backs and clogs the footsteps of the laggards. To drop metaphor, superstitions survive because, while they shock the views of enlightened members of the community, they are still in harmony with the thoughts and feelings of others who, though they are drilled by their betters into an appearance of civilization, remain barbarians or savages at heart.

The great unwashed are thus much more backward and depraved than the label "Aryan peasants" would imply, for they are really virtually irredeemable in their stupidity.

Once again, as with Henry Mayhew and the other Victorian social investigators, we are in the presence of the phenomenon of the two nations, in which even the most educated have no idea of the "extent to which relics of savage ignorance survive at their doors." (Nineteenth-century accounts of the "two nations" – whether they are savages or the poor – oscillate between including them as part of humanity and excluding them as a race apart.) All credit therefore must go to the Brothers Grimm, who went out into the countryside and brought back the first reports, since confirmed by many others, of the "astonishing, nay, alarming truth that a mass, if not the majority, of people in every civilized country is still living in a state of intellectual savagery, that, in fact, the smooth surface of cultured society is sapped and mined by superstition."

As this point Frazer's idea of civilization as a precious, fragile artifact secreted mysteriously by the minds of the enlightened leaders of mankind acting in concert, and improbably elaborated despite the forces of darkness lapping at the margins on all sides, is embodied in visionary language that takes on an apocalyptic force.

Only those whose studies have led them to investigate the subject are aware of the depth to which the ground beneath our feet is thus, as it were, honeycombed by unseen forces. We appear to be standing on a volcano which may at any moment break out in smoke and fire to spread ruin and devastation among the gardens and palaces of ancient culture wrought so laboriously by the hands of many generations. After looking on the ruined Greek temples of Paestum and contrasting them with the squalor and savagery of the Italian peasantry, Renan said, "I tremble for civilization, seeing it so limited, built on so weak a foundation, resting on so few individuals even in the country where it is dominant."

Frazer can go no further. Rationalism and the comparative study of human behavior have brought him to this abyss of darkness, into which he can but stare. Not only is he no politician himself, but his vision of primal confusion – a kind of societal id – is so far-reaching and total as to be beyond the scope of any meliorist recipe for education or reform. Here he gives us his sense of the immutable essence of human nature and social institutions. Society is inherently and steeply pyramidal in shape and will always rest on a vast dark underclass. Rewriting the Gospels, he says that the ignorant will always be with us, for by the time the ideas of their betters manage to percolate down to the masses (if they ever do), they will be so out of date and incorrect that the mental distance between top and bottom will never shrink.

This little-known passage – the lecture is one of the few pieces he chose not to collect and reprint – ranks with Ruskin's haunted and haunting vision, expressed in meteorological imagery, of *The Storm Cloud of the Nineteenth Century* (1884) that was swirling over Europe and would soon sweep everything away. Frazer himself was unable to maintain this vatic intensity, and having discerned clearly the boiling mass of human magma beneath our feet, recoiled from both what he had seen and the impossibility of ever changing it. This marks the utter negation of all his beliefs in progress and the power of the reason. Never again will he intimate to his readers these grim consequences of anthropology, and it will be as if this lecture was never pronounced. The next link in this chain of prophetic utterances that marks the problematic modern sense of culture, and whose other late-nineteenth-century representatives include Nietzsche and Dostoyevsky, will be that of his contemporary Freud, when he goes beyond Frazer in his investigations into the volcano.

Although Frazer did not leave Liverpool until September, he knew immediately that leaving Cambridge had been a mistake. Already by 5 May, a week before the inaugural and after less than a month in Liverpool, there is mental depression and physical withdrawal in the dark and ambivalent tone of a letter to his good friend the classical scholar Hermann Diels in Berlin.

My real work is done in my study, which I never quit willingly to appear in public. I am not at home in a professor's chair and doubt whether I shall long occupy it. It is a great change from the pensive beauty and historical memories of Cambridge to the bustle and tumult of a great commercial seaport. I seem to have left my heart on the willows by the Cam and cannot say how soon I may go to reclaim my lost property![38]

He seems to have decided to return virtually as soon as he arrived. It remained only to notify the university of his decision, which he did on 8 July. In a letter to the Vice-Chancellor he says that although he had come fully intending to put down roots and remain in Liverpool, it simply had not worked out, and he would therefore be returning to Cambridge before the beginning of the next term.

Experience has proved that my attachment to Cambridge – my home for more than thirty-three years – was deeper than I knew, and that my roots, like those of Polydorus, could not be pulled up without blood. In fact I find it essential to my happiness, and therefore to the doing of my best work, that I should return to residence in Cambridge.[39]

In Cambridge Frazer had created a way of life that catered to his crotchets and enabled him to block out all irritants and distractions. He found Liverpool antipathetic from the start. Perhaps it was the noise, the crowds, or the new people to meet. Whatever it was, withdrawal was now impossible: he was married, he was a professor with social obligations, he was living in a big city and not a university town. He found himself unable to elaborate a new version of the routine that had become absolutely necessary for his work and therefore his life, and he seems to have come to a total halt. (Might this have been the breakdown that Malinowski incorrectly attributed to the attacks of Andrew Lang?) In a second letter to Diels (29 August 1908), he repeats that he is bereft and heartbroken – "I am leaving Liverpool to find my heart where I left it on the banks of the Cam" – and, typically, quotes Heine: "Ich hatte einst ein schones Vaterland / Der Eichenbaum wuchs dort so hoch."

And finally we have Lilly Frazer's reaction, in a candid letter (1 September 1908) to her good friend M. J. Lewis, Professor of Mineralogy at Cambridge:

I leave Liverpool with intense regret – tho' I look forward to renewing relations with such kind friends as you are – I cannot help feeling J. G. is making a huge mistake, for work's sake etc., but one cannot reason with imagination and it is my province just now to pack and unpack etc. and never mind the rest![40]

Liverpool was a large and humiliating failure. His expeditionary fund foundered on Spencer's commitments in Australia and Roscoe's in Africa, his proposal for an imperial Smithsonian Institution got nowhere, and like a child sleeping away from home for the first time he was miserable and could not adjust to new surroundings. From his point of view, worst of all was that planning and agonizing over the move, leaving Cambridge and installing himself (and being wretched) in Liverpool, and then reversing the process, together cost him most of a year. Further, because the position was unsalaried, he was also penalized by two very large outlays for moving house in one year, the effects of which were felt in the family exchequer for several years to come. Finally, and not at all to be ignored, the decision to leave can have been taken only after dozens of anxiety-producing conversations with Lilly. Although the end seems to have been ordained from the start, and he got what he needed – the return to Cambridge – it is clear that the question was not at all settled from her point of view.[41] They had returned to Cambridge in defeat, but it was only a matter of time until she could find a way to leave for good. It would take six years, but as soon as J. G. had completed the third edition in 1914, they moved to London and never lived permanently in Cambridge again.

By the end of September the Frazers were back in Cambridge. Unable to move back into their own house, which had been let, they rented another, a large house called St Keyne's, on Grange Road. Between the departure from Liverpool and arrival in Cambridge they had been in Oxford, where they attended the Third International Congress for the History of Religions in mid-September. Even before he left Liverpool the idea of the imminent return to Cambridge had buoyed his spirits, and he wrote to Cook (18 August) that he expected to resume their walks and talks and to bring him back "up to Hebrew scratch again."[42] By 29 September he was writing to Macmillan about his plans for the completion of *Totemism and Exogamy*. The first fruits of his mental revival upon returning to Cambridge was the speculative lecture he gave at the Royal Institution on 5 February 1909 entitled *Psyche's Task*.[43]

The task in question, according to legend, required Psyche to sort a huge mass of mixed seeds into its constituent kinds. Frazer, as the modern Psyche, and assuming the role of devil's advocate, sets out to demonstrate how difficult the task is because of the similarity of the seeds of good and evil and the thoroughness with which they are intermixed. When Macmillan wondered whether the title was not both strange and uninformative, he explained it (13 February 1909):

The book is an attempt to sort out the seeds of good from the heap of evil which we call superstition, just as Psyche was given the task of sorting out the different kinds of seeds. In a deeper sense the principle of life (Psyche) exists by choosing the good and avoiding the evil, which is death. Thus I think the title may be justified on philosophic grounds, and it has the advantage of introducing just that touch of imagination and poetry which vivifies a dry scientific enquiry. . . . Then from the practical point of view of bringing the book to the notice of readers I believe "Psyche's Task" to be a much better title than "The Influence of Superstitition on the Growth of Institutions." The latter is not so much a title as a description. . . . The former is compact, clear, and striking. . . . In exactly the same way I believe that the title of *The Golden Bough* has won very many readers who would not have looked at the book if it had been called by a long abstract title such as "Studies in the Early History of Magic and Religion". . . . Do you not think that Ruskin's books owed some of their success to their picturesque and poetic titles?

His basic contention is that four of the most important and valuable pillars of modern life – the respect for (monarchical) government, the respect for private property, the respect for marriage and sexual morality, and the respect for human life – owe their origins to "superstition." As he had already indicated in *Kingship*, he was no longer ready as he had been in his more confident younger days to dismiss superstition – by which he means any belief or behavior not founded on reason – simply as Error. No longer does he conceive that the evolution of mankind was achieved entirely by exceptional individuals thinking their way out of the primeval muddle in which they found themselves.

Man is a curious animal, and the more we know of his habits the more curious does he appear... Yet the odd thing is that in spite, or perhaps by virtue, of his absurdities man moves steadily upwards... From false premises he often arrives at sound conclusions: from a chimerical theory he deduces a sound practice.[44]

From this paradox Frazer drew a conservative conclusion: even if these central institutions were founded on confusion or even lies, as he believed they were, it does not follow that they were therefore rotten or that they should be either reformed or discarded.

A tension is introduced in the introduction to the lecture. Having stated his thesis – that superstition needs an advocate because there is an argument to be made on its behalf – he then limits his subject somewhat, to make it manageable. He will deal only with secular or civil institutions, but he remarks ironically, "of religious or ecclesiastical institutions I shall say nothing. It might perhaps even be possible to shew that even religion has not wholly escaped the taint or dispensed with the support of superstition," but that is not his brief now.[45] This seems both fair and urbane, for he wishes to cast a new light on the familiar bases of social life rather than engage in religious polemic. But that is not what emerges in the most interesting of the four sections, on the institution of marriage.

He offers his usual overfull complement of examples from around the primitive world to show how widespread is the belief that the gods require strict punishment of all who break the sexual code. The belief originated in the supposed sympathetic (or magical) connection between human fertility and that of animals and fields. If illicit sexuality between individuals occurs and is not punished, then the community's food supply will be endangered. Then when magic gave way to religion, the source of the prohibition changed from natural to supernatural and was lodged in divine commandment. But, Frazer says, simply changing the locus of punishment from this world to another is inadequate. "For we must always bear in mind that the gods are creations of man's fancy; he fashions them in human likeness, and endows them with tastes and opinions which are merely vast cloudy projections of his own."[46] Now of course the context is that of paganism, but this is Aesopian language: he has at least potentially offended some of his audience after promising not to do so. The irredeemable foolishness of religion seems to be an *idée fixe*, and in this light one may wonder about his refusal of the teaching post at Manchester. Perhaps he knew himself well enough to doubt whether his self-control would always be adequate to spare the students' beliefs.

This discussion has an added interest. For having once again recapitulated the magic–religion dichotomy, he goes further. Behind primitive religious prohibitions is a still deeper and more mysterious question: how or why is it that, although societies differ greatly, each classifies some sexual relationships as immoral? That is, the judgment that such immorality upsets the natural order must have been arrived at only after people decided that some relationships were in themselves wrong.

The question brings us face to face with the deepest and darkest problem in the history of society, the problem of the origin of the laws which still regulate marriage and the relations of the sexes among civilised nations; for broadly speaking the fundamental laws which we recognise in these matters are recognised also by savages, with this difference, that among many savages the sexual prohibitions are far more numerous, the horror excited by breaches of them far deeper, and the punishment inflicted on the offenders far sterner than with us. The problem has often been attacked, but never solved. Perhaps it is destined, like so many riddles of that Sphinx which we call nature, to remain for ever insoluble. At all events this is not the place to broach so intricate and profound a subject.[47]

It seems appropriate that this lecture was written while Frazer was occupied with *Totemism and Exogamy*, which in turn sparked Freud to compose *Totem und Tabu*, where (among other places in his work) this question is directly addressed.

I have already described the unplanned genesis of *Totemism and Exogamy*, how Frazer "insensibly" found himself appending a grand conspectus of all the occurrences of totemism among primitive peoples throughout the world to the reprints of his earlier work on the subject. In making this compendium he rendered a great service to the anthropologists of his day. Until *Totemism and Exogamy* investigators could be pardoned for specializing in some one area only. But that work, gathering together and examining as it did totemic behavior around the world, henceforth required anyone aspiring to the name of comparativist to assess the local information within a global context. In this sense the unexampled scope of the survey acted as a powerful agent for rethinking the entire subject, and no doubt suggested subjects for further investigation. Indeed, the *Totemism* of 1887, in virtually creating and defining the subject for the earlier generation of fieldworkers, had served to produce many of the data that he was now able to present in *Totemism and Exogamy*. Furthermore, that earlier monograph had itself caused a number of people to become totem-happy, seeing totemism or its traces everywhere. The massiveness and authority of *Totemism and Exogamy* probably had the effect of damping down that particular silliness.

The survey, contained in the first three volumes, is organized geographical-ly; it begins in Australia (Spencer and Gillen having put the study of totemism on a new footing, the place of honor belongs to them) and proceeds to describe totemism among the peoples of Oceania, India, Africa (including much new material from Roscoe, in Uganda), and the Americas. It also describes exogamy when found among totemic peoples, but Frazer insists that no necessary relation exists between these two phenomena.

The fourth volume, which contains the summary and conclusions, along with notes and corrigenda to the first three volumes, has a different sort of interest. Its title notwithstanding, the section is not so much a summary as an analysis, in which Frazer attempts to tease out the characteristic features of these two complex and intertwined institutions. He believes that through an understanding of totemism and exogamy, which are "obviously" primitive, we come as close as possible to origins of human institutions.

His discussion of totemism holds no surprises to a reader of his *Fortnightly* essays of 1905. There are of course new data – in the Banks Islands W. H. R. Rivers has turned up "the original pattern, the absolutely primitive type of totemism" – but he continues to maintain the idea of "conceptional" totemism he put forward in 1905. Regarding the origin of exogamy the answer is less clear. He is of two minds about how the extraordinary complications that characterize exogamy (in which the clan is split into two and sometimes four or eight classes, from only one of which any community member is permitted to find a marriage partner) may be supposed to have begun. He follows Spencer and Gillen in proposing that (at least in Australia) the entire system sprang full-blown from the mind of some primitive lawgiver who, seeing his fellow tribesmen were uneasy about, or prejudiced against, marriages between near kin, promulgated a code forbidding such unions.[48] This suits his predisposition to see the actions of primitives as the products of sustained thought, which in turn authorizes us to criticize such actions as we would those of modern people.

At other times, however, he finds this idea inherently improbable, as in his discussion of North American exogamy. Lewis Henry Morgan, the American anthropologist who first understood the importance of the classificatory system of social relationships, had claimed that the Iroquoian clan system was the result of an all-wise Indian Moses or Lycurgus, who long ago devised it. To this Frazer responds:

It is no longer possible to attribute the institution of these totemic clans to the sagacity of savage law-givers who devised and created them for the purpose of knitting together the various tribes by the ties of marriage and consanguinity. Yet that the subdivision of the whole community into clans had this effect is undeniable.[49]

He seems to be unaware of the contradiction.

For anthropologists today the work holds no interest, although not because of its subject.[50] Totemism as a phenomenon no longer matters because we no longer are obsessed with notions of alleged primitive promiscuity and because the beliefs and behavior that Frazer lumped under the single heading of totemism are now analyzed structurally and functionally rather than genetically. Exogamy, however, as a central concept in the study of social classification and kinship, continues to be of the greatest theoretical interest. Instead, the book has been swept away because its ideological presuppositions have been rejected.

After perhaps thirty years during which "evolution" was virtually unmentionable (largely because it had been taken as the key to all social phenomena in Frazer's generation), anthropologists once again recognize its importance. No one, however, now understands the course of human history as a more or less steady upward march from savagery to civilization, with the presence or absence of institutions like totemism or exogamy as telltale indicators of the stage of development attained. Likewise no one today envisages totemism (or any other social institution) as a "picturesque" fruit of the great overarching banyan tree of superstition, as he did.[51] The condescension implied in "picturesque" has an uglier side too, for the study of totemism, in Frazer's eyes, leads to racist conclusions as well. In view of the content of this passage, it is especially ironic that in his mind this justification of racism commends itself to the observer who "excludes hypotheses and confines [himself] to the facts."

If we exclude hypotheses and confine ourselves to facts, we may say broadly that totemism is practised by many savage and barbarous peoples, the lower races as we call them, who occupy the continents and islands of the tropics and the Southern Hemisphere, and whose complexion shades off from coal black through dark brown to red. With the somewhat doubtful exception of a few Mongoloid tribes in Assam, no yellow and no white race is totemic. Thus if civilisation varies on the whole, as it seems to do, directly with complexion, increasing or diminishing with the blanching or darkening of the skin, we may lay it down as a general proposition that totemism is an institution peculiar to the dark-complexioned and least civilised races of mankind who are spread over the Tropics and the Southern Hemisphere but have also overflowed into North America.[52]

Today such interest as *Totemism and Exogamy* may be said to possess lies in the fact that Freud used it (along with J. J. Atkinson's 1903 essay, "Primal Law") as the anthropological basis for his metapsychological fantasy *Totem und Tabu* (1913). Freud's subtitle is "Some Points of Agreement between the Mental Lives of Savages and Neurotics," and he employs Frazer's analysis of totemism and exogamy to embed his own description of the psychosexual development of the individual in the larger context of the mental evolution of the entire human race. For Freud, totemism and exogamy are of interest because, as manifestations of archaic modes of thought, they present suggestive analogies to the habits of thought that he sees in the mental life of contemporary neurotics. *Totem und Tabu* has not been judged to be among the more successful of Freud's speculations, although not because of its dependence on Frazer.[53] Rather, it has received most criticism because of the just-so story he took from Atkinson that describes the eviction in the "dreamtime" (as the Arunta would call it) by the Father of his Sons as a result of their struggle for sexual supremacy in the Primal Horde.[54]

From the biographical point of view, however, *Totemism and Exogamy* is of interest for two reasons:

1. It offers the best of many examples of Frazer's obsessive trait of discarding nothing and recycling everything. In the preface he never really explains why he is reprinting his earlier work, with which he no longer agrees. Anyone else would have extracted whatever remained valid or useful and jettisoned the rest, but not Frazer.

2. Frazer chose to avoid the vexed question of totemism among the Semites.[55] Although he says that he elected to do so because of the state of the evidence, this omission marks yet another step in his effort, conscious or otherwise, to distance himself from Robertson Smith, for Semitic totemism was virtually synonymous in the public mind with Smith. It may also represent an unwillingness on Frazer's part to enter into religious controversy once again, for any discussion of Semitic totemism must have implications for Judaism and Christianity, and he had had enough polemic in 1901 to last him a lifetime.

13 · FRAZER AND HIS CRITIC MARETT

THE FRAZERS marked the completion of *Totemism and Exogamy* in April 1910 with a long holiday abroad. Both were tired, although it is impossible to know J.G.'s real condition because in their letters Lilly depicts him as exhausted, whereas he describes himself as feeling fine.[1] The fact is, however, that J.G. had been working uninterruptedly and at full stretch (except for the fiasco of Liverpool) since 1901. Although his robust health was proof against seemingly any exertion, even he might have gone a bit stale.

On her side Lilly, who was always prone to respiratory complaints, and had undergone long sieges of illness, had also been experiencing a marked hearing loss. Frazer wrote to Galton on 2 October 1909 that she had been virtually deaf in one ear for some time, and now the hearing in her good ear was going as well. Over the next few years she became nearly totally deaf, and henceforth used hearing aids. In those days, their reliability was poor, and a number of stories have come down about them – a large round apparatus worn on a chain round her neck lavallière-style, or else an ear trumpet when the other was not working, which happened frequently.[2] Like many people whose hearing deteriorates over time, she seems to have become increasingly irritable and suspicious. By the 1930s when Downie came to know her this process was far advanced, and he describes her as quite paranoid, although the subject of her concern was always J.G., never herself. Since the beginning of their life together she had had an *idée fixe* that other scholars were interested only in pumping her good-hearted husband for information and gave him nothing in return. From her point of view they represented only a distraction from his all-important work, and were to be kept away if possible. As she became progressively less able to hear what his callers were saying and to take part in conversation, it became easier for her to believe the worst about their intentions, and she became less willing than ever to allow anyone in to talk with him.

The holiday, which took them to Paris, Munich, Baden-Baden, and then Pontresina in the Engadine, was a success. J.G. had a grand time walking and climbing, while Lilly, never one for strenuous outdoor exertion, nevertheless enjoyed the good air and meeting new people. Both, but Lilly especially, were sad to see the time draw to a close. Writing on 13 June 1910 from their hotel at Pontresina to M.J. Lewis in Cambridge she regrets having to cut short the holiday, especially because the reason for their return is that they cannot afford to stay longer. This is the cue for yet another screed on the injustice of it all. Although nearly two years have passed since their departure from Liverpool the memory still rankles:

At times it seems a little hard that Cambridge has never done anything for J. G. and it was a piece of folly to return to it from mere sentiment from Liverpool where J. G. had found recognition and would have had remuneration if he wished. He, now, as well as I – regrets it bitterly. But for you and two or three friends we are left miserably lonely in the needless grandeur of St Keyne. But there is nothing for it but grin (or groan) and bear it and also J.G. is so tired (tho' unaware of it himself) that he could hardly bear the noise and strain of a great city.[3]

All told they were away for about eleven weeks, coming back to Britain at the beginning of July to face the old problem of lack of money. The grant from the Royal Literary Fund that had extricated them from embarrassment in 1904 had been spent long ago. The £200 pension of course helped, but the other side of the ledger showed many large expenditures. Royalties were down because *The Golden Bough* was out of print and *Totemism and Exogamy* had yet to produce anything, and the expenses incurred in the double move to and from Liverpool had been very high. St Keyne's, their new house in Cambridge, was much too large and therefore very costly to run, but it was the only one available that was even remotely suitable when they returned on short notice, and for that reason they had taken it despite Lilly's misgivings. The predictable result was that Frazer found himself nearly at the end of his savings and heavily overdrawn at the bank.

Lilly, who ran the household, always shielded J. G. from unpleasantnesses like overdrafts because she knew that such information would only make him anxious and therefore prevent him from working. But she could not keep the facts of financial life from him forever, and he was already aware of the bleak realities while they were still on the Continent. He therefore wrote from Switzerland to Macmillan, asking the company to advance him £300 against royalties on the third edition to clear the overdraft, which they promptly did. But as this was only a palliative, on 17 June 1910 he wrote once again to his benefactor Gosse. He outlined all that he had accomplished since he had last been aided by the Royal Literary Fund, explaining that he needed help for only a few more years, until the completion of the third edition would bring with it financial deliverance.

A week later (on 25 June) Lilly also wrote to Gosse; the description from this letter of the early days of their married life has already been quoted. She itemizes their outlays, explaining where their income goes: an unusually high rent (because the owner has just put in electricity), J. G.'s terrifying bills for books and journals, the "one necessary servant." Once again she airs her unhappiness at the decision to leave Liverpool, but J. G. experienced such "an attack of *Heimweh*, uncontrollable at the time," that there was nothing to be done but return. She closes, once again, with her complaint that Cambridge is purblind in ignoring the qualities of a scholar like him.

It has taken all his time, strength and energy to publish as he has – and *Totemism* (we hear from many) would have satisfied many a scholar as the book of his life-time. It has been produced in less than 2 years 1/2!! without *one* single day's break. Is it therefore unnatural if after the completion of such a task a man wishes for some reward from his University or from his Country on whom he has thrown lustre by his industry and intelligence? And can such a reward not be merited without the claim of actual penury?

Although she is an interested party, her contention is not unreasonable. Neither Cambridge nor any other university contains many scholars of Frazer's eminence and productivity at any moment, and it does sometimes happen that such persons are not recognized. The problem, however, had nothing to do with the merits of J. G.'s scholarship. Perhaps because she was brought up in France, and therefore accustomed to a centralized educational system, she seems never to have understood Cambridge's organizational peculiarities. (To be fair, Cambridge's oddities have puzzled many other foreigners, as well as Britons too.) Although the university had been strengthened *vis-à-vis* the colleges in the reforms of 1882, it was still quite weak and insubstantial, especially in financial terms. If the Vice-Chancellor ever thought about it, no doubt he would have said that Cambridge had done nothing for J. G. because the latter, as a college Fellow, had practically nothing to do with the university, at least in its educational aspect. Frazer had his life fellowship from Trinity, but the college was unable to do more either financially or in terms of appointments because he was uninterested in lecturing and no college positions in anthropology existed in any case.

For the first time nothing was forthcoming from Gosse. The Frazer file at the Royal Literary Fund contains nothing from 1910, which is to say that no formal request for assistance was ever made, by either Frazer or Gosse. In the absence of documents it is impossible to know why Gosse and/or Frazer decided not to go forward. It is nearly certain that Gosse could have produced a third grant, for he carried a great deal of weight on the committee and was able to get his own way pretty much at will. An inspection of the Fund's minute book for the five years between Frazer's grants of 1899 and 1904 shows that during that period at least one favored applicant (a journalist named Tom Taylor) was awarded a sixth grant, and that most of those who were helped received amounts under £100, with many getting £50 or less. During those five years, only one person, Joseph Conrad, received more – £300 – and only two others besides Frazer received £250. The Fund was very good to Frazer.

Whatever the reason, Frazer was soon made aware that Gosse and the Fund would be unavailing this time. Less than a month later Frazer writes (on 19 July) to Henry Jackson to ask whether any help might be forthcoming from Trinity College.[4] He candidly outlines his financial situation and concludes that unless he gets some help, he will have to exhaust his "much diminished capital" (a horrifying thing for a nineteenth-century gentleman, fraught as it was with the possibilities of dropping out of the middle class) or else

> look out at once for remunerative employment of some other kind, which at my time of life (I am over fifty six) might not be easy to find and which even if it could be found I should be reluctant to undertake, because it would involve the interruption of the work of literary research to which my whole life has been dedicated.

Jackson's reply has not survived, but it must have been to the effect that the statutes did not permit any such expedient. Apparently Frazer felt unable to approach any of his friends or family for a loan, so it looked as if he would be forced to go ever deeper into debt as he continued to write. For someone with Frazer's capacity for anxiety, such a way of life would soon have become intolerable. But his remarkable luck did not desert him, and he had not to wait long before deliverance was at hand once again. He had resumed work on *The Golden Bough* for only six months when, in February 1911, he was invited to offer two sets of Gifford Lectures at the University of St Andrews. The prestigious and well-paying Gifford Lectureship had been founded at the end of the nineteenth century by a bequest of Adam Gifford (1820–87), a wealthy Edinburgh lawyer and later a Scottish law lord, who proposed that each year a speaker deliver a course of ten lectures on a subject pertaining to the evolution of religion, considered either historically or philosophically.

Frazer accepted immediately. For his subject he chose the belief in immortality and the worship of the dead, to be surveyed historically rather than philosophically. This, he says in a letter to the head of the faculty of St Andrews, is a project that he has "had in contemplation for a number of years."[5] For financial reasons he preferred to start at the earliest possible date, and in fact delivered the first course in October 1911, the second the year following.[6] The payment for each course was a generous £400, which for Frazer meant nearly a year's income; the £800 relieved the financial pressure at home immediately. He therefore set aside *The Golden Bough* for a second time and began preparing the lectures, quarrying them from the notebooks that he had filled in twenty-five years of reading.

While he was doing so, he had a brief but revealing exchange with R. R. Marett. The letters bring together a number of the themes, both personal and theoretical, that go back to the earliest days (the origin and meaning of mythology and the opinions of Robertson Smith) and provide an index of how far he was from the direction in which the analysis of primitive religion was moving. The exchange is especially valuable because his dislike of controversy and his devotion to facts for their own sake together meant that only rarely did he engage in a theoretical discussion, much less a dispute. Finally, the letters show how extensively Frazer had, for his own psychological reasons, re-created and rearranged the ideas of Robertson Smith to make him ratify his current position.

The circumstances were these: in 1910 Marett had been named Reader in Anthropology at Oxford, succeeding Tylor, and on 27 October of that year he delivered his inaugural lecture, entitled "The Birth of Humility," a copy of which he had sent Frazer shortly thereafter.[7] Only on 11 May 1911, about six months later, did Frazer get round to thanking him. Frazer made it a practice of thanking scholars for their books immediately upon receipt and before reading them, so as not to be obliged to express an opinion on the contents. Because he and Marett were by this time good friends he could for once allow himself to react frankly and did not have to be cagy or diplomatic.

Marett was one of a number of scholars who were developing a new critical social psychology, one not based on the old association of ideas, and applying it to primitive religion; he decided, therefore, to make of his inaugural something of a manifesto. Others of this tendency included William McDougall (1871–1938), Lucien Lévy-Bruhl (1857–1939) and, although they are not named in his letter, Arnold van Gennep (1873–1957) and Emile Durkheim (1858–1917). They all rejected Tylor's and Frazer's intellectualist psychology of religion. They rejected the notion that the primitive community was composed of a collection of discrete minds, each separately thinking its own fully formed thoughts, which were directed to the rational evaluation of magical ceremonies and religious doctrine. Instead they were engaged in working out a social psychology that was essentially an analysis of collective ("mobbish" is Marett's jocular word) rather than individual phenomena, one that understood the interaction between individual and group as both complex and all-important, and one that took nonrational states of mind and feeling seriously rather than dismissing them out of hand as superstition or hysteria. Further, like James Ward (and F.H. Bradley), they were willing to make finer discriminations between mental states, to distinguish more different grades of attention than the associationists had previously been willing to acknowledge. From a wider perspective, they were an important part of a wave of interest in the irrational, whether in its vitalist, collectivist, or psychoanalytic forms, that was crescent at the turn of the century.[8]

Which brings us to the letters themselves. After apologizing for not having thanked Marett earlier, Frazer immediately moves to correct what he regards as a "mistake" on Marett's part. In the lecture Marett had explicitly criticized Frazer's intellectualism as inadequate because it did not take account of all the observed facts and had suggested how its explanation of religious psychology might be improved. Specifically, if Frazer was right about magic being superseded by religion, then something more had to be said about the "birth of humility," Marett's phrase for the complex sentiment of self-distrust and self-abasement that must have been experienced by the keenest thinkers in the primitive community as they turned to religion out of their disappoint-

225

ment with magic. For Marett, the failure of intellectualism lay in its inability to recognize the importance of the emotional life of the group (as opposed to its individual members) and to understand that emotion is propagated in crowds because its members take on the feeling "by imitating its outward expression."[9] Marett is referring to recent work in psychology (associated with William James and C. G. Lange) that proposed to understand emotion and behavior associated with it as originating in physiological (that is, subcortical) and not mental stimuli.[10] According to this theory the sensory image of the charging bull suffices to cause adrenalin to be secreted, the heart to beat faster, and the body to mobilize its defenses (in this case, to prepare to run); only *after* and *because* all this happens does the person mentally register "fear." For Marett, who wished to break down the rigid intellectualist distinction between mental and nonmental states, this physiological formulation suggested an analogy in the sphere of religious psychology: that "ritual, or in other words a routine of external forms, is historically prior to dogma [, which] was proclaimed years ago by Robertson Smith and others."[11] It is here that Frazer picks him up.

Allow me to correct what I believe to be a mistake on your part.[12] So far as I know Robertson Smith's views from intimate personal acquaintance as well as from a study of his writings, he never proclaimed that "ritual is historically prior to dogma," as you say he did. On the contrary I believe that he would have rejected such a view (as I do) as a manifest absurdity. What he did say, with perfect justice (and I entirely agree with him), is that many dogmas or myths are historically posterior to the rituals which they profess to explain and are therefore worthless as explanations of them, being mere deductions from them. But to generalise and affirm that myth or dogma is universally posterior to ritual is, I believe, an idea that never occurred to him. On the contrary he always assumed that dogma was prior to ritual, and the whole aim of his investigations was to discover the idea (dogma, myth or whatever you please to call it, in short the thought) on which ritual is founded. That, for example, is his procedure in regard to sacrifice. He assumed, or rather tried to prove, that men sacrificed because they had the idea of communion with a deity and wished to put it in practice. He did not, as I understand you to do, suppose that men sacrificed first and invented a theory or dogma for it afterwards. That is, I believe, in his opinion (as it is in mine) to invert the true relation of cause and effect. But of course he held and proclaimed that the original idea on which a ritual is founded has often been forgotten, and that men then have often invented false and worthless explanations, which the student of the history of religion can and ought to set aside. If you read his remarks on the subject again carefully (in his *Religion of the Semites*), I think you will see that I have interpreted his views correctly. I entirely agree with his views, as I interpret them, and have always acted on them in my writings, laying more stress on ritual than on myth (dogma) in the study of the history of religion, not because I believe ritual to be historically prior to dogma or myth (that I regard as absolutely false), but because ritual is much more conservative than dogma and far less apt to be falsified consciously or unconsciously, and therefore furnishes a far surer standing-ground for research. That and nothing else was, I firmly believe, my friend Robertson Smith's view.

You are not the first who has fallen into this error. A German, R. M. Meyer, in *Archiv für Religionswissenschaft*, ascribed precisely the same views that you do not only to Robertson Smith but to me! to me, who repudiate them as an absurdity.[13] Thus I am apt to think that the view of the universal priority of ritual to myth (which seems to be coming into fashion) is primarily based on a simple misunderstanding of Robertson Smith's views, and has since been supported by what I regard as a misapplication of psychology. Because it is or may be true (I am not able to pronounce an opinion on the question) that in the lowest forms of animal life – protozoa, infusoria, or whatever they are – movement precedes thought or whatever corresponds to thought in these lowly beings, it has been inferred that religious ritual must universally have been performed first and a theory or a dogma of it invented afterwards. I do not think that we have any right to make this prodigious intellectual leap from protozoa to men. Religious ritual even of the lowest savages is a highly, enormously complex phenomenon of thought, sensation, and action, and to compare it to, and to treat it on the same level with, the instinctive twitchings and motions of protozoa, infusoria, or molluscs or the like is, in my opinion, quite illegitimate. Savage ritual, as I have studied it, seems to me to bear the imprint of reflexion and purpose stamped on it just as plainly as any actions of civilised men. Whether that is so or not, you should not claim the support of Robertson Smith for views which I feel sure he would have unhesitatingly rejected. I have some idea of publishing this correction in *Man* in order to prevent others from falling into the same mistake again.

Two days later Marett replied from Oxford.

Now to discuss my alleged mistake in stating that Robertson Smith proclaimed that "ritual is historically prior to dogma." I think you have altogether missed my meaning, owing doubtless to the obscure way, and the (necessarily) cursory way, in which I have expressed it. As the general context was intended to make clear, I meant by *dogma* precisely what Robertson Smith meant by it. See, for instance, *Relig. of the Semites*, 18: "in all the antique religions mythology takes the place of dogma." What he meant by dogma is, I think, manifest from many passages, as, for instance, the following (p. 21):[14] "In ancient religion the reason was not first formulated as a doctrine and then expressed in practice, but conversely, practice preceded doctrinal theory. Men form general rules of conduct before they begin to express general principles in words; political institutions are older than political theories, and in like manner religious institutions are older than religious theories." Dogma in short means, for him, theory or *reasoned* belief. In the absence of any proof that at the back of ancient religion there were "great religious innovators" – men who thought *conceptually* and didn't merely get along with the help of perceptual processes such as imitation – he even goes so far as to speak of "unconscious forces" as having caused the ancient religions to have grown up, and terms the religious tradition itself "unconscious" (see p. 1) – a use of the term in which I could hardly follow him. Well, *that* is what he meant, and what I meant too – that and nothing more. I certainly wasn't thinking about protozoa; and would go further than you apparently would, in doubting whether the protozoon is *entirely* destitute of the rudiments of "thought" in the wide sense that covers perception (as opposed to mere sensation, if there be such a thing) no less than conception.

As to your statement "savage ritual, so far as I have studied it, seems to me to bear the imprint of reflexion and purpose stamped on it just as plainly as any actions of civilised men" (if "reflexion" here means what it ordinarily means in psychology or indeed in plain English), I entirely disagree with it. If you print your view in that form, using the word thus unqualified, I believe that every psychologist in Europe, including

Ward, will be down upon you. No one would be such a fool as to say that there was *no* reflexion at work in savage religion; these things that we distinguish as higher and lower, conceptual and perceptual, processes shade off into each other, so that the difference is always one of *degree* rather than kind. But to say that the stamp of reflexion is *"just as" plain* seems on the face of it to say that both types of religion – the savage and the civilised – are *equally* reflexive, or each in its way as reflexive as the other. If, however, you mean that plainly there is a *very little* reflexion at work in savage religion, and, equally plainly, there is a *great deal* of it at work in civilised religion, then no one will deny that; but they will claim the right, when drawing a broad contrast, to call the former "unreflective" as compared with the latter. And Robertson Smith went further; he called it "unconscious."

Dear me! I seem to myself almost over-vigorous in my style of counter-argument, but, when one is up against a giant like you, one has to lay on hard, or he crushes one with a tap of his finger!

All that some of us – McDougall, for instance, and Lévy-Bruhl, etc., in France – have been trying to do is to emphasise the *mobbish* character of primitive religion and primitive life. Perhaps we have overemphasised it, but it doesn't much matter; there's always a tendency to oscillate before reaching equilibrium.

You, on the other hand, have Howitt and Spencer behind you when you insist that in Australia a primitive legislator was capable of organising the marriage system, etc. Well, such a question must be decided on its merits. Nothing that any psychologist may say about the general "mobbishness" of savages can weigh against the evidence of facts in such a case, supposing the facts to be forthcoming. In your *Totemism and Exogamy* you made out a very good case for an Australian Lycurgus. Well, all the same my saying that they "dance out their religion rather than reason it out" applies, I believe, broadly and on the whole.

Thus I don't believe we greatly disagree about the facts after all.

To this onslaught, Frazer's somewhat abashed but by no means completely defensive response came four days later.

Many thanks for your explanations. I am very glad to find that I had misunderstood you, and that our ways of looking at these matters are not opposed to each other so sharply as I had feared they were, judging from your inaugural lecture. The passages of Robertson Smith to which you call my attention certainly support your interpretation of his view more fully than I had supposed. But I still incline to think that he was emphasising a novel view (the importance of the study of ritual as compared with myth or dogma) and that in doing so he omitted to state (what he probably assumed) that every ritual is preceded in the minds of the men who institute it by a definite train of reasoning, even though the train of reasoning may not be definitely formulated in words and promulgated as a dogma. That at least is my view, and I believe that Robertson Smith would have assented to it. I do not say that savage ritual bears the impress of as much thought as some actions of civilised men; but I do think that it bears the impress of some thought and purpose quite as clearly as many actions of civilised men. That is not, I think, a matter which psychologists are more competent to decide than men who have made a special study of savage ritual. Certainly I do not think that my friend James Ward (with whom I have walked and talked on all subjects in earth and heaven on an average once a week for many years) would claim superior competence as a psychologist in such matters.

There is a notable paradox here. Although Frazer was generally a hard-line rationalist, in writing the prehistory of humanity he stands in the tradition of nineteenth-century romantic historiography in his assumption that the principal causative agent for change was always the individual great man – or in this case, the individual great mind. Translated into primitive psychology, this assumption emerges in the form of his glorification of the unknown heroic proto-scientific thinkers who in their disinterested efforts to understand the natural world first devised magic, and who then forsook it when they saw its fundamental flaws. It is also to be seen in his contempt for the general cloddish mass of the primitive community, who, profoundly conservative in their inclinations and wholly uninterested in thought for its own sake, resist change and only with difficulty can be made to go along with the innovations that their betters, the great thinkers, put forward.

Marett had been right not merely on Robertson Smith's views on myth, dogma, and ritual but in placing him in the anti-intellectualist tradition. Smith, who had his rationalist side, nevertheless had been the first in Britain to put forward an explanation of primitive religion that was essentially sociological rather than psychological.[15] According to Smith, what the ancient religious community really worshiped, and therefore what the gods represented, was the social order – society itself – idealized and divinized. That is, ancient religion provided what we should call supernatural sanctions that legitimize the existing order of things, an order that seemed to the primitive person to be natural and inevitable and therefore divinely ordained.

Because "ancient religions had for the most part no creed; they consisted entirely of institutions and practices," Smith's examination of Semitic religion concentrated on ritual, which was largely totemic and sacrificial in character.[16] In the most notable form of Semitic sacrifice, the tribe consumed the sacrificial animal victim that was their ordinarily taboo divine totem-brother. As Frazer himself had written in his obituary, "Smith was the first to perceive the true nature of what he has called mystical or sacramental sacrifices," the peculiarity of these being that in them the victim slain is "an animal or a man whom the worshippers regarded as divine, and of whose flesh and blood they sometimes partook, as a solemn form of communion with the deity."[17] Smith's idea of the dying god was powerfully and directly influential: as Frazer acknowledges in the preface to the first edition of *The Golden Bough*, "the central idea of my essay – the conception of the slain god – is derived directly, I believe, from my friend [Robertson Smith]."[18]

Smith, then, placed the result of primitive religious ritual in the forefront of scholarly consciousness by asserting that the rite in antiquity took the place of the creed. Rather than attempt to use the myths to shed light on the rites, which seemed only "natural" to Christians who were historically focused on creeds, Smith argued that the true relation would be found to be the other way round. The myths only offered explanations of what the worshiping community was doing in its rituals but were not binding in a doctrinal sense on the worshiper, and therefore the tribesman would not have been bothered by varying interpretations of the same rite, although he would have been made intensely unhappy by varying performances of it. In such a community, in which religion was understood not as a series of propositions to which assent had to be given but as a body of practice and an all-pervasive outlook on life, belief was not obligatory: "what was obligatory or meritorious was the performance of certain sacred acts prescribed by religious tradition."[19] And here is the key sentence:

So far as myths consist of explanations of ritual, their value is altogether secondary, and it may be affirmed with confidence that in almost every case the myth was derived from the ritual, and not the ritual from the myth; for the ritual was fixed and the myth was variable, the ritual was obligatory and faith in the myth was at the discretion of the worshipper.[20]

Basically, Smith asserted, myths have grown up as elaborations upon rituals, and only achieve autonomy when the original sense of these rituals has been misunderstood or forgotten. It follows, then, that the proper way to understand a myth is to examine the ritual it attempts to explain, or if the ritual is no longer extant, then to read backward through the myth and thus to reconstruct the ritual. Smith's description of the formation of myth and his prescription for its study is thus the opposite of Max Müller's, for whom the myths were the inevitable products of linguistic rather than social processes, and for whom ritual was therefore an irrelevance.

Frazer, however, was as generally uncomfortable with Smith's theory of mythogenesis as he was with Smith's theory of sacramental sacrifice. He adopted the former as he did the latter, in the earliest days – the first edition of The Golden Bough – when Smith's influence was strongest. But the letters of 1888 to Jackson and Black show that he had already begun to go his own way early on, even if neither Frazer nor Smith ever publicly acknowledged the growing distance between them. The process of separation from his "ever-to-be-lamented" and "revered" friend had continued in the preface to the second edition of The Golden Bough, where he expressly dissociated his theory of the slain god from Smith's theory of sacramental sacrifice. In 1900 too he was baffled at the way that Hubert and Mauss persisted in connecting him with Smith; now he cannot understand how Marett and Meyer made a similar mistake. Regardless of the passage of time and the intellectual gulf that had opened up between himself and Smith, Frazer found it emotionally necessary to retain Smith's posthumous approval, even if it meant that by 1911 he had to engage in a kind of creative amnesia in order unconsciously to refashion in his own mental image a wholly new Smith, one who agreed with, and thus legitimized, his current position.

All of which leads one naturally to ask where Frazer stood on the questions of the origin and meaning of myth and its relation to ritual, which obviously are central to the survey of the world's mythology carried out in *The Golden Bough*. The answer is that it is not easy to say. The comparison with totemism is illuminating. Regarding totemism Frazer changed his mind twice, in print, and rather than suppressing his earlier ideas he buried them under his new speculations, but at least it is clear that in 1899 and again in 1905 he knew he was changing his mind. Regarding myth and ritual, on the other hand, he seems never to have realized that his many statements were at variance and even incompatible with one another. Only once, and that after he had completed the third edition, does he make an explicit theoretical statement on myth that permits one to say unequivocally what he believed – at least at that moment.

One can find, strewn through the three editions and seventeen volumes of *The Golden Bough*, statements that simultaneously support three different and mutually exclusive theories concerning myth: euhemerism, cognitionism, and ritualism. The first is a hardy perennial dating back to ancient times and much embraced by Enlightenment *philosophes*: that myths are based, however loosely, on real events in the lives of real heroes and kings, who are thus the originals of the gods. Frazer inclined toward euhemerism, especially in his frequent anticlerical moods, because this approach naturally falls in with any attempt to show up religion as an error founded in confusion, imposition, and fraud. To indicate how the three theories coexist side by side, I shall offer one example of each kind, all drawn from the third edition. Inasmuch as this statement of euhemerism appears in the second volume of *Balder the Beautiful*, the last volume in the work, perhaps it may be taken as Frazer's last word (up to 1913):

The acceptance of this hypothesis [that Balder was a real man] would not necessarily break the analogy which I have traced between Balder in his sacred grove on the Sogne fiord of Norway and the priests of Diana in the sacred grove at Nemi; indeed, it might even be thought rather to strengthen the resemblance between the two, since there is no doubt at all that the priests of Diana at Nemi were men who lived real lives and died real deaths.[21]

The second, cognitionism, is Tylor's idea that myths arise from attempts made by primitive mankind to ratiocinate. The results are aetiological tales that explain how the world came to be the way it is: myths are mistaken efforts at scientific explanation. This finds special favor with Frazer in the second edition, when he was most confident that magic is simply a precursor of science, but is to be found often enough in the third edition as well.

But we will have to ask, how did the conception of such a composite deity originate? . . . Was it the attempt of a rude philosophy to lift the veil and explore the hidden springs that set the vast machine in motion? That man at a very early stage of his long history meditated on these things and evolved certain crude theories which partially satisfied his craving after knowledge is certain; from such meditations of Babylonian and

Phrygian sages appear to have sprung the pathetic figures of Adonis and Attis; and from such meditations of Egyptian sages may have sprung the tragic figure of Osiris.[22]

The third, ritualism, begins with two assumptions. The first is that religion originated in man's attempt to control the world by magic, or self-efficacious ritual. The second, derived from Mannhardt and Smith, asserts that man is first and foremost an actor. He *does* something to cause his gods to shine their countenances upon him; he may sing or chant and he will certainly dance.[23] When he moves he acts out what he wants the gods to do for him: assure him a plentiful catch, a bountiful harvest, or a good hunt; make his women or his fields or his cattle bear. Myth arises when, for some reason – a religious reform, or the passage of time that brings with it simple forgetfulness and/or misunderstanding – the ritual falls into disuse, with the result that the words, which had been only (or mainly) the accompaniment to the sacred action, now take on an independent life of their own.

What do these words say? They originally came into being as a "libretto," a description of what the performers or dancers were doing as they imitated the gods enacting something desirable; they now become the stories of the gods' actions themselves – myths. Thus anterior to the myth is the archaic, superseded ritual, and it is the ritual that permits us to examine how primitive man truly thought of himself in relation to the universe. Myths, then, are secondary elaborations of the basic (because older) rituals, and are in that sense less important than those rituals. And of course rituals are more reliable for the study of the history of religion than myths because they are more conservative, whereas myths, made of words, have all the possibilities for textual corruption that Frazer and the other classically trained scholars knew so well.

We shall probably not err in assuming that many myths, which we now know only as myths, had once their counterpart in magic; in other words, that they used to be acted as a means of producing the events which they describe in figurative language. Ceremonies often die out while myths survive, and thus we are left to infer the dead ceremony from the living myth.[24]

With all these explanations floating around together, and with Frazer seemingly untroubled about their coexistence, what is one to think? The simplest answer, already suggested, is that Frazer either did not pursue or did not care about the inconsistent implications of the several theories that he simultaneously embraced; those who regard him as a man without analytical ability will no doubt look no further for an explanation. But other possibilities exist as well. Marett for one returned to the question a few years later, in 1914, in a long review-article on the occasion of the completion of the third edition.[25] There he noted that the distance between Frazer and Smith had increased as *The Golden Bough* had grown. He surmised that Frazer had jettisoned Smith as a matter of intellectual necessity because his new approach to totemism, which insisted that the "magical" totemic and sacramental behavior of the earliest people had to be strictly differentiated from and opposed to anything that might be construed as "religious," required it. This may well be the case, except that it entirely ignores the personal relationship between Frazer and Smith, the complexities of which Marett would not have known. On the other hand, fifty years later Stanley Edgar Hyman, offering a psychological explanation, suggests that such changes in attitude betray a continual, never-ending dialogue within Frazer's mind about religion:

There is a sense in which no one and no evidence ever convinced Frazer, but in which his ambivalent and shifting mind each time found statements and evidence to reinforce positions it had already reached. Thus Mannhardt and Smith appear when Frazer is moving away from the Trinitarian Christianity of his Presbyterian upbringing, Roscoe and Budge when he is moving back to a Unitarian Christianity of his own devising.[26]

I am inclined to go along with Hyman, but I wish the evidence permitted us to specify more clearly the sense in which Frazer continually oscillated and never concluded his spiritual odyssey. The letters of 1888 show that the pre-*Golden Bough* Frazer was aware that the anthropologist had to be alert to his own epistemological assumptions or else run the danger of completely misreading primitive behavior. At the same time it is undeniable that in most of this work such sensitivity and self-consciousness are absent. It does seem as if Frazer was constitutionally unable, except at scattered moments, to maintain the open mind and restrain the rush to moral judgment implied by such a relativistic outlook, perhaps because of the strength of his resentment at the fraud that Christianity represented in his mind. Furthermore, the views of Marett and Hyman are not mutually exclusive, and it is possible that both are right. Whichever (if either) of these interpretations is correct, one is driven to conclude that although Frazer never wavered about rationalism or evolution or the value of the comparative method, he seems to have been willing to change his mind about nearly everything else, and often did exactly that.

To speak decisively, therefore, about Frazer's ideas concerning the origin and meaning of myth and the relation of myth to ritual at any one moment during the quarter-century represented by the writing of *The Golden Bough* is impossible because of the theoretical confusion that obtains on this question in the work. Only if one were prepared to cull what must be scores of utterances on the subject scattered through its pages and then to collate and compare them chronologically could one track how and when his view developed. Such laboriousness, however, could not and would not answer the crucial question of whether he realized at the time that he had in fact changed his mind and the theoretical consequences of such changes. And even if one knew that he was aware that he had altered his position, the result would still be problematic because of his seeming indifference to theoretical self-contradiction. It is important always to keep in mind his statement, often repeated, in the preface to the second edition of *The Golden Bough* about the relative importance of fact and theory:

It has been my wish and intention to draw as sharply as possible the line of demarcation between my facts and the hypotheses by which I have attempted to colligate them. Hypotheses are necessary but often temporary bridges built to connect isolated facts. If my light bridges should sooner or later break down or be superseded by more solid structures, I hope that my book may still have its utility and its interest as a repository of facts.[27]

There being no point, therefore, in compiling such a variorum *Golden Bough*, one notes that the last statement he made, in the final volume of the work (written in late 1913), was definitely euhemerist. But he did emerge from this muddle once and speak unequivocally to this question, in the introduction to the first major work he published after the war – his edition in the Loeb Library of Apollodorus' *The Library* (1921). *The Library* being a survey of Greek myth, it was an appropriate place for Frazer, who had immersed himself in mythology for his entire working life, to describe the nature of his elusive subject:

By myths I understand mistaken explanations of phenomena, whether of human life or of external nature. Such explanations originate in that instinctive curiosity concerning the causes of things which in a more advanced stage of knowledge seeks satisfaction in philosophy and science, but being founded in ignorance and misapprehension they are always false, for if they were true, they would cease to be myths.[28]

A better enunciation of cognitionism may not exist in the works of Tylor. But the point surely is that this passage marks no real change in Frazer's views. He was always a rationalist, even in his ritualist moments. Even when he saw the primitives engaged in re-enacting the stages in the sacred life of the god, in which the ritual was primary and the myth secondary, he still conceived of the myth as being "devised" later to explain the rite fallen into disuse. And of course euhemerism is ultimately just as rationalistic as cognitionism in that both explanations discern in myth some form of conscious, purposive mental activity, either of a speculative–philosophical or a historical–allegorical kind.

But Frazer was not content to rest with this ringing affirmation of intellectualism. Although no one else had repeated Marett's "mistake," evidently his impatience and irritation over the years with those who connected him with Smith and ritualism had been growing. Accordingly, in a footnote appended to this very passage he went out of his way to attack those in the next generation of scholars – the Cambridge Ritualists – who had carried on the ritualist view that he had championed, however uncertainly:

By a curious limitation of view, some modern writers would restrict the scope of myths to ritual, as if nothing but ritual were fitted to set men wondering and meditating on the causes of things. No doubt some myths have been devised to explain rites of which the true origin was forgotten; but the number of such myths is infinitesimally small, by comparison with myths which deal with other subjects and have had another origin. . . . The zealous student of myth and ritual, more intent on explaining them than on enjoying the lore of the people, is too apt to invade the garden of romance and with a sweep of his scythe to lay the flowers of fancy in the dust. He needs to be reminded occasionally that we must not look for a myth or a rite behind every tale, like a bull behind every hedge or a canker in every rose.

Frazer's epistemology has led him up a blind alley, and in the end he seems to have despaired of making any sense of the extraordinary diversity of myth and ritual that he has so successfully displayed to the reader. His metaphors here provide the index to his confusion. Myths, which are the results of "men wondering and meditating on the causes of things," are also and at the same time "flowers of fancy" growing in the never-never "garden of romance"; scholars "invade," cut down the flowers, and make waste. A neater demonstration of the limits of his understanding of the power and function of myth and the methods and utility of mythography could hardly be asked for.

Although the exchange with Marett in 1911 shows Frazer plainly irritated by the way that critics insisted on misunderstanding him, the entire affair was a scholarly disagreement between friends. It never threatened to become ugly, like the controversy with Lang a decade earlier. On the other hand Marett, who could be a formidable polemicist when so inclined, was always gentle with Frazer. He valued their friendship, which meant that whereas he always and unmistakably made known his differences with Frazer, he was at the same time always and genuinely respectful of the older man. As a result, Frazer was always pleased when Marett reviewed his work. Much later, in the thirties, when Lilly Frazer, out of her obsessive need to keep J. G. in the public eye, kept bringing out updated versions of his older work and barely warmed-over collections of his essays, loyal Marett reviewed them all eulogistically, out of a friendship that had withstood many strains for a third of a century.

14 · THE THIRD EDITION

ALTHOUGH IT IS CUSTOMARY to date the third edition of *The Golden Bough* as 1911–15, it really begins with the first version of *Adonis Attis Osiris* in 1906, which Frazer always intended to be one of its parts. Aside from its larger size, the main difference between the 1906 *Adonis* and its counterpart in the second edition of *The Golden Bough* is its increased attention to the scenic element.

Frazer had always paid great attention to the description of landscape, as the publication of *Pausanias and Other Greek Sketches* shows. That collection of scenic gems from the large Pausanias was meant for readers who lacked either the scholarship or the six guineas but who might nevertheless enjoy Frazer's talent for capturing the spirit of place. If we turn the pages of that volume today his evocation of Greece seems hopelessly literary. During the century that has elapsed since he wrote, travel writing has changed as much and in the same psychological direction as fiction. Nowadays the subject is the sensibility of the traveler as much as it is the landscape and what takes place in it. Likewise the style of travel writing has undergone the same realistic flattening as other kinds of narrative. No one today employs so high a style, with so many unusual and archaic words and constructions, as does Frazer.

It is important to realize that this heightening was not superimposed later on, that he did not slog his way through Greece and then invent or re-create its romance and grandeur in the comfort of his Cambridge study. Rather, he seems to have been constitutionally unable to describe what he saw in front of him, and always and immediately abandoned prosaic reality for "fine writing." One can say this with assurance because his field notes from the 1895 trip to Greece have survived. Because he mistrusted his poor memory, his practice in Greece was to write his first impressions in pencil, on the spot, then in the same notebook the same night amplify his pencil notes in ink. The passages in ink then became the working notes for the text. When one compares his diary with the published work, it is remarkable how often the pencil notes have survived virtually untouched and been incorporated directly into print. Here, to take one example of many, is Frazer's description of Daulis, October 1895, written in pencil on location, without erasure or other correction, and therefore offering as direct a transcription of his immediate impression as exists: it was published verbatim in the printed text.

The wild romantic beauty of its [Daulis'] situation well entitles it to its place in the old poetic legends of Greece. This mountain fastness, looking down from its precipices as from an eagle's eyrie on the broad champaign country at its feet, is well fitted to have been the hold of a wild wicked lord like Tereus, of whose bad deeds the peasantry might tell tales of horror to their children's children.[1]

This is an extract from an *aide-mémoire* and meant for no eyes but his own. It therefore cannot be understood as intended to impress a reader; instead, it is a manifestation of his seemingly irresistible instinct to elevate what he *saw* (the sensory channel that counts most is always the visual) into "literature." He did not save this grand style, with its eighteenth-century echoes, for special effects in his books. He wrote like this all the time.

This description of Daulis was extracted from the commentary to an ancient tour round Greece, in which the scenic element is obviously both important and appropriate. *The Golden Bough*, as a contribution to the new science of comparative religion, could not easily offer much outlet to his powerful pictorial tendency. With the exception of the set pieces like the Turnerian opening and the Renanian closing, that impulse had accordingly been largely exiled to the prefaces. But Frazer has now found a justification for enlisting his literary penchant in the service of the immensely enlarged third *Golden Bough*, his *magnum opus*. In the preface to *Adonis* he says that he will be paying more attention to natural surroundings than he had formerly

because I am more than ever persuaded that religion, like all other institutions, has been profoundly influenced by physical environment, and cannot be understood without some appreciation of those aspects of external nature which stamp themselves indelibly on the thoughts, the habits, the whole life of a people.[2]

Although he presents this as a new-minted thought, it is a cliché, going back at least as far as Herder in the 1770s, who proclaimed that the primitive *Volk* had come to self-consciousness through its dialectical relationship with the environment (*Klima*). The interesting point lies in what follows: Frazer says that because he has never been out East, he cannot rely on his own observation to supply this necessary background. He intends, therefore, to overcome this shortcoming

by comparing the descriptions of eye-witnesses, and painting from them what may be called composite pictures of some of the scenes on which I have been led to touch in the course of this volume. I shall not have wholly failed if I have caught from my authorities and conveyed to my readers some notion, however dim, of the scenery, the atmosphere, the gorgeous colouring of the East.[3]

In truth this statement is self-serving because there is little evidence in *Adonis* or the rest of the third edition of any sense that religion has evolved at least in part in response to geography, and by implication to other nonintellectual factors. Instead it acts as a license for him to work up, out of his reading and imagination, the brilliant descriptive set pieces filled with "the scenery, the atmosphere, and the gorgeous colouring of the East" that so characterize the third edition.

This practice of melding various sources into a composite for scenic effect is no different from his handling of anthropological sources. Although his text is studded with footnote numbers, he always believed it to be not merely his right but his obligation to combine the raw data into a pleasing whole. He always understood anthropology to be the science of mankind, which meant that it ought to be accessible to any educated reader. His were the literary imperatives of an eighteenth-century historian – to present his materials in an engaging manner, to delight as well as to instruct.[4]

Aside from this increased attention to scenery – of which there is a great deal – and the immense multiplication of example and incident, the volume contains some wholly new elements. Most noticeable of these is that Frazer spends less time than he had in the second edition in drawing parallels between the religion of Greece and Rome and that of the "lower races." There are fewer speculative leaps from primitive and geographically remote peoples to those of the eastern Mediterranean, fewer conjectures about ultimate origins, less speculation than might have been expected about, say, the origin of sacred prostitution being found in the alleged sexual communism of the primeval horde. Appropriately, the largest part by far of his evidence comes from the history and archaeology of the Near East; much less is heard about Australia and the other exotic locales that featured so prominently in the second edition. Perhaps such (relative) discipline[5] means that he had taken to heart the misgivings of some classical scholars, who were becoming increasingly uncomfortable as Frazer and those who followed him proceeded to annex classical religion to ethnography.[6]

At the heart of the book, of course, stand Adonis, Attis, and Osiris, who continue to be conceived as incarnations of the spirit dwelling within vegetation and whose rituals continue to be understood as the dramatic enactment of the despair of the worshipers at the apparent death of the green world, followed by their joy at the return of life in the spring. No opportunity is missed to point out resemblances between those often bloody and "obscene" cults and that of Christianity. Sometimes the parallels are merely mentioned, without elaboration, in order to underline the idea that human needs and wishes are the same everywhere and at all times, and to make the reader see that motifs regarded by Christians as uniquely their own appear in other epochs and other places. At other times they furnish occasions for irony, especially when he can score at the expense of a clerical establishment. Here, for example, he gratuitously yokes the sacred prostitute of the ancient Near East and the modern nun:

[The prostitutes'] vocation, far from being deemed infamous, was probably long regarded by the laity as an exercise of more than common virtue, and rewarded with a tribute of mixed wonder, reverence, and pity, not unlike that which in some part of the world is still paid to women who seek to honour their Creator in a different way by renouncing the natural functions of their sex and the tenderest relations of humanity. It is thus that the folly of mankind finds vent in opposite extremes alike harmful and deplorable.[7]

The final sentence illustrates why Gibbon was the historian whom Frazer most admired.[8]

Already in 1906 he is drawing back from the aggressive irreligion of the second edition. Although they are geographically appropriate, the Sacaea, the Saturnalia, and Purim, of which so much was made in 1900, are absent. He takes pains to dissociate himself from the notion that Jesus was a mythical being, as some of the hard-line brethren in the rationalist camp had recently been arguing.[9] Instead he compares Jesus with Buddha, whose historical reality he affirms as well; forsaking Gibbon for Matthew Arnold, he says that both are "beautiful spirits," such as appear from time to time to "support and guide our weak and erring nature."[10]

Whatever their theological role, Jesus, Buddha, and other such ethical reformers are absolutely necessary to Frazer's epistemology and philosophy of history. For he finds it impossible otherwise to imagine how humanity made the great leaps forward from primeval stupidity to magic, and then from magic to religion, and finally from religion to science. "The attempt to explain history without the influence of great men may flatter the vanity of the vulgar, but it will find no favour with the philosophic historian."[11] Clearly Frazer sees himself as of the company of such historians, with his unique subject being the philosophical description of those unable to aspire to philosophy themselves. The euhemeristic note struck here in *Adonis*, the affirmation of historical originals behind the gods, becomes increasingly important through the third edition.

Once *Totemism and Exogamy* had been completed and he and Lilly returned from their holiday in July 1910, he was at last free to turn to the long-delayed completion of the third edition. In his special interleaved copy he had started to update and rework the second edition as far back as 1902 and had kept steadily at it throughout the first decade of the century. By 1910, therefore, he already had a good deal of manuscript in hand. Now it finally began to flow to the printer, and in a stupendous sustained eruption of continuous reading, writing, and proofreading that lasted for four years the entire third edition appeared. Whatever one thinks of *The Golden Bough*, this episode is so prodigious as a feat of scholarly industry that its details bear recapitulating.

He first brought out Parts I, II, and III, in that order, in rapid succession: in March 1911 the two volumes of *The Magic Art and the Evolution of Kings*; two months later *Taboo and the Perils of the Soul*: five months after that, *The Dying God*. (These four volumes of 1911 alone came to 1594 pages, the mere

239

proofreading of which would suffice to occupy most people for months.) Part IV, *Adonis Attis Osiris*, having already appeared in 1906, he then passed directly to the two volumes of Part V, *Spirits of the Corn and of the Wild*, which came out in July 1912; September 1913 saw the publication of Part VI, *The Scapegoat*, and the two volumes of the final section, Part VII, *Balder the Beautiful*, appeared in December 1913. (These five volumes amounted to a further 1798 pages.) He then reread *Adonis* in the light of the third edition, found it wanting, and expanded it to two volumes (640 pages) in April 1914. The twelfth volume, the Index (536 pages), amalgamating the indexes of the separate volumes, and including a master bibliography, came out in April 1915.

While the third edition was thus cascading forth, he also found time to write and deliver twenty Gifford Lectures in 1911 and 1912 and see them through the press as *The Belief in Immortality* in March 1913 (a mere 495 pages); edit in June 1912 two volumes of the letters of William Cowper, which he prefaced by a 100-page biographical introduction; rewrite (that is, enlarge) *Psyche's Task* in September 1913; and write a brief contribution to the Festschrift for his friend William Ridgeway in December 1913. As Marett humorously protested in his review of *The Magic Art*, "Dr Frazer writes faster than his disciples – and all of us are such – can read."[12]

The Magic Art is no exception to the rule that Frazer's prefaces repay close reading: here the interest lies in its confessional tone. The tactical retreat from irreligion continues but on a broader scale. He is now willing to admit the adventitious nature of the priest at Nemi. He acknowledges that the priest is and has always been little more than a rhetorical device to aid the reader in moving through the tangled undergrowth of the argument. Not only was the priest a convenient way for the reader to keep in mind the direction and meaning of the narrative, but he also had his artistic value, which Frazer renders in a typically pictorial metaphor:

By discarding the austere form, without, I hope, sacrificing the solid substance, of a scientific treatise, I thought to cast my materials into a more artistic mould and so perhaps to attract readers, who might have been repelled by a more strictly logical and systematic arrangement of the facts. Thus I put the mysterious priest of Nemi, so to say, in the forefront of the picture, grouping the other sombre figures of the same sort in the background, not certainly because I deemed them of less moment but because the picturesque natural surroundings of the priest of Nemi among the wooded hills of Italy, the very mystery which enshrouds him, and not least the haunting magic of Virgil's verse, all combine to shed a glamour on the tragic figure with the Golden Bough, which fits him to stand as the centre of a gloomy canvas.[13]

Therefore, although *The Magic Art* begins the way that readers have come to expect, with an expanded[14] version of the Turnerian and Virgilian prologue, and although Frazer says in the preface that he will from time to time continue to connect the argument of the entire *Golden Bough* to the explication of the riddle of the grove, yet he is already preparing the reader for the possibility that the sacrificial priest may himself have to be sacrificed. Behind this maneuvering lies Cook's cogent criticism of 1902: that Frazer was unwise to rest so heavily on the mystery of Nemi because the appearance of a better explanation of that ritual might mean the dismissal of the entire *Golden Bough*.

Even if it should appear that this ancient Italian priest must after all be struck from the long roll of men who have masqueraded as gods, the single omission would not sensibly invalidate the demonstration, which I believe I have given, that human pretenders to divinity have been far commoner and their credulous worshippers far more numerous than had hitherto been suspected. Similarly, should my whole theory of this particular priesthood collapse – and I fully acknowledge the slenderness of the foundation on which it rests – its fall would hardly shake my general conclusions as to the evolution of primitive religion and society, which are founded on large collections of entirely independent and well-authenticated facts.[15]

The Magic Art is unique within the third edition in that it represents a revision not of the second edition but of an intervening text, the *Lectures on the Early History of the Kingship*, much of which it incorporates. From *Kingship*, then, the main theoretical change is some misguided blurring of the hitherto sharp antithesis between magic and religion in response to Marett's continued criticism. Acknowledging that Marett has caused him to rethink the issues, Frazer comes up with a confused formula that is both inconsistent with his own individualist associationism and does not go far enough to satisfy a "mobbish" social psychologist like Marett. As in the exchange of letters he will have with Marett a few months later, in 1911 (see Chapter 13), he concludes that the difference between them

seems to be mainly one of words, for I regard the supposed mysterious force, to which he gives the Melanesian name of *mana*, as supplying, so to say, the physical basis both of magic and of taboo, while the logical basis of both is furnished by a misapplication of the laws of the association of ideas. . . . However, in deference to his criticisms I have here stated the theory in question less absolutely than I did in my *Lectures*.

His insistence that their differences are only quibbles means that he never really understood what Marett was saying. In the end he emerges with a fudged statement that "the whole doctrine of taboo, *or at all events a large part of it*, would seem to be only a special application of sympathetic magic, with its two great laws of similarity and contact."[16]

This "doctrine of taboo," thus understood as negative magic – the system of prohibitions regulating what may not be done, as charms describe what may be done – is the subject of Part II, *Taboo and the Perils of the Soul*. With the exception of the preface and thirty-three pages on the taboos affecting hunters and fishermen, it consists entirely of material from the second edition, amplified and brought up to date. In the first and second editions he had investigated taboo as the divinity that doth hedge about the sacred priest-king. The preface and the new pages, however, indicate that the issue raised in *Psyche's Task* – the complex and ambiguous relationship between "superstition" and the evolution of morality – had become a theme of abiding interest for Frazer. This large question, however, was not easily accommodated within the structure of the second edition. For this reason the tension between the direction in which the logic and structure of the second edition is taking him and the direction in which he would like to move produces a distinctly regretful preface, in which he chafes at being unable to treat the whole of the phenomenon of taboo. Frazer, however, was never excessively stern with himself about keeping to the beaten path, and in the new discussion of hunters and fishermen he allows himself a digression on the larger question of the evolution of ethics.

His comments grow out of a difference of opinion with another scholar on the meaning of the custom of the confession of sins, a difference that takes on added interest because the other anthropologist is his German-American contemporary, Franz Boas (1858–1942), the leading spirit among those emphasizing the importance of history in the study of primitive society. He quotes Boas at length concerning the many taboos that must be obeyed by Eskimo whale- and seal-hunters. If a hunter violates any of these prohibitions, then he must confess publicly or else he and his fellows will be dogged by bad luck and maybe even death. For Boas, who eschews large speculations about the origins of religion, the behavior is explained parsimoniously: the transgressor confesses in order to warn others away from himself and from any objects he may have polluted as well, lest those others likewise become contaminated unknowingly. Frazer, hunting whales himself – his prey is the evolution of magic into religion – will have none of so simple and utilitarian an explanation.

It seems more probable that originally the violation of taboo, in other words, the sin, was conceived as something almost physical, a sort of morbid substance lurking in the sinner's body, from which it could be expelled by confession as by a sort of spiritual purge or emetic.[17]

He presents many examples of peoples who do indeed administer purges to expel evil, understood as a noxious physical entity within the body that must be vomited forth. From this "lower" stage, primitive humanity then moves to a more metaphysical understanding of evil as a moral taint that cannot be literally expelled. Once evil is so construed – and by implication Frazer places the Eskimos at this level of moral development – then confession takes on a new meaning, becoming an accommodation on a higher level to a more complex moral view. It now marks humanity's recognition that it cannot cope with the world on its own, that the only recourse is to admit one's failings to an all-powerful god who will then pardon repentant sinners.

This comfortable doctrine teaches us that in order to blot out the effects of our misdeeds we have only to acknowledge and confess them with a lowly and penitent heart, whereupon a merciful God will graciously pardon our sin and absolve us and ours from its consequences. It might indeed be well for the world if we could thus easily undo the past, if we could recall the words that have been spoken amiss, if we could arrest the long train that follows, like a flight of avenging Furies, on every evil action. But this we cannot do. Our words and acts, good and bad, have their natural, their inevitable consequences. God may pardon sin, Nature cannot.[18]

At this point Marett, who quotes this passage in his generally negative review of the book, can stomach no more and launches into an uncharacteristic tirade. To him these words show that Frazer's philosophy is of the eighteenth and not the twentieth century, that he is the spokesman for a "complacent and systematic rationalism of a day when evolutionism was not."[19] Further, Frazer errs in believing that the

evolution of spirit [is] to be likened to such a lifeless "flux" as the redistribution of the particles of matter. Evolution conceived as a purely mechanical process – a moving platform – is of no use to anthropology. Bad philosophy can never make good science. Dr Frazer may justly claim to have enlarged the mental horizon of his generation by his encyclopaedic labours; but the philosophic interpretation of his vast conspectus of the facts of human life is vitiated by his failure to observe the fundamental fact of all – that life is life, and, as such, is evolving towards fuller life. In other words, life is evolving, not from "God" towards "nature," but from "nature" towards "God."

To which outburst one may remark that: (1) It is not true that bad philosophy can never make good science. There is no obvious connection between merit as a scientist and merit as a philosopher.(2) Further, from our vantage point three-quarters of a nightmarish century later, some of us may be pardoned if we prefer Frazer's stern mechanism to Marett's optimistic vitalism, if only because in holding out no hopes it leads to no disillusionments. This is not to exonerate Frazer from the charge of complacency (as in "This comfortable doctrine"), especially in his earlier work. But it does seem as if, for all his bookishness, his condescension toward the primitives, and his addiction to a priori simplification, as he grew older his moral vision deepened. His rejection of ambiguity softened and became less absolute, and in the third edition he was more able, because more willing, to accommodate complexity. Although in many ways Marett was a man who touched more of life than did Frazer, Frazer may have gone further here.

Although Part III, *The Dying God*, is only fourth of the eleven volumes, it contains the symbolic heart of the work. Its subject, which grows directly out of the study of royal taboo in *Taboo and the Perils of the Soul*, is the killing of the divine king when his powers seem to flag. To the primitive mind this is necessary because such a king is no mere political leader; rather, he is a leader only because he is believed to incarnate and preserve the cosmic order, to mark the nexus of the human and sacred worlds. Thus, were he permitted to grow ill or grow old in the natural way, the doctrine of magical sympathy implies that his people and his land would decline as well, which is intolerable (in different ways) to both the general population and the primitive metaphysician.

Frazer had asserted that the primitive king had to be killed and his divine soul passed unenfeebled to his successor in order to preserve the world, but in the second edition he acknowledged that there was no good evidence to substantiate that this had ever happened.[20] Some reports both ancient and modern existed, but they were unsatisfactory because they always described events that took place in the long-ago past. This lacuna caused Edward Westermarck to suggest that if the divine king had ever been killed, it was more likely so that his holiness and not his soul might be transmitted.[21] But, just as Spencer and Gillen's description of the *intichiuma* ceremonies had arrived in 1898, exactly when Frazer needed empirical evidence for the distinction between magic and religion, so in 1911 C. G. Seligman (1873–1940) providentially produced the divine kings of the Shilluk, precisely when Frazer was writing *The Dying God*.

Charles G. Seligman – he spelled his name Seligmann until 1914 – was a brilliant physician who in the 1890s had moved from pathology into physical anthropology.[22] In 1898, despite the fact that Haddon had already decided the makeup of his expedition to Torres Straits, Seligman at virtually the last minute talked him into allowing him to come along. The trip changed his life (as it did that of everyone in the group); afterward he devoted himself entirely to anthropology, doing significant fieldwork with his wife, Brenda, in New Guinea, the Sudan, and Ceylon. It was in the second of these locales, in 1910, that he came across the Nilotic peoples called the Shilluk and the Dinka.

On 3 December 1910, newly returned to London, he wrote to Frazer, whom he did not then know, the following unsolicited letter;

Dear Dr Frazer,

I am now writing up the material I collected in the Sudan during the first half of the present year. My Shilluk and Dinka information will please you, the Shilluks have Divine Kings, incarnating the spirit of the semi-historical, semi-divine founder of the nation who according to the genealogies lived from 20 to 26 generations ago. Until the last few years the king was ceremonially killed when he began to get old or invalidish, his grave becoming a very holy shrine. The king is killed by a special family in conjunction with some of the heads of the different districts into which the Shilluk country is divided. (I use the term district rather loosely.) If the stories and beliefs of the people themselves mean anything there was before this a period when anyone (of the royal blood?) who could get at the king and kill him became king. This is of course the merest outline.

Among the Dinkas, who never seem to have been anything but a mass of independent, and often hostile tribes certain big rain-makers were killed when they became old. These people incarnated the spirits of specially celebrated ancestors. The matter among the Dinkas is complicated by the extreme fervour of their ancestor worship, and their totemism. Some tribes being almost completely totemic, others being so little totemic that without the intermediate stages one would doubt their totemism.

I shall probably have a fairly coherent sketch of these two religions ready in 6 weeks to 2 months from now.

I don't know when you will be bringing out another volume of the new Golden Bough, but if the time is favourable and if you care to have a copy of my material for publication in this I shall be pleased to send it to you.[23]

Frazer doubtless indicated the keenness of his interest to Seligman, who, true to his word, on 1 February 1911 sent him a brief typescript summing up his findings on the Shilluk and authorized him to make use of them. These were that the Shilluk regard the king as the current manifestation of their culture-hero Nyakang, who is believed to be immanent in all their kings; that the king is not suffered to weaken in his physical powers, lest his weakness be communicated to the people, and their crops wither and their animals die; and accordingly, when he is seen to be waning, he is killed in a ceremonial fashion.[24]

Seligman's information, the first modern, reliable evidence for sacral regicide, came as something of a bombshell. It subsequently had two very different effects. For Frazer, it acted to shift his area of principal interest henceforth from Australia to Africa, and consequently his main anthropological collaborator from Baldwin Spencer to John Roscoe.[25] In the anthropological world, it has been the occasion for much disputation. In the three generations since the 1920s, which have seen a thoroughgoing reaction against all things Frazerian, it has been reviewed several times, most notably by E. E. Evans-Pritchard, who denied all of Seligman's basic contentions (and Frazer's use of them).[26] He and the other anti-Frazerians find part of the problem in the fact that, like Baldwin Spencer, Seligman admired Frazer from the start, and this admiration therefore affected – which is to say, distorted – his research. Although Seligman has never been thought of as a true-believing Frazerian, that he should write to Frazer before publishing his results and that when he did publish he should describe his findings as explicitly supplying the "missing link" in Frazer's hypothesis imply that the latter's theories had indeed influenced his research and thinking.

Such influence may be judged regrettable, but it is natural and indeed inevitable. All scholars are affected by what they read, which in turn affects what and how they henceforth see and think. Moreover, it is simplistic to imagine that the effects of a book or a theory are straightforward or unequivocal in any of its readers. Malinowski was a self-described Frazerian when he went to Melanesia, and he can hardly be said to have been an intellectual disciple subsequently.

The problem (if it is one) arises from the unavoidable fact that all ideas come from somewhere. Like all English-speaking anthropologists at the time, Seligman read Frazer. It cannot be surprising, then, that Seligman, who had been moved or impressed or fascinated by Frazer's notion of divine kingship, and within whose consciousness that notion was lodged, then paid special attention when he came upon a state of affairs that seemed to correspond remarkably well with what he had been reading and thinking about. In any event, Seligman's data, as disseminated by Frazer, have subsequently acted as a mighty spur to research into the social and political structure of African societies; since the 1920s numbers of fieldworkers have claimed to discern the presence of "Frazerian divine kingship" among other African tribal peoples. Claims, some convincing, have been made on both sides; reasonably objective observers have concluded that something like this pattern of kingship does seem to have existed in several places in Africa.[27]

Part V, *Spirits of the Corn and of the Wild*, is really a continuation of *Adonis Attis Osiris*, which precedes it. That volume benefited from its geographical focus, limited as it was to three cults of the ancient Near East. These two volumes, more diverse, continue and extend the Mediterranean motif. They begin with Dionysus, the god of grain and grape and goat, whose death and resurrection as represented in myth and ritual resemble in a number of respects those of Adonis and the others. Dionysus leads naturally to Demeter and Persephone and their many worldwide analogues, from which it is but a small step to Lityerses, in neighboring Phrygia. Frazer then descends from the so-called higher (or agricultural) races to hunting, fishing, and pastoral societies. One might think that such peoples, who have occasion each day to see that their existence depends literally on the death of animals they use for food, would not range themselves under the same resurrectionist banner. This, however, would be an error, for they too believe that their animals, as incarnations of their gods, are likewise immortal. Frazer explains this behavior animistically, for the savages in their visions or dreams of dead men and animals take them to inhabit what we see as the "void" after death.

Although Frazer claimed never to see the point of Marett's criticism, and asserted that their differences were essentially verbal, these two volumes show that the truth is otherwise. In the past Frazer had been content to point to and largely deprecate the primitives' simplicity and misunderstanding, which only illustrated the size of the evolutionary gap between them and us. Now, however, whether in reaction to Marett, or to Hubert and Mauss in Paris in their complex analysis of sacrifice, or Jane Harrison in Cambridge in her sociological and psychological discussion of Greek festivals, the later volumes of the third edition do seem to show Frazer taking more of an interest in the psychological states of awe and reverence that surround and imbue the performance of magic.[28]

It would be an exaggeration to say that Frazer has changed fundamentally. The beliefs are the same, but the tone is different. In these and subsequent volumes he seems to be a little less impatient with what had been merely seen as foolish fumbling by the primitives. His new willingness not to rush immediately to judgment is illustrated in one of his extended visual metaphors:

The circle of human knowledge, illuminated by the pale cold light of reason, is so infinitesimally small, the dark regions of human ignorance which lie beyond that luminous ring are so immeasurably vast, that imagination is fain to step up to the border and send the warm, richly coloured beams of her fairy lantern streaming out into the darkness; and so, peering into the gloom, she is apt to mistake the shadowy reflections of her own figure for real beings moving in the abyss. In short, few men are sensible of the sharp line that divides the known from the unknown; to most men it is a hazy borderland where perception and conception melt indissolubly into one. Hence to the savage the ghosts of dead animals and men, with which his imagination peoples the void, are hardly less real than the solid shapes which the living animals and men present to his senses; and his thoughts and activities are nearly as much absorbed by the one as by the other.[29]

Humans attain knowledge only where the pale cold light of reason shines – the old Frazer once again – but the area of our knowledge is now pitifully small in comparison to our ignorance. In view of that fact, the mistakes that the primitives make in confusing wish and reality are not so much derisory as all-too-human and understandable. He seems somehow to have achieved a new compassion, if not a new understanding, for those mistakes and by extension for the people who make them.

This budding sense of complexity is heightened by Frazer's willingness to acknowledge that primitive religion is more than merely the inflation to mythic dimensions of the basic biological need to survive. Obviously we must eat and drink, but as soon as those needs have been satisfied, the sexual instinct must be reckoned with as well.

The study of the various forms, some gross and palpable, some subtle and elusive, in which the sexual instinct has moulded the religious consciousness of our race, is one of the most interesting, as it is one of the most difficult and delicate tasks, which await the future historian of religion.[30]

This statement about sexuality shows Frazer edging into new territory. An analysis of the connection between the sexual instinct and religion is a task not for him but for "the future historian of religion." Nevertheless, he senses that the light by which he has been steering until now is somehow inadequate, and he seems also to have gained some idea of the quarter in which additional illumination is to be sought.

Nor is that all. Frazer now sees that human social development is the result of more than the play of powerful instincts within the boundaries established by the regulations devised by primitive savants. He says that much that is uniquely human arises from purely social (as opposed to biological) forces, which amounts to an admission that individual psychology alone is insufficient to explain human development. Unfortunately Frazer the would-be sociologist is a will-o'-the-wisp; whatever he may have glimpsed, it has all come too late. He was unable to abandon the habits of a lifetime, but it is nevertheless worth noting his response to a tendency very much "in the air" at the time. Thus:

The need of mutual protection, the economic advantages of co-operation, the contagion of example, the communication of knowledge, the great ideas that radiate from great minds, like shafts of light from high towers, – these and many other things combine to draw men into communities, to drill them into regiments, and to set them marching on the road of progress with a concentrated force to which the loose skirmishers of mere anarchy and individualism can never hope to oppose a permanent resistance. Hence when we consider how intimately humanity depends on society for many of the boons which it prizes most highly, we shall probably admit that of all the forces open to our observation which have shaped human destiny the influence of man on man is by far the greatest.[31]

Up to this point, however, as its title implies, *Spirits of the Corn and of the Wild* is essentially an overgrown but nonetheless direct descendant of the Mannhardtian discussion of the first and second editions, where the general behavioral pattern, as well as the psychology that underlies it, were built up from a massive mosaic of the folklore of the farmer and woodsman. To be sure, preagricultural societies have been levied upon as well, thus broadening the picture, but the overall pattern is the same. If the first volume of *Spirits* illustrates the legacy of Mannhardt, however, the second (*mutatis mutandis*) is all Robertson Smith. Here the focus is on the propitiation, sacrifice, and eating of the divine animal, and we are next door to totem sacraments. Twice – and both times it comes as something of a shock – Frazer remembers the priest in Nemi, who is now like Uncle Toby in *Tristram Shandy*, whom Sterne left for many chapters climbing the stairs, with one foot suspended in the air.[32] But otherwise he makes no attempt to connect the overall argument, which is based (especially in the second volume) on the folklore of the world, to the goings-on at Nemi, which now seems very far away indeed.

In comparison with the corresponding section in the second edition, there is only one change in Part VI, *The Scapegoat*, but it is an important one. In his discussion of the greatest scapegoat of them all, Frazer retracts his inflammatory speculation that Jesus had been crucified as Haman in the Palestinian Jewish version of the Near Eastern death-and-resurrection ritual. Being Frazer, however, he could not suppress it totally but instead reprinted it as a note at the end of the book. His interesting reasons for doing so are these:

The hypothesis which [these pages] set forth has not been confirmed by subsequent research, and is admittedly in a high degree speculative and uncertain. Hence I have removed it from the text but preserved it as an appendix on the chance that, under a pile of conjectures, it contains some grains of truth which may ultimately contribute to a solution of the problem.[33]

In fact he had attempted to prop up the theory before semi-abandoning it as he has. Although he does not specify his "subsequent research," it was this: in 1900 A. A. Bevan (1856–1930), Professor of Arabic in Cambridge, sent a copy of the new second edition of *The Golden Bough* as a gift to his teacher, Theodor Noeldeke (1836–1930), a well-known Orientalist at Strasbourg.

Noeldeke wrote two letters to Bevan about the book, one of which (dated 12 January 1901) has survived in part.[34] Noeldeke, although unwilling to accept all of Frazer's theories – he was critical about Frazer's willingness to believe that the ubiquity of *Märchenmotiven* was the result only of diffusion, and he rejected out of hand the speculations about the Haman–Jesus connection – was generally more favorable in his response than most British reviewers had been. He certainly went along with Frazer's assumption that the "superstitions" widely found among European peasant folklore were directly inherited from the ancient world, and that one might therefore employ, as Frazer did, examples drawn from contemporary peasants to illustrate modes of thought allegedly current thousands of years ago.

With Noeldeke's permission Bevan showed the letters to Frazer, who did not attempt to reply to their objections. Instead, encouraged by Noeldeke's moderate tone, Frazer wrote to him directly (on 11 May 1901) to ask his opinion about a different, albeit related, matter.[35] J. S. Black had sent Frazer an article on the Book of Esther by a German scholar named Winckler, who said that the Persian gods Homanos and Homadatis mentioned by Strabo as having been worshiped at Zela had been identified by a scholar named F. C. Andreas with Haman and his father Hammedatha. Frazer asked Noeldeke, who knew Andreas, what he thought of these identifications. If Noeldeke were to agree with Andreas, then Frazer might be well on his way to another scholarly coup. He would have come up with crucially important support at exactly the right time for an admittedly speculative but potentially explosive theory.

If Noeldeke agreed with Andreas, Frazer writes that he was then prepared to pile conjecture upon conjecture as follows: (1) in the passages in question Strabo was writing about the mound of Semiramis, "whose identity with Ishtar (Esther) was made highly probable by Robertson Smith"; (2) the Persian goddess Anaitis "had doubtless succeeded to the position formerly occupied by Ishtar at this place; probably the old worship went on as before with nothing but a change of name due to the Persian conquest." This means (3) that at least at Zela

both Esther (Ishtar) and Haman were worshipped down to the time of Christ, and as we both know from Strabo that the Sacaea was celebrated at this very sanctuary, the identification of Purim with the Sacaea becomes almost certain. Further, one of the strongest objections which has been made to my theory of the Crucifixion and its effects would be removed. It has been objected that even if Christ had been crucified as Haman, this could not have helped to spread his religion in Asia Minor, since no one then any longer regarded Haman as a deity. But if Andreas is right, Haman was worshipped as a deity down to the time of Christ in that very part of Asia Minor (eastern Pontus) where we know from Pliny that Christianity had struck firm roots by the end of the first century. This, you will see, squares exactly with my theory that the crucifixion of Christ in the character of Haman materially contributed to secure his recognition as a god among Asiatic peoples who were already familiar with the conception and the ritual of the death and resurrection of a god, whether he was called Tammuz, Adonis, Haman, or what not.

Noeldeke apparently replied quickly, for Frazer begins his response of 26 June with an apology for not having written sooner. The delay had arisen because he had been making other inquiries among historians of Iranian religion elsewhere, consulting among others the Cambridge Sanskritist E. B. Cowell (1826–1903) and the Belgian Orientalist Franz Cumont, along with his friend J. H. Moulton. Noeldeke must have expressed grave doubts about Andreas's identifications, and these were echoed by Moulton. From his sources Frazer learned that the similarity between the names was entirely coincidental and therefore without significance: the Iranian Vohumanah was in fact a personification of wisdom and goodness, which is as far from the villainous Haman as could be imagined. Frazer tells Noeldeke that he has therefore decided to dismiss Andreas and to forget the dazzling string of speculations that he had been ready to advance. He concludes:

I thank you sincerely for your criticisms of my suggestion that the crucifixion of Christ in the character of Haman (if it took place) may have contributed to the deification of Christ and the spread of his worship to Asia Minor. I give much weight to the objections you make to that suggestion, so much indeed that I am at present inclined to withdraw the suggestion entirely. Perhaps before a new edition of my book is called for, some fresh and decisive evidence may turn up to confirm or refute my theory.

In the face of this unanimous chorus of expert disapproval Frazer will *not* give up. Everyone has poured cold water on the suggestion, and he knows that he must retreat, but he is still unwilling: "Perhaps some fresh and decisive evidence may turn up." Frazer's luck ran out here, however, for nothing did turn up. To anyone else this would imply that the theory was worthless and should be discarded; Frazer could never bring himself to delete anything, so the theory is exiled to an appendix.

His explanation, quoted above, for reprinting is worth attention. He is doing so, he says, because this theory, its admitted inadequacies (that is, no evidence in favor and much against) notwithstanding, "might contribute to a solution of the problem." To which one might well ask: *which* "problem"? The so-called problem exists only because Frazer has created it in his equation of Jesus and Haman, which in turn rests on his identification of Purim with the Sacaea, which in turn stands on the putative connection to the Saturnalia, and so on in a chain of conjectures that extends out to the intellectual horizon. That he has no evidence whatever seems not to disturb him at all; not many scholars could remain so confident in the face of such odds. The combination of intellectual toughness and a mild and retiring disposition constitutes an abiding paradox in his life and work.

The two volumes of *Balder the Beautiful* (Part VII) bring *The Golden Bough* to an end. At the same time that they finally return the reader and the narrative to the priest at Nemi, they continue the revisionist trend. Having already scrapped the equation of Jesus and Haman, here at the conclusion of this longest journey Frazer proceeds blithely to announce that the very identity of Balder is now open to question, seemingly regardless of the fact that in doing so he destroys the theoretical coherence of the entire work. In 1900 Frazer had argued that the tree guarded by the priest was an oak and the golden bough a branch of mistletoe with which his challenger sought to kill him. If this were the case, then the priest as a representation of the vegetation spirit of the tree might be compared with the otherwise invulnerable Balder, who was killed by just such a branch of mistletoe. In both cases the mistletoe contained the external soul of each.

Now, however, in the final preface (dated 17 October 1913), in which he sums up as he takes leave of the entire enterprise that has "occupied and amused me for many years," he says that, far from insisting that both are members of the same class of sacred beings, the entire question has become virtually a matter of indifference to him.

Though I am now less than ever disposed to lay weight on the analogy between the Italian priest and the Norse-god, I have allowed it to stand because it furnishes me with a pretext for discussing not only the general question of the external soul in popular superstition, but also the fire-festivals of Europe, since fire played a part both in the myth of Balder and in the ritual of the Arician grove. Thus Balder the Beautiful in my hands is little more than a stalking-horse to carry two heavy pack-loads of facts. And what is true of Balder applies equally to the priest of Nemi himself, the nominal hero of the long tragedy of human folly and suffering which has unrolled itself before the readers of these volumes, and on which the curtain is now about to fall. He, too, for all the quaint garb he wears and the gravity with which he stalks across the stage, is merely a puppet, and it is time to unmask him before laying him up in the box.[36]

In short, *The Golden Bough*, which began a quarter-century earlier as a digression from a general work on primitive mythology, is finally revealed to have been that mysterious general work all along. The priest at Nemi, the golden bough, and Balder, along with all the other topics he has discussed at such length, are mere puppets, narrative devices to hold the reader's interest while their creator stalks bigger game: nothing less than the evolution of the human mind itself in its slow and often crabwise climb to the full rational self-consciousness that we know as science. Having admitted that he has really had his eye all along on such larger matters, however, he is now strangely unable to give a clear account of the real subject of the work, or of the conclusions that will stand in place of the now-discarded mummery with the priest and the bough. It is as if he can no longer recall the path he has blazed through the trackless forest. The best he can manage is a statement of the difficulties that beset any such labyrinthine inquiry: in addition to the obvious matter of the absence of records, there is the problem of dispelling the mists of prejudice from before the reader's eyes that make it virtually impossible for us to inhabit the mental world of the primitive.

Having said that, he offers a few statements that, so far from being novel, might have been taken verbatim from the preface to the first edition of 1890. We have once again the "essential similarity of the working of the less developed human mind among all races, which corresponds to the essential similarity in their bodily frame as revealed by comparative anatomy." But, whereas the outline and direction of physical development is unequivocal, the critical difference introduced by the fact of cultural diffusion makes it impossible finally to be sure about the true course of social and mental evolution. This is virtually the first time that he has recognized the existence, much less the importance, of diffusion, not to mention the problems it poses for a theory like his that has insisted that the ratiocination of numerous individual thinkers, meditating solitarily and disinterestedly on the constitution of the world, is the principal means by which humanity has progressed.

But the equation of the priest and Balder is by no means the only important question on which he has changed his mind. He now jettisons his older theory about the nature of European fire festivals. Under the influence of Mannhardt, he had understood them as essentially inspired by sympathetic magic, as performances intended to renew the power of the sun. Although he continues to believe that this view has some merit, he now accepts Westermarck's explanation that they are primarily purificatory in their purpose, so that the bonfires are meant to burn away all the noxious entities, physical and spiritual, that threaten human life.

Having gone that far, he goes further: he now believes that the evil against which these fire festivals were directed was witchcraft, and the ritual climax of these festivals either actually or potentially was the burning of witches.[37] This prompts a reflection that again only resurrects a remark in the 1890 preface, except that now it is pronounced as the product of twenty-five more years of continuous reading, writing, and thinking on the subject. As such, it has a gravity that recalls the apocalyptic warning that he sounded (using the same metaphor) in *Psyche's Task*, four years earlier. In his view the defeat of witchcraft and other such irrational obsessions was not and never can be final, and that if ever the vigilance of the rational governing classes were to slip, the old insanity would start back to life and come boiling up. In an amazing throwaway remark he says that our only reason for hope lies in the fact that the peasants have been leaving the land and migrating to the city, where they adopt new and more progressive modes of thought. Once again we have a fleeting sociological gleam:

The truth seems to be that to this day the peasant remains a pagan and savage at heart; his civilization is merely a thin veneer which the hard knocks of life soon abrade, exposing the solid core of paganism and savagery below. The danger created by a bottomless layer of ignorance and superstition under the crust of civilized society is lessened, not only by the natural torpidity and inertia of the bucolic mind, but also by the progressive decrease of the rural as compared with the urban population in modern states; for I believe it will be found that the artisans who congregate in towns are far less retentive of primitive modes of thought than their rustic brethren.[38]

The master metaphor of progress that informs the entire *Golden Bough* implicitly sets up expectations that, in rhetorical terms, are completely undercut by *Balder the Beautiful*. In discarding the priest at Nemi, whose presence had so powerfully affected the work's structure and atmosphere, in changing his mind about fire festivals, and in reiterating at the end of the third edition only what he had said at the beginning of the first edition, Frazer in one sense is pulling the rug out from under the entire enterprise. For this reason, and in view of the length of the arduous ascent of humanity toward the light – not to mention the length of the third edition of *The Golden Bough* – it is easy for us to imagine a reader of the whole work disappointed at having traveled so long and so far only to find that in a sense he had never departed at all. But in fact such was not the reaction at the time; few if any felt let down in that or any other way. Although scholarly critics continued to point to shortcomings in each part as it appeared, the work was widely reviewed in the public press, and there the reaction to the whole was overwhelmingly favorable.

There is another important question on which Frazer has a new position in *Balder*, although it does not figure in his catalogue of recantations in the preface. The issue, already touched upon in Chapter 13, is the origin and meaning of mythology, and it is ignored perhaps because he was unaware that he had changed his mind. Despite his continuing theoretical inconsistencies, Frazer had steadily been moving away from ritualism and toward euhemerism. In the *Adonis* of 1906 he found it necessary to affirm the historical reality of Jesus. In the years that followed he was tugged further toward euhemerism by the work of two scholars: his friend John Roscoe and the leading Egyptologist (Sir) E. A. Wallis Budge (1857–1934).

In 1907 Roscoe published a brief article on "Kibuka, the War God of the Baganda," in *Man*.[39] It had originated in the following circumstances: during the civil wars in Uganda of 1887–90 the Muslims managed to burn down many temples of the old religion, including the large shrine dedicated to Kibuka. But before this happened Kibuka's priest had prudently emptied the sanctum and buried the sacred relics, among them the god's shield, jawbone, umbilical cord, and mummified genitalia. Roscoe had then met the priest, whose financial embarrassment was greater than his scruples about selling the sacred objects. Roscoe bought them sight unseen. Having promised the priest that he would not open the parcel containing the remains within Uganda, Roscoe sent it to the Museum of Ethnology in Cambridge. When he returned to England in 1907 he opened the parcel, there to find the abovementioned items. So far as he was concerned, this was proof positive of the human origins of Kibuka. He therefore wrote that "Most people [among the Baganda] now believe Kibuka to be a spirit only; but the fresh light thrown upon his history, together with the indisputable fact of his corporeal relics, prove the deity to have been a human being." Because of the use to which Frazer subsequently put this narrative, there is no doubt that Roscoe had convinced him as well of Kibuka's human origins.

In 1911 Budge published the massive two-volume work, *Osiris and the Egyptian Resurrection*, in which he argued that Osiris was to be identified with a real man, King Khent-Amenti of the shadowy First Dynasty, and that the undoubted vegetational aspects of his cult were later accretions. The evidence for this was that the god incorporated the attributes of the saintly Khent, that the tomb of Osiris was traditionally identified with that of King Khent, and that (in Frazer's words) "in this tomb were found a woman's richly jewelled arm and a human skull lacking the lower jawbone, which may well be the head of the king himself and the arm of his queen."[40]

In a speculative leap that is amazing even for Frazer, he now connects these Egyptian finds and Roscoe's Kibuka. It seems that the tomb of "Osiris–Khent" is about a mile and half from Osiris' temple at Abydos.

There is thus a curious coincidence, if there is nothing more, between the worship of Osiris and the worship of the dead kings of Uganda. As a dead king of Uganda was worshipped in a temple, while his headless body reposed at some distance in a royal tomb, and his head, without the lower jawbone, was buried by himself near the grave, so Osiris was worshipped in a temple not far from the royal tomb which tradition identified with his grave.[41]

That is, because Osiris and Kibuka, separated by a mere five thousand years and two thousand miles, have in common the fact that their *membra* were indeed *disjecta*, separated from the place where they were worshiped, Frazer concludes that

Perhaps after all tradition was right. It is possible, though it would be very rash to affirm, that Osiris was no other than the historical King Khent of the first dynasty; that the skull found in the tomb is the skull of Osiris himself; and that while it reposed in the grave the missing jawbone was preserved, like the jawbone of a dead king of Uganda, as a holy and perhaps oracular relic in the neighbouring temple. If that were so, we should almost be driven to conclude that the bejewelled woman's arm found in the tomb of Osiris is the arm of Isis.[42]

This amazing farrago of nonsense has its exact analogue at the end of *Balder the Beautiful*. In the text, after an exhaustive survey of the fire festivals of the world, Frazer concluded that the Balder myth, and especially the narrative of his death, bore a strong resemblance to the many European customs in which mock victims are thrown into the fire. Inasmuch as these latter are most probably survivals of primitive times when human representatives of the spirit of vegetation were sacrificed, Balder's myth was probably best understood in the same way, that is, ritually:

If I am right, the story of Balder's tragic end formed, so to say, the text of the sacred drama which was acted year by year as a magical rite to cause the sun to shine, trees to grow, crops to thrive, and to guard man and beast from the baleful arts of fairies and trolls, of witches and warlocks. The tale belonged, in short, to that class of nature myths which are meant to be supplemented by ritual; here, as so often, myth stood to magic in the relation of theory to practice.[43]

In the notes to the same volume, however, Frazer tells a different story. Note III, entitled "African Balders," brings together a number of accounts of African chiefs who allegedly could be killed only by an apparently insignificant weapon and who were "real men of flesh and blood who lived not long ago and whose memory is still comparatively fresh among their people."[44] A comparison of these stories with that of Balder now confirms Frazer

in the suspicion that Balder himself may have been a real man, admired and loved in his lifetime and deified after his death, like the African sorcerer, who is now worshipped in a cave and bestows rain or sunshine on his votaries. On the whole I incline to regard this solution of the Balder problem as more probable than the one I have advocated in the text, namely that Balder was a mythical personification of a mistletoe-bearing oak. The facts which seem to incline the balance to the side of Euhemerism reached me as my book was going to press and too late to be embodied in their proper place in the volumes. The acceptance of this hypothesis would not necessarily break the analogy between Balder in his sacred grove on the Sogne fiord and the priest of Diana in the sacred grove of Nemi; indeed, it might even be thought rather to strengthen the resemblance between the two, since there is no doubt at all that the priests of Diana at Nemi were men who lived real lives and died real deaths.[45]

Thirteen years earlier, in the preface to the second edition, Frazer had presented himself as the servant of the truth, following the facts wherever they might take him. But in following these African facts down the euhemerist trail, he has succeeded in making a complete hash of the argument of *The Golden Bough*. The confusion here is total. The "African Balders" were real men, therefore the Scandinavian original was too. The priest of Diana in Nemi was a real man, albeit one killed as a representation of the mythical spirit of the oak; therefore, by some inverted logic, the real men round those Norse bonfires may have been serving a god who was once a man but who has become mythic. I am unsure whether this is what Frazer has in mind. Whatever he intended, the text is unintelligible.

The inconsistencies and illogicalities undoubtedly exist – although nothing comes close to this muddle at the end of *Balder* – but it would be a mistake to exaggerate their importance. For in the overall context of the whole third edition, they are as nothing. As the volumes appeared, and its immense scope began generally to be appreciated, it was universally acclaimed despite its inadequacies as one of the intellectual monuments of the age. It was often said that *The Golden Bough* as a whole had fundamentally changed the way that educated people understood both human history and contemporary behavior and institutions. Because the volumes of the third edition received such extensive critical attention, Frazer's ideas – or at least their general drift, along with a few central images and metaphors – quickly passed into intellectual currency in the English-speaking world in the 1920s. In addition, many people who could not afford the ten-shillings-per-volume price sought the work out in the public libraries. He had something for everyone: educated persons enjoyed his prose style and were impressed and moved by the immense intellectual sweep of the work, which seemed to comprehend and clarify so much, and implicitly justified the role of the British Empire as well; the new and not-so-well-educated middle class were told by the newspapers that *The Golden Bough*, at least in its abridged form, was one of those books that any thoughtful person *had* to know about; the self-educated among the working class and aspiring intellectuals and radicals read *The Golden Bough* for its explanation of how society and religion had begun in primitive confusion and misunderstanding.

From this point onward Frazer may be said to have two reputations. For anthropologists, increasingly interested in studying social structure and function in primitive societies rather than in assigning them to places in the evolutionary hierarchy, he seemed more an irrelevancy than anything else. Even as honors came to him, he was dismissed by his colleagues, especially the younger ones, as out of date. On the other hand, however, by the majority his works were hailed as those of a prophet and seer. From our perspective it may seem as if there was some truth in both judgments.

As a publishing venture the third edition was a thundering success for both publisher and author. Frazer had been right to believe that if only he were able to complete the third edition, his financial worries would be over. At some time unknown he had changed the basis of his publishing arrangements with Macmillan: he now had a royalty contract. For the third edition of *The Golden Bough*, his royalty (in Britain) was an extraordinary 25 percent, and with the success of the work the sums in question must have been very large.[46]

It is received wisdom among publishers that, however glowing the reviews, reader interest in multivolume works or series falls off rapidly, and therefore one prints fewer copies of later volumes than of earlier ones. In the case of *The Golden Bough*, however, interest remained so high throughout that this maxim was nearly belied. Macmillan began by printing 1500 copies of the early parts because that had been the size of the print run for the second edition. These sold out so quickly that they had to be reprinted at the same time that succeeding parts were appearing. By the time the last two parts were ready, Macmillan ventured a first run of 2000 copies, and they too had to be reprinted virtually immediately. The sales were huge in absolute terms, and not merely in comparison to Frazer's earlier books or to other anthropology or other nonfiction. Between March 1911, when *The Magic Art* came out, and November 1922, when Frazer's own one-volume abridgment appeared, no fewer than 36,000 copies of all volumes of the third edition were printed. Even after the publication of the abridgment (which in eleven years sold more than 33,000 copies at a price of eighteen shillings per copy), the twelve-volume edition remained in print throughout the 1920s, and each volume was reprinted two or three times during that decade.[47] The epitome has remained in print continuously (in paperback since 1957), and the twelve-volume edition was reprinted by Macmillan as late as 1977.

15 · HONOR TO THE KING

THE PREFACE TO *Balder* is dated 17 October 1913. At longest last *The Golden Bough* was complete.[1] I suspect that J.G. had promised Lilly when they returned ignominiously from Liverpool five years earlier that they would leave Cambridge once he finished the third edition. Promise or not, the time had come. In late 1913 Frazer announced that he and his wife would be leaving for London in the new year, their date of departure to depend upon the sale of their Cambridge house and the access to their new home, 1 Brick Court, in the Temple.

Frazer's having dutifully studied law nearly forty years earlier had an unforeseen but happy result. Because he had been admitted to the bar from the Middle Temple, he was entitled to apply to live in one of the residential chambers there. Here was the answer to Lilly's prayers: a desirable address in London, at a reasonable rental, in a pleasant flat large enough for the two of them (and most of his library) and yet small enough for her to manage on her own. Furthermore, in this new existence, their lives would be organized somewhat more equitably than they had been in the past. No longer would the furthering of his work be the *sole* criterion for any decision or arrangement; henceforth her wishes would be catered to as well.

It had not escaped the notice of his friends and colleagues that the completion of *The Golden Bough* and the end of his residence in Cambridge would coincide very nearly with his sixtieth birthday, on New Year's Day, 1914. On such occasions a gift or other token of remembrance was customary, and a group of his friends gathered to decide what it should be. No doubt the usual portrait and Festschrift were mooted. It cannot have been easy to think of something that would genuinely please him, for Frazer was a man totally without vanity and had no interests other than his work. Someone came up with the perfect idea: a Frazer Anthropological Research Fund, its *raison d'être* the award of travel grants to anthropologists to do fieldwork. F. M. Cornford, secretary of the committee, wrote to explain the proposal to Frazer and ask whether it met with his approval; if it did, the committee would act.

There then ensued a series of letters at once touching and comical.[2] On 1 February Frazer wrote to Cornford that he was pleased by the idea and flattered to be associated with it. He would prefer that his name not be used, but if the committee thought it advisable to name the fund after him, so be it. A week later (8 February), however, he had second thoughts. He still liked the idea, but "I see objections, which I regard as insuperable, to the proposal to institute such a fund in my honour." His scruple lay in the fact that his friends would be levied upon to contribute to a project, however worthy, in order to do him honor. "Most of my friends are poor men, many of them with families to support and with many pecuniary claims upon them." (Who did he have in mind? When nearly all scholars were gentlemen, perhaps only Haddon, Roscoe, and Malinowski among his academic friends were in relatively straitened circumstances. For none of the nonacademic group was the prospect of a subscription of a guinea or two calamitous. But even one impecunious friend would have been enough for him to think the worst.) In his imagination he had already foreseen that some would give though they lacked the means to do so, and thus stint themselves or their loved ones, or else they would refuse to give; either way he would give them pain and cause them to resent him. Therefore, although he continued to think the idea of a research fund admirable, and was even willing to join the organizing committee and support it financially, he could not agree to lend his name to it.

Cornford's response may be inferred from Frazer's next letter to him (14 February). Cornford seems to have said that, an anthropological travel fund being fairly recherché among good causes in this world and human nature being what it is, the chances for the fund's success were nil if it were not named for him. Sadly recognizing the justice of this argument, Frazer then agreed and for a second time allowed his name to be used.

Cornford immediately began writing to a long list of possible supporters within the worlds of scholarship and letters.[3] A number of replies, all dating from spring 1914, are extant, and with one exception all were in the affirmative: among them were Lord Gower, A. J. Balfour, Viscount Bryce, and A. H. Hawkins in politics; Cumont, Diels, Doerpfeld, Durkheim, Westermarck, and Wissowa among the scholars. The exception was Sir Walter Raleigh, professor of that new subject, English literature, at Oxford. Raleigh (1861–1922) may have been a lightweight as a scholar, but he was an astute critic. He would send Frazer a personal gift to mark the occasion but was not interested in associating himself with Frazerian (or any other kind of) anthropology:

Frazer is (a beautiful writer, but) essentially a hard-bitten eager rationalist, whose work is a long statistical satire on religious belief. I love him, and I don't believe a word of it. Man is a creature that plays fast and loose, but always plays. Frazer takes the good Lord too seriously. He'll be frightfully put out when he's told that God in his private capacity (as the Scotchman said) is often facetious about the acts he feels bound to perform in his public capacity.[4]

Others (unnamed) raised a different objection, based on the inherently costly nature of fieldwork as an activity. Unless supporters were prepared to replenish the fund when, inevitably, it ran low (as it would fairly quickly, after only a handful of expeditions had been financed), the whole enterprise might prove embarrassingly short-lived.[5] This was the state of play, with numbers of people approached and agreeing to participate and with some money actually collected, when, like most other scholarly projects, the fund was put aside at the outbreak of the war.

The Frazers became tenants of their chambers, which consisted of four rooms on the third floor, in March 1914 and gradually installed his library.[6] They actually moved into the Temple in mid-June. He fell in love with it immediately: as he wrote to Gosse on 27 June, "I have already fallen under the spell of the place, which seems to me an enchantress hardly less potent than Trinity." Part of this enchantment was its associations with one of his favorite writers, Joseph Addison, whose essays he edited in two volumes as the first work he undertook in his new life in the Temple. The Addison, which appeared in February 1915, was a literary *divertissement* that he allowed himself as an indulgence upon completing *The Golden Bough*. Although none of the *Spectator* papers relates directly to the Temple, the place is itself a splendid example of Queen Anne London. With his sensitivity to landscape and his lifelong sympathy with the early eighteenth century, perhaps all that was needed was the view from his window to set his imagination working. Frazer in the Temple was the very opposite of Frazer in Liverpool. This time there was total harmony between man and setting.

The introduction to the essays shows his delight in the Addisonian atmosphere. Instead of something solid, such as the sizable biographical essay that he wrote to preface his edition of Cowper's letters of 1912, he produced a bubble: an unexpected and for that reason all the more successful imitation of Addison in his Sir Roger de Coverley style. The preface purports to be a newly discovered *Spectator* paper that he (Frazer, the editor) has found. He continued in this vein in a charming series of further occasional papers that claimed to be unpublished essays by Addison about Sir Roger. These appeared in magazines in 1915 and 1916 and were later collected as *Sir Roger de Coverley and Other Literary Pieces*, in 1920, and then once again, with further Sir Roger papers, in *The Gorgon's Head*, in 1927.

On 22 June Frazer was knighted. As is so often the case, this honor led to others. In June 1920 he was inducted into the fellowship of the Royal Society, the first anthropologist to be so recognized. The same month he received an honor that must have been especially esteemed by Lilly: at long last he was made D.Litt. by Cambridge: at the same ceremony his friends Ward, Gosse, and J.J. Thomson, along with Henri Bergson, also became doctors of the university. In 1925 he became a member of the recently founded Order of Merit, a high distinction in that the Order, composed entirely of persons who have distinguished themselves in science, literature, or the arts, never has more than twenty-four members at any one time and usually has fewer.[7]

The normally retiring Frazer seems to have accepted these marks of public recognition largely to gratify his wife. She reveled in being Lady Frazer and never let anyone forget who she was.[8] Lilly Frazer was in every way a more vivid personality than J. G. Unencumbered by the need to maintain the persona of the serious scholar, she was far more outspoken and direct and certainly wrote more exciting and excited letters than he did, in her inimitable Franco-English style and with her own breathless punctuation. Among the best of these is a series to their old friend, M. J. Lewis. The Frazers had been friendly with the Lewises for some years before the move to London. After the move Lilly, whose deafness made the use of the telephone impossible, kept up with Lewis by post. Here is part of the first London letter from Lilly, dated 26 July 1914: it replies to one of Lewis's that warmly congratulated J. G. on the knighthood. From it we learn that not all Frazer's friends were so magnanimous.

All I do know is that your letter was particularly nice and gave us both *very* great pleasure. I read it out to J. G. and (I *confess* to *you*) I passed [over] the word *condole* you used in fun – "Congratulate with him and (condole) with him" – the reason being that a former fellow of Trinity – (I may as well mention him to you – feeling that you will not refer to it in *any* way) Mr Wyse – has caused us deep and bitter harm by two horrid letters which point almost to mental derangement *and against* the title [namely, the knighthood], against our dwelling here, against Everything! By an unfortunate chain of circumstances the first Reproach!! reached here just as J. G., beaming in countenance and resplendent in (borrowed) millinery returned from the Investiture having appreciated the beauty of the Palace and the gorgeous spectacle of all the uniforms blazing on that sunny day of June. It *did* cloud our brilliant sky and it did *hurt* and therefore your kindly fun – "condole" was surpressed [*sic*] by me, reading aloud! Mr Wyse knows perfectly, as you all do who know J. G., that if he accepted the title [it] was so that *I* had a chance of sharing publicly in his honour – ; he also thought that had his Mother been alive she would have *wished* him to accept simply, as being more dignified than a haughty refusal, etc. – anyhow he was (after some first *jibbing*) and is pleased – Mr Wyse, who is ill and was always a mass of cramped prejudices, only tried to wound *me*, but he little knows his friend. To wound J. G. *thro' me* is to doubly wound him! That was our *only Gnat* in the ointment and your friendly congratulations came all the more welcome as they followed a second and still more violent leter from Mr W! J. G. will soon forget it all in work and he is very well and very fit and in full swing of work again. . . . J. G. is always highly strung and far more sensitive – almost touchy, than one could guess from his manner – the result of overwork – I am doing my best to reduce that and have succeeded so far in his consenting to give up work after dinner . . . P.S. I do hope people will not arouse Heimweh in J. G. by saying (as many do) "How could you ever tear yourself away from Cambridge." It is just a mere form of speech but J. G. takes *all* literally![9]

It is fitting that Frazer's knighthood came in June 1914, for that brilliant summer provided (metaphorically speaking) the last good weather that Britain would see for more than four years. Long before the leaves had fallen war had come. As with many middle-aged and elderly Britons, the war at first seems to have changed little in Frazer's life. One says "seems" because relatively few of Frazer's letters are extant from the latter half of 1914. One reason may be that his brother Samuel, whom Downie described to me as "near-alcoholic," died in May of that year, and J.G. as elder brother and titular head of the family was doubtless involved in settling the estate and other family matters. Accordingly one must focus on his publications, for despite family upheavals and the travail of moving house and library, Frazer never stopped working, nor is there a gap in the letters to Macmillan.

Once he was again installed among his books, he was eager to get back to work. In late 1914 he was occupied with the Addison essays and the index volume to *The Golden Bough*, which duly appeared in February and April 1915. Once they are out of the way (he writes to Macmillan on 27 May 1914), the next major item on his long agenda is to be *Folk-Lore in the Old Testament*, on which he had been working fitfully since 1907. He plans to use the essays he had contributed to the Tylor, Darwin, and Ridgeway volumes as its nucleus, to which he would add the results of his continuing study of the Old Testament.[10] The most important of these additions was a long dissertation on the worldwide legend of a great flood that he would be giving as the Huxley Memorial Lecture in November 1916.[11] He expects (he writes) to have completed the (single) volume by the end of the year. On 12 April 1915 he is still describing *Folk-Lore* to Macmillan as "a comparatively small book in one volume." Needless to say, it did not appear until three years later, in November 1918, and when it did, it had become three large volumes. The delay was largely but not entirely a matter of his compulsion to expand his books endlessly. Even for one so singleminded in his devotion to work as Frazer, the war did gradually come to make a difference.

Along with *Folk-Lore* Frazer was also working on the second volume of *The Belief in Immortality and the Worship of the Dead*. The first volume, published in 1913, contained his Gifford Lectures of 1911 and 1912; it had been rather lost in the great flood of *The Golden Bough*. But even if it had not been obscured by the timing of its publication, it is hard to envisage its intended audience, for it is nearly entirely given over to minutely detailed reports of native beliefs about the afterlife.

It is a survey, organized geographically, of the universal belief in some form of life after death: this volume is devoted entirely to the aborigines of Australia and the natives of New Guinea and Melanesia. Volumes two and three, describing in like manner the beliefs of, respectively, the Polynesians and Micronesians, appeared in 1922 and 1924.

As such it resumes the theme of his first independent foray into anthropology, the paper on funeral customs delivered to the Anthropological Institute back in 1885. A comparison of the two shows that although Frazer now knows immensely more than he did thirty years earlier, not much has changed on the theoretical side. Characteristically, like the essay of 1885, the book's intellectual framework is implicit and is presented allusively: Frazer simply assumes (à la Tylor) that the basic evidence among savages for life after death is that provided by dreams. And, as in 1895, Frazer's second assumption throughout is that the vast engine of funeral superstition is powered only and entirely by fear of the dead and of ghosts. Nowhere does he intimate that the natives might be motivated by affection or reverence for the departed or that they might even be indifferent to those gone on before. In short, the psychology is exactly that of the letters to Jackson and Black a quarter-century earlier, when the question was whether religion was rooted in fear or love of the gods. Frazer, that last best son of the Enlightenment, comes down unquestionably on the side of fear. All three volumes of *Immortality* employ the same rhetorical strategy as *The Golden Bough*, in that he never misses a chance, in an ironic or sarcastic aside, to remark resemblances between "savage" beliefs and Christianity.

Until 1914 Frazer, in common with most Western intellectuals, admired Germany as the world center of scholarship and science. With the advent of war, like nearly all Britons he became a patriot, which is to say intensely anti-German. Perhaps his patriotism was all the keener because, aged sixty and with no practical skills to put at the service of his country, he was unable to convert his sentiments into action. Despite the relative paucity of his letters from the war years, there is some evidence of his activities in this direction.

He did make several quasi-political gestures. The first took place at the outset of the war. In October 1914 Gilbert Murray, who had by then given himself over nearly totally to Liberal politics, circulated a manifesto among scholars and writers supporting the war; among others he asked Frazer to sign. Frazer declined, wholly out of native caution – the document referred to German statements that he had not seen – but the possibility that he was simply ignorant of the issues should not be ruled out.[12] In a letter to Lewis, Lilly says that at this period Frazer never even glanced at the newspaper, despite the fact that it was filled with war news that most people found gripping. Inasmuch as his productivity was due in part to his willingness to screen out *everything* not connected with his work, and Lilly conceived it part of her wifely office to keep the number of scholarly visitors to a minimum, his inattention to current affairs may have been of long standing.

The second occasion was the *cause célèbre* in 1916 surrounding Bertrand Russell's lectureship at Trinity.[13] Even before Russell's case made the headlines, the public felt, and not without reason, that Cambridge was full of supporters of conscientious objection, anticonscription agitation, and other similar "unpatriotic" causes. On 22 January 1916 a special meeting of the Fellows was convened to discuss whether a Fellow might hold meetings in his rooms of "members of a society invited to promote its objects, these being neither illegal or immoral." This meeting, which came to be seen as a vote of confidence in the College Council's management of college affairs, had been called in response to the Council's banning of a meeting in a Fellow's rooms of the Union of Democratic Control, an organization critical of the conduct of the war. Although Frazer generally took no interest whatever in public questions, he loved Trinity and cared deeply about its welfare; accordingly, he made what was for him a considerable effort, forsook his work for an entire day, and attended. Although the votes of individual Fellows were not recorded, the conservative group carried the day and endorsed the Council's action; in the light of later events, it is safe to assume that he voted with them.

By 1916 Russell's support of pacifist causes had made him notorious. In June of that year he was convicted of publishing "statements likely to prejudice the recruiting and discipline of His Majesty's forces" under the Defence of the Realm Act and fined £100 and costs. Because of this conviction, the Council in July voted to strip Russell of his lectureship. The reaction was a little while in coming, but in November of that year, twenty-two Fellows sent a memorial to the Council expressing their dissatisfaction with its action. Cornford, though at forty-two too old for active service, had become a gunnery instructor in the army; he nevertheless remained interested in college affairs and asked Frazer to sign the petition. He refused; in a letter of 16 November 1916 he replied that he would not sign because "I take a serious view of Mr Russell's offence, and am of opinion that the Council of the College was right in depriving him of his lectureship. I will not go into my reasons now. Perhaps I may have an opportunity of seeing you soon when we could discuss the matter, but I am not likely to change my opinion."[14]

Russell was convicted again in 1918, but by that time he was no longer a member of the college, having taken himself off its books after the Council's action two years earlier. After the war, as a gesture of reconciliation, twenty-seven of the Fellows (nearly all of them the younger men who had actually served in the war) sent a memorial to the Council asking that Russell be reinstated. Once again Frazer was not of their number. This time their petition was successful, however, and Russell was restored, but never took up his position again.

A postscript to the affair from Frazer's point of view is supplied in a letter of 28 December 1919 to Lewis. As the mathematician G. H. Hardy had been one of the chief organizers of the pro-Russell faction within Trinity, not surprisingly Frazer notes with some complacency Hardy's move to Oxford:

I do not imagine that Hardy's departure for Oxford will be much regretted in the College; the line he took in the war, if I mistake not, was neither wise nor patriotic. He struck me as a man lacking in judgement and common sense, however great his mathematical abilities may be. Bertrand Russell I take to be a man of the same sort.[15]

In view of the fact that Russell had been reinstated at the urging of as many as twenty-seven of the Fellows, Frazer was mistaken – unlike Russell's, Hardy's departure had been felt as a loss by most of the college – and his tone can be described only as smug.

L'affaire Russell was very much the exception, however. Most of the time Frazer's life lacked any touch of the dramatic, much less the melodramatic. We have a splendid snapshot of the domestic habits of the Frazers in the mid-war years thanks to another of Lilly's vivid letters (dated 5 April 1916) to Lewis. It begins with a comment about a sudden severe storm a few days earlier in which Lewis had been caught.

It was not till we put out the lights that I saw it was a *bad* night, for I draw *back* the blinds *then* – as J. G. rises at five a.m. – it saves him trouble and prevents his making any breakages with banging about curtains etc. We are so absorbed in work – "Folk-Lore in the Old Testament" – that we live quite a life of our own, hardly knowing what goes on excepting for a glance of mine, at the *Times* – J. G. never looks at it. It is no use following the war step by step for we can do nothing! not even pray for Peace, for that also seems wrong? according to some authorities. All we can do is imitate you and economise, and we do so – religiously. Even J. G. says it would be impossible to simplify further! the only thing we might now reduce is his barber's fee. He speaks (J. G.) of cutting off his own hair (or what is left of it) but so far – tho' barbers have also raised their prices – he has had recourse to them every few months!! His chief operator was . . . an alien in early 1914 but has since discovered that he is a Serb! We keep no servant, a woman comes thrice a week to clean and wash – it is *very* peaceful. We cook our own breakfast – I make the study and kitchen fires while J. G. partakes his grape-nuts in the dining room which has a gas stove and he takes (the Hebrew Bible helping!) a long time over that meal. We go out to our midday dinner to a little club that I belong to, five minutes walk from us – the "Writers" – and get a most excellent meal for one shilling for me and 1/3! for J. G. who is my guest. We make our own supper or rather it almost makes itself out of cheese – and turn out lights by 9.30–10. Quite a conventual life, varied by a few lectures etc. at the R. Institution where the other day explosives (such as Cordyte [*sic*]) were made in our presence and reminded us of the realities and atrocities of the present moment.[16]

Lilly called their life conventual, and in fact they both worked long and hard. The war made more of a difference in Lilly's life than in J. G.'s, for she immediately stopped writing stories and playlets for schoolchildren in French and became active as a translator from the French.[17] The Allies produced an incredible amount of anti-German propaganda in order to buoy up the spirits and stoke the furnace of outrage of those on the home front. This was true even more in France than in Britain, for France had the hated enemy on its sacred territory; it was in the translation of this sort of material into English that she specialized. In 1916 her renderings of André Cheradame's *The Pangerman Plot Exposed* and Philippe Millet's *Comrades in Arms* were published, in 1917 Paul Loyson's *The Gods in the Battle*, and in 1918 Loyson's three lectures entitled *France the Apostle and the Ethics of the War*. (In her foreword to *The Gods in the Battle*, she thanks her husband for having helped with the proofreading of that volume.) She also enlisted her daughter, Lilly Mary Grove, into the effort, for in 1917 Lilly Mary translated *The Victory of the Marne*, by the well-known French writer Louis Madelin.

J. G.'s part in the family cottage industry, though small, was not confined to proofreading, for in 1917 he wrote a preface to a volume that before 1914 he would never have even picked up, much less read: *The Reconstruction of South-Eastern Europe*, by Vladislav R. Savić. The book is a plea, on the grounds of both justice and expediency, for the creation after the war of a Serbian state, and Frazer's two-page preface (dated 22 December 1916) warmly endorses the author's position. How Savić swam into the orbit of the Frazers, what J. G. knew of Balkan politics, and how he was induced to write the preface, are all unknown; one guesses that Savić might have been an acquisition of Lilly's. In terms of explicit political gestures, this is as far as Frazer would go.[18]

By 1914 Frazer, through his erudition and his publications if not through his personal qualities or institutional position, had become an elder statesman and a mentor to at least a few younger men. There cannot have been many because his shyness, his punishing work schedule, and his isolation from the slowly developing academic anthropological establishment meant that he did not meet many of the rising generation. The two whom he helped most have already appeared in this narrative: Bronislaw Malinowski and John Roscoe.

Malinowski was in Australia and Melanesia in 1914 and could not return to Europe, even if he had wished to do so, until the German naval raiders besetting the Pacific were put out of action. Frazer did what he could for him, writing to Gilbert Murray in February 1918 to intervene with his brother Hubert, Governor of New Guinea, to permit Malinowski, as a Pole technically an enemy (Austrian) alien, to carry on working undisturbed.[19] This letter aside, we know that Frazer and Malinowski wrote to one another throughout the war, for their correspondence figures in the latter's *Diary in the Strict Sense of the Term*.[20] None of the early letters is extant. In the surviving correspondence, which consists of a large number of letters from Malinowski to both the Frazers, the earliest item dates from 1917.

Here is the beginning of that important first letter (25 October 1917), written aboard the SS *Makambo*, en route to Papua.

I could not have been given a more kindly and stimulating encouragement than that which I received in your letter of July the 5th 1917. Every ethnologist naturally looks up to you as the leader in our branch of learning and your approval so kindly and generously expressed has been and will be the most efficient impulse for my future work.

At the time, when I received your letter, I needed a stimulus very badly, because I was resuming work after a pause of almost a year, due to ill health. This delayed my third trip to New Guinea, but now I am much better and I am off to the Trobriand Islands once more.

As you have been so kind and allowed me to report on my work, I shall tell you my plans and I also shall be bold enough to write to you from time to time, giving an account of what I am doing ethnologically. Should you be as kind as to give me in return the benefit of your advice and criticism, I shall be always most grateful and I shall make it my ambition to improve my methods accordingly.

Through the study of your works mainly I have come to realise the paramount importance of vividness and colour in descriptions of native life. I remember how helpful it was to find in your *Totemism and Exogamy* a picturesque account of the country, where the respective tribes live. In fact I found that the more scenery and "atmosphere" was given in the account, which you had at your disposal, the more convincing and manageable to the imagination was the ethnology of that district. I shall try to give the local colour and describe the nature of the scenery and *mise-en-scène* to the best of my ability.

As far as native psychology is concerned, it was a great pleasure to see that you approved of my sally against the "Collective Consciousness."[21] Such metaphysical concepts, shrouded in the worn out rags of Hegelian pomp, only slightly trimmed and repainted to suit the modern craving after greater sobriety, are bound to play havoc with field work: they obscure the real issues and, if blindly followed, would produce artificial and twisted methods of observation.

You are probably aware that there is now a tendency, supported among others by one or two leading field ethnographers and an eminent Egyptologist, to attack what they call the "psychological method."[22] Personally I think that we cannot study separately the institutions of a people and its mentality. Only by investigating them side by side, by seeing how certain ideas correspond to certain social arrangements, can both aspects become intelligible. The comprehension of an institution in a foreign country, can be measured by an individual's ability to "live" in that country, that means to fit into its institutions. A foreigner in England, who would not understand the language, the temperament, the current ideas, the tastes and fads of the outlook there, would not be able to live in English institutions: to enjoy their sports and amusements, to fit into English schools and Universities, to make himself at home in English social life or to take part in English politics. On the other hand, he would never be able to penetrate into the depths of the British mentality, if he kept aloof of the British institutions. The same refers, *mutatis mutandis*, to a native society, as far as I can see. Living among them, learning their language; fitting into their customs and institutions and constantly examining the ideas, which refer to these customs and institutions; doing what they do (as far as this is possible) and trying to understand their instincts, their likes and dislikes – these are the two lines of inquiry which, I think, ought to run parallel in the study of a native race.

As far as the subject matter of my inquiries is concerned, I am endeavouring to cover the whole field and not to neglect any aspect that really matters. I am personally most interested in the mental life of the natives, in their beliefs and their ideas of the Universe. But I realise that this can be understood only after the concrete manifestations have been studied. The study of your works, and more especially of *The Golden Bough*, has convinced me of the intimate relationship between magic and religion on the one hand and economic pursuits, such as gardening, fishing and hunting, on the other. And I have tried carefully to study the economic aspect of native life.[23]

The first and third paragraphs are somewhat fulsome, but to emphasize this note would, I think, distort the relationship between the two men. With Tylor gone – he died in 1917 but had been intellectually inactive since the turn of the century – Frazer in truth *had* become "the leader in our branch of learning." In addition, Frazer was a friend, and remained one lifelong, so that any servility on Malinowski's part was alloyed with affection.

The letter contains the germ of Malinowski's later thinking about both ethnographic method and how ethnography should be written. It shows his recognition of the importance of setting behavior and belief within a vividly rendered context, one that gives the behavior meaning and makes the action comprehensible to the reader. Their disagreements notwithstanding, Malinowski was impressed by Frazer's style and probably took him as one of his prose models.[24] Where the two differ, of course, is in what the appropriate context for behavior and belief should be. For Malinowski magic and religion are both cause and effect within a complex process of social interaction, whereas Frazer was interested only in what the behavior "meant," with meaning reductively understood in Western intellectual terms and measured by an externally imposed evolutionary scale. The letter, in short, embodies much of the program of the new anthropology, and it is both appropriate and poignant that its recipient should be the incarnation of the old anthropology.

That Malinowski held Frazer in genuine esteem and respect does not prevent ironic criticism from creeping in; such comment, if it is to be delivered to one's friends, must be done obliquely. The last paragraph, in which Malinowski says that *The Golden Bough* showed him the connection between magic and religion on the one side and economic activity on the other, is a good example. If *that* is the lesson of *The Golden Bough*, no one else seems to have learned it. Perhaps his reading of *The Golden Bough* caused Malinowski to become interested in everything that Frazer left out. Indeed, Frazer recognized that not only he, but anthropologists in general, had overlooked the economic basis of primitive societies. In his eulogistic preface to Malinowski's *Argonauts of the Western Pacific* in 1922, he admitted as much:

Little reflection is needed to convince us of the fundamental importance of economic forces in all stages of man's career from the humblest to the highest. . . . If anthropologists have hitherto unduly neglected it, we may suppose that it was rather because they were attracted to the higher side of man's nature than because they deliberately ignored and undervalued the importance and indeed necessity of the lower.[25]

Whatever Malinowski's complex intentions, the excessive deference of the *Makambo* letter acts to distance him from Frazer. That deference is entirely self-imposed, for Frazer always made clear his immense gratitude to the field researchers, whose energy and courage made his own kind of comparative work possible. His willingness to change his mind and his continual emphasis on the provisional nature of his findings combined to produce the most modest sort of professional persona, one as far as possible from the dictator laying down an orthodoxy that must be followed at all costs. And certainly Frazer in person, as Malinowski well knew from their meetings, was the opposite of prepossessing. Frazer was always willing to make his views known when asked, but he never thought that Malinowski (or anyone else) would or should leap to "improve their methods accordingly."

On the other hand Malinowski, when he achieved a position of ascendancy within anthropology at the London School of Economics in the 1920s and 1930s, exercised near-total control over the personal as well as professional lives of many of his students.[26] This may be an example of psychological projection at work, in which Malinowski imputes his own motives to Frazer. Alternatively one can read this pastoral concern for the nonacademic welfare of his students as an example of Malinowski's greatness as a teacher. Frazer, on the other hand, perhaps out of his constitutional shyness, was unable to strike up even the semblance of a personal relationship with any of the younger generation except Malinowski, who had sought him out upon arriving in Britain.[27]

Of the brilliant first generation of Malinowski's students, Sir Raymond Firth perhaps knew his teacher best. Firth has testified to Malinowski's willingness to flatter people, sometimes outrageously, and then to mock them afterward to others. I do not believe that this letter of 1917 is an example of such mockery. Firth speaks of Malinowski's "somewhat contemptuous affection" for Frazer. By that he means that the contempt was directed against Frazer as a thinker, and the affection (and respect) reserved for the man. Firth says that Malinowski often had his students read Frazer in order to act as a foil to his own criticism. He would not have used Frazer at all if he thought nothing of worth was to be found there, despite the fact that he saw Frazer as *passé*.[28]

After the war Malinowski returned to Europe in poor health. He was forced to spend much time resting while writing up his Trobriand results. Throughout, he stayed in close touch with Frazer, letting him know what he was working on and how he was getting on. Although he genuinely liked Frazer, he also was aware that Frazer might prove useful, and he certainly was not averse to laying it on thickly. Thus, in a letter of 10 February 1921: "I shall be very grateful indeed to receive a reprint of your Ernest Renan lecture and I hope you will be able to send me one. Anything you have to say about Comparative Method and more especially about its application to religious problems is of utmost value and importance to modern anthropology!"[29] This surely is Malinowski being fulsome.

For his other protégé, John Roscoe, the case is completely different because their friendship was without ambivalence on either side. Roscoe had returned to Uganda in 1907 after having spent several months in England. In Uganda he distributed copies of Frazer's expanded questionnaires, and made inquiries in order to answer the latter's specific queries about kinship rules and exogamy among the Baganda. As a result, his information was prominently featured in the African volume of *Totemism and Exogamy*. Returning to England in 1909, he retired from active service in the Church Missionary Society, and with Frazer's encouragement produced two volumes on African ethnography that are still useful today: *The Baganda* (1911) – dedicated to Frazer – and *The Northern Bantu Tribes* (1921). One reason they retain their value is that Roscoe in his fieldwork enjoyed certain advantages, over and above his fluency in the native languages and his sympathy for the people, that were unique. Because he had befriended the native prime minister, the *katikiro*, the latter virtually commanded everyone, especially the old people who remembered the time before the white men came, to answer Roscoe's questions fully, thus affording him information he might never have obtained otherwise. In 1910, partly through Frazer's efforts, Cambridge awarded him an honorary M.A. for services to ethnology and anthropology, and perhaps more important, an ecclesiastical living in Norfolk that was in its gift.

Roscoe, now free at last of missionary commitments, was eager to get back to the bush in an anthropological capacity, and Frazer did all he could to help. In the next few years he tried to interest various charitable bodies – notably the Carnegie Trust in both the United States and Britain – to sponsor an expedition, with no success. With private backing unavailable, he then turned to official channels, and in April 1914, after many months of petitioning and politicking, actually succeeded in getting the Colonial Office to offer Roscoe a year's contract to carry out anthropological research in Uganda.[30] The outbreak of war, of course, meant the suspension of the project, and with that suspension Roscoe doubtless believed that his days in the field and indeed in Africa were over. But remarkably, through Frazer's persistence, after the war Sir Peter Mackie agreed to sponsor an expedition to Africa, administered by the Royal Society, with Roscoe as its leader. In 1919–20, then, at the age of nearly sixty, Roscoe returned to Uganda to investigate several tribes with whom he had had little contact during his earlier sojourns. His results are to be found in *The Bakitara* (1923), *The Banyankole* (1923), and *The Bagesu* (1924).

Frazer's main scholarly project during the war was *Folk-Lore in the Old Testament*, published on 12 November 1918, the day after the Armistice was signed. Appealing to the readership that *The Golden Bough* had created, along with the large audience always interested in religious questions and the Bible, it was an immediate publishing success: despite its high cost (37s 6d for the three-volume set), the first printing of 2500 copies was quickly exhausted, and two more printings totaling 4000 more copies were called for within eight months.[31]

Although the idea of discussing the folkloric elements in the Hebrew Bible is a good one, and as a commentary the work lies congenially to Frazer's expansive and discursive predilections, yet, its popularity notwithstanding, it may be his most disappointing major production. As one would expect, it is well written in his ornate manner; nevertheless, its good qualities are outweighed by a number of major shortcomings – in comprehensiveness, in proportion, in method.

A comparison of *Folk-Lore* to the commentary on Pausanias, the work that it seems to resemble most, is illuminating. At first glance *Folk-Lore* has advantages that should make it the better of the two: it is about half the length of Pausanias, and was written uninterruptedly in three years rather than sporadically over fourteen. In addition, it is composed of a relatively small number of long – sometimes very long – essays rather than of thousands of short notes, as Pausanias is. These should add up to a work that is tighter and easier to read.

The reality is otherwise. Although the final version of *Folk-Lore* did take three years to write, in fact its contents were composed over about eleven years, for it owes its conception and method to the notes on biblical folklore that Frazer contributed to the Tylor Festschrift of 1907. If suffers from the casual way in which most of it was compiled, with Frazer stitching together and amplifying those earlier essays and then adding to that large mass further essays and notes written in no particular order.

Of course the inherently elastic nature of a commentary tends to forgive such heterogeneity; after all, texts contain no markers within them that indicate what does and does not deserve discussion, nor the amount or kind of discussion that is appropriate. But for that very reason the commentator must somewhere explain the criterion on which he makes that most basic decision – to speak or to pass by in silence, especially in a work like this one that is directed to a general audience unfamiliar with the relevant scholarship. Frazer never really explains how he knows that folklore is present, except of course that the passage in question resembles, or reminds him of, some belief or custom somewhere.[32]

To be fair, he does address this question, albeit unsatisfactorily, in the preface. There he not only implies the existence of seemingly objective guidelines that direct him, but he opens prophetic vistas for the subject as it will no doubt be developed by scholars in the future:

The instrument for the detection of savagery under civilization is the comparative method, which, applied to the human mind, enables us to trace man's intellectual and moral evolution, just as, applied to the human body, it enables us to trace his physical evolution from lower forms of animal life. There is, in short, a Comparative Anatomy of the mind as well as of the body, and it promises to be no less fruitful of far-reaching consequences, not merely speculative but practical, for the future of humanity.[33]

Having made so promising a start, he then gets distracted into sketching the history of the comparative method as applied to Hebrew antiquities, and never returns to the matter at issue: how one *knows* that one is in the presence of folklore, and thus that the comparative method ought to be applied in order to explicate its meaning. The reason he slides off this question is that in truth he has no method, or rather that he would say that the presence of folklore is self-evident – at least to an expert such as himself. Folklore by its very nature being a meaningless survival from an earlier epoch, it makes itself known as a snag in the otherwise rational and sensible texture of the narrative into which it has obtruded. Changing the metaphor, it is like the boulder that breaks the smooth expanse of the Italian lawn to which he compares the strange rite at

Nemi in the early pages of *The Golden Bough*. In other words, we detect folklore by contrast, by comparing it to what it is not: culture.

Frazer is so committed to the comparative method that he simply dismisses anything that the comparative method does not illuminate. An example is the question of independent invention versus diffusion as the mechanism by which myths and legends originated and disseminated. That is, if the human mind is essentially everywhere the same and evolves in response to an evolutionary program, as he had been maintaining since 1885, then it follows that at best all that the comparative method can do is collect and juxtapose examples of the same mentality.

On the face of it, the comparative method seems better adapted to studies of cultural diffusion, where careful collocation of variants may indeed give clues as to the manner in which a folktale or motif spread. But Frazer is not interested in such small fry as the dissemination of a tale or motif. For him, the virtue of the comparative method lies in its power to take us as close as is possible to the workings of our mental "anatomy."

Further, to compare like with like, it is important that the information all come from societies (or minds) that have reached the same stage of development; to compare unlikes would vitiate the method. But Frazer is not careful about this basic point, and as a result much of his comparison is meaningless. A good example is to be found in the first essay, in which he discusses the creation of mankind (Genesis 1–3). He points out the presence of two different accounts in Genesis and, after analyzing the (presumably) earlier of the two, presents as parallels a large number of more or less similar narratives. Those that are "more similar" come from societies that were roughly on the same level of social development as the Hebrews, whereas those "less similar" are taken from much less well-developed cultures. Although he says that he "cannot doubt that such rude conceptions of the origin of mankind, common to Greeks, Hebrews, Babylonians and Egyptians, were handed down to the civilized peoples of antiquity by their savage or barbarous forefathers," logically that constitutes no proof whatever of any such transmission.[34] The possibility of independent invention, especially about a subject of such universal interest as the origin of the human race, cannot be dismissed so lightly. This lack of proof is especially incongruous in the light of the metaphor of comparative anatomy. If our minds, like our bodies, follow inbuilt laws of development, then one should expect the same results everywhere unless exceptional conditions supervene, so that it would not be necessary to discuss how "such rude conceptions . . . were handed down" and indeed their "savage or barbarous forefathers" need never be invoked at all.

Putting this methodological confusion to one side, when one considers the variety of genres represented in the Old Testament and the geographical, chronological, and cultural distance that separates us from its peoples and times, any commentary on it, whether its focus be folkloric or otherwise, requires a great deal of planning if it is to achieve proportion as well as scope. Especially is this true at the outset, where the pitch of comment sets the scale for the whole work and indicates to the reader explicitly or implicitly what the commentator regards as important. In short, a large-scale work such as this one requires *architecture*, about which Frazer seems never to have bestirred himself. This seems to have been inherent in his rather offhand view of the Bible project from the start. Recall his letter to Macmillan in 1907 in which he says that a book on folklore in the Old Testament would be easy to do because it would consist of detached notes and therefore could be extended indefinitely. He seems never to have thought of the work as a whole or weighed the need for a framework other than that provided ready-made by the sequence of the books of the Bible.

The result is that *Folk-Lore in the Old Testament* is shapeless or, more precisely, misshapen. The reason the first volume contains 569 pages is entirely a matter of the mechanics of printing and bookbinding, for it does not correspond to anything in the Bible. The volume does not even exhaust the cycle of stories about Jacob, much less the entire book of Genesis. Furthermore, it contains only seven essays, of vastly different lengths. The two shortest, on the mark of Cain and the tower of Babel, are each only twenty-five pages long. By comparison, the two longest, on Noah's flood and on ultimogeniture – the legal system by which inheritance passes to the youngest son (Jacob) rather than the eldest (Esau) – occupy 257 and 137 pages, respectively, or together fully two-thirds of the book.

The only valid reason for such massive disproportion, which distorts the first volume and to that extent weights the entire work inordinately toward the Pentateuch (and toward Genesis within the Pentateuch), would be the overwhelming importance of these two topics in themselves, and even then the quality of the commentary itself would have to be outstanding to justify so extensive a coverage. The real reason, however, that these sections are so distended has little or nothing to do with such intrinsic considerations. Instead it is, I believe, psychological: having done the research, Frazer could not bring himself to exclude any of it. On the contrary, because his Huxley Lecture on the Deluge narratives could not run much more than an hour, he had had to restrain himself severely on that occasion. No such limitation prevailed, however, on the page, and there he could and did present *everything*, at stupefying length. That very little of it had any historical or other relation to the tale of Noah's flood was in the end immaterial. The juggernaut of Frazer's erudition, combined with whatever it was within him that worshiped facts and could not bear to leave one of them unmentioned, would not be denied.

An excellent example of this omnivorousness-cum-compulsiveness is furnished in the second-longest essay, on ultimogeniture. It is unclear how and when he became interested in the subject. It was not part of the miscellany of 1907, nor does it appear *en passant* elsewhere. Wherever it came from, in it Frazer presents all the many instances known to him of this system of inheritance. He then concludes that its origin is easily understood: among pastoral peoples in a sparsely populated world, each son as he comes of age takes some cattle and strikes out on his own, thus leaving the youngest brother at home to inherit whatever remains. This custom having long been forgotten by the time the pastoral Hebrews became farmers, the later Jahvist or Elohist writer, who knew only primogeniture, could explain this seeming aberrant system of inheritance by the youngest only through making Jacob into a trickster. Having come to this sensible conclusion, however, Frazer now suddenly returns to two farfetched theories about the origins of ultimogeniture that he had mentioned and *already dismissed*. This furnishes him with the pretext for two long digressions, the first on the *jus primae noctis* and the second on polygamy. They are wholly gratuitous because, as Frazer acknowledges *after* the lengthy sifting of the evidence, the *jus primae noctis* is a fiction, at least in Europe, and the connection between ultimogeniture and polygamy is at best tenuous and probably nonexistent; neither has any connection whatever with Jacob.

The architectural problem is aggravated by the fact that the first volume and two-thirds of the second – fully 1000 pages all told – deal only with Genesis, which means that the rest of the Pentateuch and the whole of the Prophets and the Writings must be crammed hurriedly into the last 500 pages. Furthermore, Frazer is wholly uninterested in the fact that Genesis is made up of stories composed with consummate literary skill. He understands his subject to consist entirely of the illustration at length of the mental outlook and epistemological development of the writers and protagonists of the narratives, and the ways in which that outlook and development resemble those of the "lower culture" round the world. Therefore he is not interested in what the writers of Genesis *did* with the folklore that they certainly knew and employed; it is enough for him merely to demonstrate and reiterate through the comparative method the existence of a folkloric stratum.

Such commentary as he offers on the scriptural stories is thus nearly all oblique, for like a preacher the text serves as pretext; having announced the chapter and verse in question, immediately he is off and running, amassing savage comparisons, and leaving the Bible far behind. Thus, the point of the immense cornucopia of flood narratives is this: because both patriarchs and primitives believed in stories of a great deluge, this means that the mind of the patriarchs was as undeveloped as that of the primitives. Because Frazer deals entirely with epistemology, the obvious evidence that the Hebrews or northwest Semites were more technologically developed than, say, the aboriginal societies of North America is of no interest to him and is never mentioned even as their flood stories are juxtaposed.

Folk-Lore is therefore a collection of analogues to and "survivals" from primitive societies that exemplify the workings of the same savage mind that was described at such length in *The Golden Bough.* Despite the obligatory doffing of his cap in the preface to the "high moral and religious development of the ancient Hebrews," the implicit purpose of the work can be simply stated: to undermine the Bible and religion by insisting on its folkloric stratum, thereby associating it with savagery. *Folk-Lore in the Old Testament* is really a huge tract in which Frazer employs his immense erudition in order to make a single simple point repeatedly about the Hebrew Bible, and therefore by implication about the religions that are founded on it.

So much for what *Folk-Lore in the Old Testament* is not; to be fair, one ought also to say what it is, which may help to explain why it became so popular. Here is a brief representative passage. Frazer's subject here is "the bitter water," the text in Numbers (5:11–28) where a woman charged with infidelity is given a bitter drink as a trial by ordeal to ascertain whether she is telling the truth when she swears her innocence. His discussion, such as it is, takes all of *three* pages, of which fully half is given over to the passage itself. After explaining certain oddities of the text (such as why certain elements are repeated), he describes the ordeal ceremony again in his own words. He then delivers himself of the following opinion, which functions as a conclusion – except that no argument has preceded it – after which he continues for more than *one hundred* pages on the poison ordeal in Africa, India, and other exotic parts. Here is his "conclusion":

For trial by ordeal, wherever it flourishes, is a mode of ascertaining guilt as barbarous as it is ineffectual; and though, by reason of the conservative nature of law and custom, it may long linger among peoples who have attained to a considerable degree of civilization, it can only take its rise in ages of gross ignorance and credulity. The different forms of ordeal by which men have sought to elicit the truth are many and well fitted to illustrate the extent and variety of human folly.[35]

Inasmuch as no proof whatever for this statement is offered, the rhetorical position must be one of preaching to the persuaded. This biblical survival (as he views it) of an earlier time and culture when primitive rituals such as ordeals prevailed is served up unglossed and ungarnished, on the assumption that it speaks for itself and that no other conclusion is conceivable. Of course it does not speak for itself, and the same sort of objections can be made to the hundred pages of poison ordeals that were made about the creation narratives. Frazer's mournful, Gibbonesque indictment of the Bible as a tissue of ignorance, barbarism, and folly exists wholly on the level of rhetoric; the reader is supposed to be convinced of the truth of this general proposition by the cumulative effect of the comparative data that are adduced, despite the fact that there is usually no logical or historical connection whatever between those data and the Bible.

Despite the fact that most of the work thus constitutes a gigantic piece of pseudo-argumentation, it was very popular. Such popularity must be due in part to the moment of its publication. To the extent that the end of the war marked "good-bye to all that," such a sustained undermining of one of the central pillars of the social order must have appealed directly to those enervated by the mood of exhaustion and cynicism that prevailed at the end of four years of true primitivism and savagery. Indeed, to many readers it must have seemed as if the point of *Folk-Lore* – that the Old Testament was founded on and suffused by savage modes of thought – explained a great deal about the postwar world. It is easy to imagine disillusioned readers dipping into the volumes and coming away confirmed in the belief that the foundation of society was rotten; indeed, that it must always have been so, a fact that had been kept from the world until a courageous man like Frazer shed light where there had been darkness.

Among scholars, on the other hand, the reception was quite different. Although Frazer was felt to be an authentic Great Man, and beyond personal criticism, the generally negative reception of the second and third *Golden Boughs* continued. As one might expect, the most searching discussion was that of Marett, who had by now inherited Lang's role if not his manner and become Frazer's more or less official critic.[36] Marett used the occasion of the publication of *Folk-Lore* not only to criticize that work but also to analyze the theoretical assumptions underlying the study of folklore as it had developed since the middle of the preceding century. He argued that those assumptions were not merely inadequate to deal with its real subject, but had in fact succeeded in obscuring that subject from view. If folklore was to be anything more than enumerative and taxonomic, it had to become sociological and psychological. Because traditional folklorists – and Marett acclaims Frazer as the greatest of them – had no social psychology worthy of the name, and because they assumed that the processes that created folklore were essentially simple and clear, their field had become sterile, a branch of museum studies. In the light of these deeper criticisms he then evaluated Frazer's performance as a biblical folklorist, focusing especially on his psychological limitations.

For Frazer, the psychology of the folk is not an issue. He knows their minds in the same way that he knows the minds of the primitives in *The Golden Bough*, from the quality of their behavior or, in this case, their lore. Just as the boulder of savagery interrupted the smooth expanse of the Roman lawn, so the folk's rude beliefs and actions break into the moral exaltation of the Hebrew lawgivers and prophets. Because Frazer is uninterested in biblical history, however, he never thinks to ask whether the primitive behavior may not have begun at some intermediate period but instead places its origin entirely in the dim immemorial past.

The burden of Marett's criticism obviously goes far beyond *Folk-Lore in the Old Testament*. Since World War II the field of folklore has found itself in crisis. What are its subject-matter and methods? How does it differ from other related disciplines? What is its relation to the "folk"? In the event, most of Anglo-American folklore has eschewed the sociological and psychological path suggested by Marett, although its practitioners have largely discarded the old-style fossil hunting as well. But Marett's critique, occasioned by the appearance of *Folk-Lore in the Old Testament*, one of the last of the old-style works on the grand scale, was an important step in this important intellectual reorientation.

16 · RETURN TO THE CLASSICS

F RAZER had always to be working; life without a major project – or two or three – in hand was unimaginable. With *Folk-Lore in the Old Testament* finally behind him, and with prospects for substantial royalties, he turned to something that did not need to make money. On 27 September 1918 he wrote to his old friend W. H. D. Rouse, now coeditor of the Loeb Library, about the possibility of editing a title in that series. This approach led directly to his edition of Apollodorus' *The Library* (1921) and indirectly to that of Ovid's *Fasti* (1929). Frazer's significant work in the twenties – which is to say, his last significant work – was all classical.

Although the letter to Rouse brought about his return to classical studies, it was by no means his first connection with the Loeb Library, for he had been involved from its inception.[1] On 15 October 1910 Frazer had written to George Macmillan that its founder, the American banker and classical amateur James Loeb (1867–1933), had asked him to be the Library's first director, at the splendid salary of £600 per year. Frazer was strongly inclined to accept, for such an income would surely mean the end of his recurrent financial embarrassments. In the end, however, he refused, for two reasons. He told Loeb that he would consider the position only if Macmillan agreed to be its publisher, and Macmillan turned down the ideas as commercially risky.[2] He was also fearful that direction of the series would take too much time from his writing; no matter how much Frazer sought financial security, it could not be bought at the price of his work.

Frazer was tempted for more than financial reasons, for he must have found Loeb's combination of humanism and liberalism quite congenial. His affinity for Jews would have been an advantage as well, as Loeb would hardly have been comfortable with an anti-Semite. Certainly Lilly supported it, for to her it must have seemed the long-awaited, heaven-sent ticket out of Cambridge, combining the income they needed, a prestigious position, and time for J. G. to carry on his own work. But he had to have his friend Macmillan at his side as business and publishing advisor. When Macmillan demurred, Frazer could not contemplate entering into such a relationship with anyone else. In view of Frazer's fears and scruples, he was right to decline; the possibilities for anxiety and misery were too great.

The series went ahead, of course, with W. H. Heinemann and the veteran T. E. Page (1850–1936) in place of Macmillan and Frazer, and it was Page who brought in Rouse. The classical establishment greeted the new series with indifference: a historian has written that "the great were scornful."[3] The Library had barely begun when the war broke out, and along with most scholarship went into hibernation. Despite the initially frosty reception, it became increasingly popular after the war because of the gradual decline in classical education. Perhaps Frazer, who had just completed *Folk-Lore*, wished to make a gesture to Loeb, with whom he had become friendly, for not having accepted the editorship. Whatever his reasons, he thought to take some classical recreation in the form of editing a title in the series.

This was the background to his approach to Rouse. The extant correspondence with Rouse begins *in medias res*. He must earlier have expressed interest in Herodotus – a "natural" author for him because of the ethnographic possibilities – for on 5 June 1918 he thanks Macmillan for approving the idea of an edition and commentary on that author. (As he says nothing about Macmillan's publishing such an edition, he must be referring to the Loeb series.) He has just learned, however, that A. D. Godley was interested in editing Herodotus and therefore gladly yields to him."He will probably do it much better than I should, with a lighter touch and greater freshness of style."

If not Herodotus, then who? He tells Rouse that he knows what he is looking for:

a less familiar and well-thumbed author than Herodotus, by preference one that had not been already translated into English, though that might be difficult to find. I find it irksome to tread the beaten path, I prefer to strike out as an explorer into the untrodden wilds. Among the authors that have occurred to me are Apollodorus (the *Bibliotheca*), Porphyry (*De abstinentia* and *De antro nympharum*), and Dionysius Halicarnasensis (the *Roman Antiquities*). In Latin I am attracted both by the matter and the fine flowing style of Lactantius. Are any or all of these already earmarked for the Library? If not, I might undertake one of them, probably Greek rather than Latin. But in that case I hope you would be so kind as to leave me free to take my own time over it; I have been so long accustomed to choose my own work and at my own time that anything like compulsion is apt to have the effect of preventing me from doing anything.

By the way, what about Plutarch's *Moralia*? They are very interesting and written in a better (because less pretentious) style than his *Lives*. But I fancy they have often been translated, and you may already have arranged for them.[4]

Although the letter is clear enough, Rouse must have misunderstood it, for Frazer in his next (17 October) has to set him right. The last thing in his mind had been to pre-empt any, not to mention all, the authors he named. His purpose had been only to inquire whether they had been spoken for, and he is glad to learn that all but the *Moralia* remain unassigned. Of those he mentioned, he would be choosing only one. Finally, whichever it is, he enjoins Rouse to make no announcement of any kind until the work is well under way; a premature announcement would set his teeth on edge and cause him to withdraw. He then goes on to muse aloud about other authors and texts that he might enjoy working on: some of Cicero's philosophical works, especially the *Tusculan Disputations* and *De natura deorum*; Isaeus, Isocrates, Antiphon, Lysias, etc. There are more Greek authors than Latin, and some (for example, Cicero) offer no obvious possibilities for folkloric commentary, so that was not the only thing in his mind.

Several letters that have not survived must then have passed between them, and quickly at that: an invitation from Rouse asking Frazer to choose a title, a response from Frazer in which he names Apollodorus, and a formal authorization from Rouse and contract from Heinemann. For the next we hear, it is all done. Only three months later (27 January 1919) Frazer writes, "I have completed a translation of the *Bibliotheca* of Apollodorus for the Loeb. It would, with the Greek text, make a single volume. There are two English MSS (one at Oxford, one at the British Museum) which I wish to consult before sending my text and translation to the printer."[5]

Rouse had been one of those in Frazer's anthropological circle in the late 1880s. After a classical fellowship at Christ's College from 1888 to 1894, he had studied and edited modern Greek and Indian folklore, and in 1902 had become headmaster of the Perse School in Cambridge. There he had been a pioneer in the teaching of classical languages by the oral–aural method (and in the process worked with Lilly Frazer, who was interested in the possibilities of the phonograph in teaching languages). As such he knew how prodigiously hard-working Frazer was. Even so, he probably could not believe how quickly the work had been accomplished. If that was his reaction, then he was right not to believe his eyes; appearances to the contrary notwithstanding, the book was anything but complete.

For Frazer says only that he has finished the translation. There can be no doubt that he always enjoyed translation, and that he acquitted himself well at it; even as an undergraduate his work in the classical Tripos had been outstanding. Nevertheless the translation was only an hors d'œuvre in relation to the real meal, the annotation. Unfortunately, however, the format of the Loeb Library does not really allow for commentary, at least on the Frazerian scale. Its volumes consist of text and translation on facing pages, with only the necessary minimum of notes needed by the nonexpert reader. The Loeb editions are supposed to provide working texts for the classical scholar and translations for the amateur and nonclassical scholar; they are supposed to embody the results of modern scholarship without an overt display of editorial erudition. Knowing Frazer's expansive predilections and his own responsibilities to the series, Rouse must have hoped that Frazer for once might elect a minimalist solution, that all that remained was the relatively brief and undemanding task of textual collation that the letter implied.

If that is what Rouse hoped, then he was to be disappointed. In Frazer's terms his letter meant only that he had come to the point where the project began to engage him fully. In the event, the introduction to Apollodorus is dated 5 April 1921, more than two years later; the edition is in two volumes rather than one; and Frazer consulted no manuscripts whatever, relying nearly entirely on the textual labors of earlier scholars.[6]

One does not wish to give the wrong impression: the large amount of annotation (by Loeb standards) was merely unusual, not scandalous or even troublesome. Frazer does present a good deal of commentary in the notes, most of which usefully compare Apollodorus' version of the myths with those found in other Greek authors. In addition, the lengthy appendix to the second volume comprises 150 pages of brief and not-so-brief disquisitions on various mythological motifs, but such commentary is neither overlong nor irrelevant. Unlike *Folk-Lore in the Old Testament*, where he ransacks the anthropological attic of the entire world for comparisons, in the notes (as opposed to the appendix) he keeps to what classical scholars would agree was germane, allowing himself only occasional excursions among the primitives.

The Library – its name in English – consists of, in Frazer's words, "a plain unvarnished summary of Greek myths and heroic legends," as found in literary sources; Apollodorus makes no claim to tap any oral tradition.[7] In fact the work is considerably more important than such a bare-bones description implies. The reason is that, as a late compilation, it often constitutes the only extant record of many earlier lost books. It is therefore invaluable for scholars interested in reconstructing lost epics or tragedies or in elucidating vase paintings. It is a distinctly significant secondary work of reference, one that Hellenists find themselves using again and again.

Nothing is known aboutApollodorus himself – Frazer places him in the first or second century A.D., but that is only a guess – or about anything else he might have written, so that the reader's attention is focused entirely on the work. Starting from the creation of mankind, Apollodorus tells the story of the Greek nation all the way through the sequels to the *Odyssey*. His style is the featureless prose of the compiler, the summarizer, the writer of anonymous articles in an ancient encyclopaedia, but at least the translator always understand what his author intends.

Frazer never explained why he chose to work on Apollodorus. Doubtless he was attracted to *The Library* because of its mythological content, which he knew he could enrich and illuminate with comparative parallels, and doubtless also by the knowledge that the text was in good condition, thus sparing him much tedious and uncongenial labor. But this entire Loeb foray has something off-center about it, for the concise format never allowed him to hit his stride as a commentator, and the blandness of the text can have offered him little literary enjoyment.

He was able to extract from the occasion at least one gratification, however: *The Library* is dedicated to "My old teacher and friend, Henry Jackson O.M." That may have been the only truly enjoyable thing about it, however, for we know that in the end he thought the project finally not worth the effort. When it appeared he naturally sent a copy to Gosse, who, surprisingly, since it lay far outside his usual literary territory, reviewed it.[8] In thanking Gosse (on 28 August 1921) for this favor he remarked,

I thank you for your kind and sympathetic review of Apollodorus. Almost you persuade me to think better of the poor old buffer than I have hitherto done. Nevertheless when I am called upon to give an account of my life before Rhadamanthys, and he knots his brows and says, "How about Apollodorus?" I fear I shall hang my head and plead guilty to having misspent nearly three years over that wretched creature. However, I shall be able to call on you as a witness for the defence.[9]

His negative verdict notwithstanding, the work is not devoid of interest, which is to be found, characteristically, in the introduction. This is given over to a brief but, by his standards, extended theoretical pronouncement on the nature of mythology.

The discussion turns on his definitions of the three key terms of myth, legend, and folktale. Myths are "mistaken explanations of phenomena, whether of human life or of external nature."[10] These explanations arise from disinterested instinctive human curiosity – the same need to get at the causes of things that, much later, will produce science. Legends, by comparison, are "traditions, whether oral or written, which relate the fortunes of real people in the past, or which describe events, not necessarily human, that are said to have occurred at real places. Such legends contain a mixture of truth and falsehood, for were they wholly true, they would not be legends but histories." The problem here as elsewhere lies in Frazer's insistence on defining legends and myths exclusively on the basis of their truth-value, and in doing so by means of an inadequate two-valued logic – legends are either true or false.

Folktales are a third kind: "narratives invented by persons unknown and handed down at first by word of mouth from generation to generation, narratives which, though they profess to describe actual occurrences, are in fact purely imaginary, having no other aim than the entertainment of the hearer and making no real claim on his credulity." Although Frazer acknowledges the universal pleasure people take in telling and listening to stories, because the criterion is once again that of the alleged veracity of history, understood as an account of things as they "really" were, such tales are deprecated as at best mere entertainment.

Whatever its shortcomings, this does at least constitute a typology of narrative that he might have used to analyze Apollodorus' text. Unfortunately he hardly goes much further in the introduction, contenting himself with listing the tales of Meleager, Melampus, Medea, Glaucus, Perseus, Peleus, and Thetis as examples that "bear traces of the story-teller's art."[11] Neither the notes nor the appendix carries this schema further. On the other hand, judging from works like *The Belief in Immortality*, in which (within a geographical area) eumeration is virtually Frazer's sole organizing principle, perhaps one should be grateful for the constraints of the Loeb format.

Otherwise we might well have had an immense naming of trees and only the barest intimation of the existence of a forest.

The translation is highflown and decorous. Frazer, given too often to archaism in his own English, is all too ready to lapse into the false-antique in rendering someone else's. To be sure, such a judgment is a matter of historically conditioned taste, but the later twentieth century in classical translation has generally esteemed most the qualities of swiftness, straightforwardness, and transparency, and has generally commended the version that effaces itself before the original. To a modern eye, Frazer's translation of the bland idiom of Apollodorus, though not especially old-fashioned in his day, has not aged well.

None of the above should be taken to mean that he was insensitive to tone and nuance; however much his interest lay in the commentary he always took translation seriously. Rouse had arranged that he receive copies of all Loeb titles as they appeared, and we have his comments on the work of three of his fellow translators. In a letter to Rouse of 8 January 1920 he commends H. Rackham's version of *De finibus* ("quite admirable") and A. T. Murray's *Odyssey*. Of the latter he says,

I am glad that the translator does not affect the archaic style of [S. H.] Butcher and [Andrew] Lang. I agree with another translator of Homer, my dear Cowper, that affectation in every form, including style, is loathsome. Why, oh why, did you allow Theocritus to be translated [by J. M. Edmonds] in that abominable mincing affected archaistic manner? Why, in many places the Greek is clearer than the English, and one has to look at it to know what the translator means. But if I am not mistaken, you actually relish this sad stuff. Well, de gustibus, etc.[12]

To which we all say amen. Because everyone except perhaps Wilde and Baudelaire agrees with Cowper and Frazer in abhorring affectation, it is all the more important to be clear here: in saying that his language is sometimes stiff, I do not mean that his Apollodorus is unreadable, only that canons of style and appropriateness have changed vastly since about 1950, and that his standards and expectations are not ours.

In the heady days after the Armistice, all Britons were united in their exaltation at the end of the war. That exhilaration passed quickly, a casualty of the cynical reversion to postwar business-as-usual, and Frazer forgot his brief flirtation with politics and returned to scholarship. He was much taken up with the plans for Roscoe's expedition to East Africa, which had suddenly come back to life and was now imminent. Frazer agreed to act as liaison between Roscoe and the expedition's backer Sir Peter Mackie on the one side and the Colonial Office and W. B. Hardy, secretary of the Royal Society, on the other. He loathed this kind of work, for he was always fearful that Roscoe might somehow be harmed by a mistake on his part, and he did it only out of friendship.

Everything had to be put aside in February and March 1919, however, when Lilly's daughter, Lilly Mary, died suddenly in France, perhaps a victim of the influenza pandemic.[13] He and Lilly spent six weeks in Paris, during which her health collapsed again. By April, however, he was back at work in London, undecided about the suggestion, put forward by several people, that he write a companion volume on folklore in the New Testament. He liked the idea, but it must take its place at the end of a long queue of projects: he had to complete Apollodorus, and he had not forsaken anthropology – the second volume of the long-interrupted *Belief in Immortality* beckoned as well.

Because of Lilly's poor health, they decided to spend the winter of 1919–20 in the sun in Greece. They never reached Greece, however, because Lilly broke down once again, and they were unable to go farther than Paris. She developed pneumonia, along with arhythmia of the heart, and just before Christmas was in a grave condition. But the crisis passed, and on 28 December 1919 Frazer could write to M.J. Lewis in Cambridge that they were comfortably installed in the Hotel Lutétia, and in fact were better off than if they were home in the Temple, for there they have no servant and are not permitted to cook in their rooms. Lilly was out of bed and able to manage a few steps unaided for the first time in weeks.[14]

Meanwhile, with the postwar resumption of intellectual life in Britain, the idea of the Frazer Fund was mooted once again. In early 1920 Cornford, still the chief organizer, brought it up in a letter to Frazer, who was in Folkestone with the recuperating Lilly. It is clear that her recovery was virtually complete, for on 24 February she was strong enough to write a long letter to Lewis, in which the following passage occurs:

I intend to write to Mr Cornford and ask him to give me an appointment any time he is in London. That matter of the Testimonial to J.G. needs sifting and reconsidering and he, J.G., is *not* – and has *not* been, reasonable about it – and squashed it in the bud. I will say nothing to him [J.G.] about it at present and I strongly wish to see Mr Cornford *by myself*.[15]

The official account of the genesis of the Frazer Lectures is that because of the great price inflation caused by the war, the misgivings about the long-term financial viability of the fund expressed before the war now seemed even more substantial.[16] As a result the organizers decided to convert the fund into a lectureship, as presenting less of a problem in terms of ongoing support.

Lilly's letter, however, implies something different: that Frazer vetoed the idea of the fund when it was revived, and that she prevailed on him to change his mind and then worked out the arrangements with Cornford. Nothing conclusive exists, but this latter version sounds more probable, given the depth of her feeling about it. The fund may indeed have become a lectureship for financial reasons, but it is clear that Lilly was instrumental in assuring that this first explicit recognition of her husband was not going to be torpedoed by a small thing like his modesty.

In the same lively letter she tells Lewis in the strictest confidence that the breakdown in her health may have shaken J. G. perhaps more than it has her. His fright at her close call has produced a predictable reaction: "at every difficult juncture in life – whether it is a chilblain on my small toe or a tooth ache or influenza – his panacea comes pat: 'Return to Cambridge'!!! It is a fixed notion in his brain such as great thinkers frequently have, and which nothing can eradicate." This *idée fixe* had grown to the extent that

last summer I gave way against my better reasoning and he applied to Mr [H. McLeod] Innes [Senior Bursar at Trinity] for College rooms and *was refused* by the Council. People or women like myself are so illogical that I *bitterly* resent that refusal – ! and J. G. felt it *desperately*. He has always looked to Trinity as a haven of refuge – ! *But*, dear friend, I also consider a move back to Cambridge – at least in *my* life time – except for a temporary stay or for a definite post – a piece of *huge folly* – ! *Where* am I to roost if he has College rooms?? Am I at my age and in my delicate state of health to resume the navette (shuttle) I used to make for years before and perpetually come and go to his rooms!? *He needs me.*

This is followed by four more pages recounting slights real and imagined to J. G., and therefore to her, who feels them so much more than he does.

It is *not* personal pride that prompts all this – it is mere truth: – J. G.'s work influences the thought of the *world* and Trinity would *regret* if it did not give him a chance. It would not hinder J. G.'s work to give a few lectures say for two terms a year, they would form a book afterwards – I believe he would accept any post even as Waiter! at the High Table!! so as to return to Cambridge – his desire is *so* great! Of course if he had a post, if his library *were* housed in College rooms, our other needs and expenses would be so reduced – that we could make frequent absences from Cambridge – and thus I might bear with the climate described by the late Sir G. Humphry as one in which one has neither the energy to live or to die in.

It is easy to smile at this and other similar passionate outbursts on her part. It was a good thing that Frazer was a self-starter who had, before he met Lilly, become so used to working on his own that he did not need the society of others, for many who would have befriended him were put off by her. It was also a good thing that he accepted her domination, or else he would have been dreadfully unhappy in the marriage, and he was not. Her children may have counted themselves fortunate that their powerful mother was so wrapped up in her husband, or she doubtless would have interfered much more in their lives. (It may not be accidental that both lived far away, Lilly Mary in Paris and Grenville in Stockholm.) And yet it is also true that she seems to have been one of those women who find fulfillment in the role of wife, a woman who cared for her children but lived for her husband. There is no doubt that she was hard to take in person – the testimony is unanimous on that point, and the prospect of her renewed presence may well have been one of the covert reasons why Trinity rejected Frazer's request – yet she was singleminded in her efforts to further his career and secure for him the recognition that was long overdue.

Frazer having been turned down at Trinity, they returned to London. They stayed in the Temple for eight years all told, until August 1922. Their decision to move was due not so much to the added costs (although their low prewar rent had been raised) as to the inconveniences of living there: namely, the need to take all their meals out and Lilly's increasing difficulties in climbing the three flights of stairs to their rooms. The postwar years were hard ones for her, and her upper-respiratory weakness, which in those pre-antibiotic days could lead to fatal influenza or pneumonia, laid her low a number of times. They left the Temple in the summer of 1922, and commenced a wandering existence for a year in Britain and Europe, living in hotels, while they had a house built for them – in Cambridge. They seem to have reached an accommodation: Lilly would be relieved of the inconvenience of living in the Temple, and J. G. would get his wish and return to Cambridge.

One of the last extant letters Frazer wrote from Brick Court was to T. E. Page, editor of the Loeb Library, on 28 April 1922:

I have some thoughts of undertaking another Loeb volume, if you are willing and a suitable author could be found who is not yet bespoken. Among the possible authors who occurred to me are Cicero, *Tusculan Disputations* and *Academics*; Ovid, *Fasti*; Isaeus; Aristotle, *De anima* and *Poetics*; Minor Greek mythographers (Antoninus Liberalis, Conon, etc).[17]

From the fact that this letter comes only nine months after the publication of *The Library*, perhaps Frazer's deprecation of Apollodorus to Gosse had been merely a touch of authorial fatigue. In any event, several of the titles he names here had appeared in the letter to Rouse in 1918, which implies long-term interest. Of these, all the Greek texts, along with the *Fasti*, offer opportunities for more or less extensive commentary from the comparative anthropological standpoint. In the end, he chose the *Fasti*. On the move and living in hotels as he was, he was able to work on the translation, but for the commentary he would need his library. The *Fasti* was duly reserved for Frazer until he should be able to turn to it.

What is not known is that at the same time he reserved a second work as well. A letter of 10 June 1922 to Miss Buckley, Page's secretary at the Loeb, says, "I am glad you are pleased that I am down for the *Tusculans* and the *Fasti*. It may be some little time before I get to work on them, as we are giving up our rooms in the Temple shortly and the whole of my library is to be transported to Trinity College, where it must be completely re-arranged."[18] Inasmuch as Cicero's *Tusculan Disputations* had been one of the possibilities in 1918 as well, we may assume that they had engaged him for many years before that.

Because the *Fasti* took much longer than had been planned, he never got to Cicero. The Tusculans are highminded Stoic discourses on the fear of death, the endurance of pain, the sufficiency of virtue for a happy life, and other such philosophical themes. Cicero may well have come to appeal more as Frazer grew older; had he translated Cicero when he was in his late seventies, the result might have been memorable. The approach of his own death might have made him a sympathetic editor of that text.

During the early 1920s, then, he was editing Apollodorus and planning future classical work, corresponding with Roscoe in Africa, and writing the second volume of the *The Belief in Immortality*. He was also doing what he could to advance the status of anthropology, which mostly meant the claims of Bronislaw Malinowski, who by now had returned to Britain and was lecturing at the London School of Economics.[19] Frazer's letters to Roscoe always contain summaries of the anthropological news, and in 1920 Malinowski begins to appear in these. On 28 May Frazer had been attending Malinowski's lectures on primitive economics, which he thought were "capital." On 7 July he and Lilly had been seeing a good deal of Malinowski, who was "first rate." On 12 October he was pleased to learn that the governor of Uganda is sympathetic to anthropology and is willing to consider the appointment of a permanent government ethnologist.

I can't make out the name of the man whom you have suggested as suitable for the post; it seems to be a name that I do not know. In time we might have a really first-rate man in B. Malinowski, who is quite willing to continue your work in Central Africa. He is a great linguist and would soon learn the language. But he could not go for about two years, as he calculates that it will take him that time to write his book on the Trobriands, for which he has much material ... After he has finished his book on the Trobriands he wishes to take up field work again, and is favourably disposed to Central Africa, the climate of which, I suppose, is better than New Guinea.[20]

On 2 March 1921 he writes to Macmillan in support of his friend, who has just submitted his manuscript on

primitive trading in the South Seas. ... I consider him decidedly the ablest, the most philosophical, and the most penetrating of the younger anthropologists with whom I am acquainted. I expect great things of him. As to the particular subject of this book I can testify to its novelty and interest, having attended his lectures on the subject last summer at the London School of Economics. ... I need hardly say that Dr Malinowski's book is based on first-hand observation continued under the most favourable circumstances for several years. He is perhaps the first observer to recognise the extreme importance of an accurate study of primitive economics.

Unfortunately, by this time the pitcher had gone to the well more than once too often. Frazer had touted too many anthropologists to Macmillan, who had grown wary of publishing books that were of "the highest scientific value" but did not sell. So he passed over *Argonauts of the Western Pacific*, and Routledge published Malinowski's book, with Frazer's eulogistic preface, in 1922.

In the years leading up to his seventieth birthday Frazer thus was working as hard as ever. It was at this time that recognition – in Lilly's view, long overdue – finally came to him. On 25 June 1920 he was made a member of the Royal Society. It was indeed a high distinction, for Frazer's induction implicitly meant the recognition of anthropology as a scientific discipline by the oldest and most prestigious learned society in the world. This honor was followed by another, for it was also at this moment that the Frazer Lectureship (Lilly of course having persuaded J. G. to go along), under the diligent and sustained direction of Cornford, at last became a reality.

It was proposed that an annual Frazer Lecture, on some topic in social anthropology, be given, on a rotating basis, in each of the universities with which its namesake had been connected – Glasgow, Cambridge, Oxford, and Liverpool. The inclusion of Oxford was distinctly an academic courtesy, as his sole official link with that university had been its award of an honorary degree upon the completion of Pausanias in 1898. And it was doubtless the same courtesy that impelled Cambridge to initiate the series at Oxford. The first address was given in 1922 by Sidney Hartland: "The Evolution of Kinship: An African Study."

The ceremony at Oxford was an impressive one, the high point of which was a brief but eloquent address to Frazer written by his friend A. E. Housman and circulated to a distinguished gathering of friends, colleagues, and well-wishers. Lilly must have savored the evening deeply.[21] As might be expected, most of the early lecturers were men with close personal ties to Frazer, including Roscoe (1923), Malinowski (1925), Marett (1927), Westermarck (1928), and Haddon (1929). Except for the hiatus occasioned by the Second World War, the lectureship has continued, and the lecturers have been among the most eminent anthropologists in the world.

The last of a triad of high honors was the award of an honorary doctorate from the Sorbonne on 19 November 1921. In one of those spasms of amity that occur from time to time in the always ambivalent relationship between France and Britain, Frazer and Rudyard Kipling, as two writers well known in France, were invited to receive degrees. The event was even more glittering than the one at Oxford in that it was not merely a public occasion but a state occasion as well. In the well-known French manner that is virtually unimaginable in an Anglo-Saxon country, the highest officials of the republic, as well as of the world of learning, presided at a ceremony to honor men of letters. (If Lilly was pleased at the honor paid J. G. by his colleagues at home, how must she have felt to see him on the platform next to, and embraced by, the President of France?)

The Frazers enjoyed an extraordinarily warm reception in France. This must in large measure be attributed to Lilly Frazer's sustained and successful efforts to make her husband's name well known in her native land. She accomplished this by seeing to it that, starting with the second edition of *The Golden Bough*, nearly all his major works were translated into French. Perhaps in order not to have to concern himself about it, and knowing that she would become involved regardless, George Macmillan authorized her early on to find and supervise the translators and to sign contracts with them. Over and above this, she translated the first part of *Adonis* and the whole of the abridged *Golden Bough* herself. The award of the doctorate therefore marks a natural culmination to nearly twenty years during which the French had become increasingly familiar with Frazer's work. To the degree should be added, as other notable moments in his French career, addresses to the Ernest Renan Society in 1920 and the Renan centenary celebration at the Sorbonne in 1923, the receipt of a doctorate from Strasbourg in 1922, and his admission as a corresponding member of the Institut de France in 1927.

The last book that Frazer prepared in the Temple was his "best seller," the one-volume abridgment of *The Golden Bough*, which appeared in November 1922. One would think that a man whose impulses all ran in the direction of expansion would have found it difficult to cut his works wholesale, but such was not the case. There are no *cris de cœur* to Macmillan about the impossibility of compressing eleven volumes into one; instead, he went about it straightforwardly and effectively. Most of the saving of space was accomplished by omitting all footnotes, and by cutting back into a manageable garden the vast jungle of examples and illustrations. The pruning made the argument much clearer and easier to follow. Of course the abridgment could not be carried out entirely by deletion. It required much new writing, if only of summaries and transitions, but Frazer carried it out speedily, impelled by the wish to see the book through the press before he left London. To provide recreation and variety from this hard slogging, he altered a resolution of fifteen years' standing and agreed to review anthropological books for *The Times Literary Supplement*. This second incarnation as book reviewer lasted from May 1922 through September 1926.[22]

During 1922–3, spent on the Continent, both Frazers continued to work extremely hard. Because he was unable to undertake any work that required access to his library, his main project during early 1923 was the abridgment of *Folk-Lore in the Old Testament*. The work of compression was not quite so drastic as it had been in *The Golden Bough*, for here only three volumes and not eleven had to be reduced to one. At first he had what he thought was a bright idea: he proposed to achieve a volume of the requisite size by deleting the lengthy analytic table of contents, marginal summaries, notes, and index, thereby retaining the text untouched. Macmillan had patiently to explain to him that the resultant work would not in any important sense be an abridgment and therefore could not be sold as much, and further that buyers of the complete edition might be unhappy to see the whole of the text they bought now selling for a fraction of the original price. Frazer saw the force of that argument and fell to cutting and rewriting.

In early 1923 Frazer had asked Macmillan for an advance of £1000.

Macmillan was willing; in return, however, he asked Frazer (24 January) to agree to a new method for calculating and paying the royalties from the large *Golden Bough*, which of course remained in print and continued to sell (slowly) despite the existence of the epitome. Frazer would henceforth receive a 25 percent royalty rather than half-profits, and the payments would be equalized when possible, thus giving both company and author a better idea of their cash flow. Frazer was pleased to accept, noting (on 25 January) that the wide fluctuations in his income under the old system were "a source of considerable embarrassment to me, as I could not count on the same income from year to year." He thanks Macmillan for having looked after his financial interest so well over the years, and for being so easy about advancing him the large sums that he needs to pay for the new house he is having built in Cambridge.

If they must return to dreaded Cambridge, then Lilly had decided that at last she would have *her* house, a small, manageable home built to her specifications, rather than make do with whatever happened to be on the market. However, they lived in the house, called Lanfine, on Hills Road, for only about five months in 1924. Downie, without stating when or where this happened, tells a story about a house that the Frazers had built for them.[23] Lilly, inspecting the place before it was quite ready for occupancy, entered the bathroom but was unable to get out because the doorknob came off in her hand. After a gigantic fit of hysterics, which ended only when a workman broke through and freed her, she vowed that she would never live there. As Lanfine was the only house they ever built, it must have been where that ridiculous scene took place.

Frazer's few statements about Lanfine say nothing about the reasons for selling so quickly: on 27 January 1924 he writes to Roscoe that "we are settling down and finding the house fairly comfortable, though not all that we could desire."[24] On 29 April he writes to Macmillan that "I hope soon to get rid of this house, which does not suit us," and on 25 July "We have sold Lanfine."

They must have put it on the market soon after they moved in; Downie says that they sold it to the first person offering a thousand pounds, which means that they took a punishing loss, for the house must have cost four or five times that amount to build. If Lilly was not going to live in her own house in Cambridge, she certainly was not going to live anywhere else in that blighted place, so they left Britain and spent another year wandering about, mostly in France.

In October 1925 they returned to London, where they moved into the large apartment house known as Queen Anne's Mansions, near St James's Park. There they stayed for about three years. Not only was the Lanfine fiasco extremely expensive, but to add to Frazer's regrets, this time (April 1924) Trinity College agreed to give him more than storage for his library; they now offered a room in which he could work as well. Thus, when Lilly locked herself in that bathroom, she also effectively locked J. G. out of his beloved Trinity as well.

Before turning to Frazer's major work of the 1920s – the edition of Ovid's *Fasti* (1929) – it is appropriate to say something about a few of the publications of this period. Besterman's bibliography has numerous entries, but most are translations of his works into foreign languages. The others are of no great importance because there is little in them that is new. Frazer had collected the materials for many books, and he resented anything that prevented him from writing them. Whenever he could, therefore, he turned to his files, and from them quickly produced a book. One of these, and by far the most substantial of the mid-1920s, is *The Worship of Nature* (1926); although the title page describes it as volume one, no second volume ever appeared. It represents the Gifford Lectures that Frazer gave at Edinburgh in 1924 and 1925, much augmented. Its subject is the worship of sky, earth, and sun among both Aryan and non-Aryan peoples; the sequel that he never wrote would have completed the survey of the worship of the sun as well as the personification and worship of other aspects of nature. The view that it offers is comprehensive, in the atomistic manner of his earlier three-volume catalogue of *The Belief in Immortality*. Like *Immortality* it is organized geographically, although Frazer, in covering the entire ancient and primitive world in a single volume, has perforce forgone *Immortality*'s overwhelming detail.

Otherwise, the publication that merits most notice is the first of his collections of earlier and sometimes fugitive pieces. *The Gorgon's Head and Other Literary Pieces*, as its title implies, conveniently brings together his nonanthropological essays, addresses, and a few poems and other scraps, together with a few unpublished items. The heart of the volume is the series of seven imitations of Addison in his Roger de Coverley mode, which are quite successful. To these he added two long descriptive lectures that he gave at the Royal Institution in 1921, one on "Roman Life in the Time of Pliny the Younger" and the other on "London Life in the Time of Addison"; four biographical sketches, of which the two important ones are the obituary notices of Robertson Smith and Fison and Howitt; and a literary miscellany. In this last lot, the most interesting, because least characteristic, is a brief, hitherto-unpublished essay entitled "Pax Occidentis: A League of the West." He wrote it in 1906 and submitted it to the *Independent Review*, which rejected it. It was then mislaid and thought lost; it probably turned up in one of the Frazers' many house moves. It is a proposal that Britain and France band together with other European countries to oppose rising German militarism. From the vantage point of 1926, it no doubt seemed to Frazer that had his or some other similar plan then been followed, the world might have been spared the ensuing bloodbath. In reprinting it twenty years after its composition, he says, "It may perhaps pass for a Sibylline leaf." A long, unpublished piece,

"The Gorgon's Head," gives the book its title. It is very early, dating from 1885–6, and was written as a respite from the task of translating Pausanias. Purporting to be a fantasy, it is a tedious and unimaginative retelling of the Perseus story.

Frazer's edition of Ovid's *Fasti* is comparable only to his commentary on Pausanias in its scope and brilliance. If there is any Latin text that is both important enough and difficult enough to merit annotation on the grand scale, and from a perspective that only Frazer could have supplied, that text is the *Fasti*. Overall, the verdict of the reviewers, despite their inevitable minor cavils and petty disagreements, was extremely favorable. It is summed up in the opening sentence, qualified though it is, of Cyril Bailey's review: "There can be no doubt that Frazer's *Fasti* is the most important full edition of a Latin classic published in England since the war."[25]

Although the *Fasti* did not figure as one of the possibilities in Frazer's letter to Rouse of 1918, it does appear on another, more significant list – the one Frazer drew up of his reading when he entered Trinity as a freshman in 1875. In Victorian Britain, if schoolboys read Ovid on their own, it was the *Ars Amatoria* and not the *Fasti*. For an undergraduate to have encountered the *Fasti*, much less read it, in the 1870s is a striking testimony to Frazer's wide-ranging curiosity. In a sense, then, he had been living with the *Fasti* for his entire adult life, and he knew it exceedingly well.

Unlike the Pausanias, neither *The Library* nor the *Fasti* was in any sense an embattled work. Neither was produced in response to a perceived scholarly need. Both had been well if conventionally edited before Frazer came to them. Neither is controversial; in neither case was there a Wilamowitz acting as a dark antagonistic presence in the background. Although both were warmly welcomed and both have proved useful for scholars, it cannot be argued that either has produced a shift in our awareness of the past in general; in both cases, however, Frazer's edition remains the standard, more than half a century later. The two editions, then, owe their existence more to Frazer's long-term preoccupations than to anything else.

Although the edition of the *Fasti* originated in Frazer's relations with the Loeb Library, obviously something happened to transform a modest single volume from Loeb into five grand volumes from Macmillan. The answer is to be found in Frazer's letter from Paris of 25 January 1923, responding to one from his publisher; amazingly, it shows that the motive force behind the large edition was George Macmillan. I say "amazingly" because one would think that after Pausanias, *Totemism and Exogamy*, and three *Golden Boughs*, Macmillan might have had enough. But conditions were now very different from the turn of the century, when both Frazer and anthropology were hardly known. By the mid-twenties the runaway success of *The Golden Bough* and *Folk-Lore in the Old Testament*, especially in their abridged forms, had created a public interested in anything that he wrote – even something so specialized as the *Fasti* – and the economic boom meant that there was a lot of money around, so that the project may not even have seemed a financial risk.

Frazer, with the text and translation already in hand for Loeb, writes that all he had in mind is "little more than a text and translation with some notes – something to occupy me in the months during which I am cut off from my library. You clearly contemplate something much more elaborate, since you speak of possibly three (octavo) volumes without the Latin text." This unique reversal of roles continues, with Frazer offering two cogent objections to Macmillan's proposal for a grandiose edition-cum-commentary:

Such a commentary is not needed, since the existing cheap editions in English and German . . . contain the necessary explanations, and I should not care simply to repeat them. . . . Such an elaborate work would take up much time, which I would rather devote to anthropology, for I have still a number of anthropological books which I wish to write and which I regard as much more important for the history of thought than re-editing a Latin treatise which has already been well edited again and again.

He agrees only to think about the idea. Six weeks later, on 10 March, Frazer writes to Macmillan that he has completed the translation. He then put the project aside for two reasons: he was away from his library and he was occupied with other work, most notably the abridgment of *Folk-Lore in the Old Testament* (1923) and the third volume of *The Belief in Immortality* (1924). The *Fasti* does not figure at all in the Macmillan correspondence for the next three years, although he certainly returned to the commentary once *Immortality* was out of the way. The silence is broken when, on 12 January 1926, Frazer describes a meeting he has just had with Rouse. Their amicable conversation led over the next few weeks to the resolution of an awkward situation that evidently had been developing for some time.

Essentially, the problem was that Heinemann, the publisher of the Loeb series, wished to bring out Frazer's one-volume *Fasti*, which was ready for the printer. Macmillan, on the other hand, with a much larger investment in the five-volume edition, on the commentary of which Frazer was still working, did not want Heinemann to publish: two near-simultaneous editions of the *Fasti* by J. G. Frazer was one too many. To Macmillan, the prior appearance of the Loeb edition could only be confusing and distracting to the public, and might seriously affect sales of the big edition when it finally came out.

The settlement, arrived at after gentlemanly negotiations, was reasonable, if rather one-sided: Heinemann agreed to delay publication until two years after the Macmillan edition had appeared. In return, Frazer waived his payment in order to compensate Heinemann for the expense of keeping the edition set up in type for those two years; Heinemann was also allowed to use a reasonable amount of the annotation from the Macmillan edition. Thus the Loeb *Fasti* would not distract from the debut of the Macmillan *Fasti*, and its

293

edition, intended in any case for a different audience, would be enriched by at least some small part of Frazer's copious commentary. Heinemann did not get much in return for being willing to wait. Perhaps the long friendship between Frazer and James Loeb, and the latter's sense of *noblesse oblige*, were responsible for so amicable a settlement.[26]

Curiously, this account, which is based on the surviving documents, does not gibe with Frazer's own version of events. In the preface to the Macmillan edition he says that he began work on the *Fasti* intending to produce only one volume for the Loeb, but that his notes quickly overspilled even the space that he had been allotted for Apollodorus (that is, two volumes). "When this was brought to the notice of Mr Loeb, he kindly and generously gave me leave to accept the offer of Messrs Macmillan and Co. to publish my commentary in full, only stipulating that the text and translation should, after a sufficient interval, be issued as a volume of the Loeb Library."[27] However, George Macmillan's letter proposing the big edition was written in January 1923, *before* Frazer had even finished the translation for Loeb, much less embarked on the commentary.

Let us leave this small biographical puzzle and turn to the *Fasti* itself. Ovid, to the extent that he lives today, is known for either his erotic poetry (*Ars Amatoria*) or his comprehensive reworking of mythology in the *Metamorphoses*. By contrast, the subject of the *Fasti* is unimaginable in modern poetry – the Roman calendar (*fasti* are the "special" days, or festivals). It is a work of the poet's maturity – he was working on it when he died – and resembles the *Metamorphoses* more than anything else, in that both are long narratives that artfully recount myths and legends. Like the *Aeneid*, the *Fasti* was to be in twelve books, but only six (January through June) were completed, the remainder in the judgment of his literary executors being unfit to be published. Although a versification of the Roman calendar sounds the most unpromising of subjects, in fact it amounts to a poetical reconsideration of the history of Rome from Romulus and Remus down to Augustus, and as such is extremely successful in its own unique terms. It is neither an epic nor a chronicle. Instead it is a kind of historical mosaic of, and commentary on, Rome, with its armature provided by the calendar, which means that the poet flits from tale to tale as he explains the origins and meanings of the many public festivals and historical anniversaries.

Perhaps Ovid conceived the *Fasti* out of a knowledge of his own strengths and weaknesses. Its episodic structure permitted him to narrate many stories, some grave and others light-hearted, without demanding of him what he did not have – the moral seriousness and staying power needed for an epic. Like Pausanias, Ovid includes in his poem not only history but religion as well, because most of the special days in the calendar have religious significance. Finally, in marking the slow round of the seasons, he presents a good deal of astronomical lore, some of it inaccurate. The whole is rendered with the finish and sophistication that distinguishes all of Ovid's work; all told, it is a major poem by a great poet.

The *Fasti* justifies and indeed requires commentary on the Frazerian scale on two counts. The first is stylistic. Because Ovid was constitutionally and continuously predisposed toward oblique and allusive expression, many lines must be glossed for the modern reader. The task here is one for the literary critic, not the anthropologist; an important source of the strength of the commentary is that Frazer does both equally well. In fact, although the reviewers' attention was focused on the ethnography, much of the annotation consists of this kind of straightforward *explication de texte*.

The second is related to the moment of the poem's composition. Ovid lived from 43 B.C. to A.D. 17, or just after the extinction of the republic. This was much more than a political change, however, for it was widely felt to mark the end of the old Roman ethos as well as the old Roman polis. In the sense that the *Aeneid* looks forward to a new imperial, cosmopolitan Rome, so the *Fasti* looks backward to a simpler, more rural Rome in which the unwritten traditions of the family and the *gens* counted for virtually everything. It is significant that when Ovid began to study the calendar for his own poetic purposes, he found that not only were the origins of most of the events commemorated lost in antiquity, but that even many of the priests did not know or care much about the old traditions. His need to carry out folkloric research within the state annals and among the priesthood testifies to both his self-consciousness and his sophistication. The results of that research – the trove of religious rites, folklore, and traditional observances, along with their then-current explanations – that he managed to collect and preserve in the *Fasti* are invaluable for our knowledge and understanding of Roman religion, even if they must be used with caution. In this sense Frazer was the ideal commentator for the work, for no one else controlled both the anthropological and the classical materials so completely.

To do justice to this important work, Frazer's edition runs to no fewer than 2000 pages, in five volumes, of which the first holds the text and prose translation, on facing pages; the second, third, and fourth each contains the commentary on two books of the *Fasti*: the final volume comprises copious illustrations, maps, figures, and two excellent indexes that make the entire edition easily accessible.

As Frazer had noted to Macmillan, the text had been well edited in the relatively recent past, so, as with Apollodorus, he was again spared a great deal of the difficult work that goes into establishing a text where the sources are poor or where many cruces vex and bemuse. Unlike Apollodorus, however, where he consulted no manuscripts, for Ovid he obtained photographs of all the important ones and compared them diligently. Unlike most editors he offered no conjectures of his own, but he felt free to use his own judgment and often adopted readings from inferior manuscripts if they clarified the meaning. The reviewers agreed that his text was a monument to good sense (rather than critical ingenuity), and many remarked that the folkloric and ethnographic dimension that he introduced often shed brilliant new light on the text.[28]

The *Fasti* is a poem of nearly five thousand lines. The translation, albeit in prose, of such a sizable work is therefore a considerable achievement in itself, and merits attention. The *Fasti* had been translated into English five times in the nineteenth century, but Frazer consulted none of these versions.[29] He gives no reason for this, but it is likely that he did so in order to approach the text without prejudice and without feeling that he had been influenced by anyone. He set great store on total freedom of action, in the literary arena as in all else.

The translation presents a number of literary problems, and Frazer's solutions are of some interest, both because of the text they produce and the hints they offer about his sensibility. The heart of the matter is this: Ovid is a great poetic stylist, and anyone who reads and enjoys the *Fasti* in Latin gets a great deal of pleasure from the poet's virtuosity. All the devices of his craft are on display: ceaseless verbal ingenuity, which takes the forms of internal echoes within the poem, constant word play, and various kinds of musical effects like alliteration and assonance that Latin permits. Any prose translation of such a poem must lose most of this verbal texture, partly because it is in prose and partly because of the fundamental differences in grammar and diction between Latin and English that prevent the transplantation or reproduction of many of the devices and effects. Like all good translators, Frazer tries to retain as much as he can, and often succeeds, so that the Latinless reader does come away with some sense of Ovid as craftsman, even if he is unaware how close Frazer often comes to the original.

At the same time, for all his inventiveness and musicality, Ovid is a mannerist. Whenever his subject permits, he tends toward archness, facility, and self-consciousness. This was a criticism leveled by his contemporaries in the ancient world, and it remains one today. In a nice piece of bitchery, Seneca remarked that Ovid "does not use words too freely except in his poems, where he does not fail to know his faults – but loves them."[30] The censorious Quintilian said that "the *Medea* of Ovid shows, in my opinion, to what heights that poet might have risen if he had been ready to curb his talents instead of indulging them."[31] Nearly two millennia later, E. J. Kenney writing in 1970 in the *Encyclopaedia Britannica* eschews moralizing but also emphasizes Ovid's bent for fantasy and artificiality:

Ovid's early training encouraged his romantic and escapist bent . . . in Ovid can be seen the beginnings of the long domination of rhetoric over poetry. . . . He is the most Alexandrian of the Roman poets. His aims can be summed up in one word: point conveyed by smoothness, fluency and balance. To achieve this he shaped the already artificial poetic diction elaborated by his predecessors into an instrument which within its inherent limitations is nearly perfect.[32]

Paradoxically, then, Frazer's own decorous tendencies toward archaism and archness that are inappropriate in rendering a bland writer like Apollodorus or a clumsy one like Pausanias are often quite suitable for a mannered writer like Ovid.

The commentary is the edition's *raison d'être*. Much of it consists (as Frazer writes to Macmillan, 29 January 1926, while he is still working on it) of

the evidence of ancient writers, inscriptions, and monuments illustrative of the *Fasti*: there is little in it of comparative folk-lore and very little of speculation. Indeed, I fear that readers who look for new light on old problems will be disappointed. For the most part I stick to the solid ground of well ascertained facts, and where the interpretation of the facts is uncertain, I indicate plainly the uncertainty.

This may have been Frazer's intention in 1926, but the declaration understates the ethnographic aspect of the commentary that he actually composed. Certainly from the point of view of the classical reviewers, most of whom had barely considered the light anthropology might shed on their subject, this novel aspect absorbed most of their attention. However, in comparison with *Folk-Lore*, with its barely concealed antireligious agenda, the commentary to the *Fasti* is a model of scholarly objectivity, and for this reason remains useful today.

But although Frazer does not have Christianity in his gunsights here, as he does throughout in *Folk-Lore*, he never wholly forgets that religion, as the vehicle of superstition, is the enemy, whether the religion in question happens to be that of Jove or Jehovah. Thus, in discussing the introduction by King Numa of an intercalary month, he notes that the Numean system of making up for the difference between the lunar and solar years was inaccurate by exactly four days.

This excess of four days in four years was clearly due to the preposterous Roman custom of reckoning the lunar year at 355 days instead of the more exact 354 days, and the error seems to have arisen, as both Macrobius and Censorinus thought, through the superstitious and absurd preference for odd numbers. It might be difficult to find a more glaring instance of the havoc which superstition can work when it is suffered to invade the province of science and of practice.[33]

And as if to show that the old comparativist lion is not asleep but only dozing, Frazer then mildly observes that "intercalary days and months appear to be commonly regarded as unlucky."[34] Having created this opening for himself, he supplies two pages of intercalary beliefs among the Aztecs, the Tigreans, the Bafioti, and other such exotic folk. The difference between such an interpolation and an analogous one in the commentary on the Bible is that after only two pages he comes back to the Romans and Ovid, whereas in *Folk-Lore* he might never have returned to the Hebrews.

There are two reasons for this difference. The first is crude but important: the flame of Roman religion having been snuffed, it can be criticized but need not be combated. Christianity, on the other hand, because it remains very much alive, requires constant and relentless confrontation. Accordingly Frazer can be more relaxed in the expression of his irreligion when he is dealing with Rome, and therefore he is able to stay closer to the text. Second, the Ovid is a true commentary, in which the nature and history of the text dictate what does and does not receive comment. Therefore Frazer cannot and does not ride his hobbyhorse endlessly because he is insistently recalled by the text.

A good example of the qualities of the annotation is offered in the 27-page note on the ancient, mysterious, and orgiastic festival of the Lupercalia (*Fasti* ii. 267). By way of introduction, it should be said that Ovid was not especially clear about it – or perhaps his sources were not – and that historians have since disagreed about its origins, nature, and significance. Therefore, Frazer's primary task as commentator is to marshal the vexed and vexing evidence, explain the numerous problems, and weigh the solutions proposed by others, offering his own ideas as contributions to a murky and embattled question. Accordingly, he first describes what happened at this obscure and baffling festival, in which naked male revelers (the Luperci) ran around and beat young girls with goatskins, and which had something to do with the native Pan-like god Faunus. He then establishes its twofold nature: it was purificatory and it also recalled an ancient rite intended to ensure the fertilization of women. On linguistic grounds Frazer argues that the ritual harks back to a time when the male role in conception was unknown.

At this point the horizon widens appreciably:

The primitive character of the ritual and of the ideas implied in it suggests that originally the Lupercalia was a magical rather than a religious rite, and hence that it did not involve a reference to any particular deity, but was simply one of those innumerable ceremonies whereby men have attempted, in all ages and all countries, to repel the powers of evil and so to liberate the powers of good, thus promoting the fertility at once of man, of beast, and of the earth. These ceremonies commonly take the form of a periodic, generally of an annual, expulsion of evils, which are usually conceived in the form of demons or ghosts; having forcibly driven out these dangerous intruders, the community fancies itself safe and happy for the time being, till the recurrence of the old troubles seems to require a fresh application of the old remedy.[35]

Contrary to what one might expect, Frazer does *not* use these two sentences as a springboard for a disquisition on the evolution of primitive mentality, in his *Golden Bough* manner; instead, he stays firmly rooted in the Roman world. Because he does, and because peoples all round the world – primitive, ancient, and modern – acknowledge in their prayers and rituals the need for periodic purification of self and community, his discussion depends on fewer a priori assumptions and is therefore both more modest and more plausible than if he sought to connect the Lupercalia with, say, the religious behavior of the Australian aborigines, who also are ignorant of the biology of sexual reproduction.

He goes on to assess three different explanations of the etymology of *Lupercal*, and comes down on the side of one advanced by his old mentor Mannhardt. Before the Luperci began to run, they slaughtered the goats whose skins would be used in the ritual beatings. When all the goats were killed, the Luperci touched the foreheads of two youths of good family with the point of the knife that had been used, the blood being wiped away immediately after. Mannhardt had interpreted this as a ritual of death and new birth. Mannhardt and Frazer assume that the Luperci as goats represent the "Spirits of Vegetation," and the symbolic death and resurrection of the two are intended to represent and thereby to hasten the rebirth of life. Although his conclusion might have been drawn straight from *The Golden Bough*, up to this point Frazer bases himself entirely on classical evidence.

Now for the first time he goes far afield, describing a similar-sounding ceremony from Kenya, in which initiates are also born again from a goat. Not only are the Kenyan and Roman rituals alike in this but they both involve a fig tree. This leads to a disquisition on the Roman midsummer rite in which the male and female fig trees were married to one another, and to the seemingly similar uses to which fig trees, with their milky sap, were put by both Romans and Kenyans in rituals for making barren women fertile.

There is more. Because the method for fertilizing the date palm also resembles that of the fig tree, and because we have sculptural representations of the king of Babylonia (whom Frazer calls a "divine king") fertilizing the dates, he then invokes the possibility that "the fertilization of the palms was celebrated by a religious festival comparable to those which the Greeks and Latins appear to have celebrated on the occasion of the fertilization of the fig."[36] He concludes with a survey of the habitat and diffusion of the fig and date in antiquity, which leads him to this grand, sweeping conclusion:

Thus it seems not unreasonable to suppose that before the rise of the great civilizations of Babylonia, Egypt, and Greece, a ruder but perhaps more homogeneous culture, based to a large extent on the cultivation of the date-palm and the fig-tree, may have prevailed throughout a zone stretching from the Tigris and Euphrates on the east along the whole of North Africa to the Atlantic on the west, with offshoots on the northern coasts of the Mediterranean in Asia Minor, Greece, and Italy; and that the religion of the people throughout this great area may have centred to some extent round the trees from which they mainly drew their subsistence. . . . But we have wandered far from Ovid. It is time to return to him.[37]

It is indeed time to return to him. When we do return, especially if we are the average conservative classicists of 1929, our eyes have been well and truly opened and some undreamed-of possibilities have been raised. No, not all of it is true – certainly the conclusion about the great prehistoric date-cum-fig culture, at least in the light of the evidence offered, must be dismissed as a fantasy. But thus to evaluate this remarkable *tour de force* mean-spiritedly is to miss its meaning. For those readers who instinctively resist anything so all-comprehensive as Frazer's conclusion, they can stop reading about two-thirds of the way through – at the first mention of Kenya – and come away with a sound, authoritative, and thought-provoking essay on the Lupercalia couched entirely in classical terms. However, it cannot be bad for a scholar every now and then to encounter broader views than are normally taken, even if in the end they are disregarded.

Of course the essay on the Lupercalia is not typical of the entire commentary, if only because of its exceptional length. But one hopes that this summary suffices to give a sense of Frazer's authority and his total mastery of the classical materials, disposed in the manner that classical scholars know and respect. Without this as a basis, none of the rest would be possible. It may seem from this example that for Frazer classics was anthropology pursued by other means. This is only partly true – there are hundreds of entries that lack even the faintest whiff of the ethnographic about them – but that it should be so is perfectly reasonable.

Through his long life Frazer produced a vast tapestry on primitive religion, within which he also threaded the religions of the three civilizations that in the West have been given the name and status of classical: Israel, Greece, and Rome. From the standpoint of the late twentieth century the books on the primitives have been measured and largely found wanting; this is not the case with the books on the classic civilizations, two of which – Pausanias and the *Fasti* – still live for scholars. Of these, the *Fasti* represents the apex of his intellectual life and is arguably the finest work he ever accomplished.

17 · AFTERMATH

Having left Queen Anne's Mansions in the autumn of 1928, the Frazers resumed their wandering existence, spending the winter of 1928–9 in Paris, where Frazer completed reading the proofs of the *Fasti* and Lady Frazer busied herself with the foundation of the Société du Folklore Français.[1] They then spent most of the spring in Lausanne, and returned to London in June, where they took a small flat in the Temple to use as a *pied-à-terre*. Henceforth, for the last dozen years of their lives, they moved restlessly and had no fixed abode; after they gave up the Temple flat they stayed at their London club (the Albemarle), in hotels in London and Paris, or in a rented flat in Cambridge.

When the *Fasti* finally appeared in October 1929 Frazer, healthy and energetic in his seventy-sixth year, looked forward to returning to anthropology. He had collected the materials for many books, the writing of which would occupy him for the rest of his life. He turned to this immense mass of notes as soon as Ovid had been seen through the press, and the immediate result was *Myths of the Origin of Fire*, which appeared in February 1930. This is yet another sterile volume of the same kind as *The Belief in Immortality* and *The Worship of Nature*, which laboriously and comprehensively presents the beliefs of ancient and primitive peoples, organized geographically, on the subject named in the title.

Not many letters have survived from this period. The Frazers were more or less permanently on the move, and the letters are often written from railway-terminus hotels, where they liked to put up. Because Frazer could do nothing that depended upon his library, most of his communications have little to do with his work. An exception is one that he wrote on 7 February 1930 from Paris to J. J. Thomson, the Master of Trinity.[2] In the mid-twenties he had been given the use of a large room in college, as part of the arrangements for their return to Cambridge. When the Lanfine débâcle caused them to leave, he stored his library in the room, keeping out only that relatively small number of books that he would need for the Ovid. He now asks the Master to exchange this room for a full Fellow's set of rooms, for he wishes to return to anthropological work in Cambridge, which means access to his library. For his part, if the college permits him to return, he undertakes to be in residence for at least 100 days a year. To his gratification, the request was immediately granted. Because of the breakdown in his health that occurred in the next year, however, he never returned to residence.

Because so much of their income was derived from his royalties, Lilly was keenly aware of the importance of keeping J. G.'s name before the public. The best way to do this, of course, was for him to write more books; he certainly did his best, but his works tended to appear at long intervals. As that could not be changed, she reasoned that the next best would be to repackage the old titles. She had done her part in 1924, with *Leaves from the Golden Bough*, "culled by Lady Frazer." This was a children's version of *The Golden Bough* – a collection of narrative extracts, in J. G.'s words, containing myths and legends, folktales, and explanations of holidays and festivals, all suitably illustrated for a younger audience.

In early 1929 she had another good idea. She proposed to Macmillan that the maps from the last volume of Pausanias be republished separately in a portfolio for the use of travelers. (Cartography in Greece then was not well developed, and Frazer's maps of thirty years earlier were still useful.) On 10 July 1929 J. G. wrote to Macmillan to supplement this proposal: to the maps should be added the plans of the major archaeological sites, and a brief explanatory text incorporating the latest discoveries. He, out of touch with archaeology these many years and therefore unable himself to write such a text, had found someone qualified to do so: A. W. van Buren, the Director of the American School in Rome. This was agreed, and the resulting volume, *Graecia Antiqua: Maps and Plans to Illustrate Pausanias's Description of Greece*, appeared in January 1930.

When *Graecia Antiqua* was announced, the noted British archaeologist A. J. B. Wace suggested to Macmillan that a full-scale supplement to Frazer's Pausanias, incorporating the findings of the past thirty years, be published in order to bring that invaluable work up to date and thereby extend its utility (and sale). Frazer was amenable, on the understanding that the new publication would be a supplement, his text to remain undisturbed. But as such plans do, this one changed under discussion, and its final version, advanced by the American Archaeological Institute and reported by Wace, proposed something quite different: that the commentary be rewritten, section by section, by different scholars to reflect the current state of knowledge, retaining only that part of the original commentary that remained accurate. To this Frazer was utterly and quite properly opposed.

In 1929 the Bodleian Library had asked Frazer for a specimen of his writing, and he decided to donate the manuscript of his fellowship essay on Plato of 1879. On 17 January 1930 he therefore asked Macmillan, in whose offices the manuscript had been stored, to be good enough to send it along. Macmillan, who until then had not known of the essay's existence, immediately offered to publish it, both for its intrinsic interest and as a homage to his friend of forty-five years. Frazer agreed, on condition that it appear unchanged, and it came out in May 1930.

His next book, *Garnered Sheaves* (1931), collects his anthropological pieces starting with the essay on funeral custom and belief of 1885, and stands as a useful companion to *The Gorgon's Head* of 1927. The other volume of that year was the much-delayed one-volume Loeb *Fasti*.

In the spring of 1931, however, an event took place that determined the remaining ten years of Frazer's life. As far back as 20 April 1920 Frazer had written to Gosse to tell him of his intention of becoming a life member of the Royal Literary Fund, out of gratitude for the help the Fund had given him at two critical moments in his life. Thereafter, whenever he and Lady Frazer were in London they attended the Fund's annual dinners, and in 1929 Frazer agreed to become a vice-president. On 11 May 1931 he was a speaker at the Fund's banquet. The entry from Harold Nicolson's diary for that date tells what happened:

Literary Fund dinner. Duke of York [the future George VI] in the chair. Speakers: the Master of Wellington and Frazer of the *Golden Bough*. The latter has written out his speech in his own handwriting and when it gets to the point, he can scarcely read it. There are vast, appalling pauses during which Lady Frazer, at his side, looks up with the bright smile of anticipation adopted by people who are completely deaf. She is always armed with a portable wireless which she wears on her bosom. When I sat next to her once at dinner, this machine gave out strange sounds of jazz interspersed with vague and distant talks on poultry farming. It took me some time to discover what had happened.[3]

Downie says that as Frazer began reading, "his eyes filled with blood and all went dark" (presumably, blood vessels in the eyes ruptured). He felt no pain, but he was blind. He had had eye trouble for thirty years, and had had several operations that had restored his sight, but this trauma came without warning. Lady Frazer immediately took him to consult the most renowned ophthalmologists in Europe but nothing could be done. Frazer never saw again.

Once the initial shock passed, and the doctors were unanimous in holding out no hope, J. G. and Lilly took stock of the new state of affairs. Despite his necessarily increased dependence on her henceforth, they decided that this blow should not and would not stop him from working. For him work was not merely a matter of routine but his very reason for living. His mind was unimpaired, he was otherwise strong and in good health – what would he do if not work? So, with the aid of readers and amanuenses, he would and did continue to write and to publish through most of the 1930s. A few of those publications were recycled early material, but most were not. Whatever one thinks of the work he brought out in this last period of his life, the most impressive thing about it surely is that it exists at all – that he was able to keep going until virtually the end.

Because a number of his helpers have left accounts of their time with the Frazers, we have more detailed information about this last (albeit saddest and least interesting) decade in their life than we do of any of those that preceded.[4] The scenes depicted are often pathetic. J. G. was blind and Lilly was deaf. As he grew increasingly helpless, she sometimes pushed him around literally as well as figuratively. He never complained, at least in the hearing of any outsider; she, on the other hand, complained enough for both of them. If his new life was difficult, hers was doubly so, for she was not only handicapped herself but had to look after J. G. as well. She was encumbered with a husband whom she loved but who was an invalid, and her normal impatience and paranoia did not help. She maintained her policy of keeping anything from him that might disturb him, so that his life remained calm, but this meant that it was all the more difficult for everyone else in the household, not least for the secretaries. They exacted revenge in their reminiscences.

Whatever his helpers may have been feeling as they skirmished daily and sometimes hourly with Lady Frazer, the tonic he wanted was occupation. He had been named Honorary Bencher of the Middle Temple in 1931, this being a rare honor, but he needed substantive work. It was therefore gratifying that he was asked in 1932 to give the Zaharoff Lecture at Oxford early in the following year. He was pleased to accept because it gave him an opportunity to pay tribute to the French savant Condorcet and, in so doing, to the qualities of order, rationalism, and decorum for which the Enlightenment stood – and for which he stood as well. In *Condorcet on the Progress of the Human Mind* Frazer, who had expressed in his inaugural lecture in 1908 a vision of the fragility of civilization, surrounded as it was by irrationality on all sides, now saw as if in a second vision the rise of modern forces of confusion and destruction. These, of which the prime example was the Bolshevik Revolution, were the result of the insane fancies of a small group of "purely speculative thinkers or dreamers." Altogether it seemed as if Europe in the 1930s resembled France in the 1790s, with only a change of names needed to make Burke's anti-Jacobin tirades directly applicable to Soviet communism. Unfortunately the outcome was now clouded and uncertain. Although Condorcet believed in the perfectibility of humankind through the use of reason, Frazer could not be so sanguine. "For unhappily in the scales of human judgement the clear dictates of reason are too often outweighed by the blind impulse of the passions."[5]

Once he resumed working, it was at the old tempo. While he was writing the lecture, he was also (with the help of his reader and secretary) quarrying from his notes another of those long-planned books. This one, *The Fear of the Dead in Primitive Religion*, marked the completion of the circle that had begun in his first anthropological essay, back in 1885. He gave this as the William Wyse Lectures at Trinity College in 1932 and 1933. Wyse, whose waspish letter to her husband had so irritated Lilly Frazer in 1914, had surprised everyone,

Frazer included, by leaving his money to Trinity to endow a lectureship not in his own subject – classics – but in social anthropology. As Wyse's close friend, and as Trinity's own great man of anthropology, Frazer was the obvious choice to inaugurate the series. His two sets of lectures, delivered in 1932 and 1933, were published in two volumes, in 1933 and 1934, and he continued for a third volume on the same subject (1936).

Meanwhile Lady Frazer decided to remind the world of J. G.'s eminence and at the same time present him with a fitting gift on the occasion of his eightieth birthday, 1 January 1934. In late 1932 or early 1933 she retained Theodore Besterman (1904–76), later an illustrious bibliographer but then only a wealthy and bookish young man, and commissioned him to prepare a bibliography of J. G.'s lengthy and complicated *œuvre* of fifty years.

By this time the economic depression had hit publishing hard, and Macmillan like all other firms had had to retrench. No longer could they afford to make handsome gestures by bringing out books like this one that had no chance of recouping their production costs, much less make a profit. Moreover, George Macmillan, with whom the Frazers had dealt for nearly fifty years, was in poor health and had virtually withdrawn from any active role in the company (he died in 1936). His successors had not had his friendship with Sir James to compensate them for Lady Frazer's continual importuning, and they were unwilling to put up with it. The firm therefore accepted the bibliography for publication, but only on a subscription basis. They would do it, that is, only if she produced enough prepaid sales to indemnify them against any losses.

Lady Frazer at first was outraged, and was not backward in reminding them how much money J. G. had made for the house of Macmillan over the years. They were adamant, and she realized that she had to accept the new order of things if the book was to appear at all. As well as being an indomitable fighter, she was a canny tactician, and therefore carefully planned this campaign – the first of many over the next few years. She enlisted the cooperation of the Folk-Lore Society, of which Frazer had been an inactive vice-president for many years, to distribute a prospectus for the bibliography to its members. More important, she wrote to all their own many friends and acquaintances in Britain and abroad, asking them to take one or more copies in honor of J. G., and canvassed as well the major research libraries. Finally, when all her efforts did not produce quite enough subscribers, she guaranteed to make good any losses that might result.

Besterman told me that the project would have been a difficult one even for a seasoned bibliographer, and he was then quite inexperienced.[6] Although he was given access to Frazer's files, it had not been at all easy to thread the labyrinth of the publications and republications, sometimes with new titles; the technical problems, however, were as nothing compared with the problems attendant on working with Lady Frazer. She kept changing her mind about the format; she would receive subscriptions, then forget to give him the names, but blame him nevertheless when they failed to appear on the list; and she was snobbishly fanatical about how the subscribers – her friends – should be styled. Despite all this, the volume appeared, on time, in January 1934.

The subscription campaign for the bibliography proved good practice for the upcoming years. The depression had not only made Macmillan uncooperative but had devastated the Frazers' exchequer, dependent as it was in such great measure on royalties and the Trinity dividend. For anthropologists Frazer was now hopelessly old-fashioned; at the same time the book-buying public had many more important things on which to spend their diminished incomes than expensive volumes of speculative anthropology. She therefore had quickly to find some new sources of income, or their expensive household would rapidly become impossible to support. But even in a depression there is money about, if only one knows where to look. When she learned that the Drapers Company sometimes made charitable grants, she put together a group of testimonials from no less than the Archbishop of Canterbury, the Prime Minister, the Master of Trinity College, and the President of the British Academy. With such support it is perhaps not surprising that in 1933 she succeeded in securing a grant of £400 a year for three years from the Company to pay for a secretary for Sir James, that he might continue to do his work. This was renewed for another three years in 1936, and in 1940 a final grant of £100 was made. These sums, only part of which were spent on secretaries, were crucial in getting them through.[7]

Although J. G. continued to dictate letters to his friends, she took over the correspondence with Macmillan, and badgered the company into bringing out a last collection of J.G.'s essays. *Creation and Evolution in Primitive Cosmologies and Other Pieces* (1935) included the talk on Condorcet and the two affecting and valuable autobiographical essays – his last original work – along with several recent obituaries and a few pieces that had somehow escaped collection earlier.

She also prevailed upon them to publish *Aftermath* (1936) and *Totemica* (1937).[8] These two volumes can be regarded as either the vestigial continuations of *The Golden Bough* and *Totemism and Exogamy* or else as the fourth and second editions, respectively, of those works. In a sense Frazer published all his books unwillingly because he conceived them primarily as repositories of facts, and publication by definition excludes some relevant information, either because it has been overlooked or else come too late for inclusion. Therefore, as soon as he received copies of his books, he began annotating and enlarging them. The next edition began, at least potentially, the moment he passed the last proof for the press.

As the long-delayed afterbirths of the works they purport to continue, they are strange productions. They assume that the reader possesses the originals, and indeed has them open on the table alongside, for each chapter in the continuation – many only a page or two long – is keyed to the relevant section of the original. They contain no new arguments, only new examples. That they represent no change or advance whatever, only more of the same, is depressing and perhaps moving as well to anyone coming to them as the final installments in Frazer's long career. The reason for this unwillingness to rethink is implied in an architectural metaphor in the preface to *Aftermath*: "In the present work I have extended and strengthened the foundation without remodelling the superstructure of theory, which on the whole I have seen no reason to change."[9] His unexamined belief in facts for their own sake (the "foundation"), atop which is uncertainly perched a quantity of theory (the "superstructure"), has survived untouched, not merely from the completion of *The Golden Bough* in 1915 but from 1885 and probably even earlier. In his view *Totemism and Exogamy* and *Aftermath* – by which is meant the facts in those two works – needed only to be kept current. This task he had now completed.

He changed nothing because unfortunately he had learned nothing. The books were reviewed – sometimes savagely or disdainfully – on the strength of Frazer's past eminence, but they are trivial productions, mainly notable as monuments to his strength of character. Few men of his age and with his disability could have written two such volumes, which are after all lengthy and sonorous in his customary style if no more, and seen them through the press. Downie, who literally wrote both of them, notes that between *Aftermath* in 1935 and *Totemica* in 1937, Frazer declined markedly. For *Aftermath* the old man could manage to concentrate for an entire day, and was able to digest and recast the materials that Downie read out to him. By the time of *Totemica*, however, he was no longer up to such mental effort, and much of that volume consists of paragraphs and even whole pages incorporated verbatim from the sources.

Although Downie developed great affection for Frazer, he found it impossible to coexist with Lady Frazer for any long time. He tells of frequent hysterics, wild accusations followed by tearful retractions, being discharged and then taken back without explanation. He left their strenuous employ after the completion of *Totemica* but was lured back the next year. This time the project was the long-mooted publication of Sir James's anthropological notebooks. Downie suggested, and Frazer agreed, that their contents be reorganized geographically, and the former carried out the work, deciding the extracts to be used and the sequence in which they would appear; his name figures on the title page as editor. The notebooks, which made four large volumes in print, were collectively entitled *Anthologia Anthropologica*; they appeared in 1939 and 1940. Macmillan was not interested, and they were brought out as an expensive vanity publication by Lund Humphries.

After *Anthologia* Downie left, to be replaced by P. William Filby, an impecunious assistant at the Cambridge University Library. His narrative is as sad and comical as that of Downie, except that by now Frazer had had a stroke, and needed a manservant to help him at all times. He remained capable of minimal intellectual effort, which to Lady Frazer meant that he was to hear readings from his own works each day. When he protested that he did not want to hear his own words but those of others, she would have none of it – she knew what was best for him – and kept popping in at odd intervals to make sure that Filby had not smuggled in any illicit reading matter. Filby then left and was succeeded by Sarah Campion, who got on perhaps least well of all the assistants with Lady Frazer; her period of service, in the spring of 1940, was therefore briefest.

In 1939 Downie was re-engaged; Lady Frazer wished him to write a life of Sir James, which he duly did. *James George Frazer: The Portrait of a Scholar* appeared in 1940. Downie said that she was unwilling that the book contain even the slightest hint of criticism, and she literally read the manuscript over his shoulder as he wrote.

This sad comedy continued until 7 May 1941, when Sir James Frazer died in Cambridge, of a combination of the degenerative effects of old age. Lady Frazer, who herself had had at least one stroke but had kept herself going by willpower alone because her husband needed her, was at last released, and she died several hours later the same day. The joke among the Fellows at Trinity College was that she would not allow him even one day's peace by himself. They are both buried in St Giles' cemetery, in Cambridge.

APPENDIX 1

ADDITIONS TO BESTERMAN'S BIBLIOGRAPHY

In the interest of completeness I offer a supplement to Theodore Besterman's invaluable *A Bibliography of Sir James George Frazer, O.M.*, which goes through 1933. It comprises both omitted items and those that appeared after 1933. Mr Paul Naiditch called my attention to the first two items.

1885a. "A Slavonic Parallel to 'The Merchant of Venice,'" *The Academy*, 27 (9 May 1885), 330–1. A letter.

1886a. "'Patria and Potestas' among the South Slavonians," *The Academy*, 29 (27 March 1886), 166–7. A letter.

1888a. "Theseus," *Encyclopaedia Britannica*, 9th edn, XXIII, 293–5. [Signed "J.G. Fr."]

1888b. "Thespiae," *Encyclopaedia Britannica*, 9th edn, XXIII, 297. [Signed "J.G. Fr."]

1897a. [Letter to Edward Clodd on folklore], *Folk-Lore*, 8: 11–12.

1906a. "Savage Childhood: The Infant Kaffir," *Daily Mail* Books Supplement (London, 24 November 1906). Review, signed, of Dudley Kidd, *Savage Childhood: A Study of Kaffir Children* (London, A. & C. Black, 1906).

1906b. "A Museum of Mankind. The Pitt-Rivers Experiment," *Daily Mail* Books Supplement (London, 15 December 1906). Review, unsigned, and probably by JGF, of A. Lane-Fox Pitt-Rivers, *The Evolution of Culture, and Other Essays* (Oxford, Clarendon Press, 1906).

1906c. "The Black Man's Mind," *Daily Mail* Books Supplement (London, 29 December 1906). Review, unsigned, and probably by JGF, of R.E. Dennett, *At the Back of the Black Man's Mind, or Notes on the Kingly Office in West Africa* (London, Macmillan, 1906). See letter to Clodd, 11 December 1906.

1907a. "The Tribes of the Lower Niger," *Daily Mail* Books Supplement (London, 5 January 1907). Review, unsigned, and probably by JGF, of A.G. Leonard, *The Lower Niger and Its Tribes* (London, Macmillan, 1906). See letter to Clodd, 11 December 1906.

1907b. "A Lady Among Cannibals," *Daily Mail* Books' Supplement (London, 9 February 1907). Review, unsigned, and probably by JGF, of Beatrice Grimshaw, *From Fiji to the Cannibal Islands* (London, Eveleigh Nash, 1907).

1907c. "Black-Fellows. The Aborigines of Australia," *Daily Mail* Books Supplement (London, 16 February 1907). Review, unsigned, and probably by

JGF, of N.W. Thomas, *Natives of Australia* (London, Constable, 1906).

1907d. "Commendatore Boni at Cambridge," *The Times* (London, 21 May 1907), p. 6. A letter.

1919a. "Preface" to Edgar A. Browne, *The Queen of Hearts and Other Plays*. London, Hodder & Stoughton. Pages vii–xiv.

1934a. *The Fear of the Dead in Primitive Religion*. Vol. II. London: Macmillan.

1935a. *Creation and Evolution in Primitive Cosmogonies and Other Pieces*. London: Macmillan.

1936a. *The Fear of the Dead in Primitive Religion*. Vol. III. London: Macmillan.

1936b. *Aftermath: A Supplement to The Golden Bough*. London: Macmillan.

1937a. *Totemica: A Supplement to Totemism and Exogamy*. London: Macmillan.

1938a. *Anthologia Anthropologica*. Vol. I: *The Native Races of Africa and Madagascar*. London: Lund, Humphries. Edited by R.A. Downie.

1939a. *Anthologia Anthropologica*. Vol. II: *the Native Races of Australasia*. London: Lund, Humphries. Edited by R.A. Downie.

1939b. *Anthologia Anthropologica*. Vol. III: *The Native Races of Asia and Europe*. London: Lund, Humphries. Edited by R.A. Downie.

1939c. *Anthologia Anthropologica*. Vol. IV: *The Native Races of America*. London: Lund, Humphries. Edited by R.A. Downie.

FRAZER'S NOTEBOOKS

Study of the working methods of a library scholar like Frazer is important, for his patterns of thought may show up in the way he handled his materials. In 1939, after the last drop of utility in the form of *Anthologia Anthropologica* had been squeezed out of them, Lilly Frazer offered fifty-five of J.G.'s notebooks to the British Museum, which accepted them (BM Add. MSS 45442–96). This bequest represented only a small part of his working materials, however. How many notebooks there had been, and what became of the rest, is unknown. Some of the gaps are obvious: e.g., this group is nearly entirely anthropological; there is virtually nothing on his classical productions. Furthermore, the notebooks contain the results of his review only of the journals, but not the books, for the second edition of *The Golden Bough* (1898–9). In addition, the archives of the Department of Social Anthropology at Cambridge contain a handful of late notebooks. How they came there no one now knows. (I wish to thank Dr Alan Macfarlane for informing me of their existence and arranging for me to see them.) There are other gaps too, as will emerge below.

The BM volumes fall into two categories. The first forty (Add. MSS 45442–81) are the so-called unclassified notebooks, which contain verbatim extracts, without comment, from anthropological books and journals, along with a few drafts of essays and notes of conversations and copies of letters received. Of this group fifteen have geographical titles ("America," "Africa," "New Guinea") and the rest are miscellaneous. From this unclassified series Downie quarried *Anthologia*. The only index each volume contains (on the inside front cover, in JGF's hand) is a list of authors, sometimes with titles, of the books abstracted within.

The remaining fifteen volumes are the so-called classified group. As their titles indicate – "Plants and Animals in Classical Authors," "Marriage Customs," "Burial and Mourning Customs" – they are organized around a single topic. Their contents are discussed below.

From changes in his handwriting and from internal evidence such as the date of the latest source abstracted within each book, used as a *terminus ad quem*, it is possible to assign many of the volumes to a period of a year or two, and all of them to within five years. Leaving aside his classical reading, if the BM cache constituted the whole of his anthropological notebooks, Frazer filled on average about one or two unclassified volumes a year, which seems much too low. There must have been many more from the early years because Robertson Smith was citing these notebooks in 1890, yet only about eight date from this period.

Frazer's note-taking system is remarkable. Once he made the crucial decision at the start to use bound books rather than loose cards, his deeply held belief in following the facts wherever they might lead explains why most of the books are unclassified, for to have adopted an a priori set of categories might have caused him to miss something.

The contents of these volumes are completely miscellaneous and accidental, depending wholly on the order in which Frazer read; therefore his indexing system is critically important. The index, such as it is, is to be found in the classified series, which naturally began at the same time as the unclassified. These classified books are mixed. The first part of each is not an index at all but contains information in its own right, and only the second half is given over to indexing citations to the unclassified series. Thus, Add. MS 45488 ("Mourning Customs and the Treatment of the Dead") begins with material that he used in his 1885 paper to the Anthropological Institute; only the latter part contains bibliographical citations on this subject. As there are only fifteen classified volumes and some of them are highly specialized – e.g., "Plants and Animals in Classical Authors" (Add. MS 45483) or "Customs and Myths from Classical Sources" (Add. MS 45486) – many facts and even whole articles could not be properly assigned to any of them, which vitiates the system.

There is one early attempt (Add. MS 45482) at a different system: a book with alphabetical tabs devoted entirely to library references. It contains, for example, under "B," entries on "bridges"; "blood, sacrifice of one's own"; "barring of door against a person in a ceremony"; "blood feud"; "blood revenge based on the belief that it is required by the ghost of the slain" – each item followed by one or more bibliographical citations. These citations, however, are to books and journals in JGF's library and the university library, *not* to his other notebooks. From its uniqueness one may infer that he may have found this method both laborious and unworkable; in any event he seems soon to have changed over to the system already described.

BIBLIOGRAPHIC NOTES

To reduce the number of footnotes, I have avoided making repeated references to a few major manuscript collections. The Frazers' letters to the Macmillan Company – directed mainly to George Macmillan – are part of the Macmillan Company papers deposited in the British Library, and are used with the permission of the British Library Board and The Macmillan Press Limited. The Frazer papers are BL Add. MSS 55134–55, as follows:

55134	1884–97
35	1898–1902
36	1903–7
37	1908–10
38	1911–13
39	1914–18
40	1919–22
41	1923–5
42	1926–7
43	1928
44	1929
45	1930
46	1931
47	1932–3
48	1934 (January–April)
49	1934 (May–December)
50	1935
51	1936
52	1937
53	1938
54	1939
55	1940–1

All the MSS of the letters from the Frazers to Sir Edmund Gosse are to be found in the Brotherton Collection, University of Leeds. Frazer's letters to Edward Clodd that are in TCC are so indicated in the notes; all others to Clodd are in the Brotherton Collection. The letters in the University Library, Cambridge, are quoted by courtesy of the Syndics of the University Library.

ABBREVIATIONS

The following abbreviations will be used in the notes for works by Frazer; in each case the place of publication is London and the publisher Macmillan.

C & E	*Creation and Evolution in Primitive Cosmogonies and Other Pieces*, 1935
FOT	*Folk-Lore in the Old Testament*, 3 vols., 1918
GB	*The Golden Bough*, 1st edn, 2 vols., 1890
GB²	*The Golden Bough*, 2nd edn, 3 vols., 1900
GB³	*The Golden Bough*, 3rd edn, 12 vols., 1911–15
GBᵃ	*The Golden Bough*, abridged edn, 1922
GH	*The Gorgon's Head and Other Literary Pieces*, 1927
GS	*Garnered Sheaves*, 1931
Paus	*Pausanias's Description of Greece*, 6 vols., 1898
PT	*Psyche's Task*, 1909
T & E	*Totemism and Exogamy*, 4 vols., 1910

Other abbreviations

DNB	*Dictionary of National Biography*
FGB	R. A. Downie, *Frazer and The Golden Bough* (London, Gollancz, 1970)
JAI	*Journal of the Anthropological Institute*
JRAI	*Journal of the Royal Anthropological Institute*
J. Z. Smith	Jonathan Z. Smith, "The Glory, Jest and Riddle: James George Frazer and *The Golden Bough*" (Yale diss., 1969)
TCC	Trinity College, Cambridge
UL	University Library, Cambridge

NOTES

Introduction: Frazer and intellectual biography

1 R.A. Downie, *James George Frazer: The Portrait of a Scholar* (London, Watts, 1940), p. 11.

2 R.A. Downie, *Frazer and the Golden Bough* (London, Gollancz, 1970).

3 Marvin Harris, *The Rise of Anthropological Theory* (New York, Crowell, 1968); Matthew Hodgart, "In the Shade of the Golden Bough," *Twentieth Century*, 157 (1955), 111–19; Edmund Leach, "Golden Bough or Gilded Twig?", *Daedalus*, 90 (1961), 371–99, and "On the 'Founding Fathers': Frazer and Malinowski," *Encounter*, 25 (1965), 24–36, rpt. with comments and rejoinders in *Current Anthropology*, 7 (1966), 560–7; Robert H. Lowie, *The History of Ethnological Theory* (New York, Rinehart, 1937).

Frazer fares no better in: E. E. Evans-Pritchard, *Social Anthropology* (New York, Free Press, 1951), *Theories of Primitive Religion* (Oxford, Oxford University Press, 1965), and *A History of Anthropological Thought*, ed. André Singer (London, Faber & Faber, 1981); George W. Stocking, Jr, *Race, Culture, and Evolution* (New York, Free Press, 1968). In 1983 Stocking began editing the annual *History of Anthropology* (University of Wisconsin Press); the second volume, despite its unfortunate title *Functionalism Historicized* (1984), is important, especially the essays in it by Jones, Stocking, and Kuper. I regret that George Stocking's outstanding volume, *Victorian Anthropology* (New York, Free Press, 1987) arrived when this work was already in proof.

4 Obituaries and notices: H. J. Fleure, *Obituary Notices of Fellows of the Royal Society, 1939–1941*, 897–914; E.O. James, *DNB*, and *Man*, 42 (January–February 1942), no. 2; R.G. Lienhardt, *International Encyclopedia of the Social Sciences* (New York, Macmillan, 1968), V, 550–3; J. H. Hutton, *Cambridge Review*, 62 (23 May 1941), 439–40, and *Nature*, 147 (24 May 1941), 635–6; H. McLeod Innes, *Cambridge Review*, 62 (23 May 1941), 439; Bronislaw Malinowski, "Sir James George Frazer: A Biographical Appreciation," in *A Scientific Theory of Culture and Other Essays* (New York, Oxford University Press, 1960; orig. pub. 1944), pp. 177–221; R. R. Marett, *Proceedings of the British Academy*, 27 (1941), 377–91, and *Nature*, 147 (24 May 1941), 633–5; J. L. Myres, *Nature*, 147 (24 May 1941), 635; A. R. Radcliffe-Brown, *Man*, 42 (January–February 1942), no. 1; H. J. Rose, *Classical Review*, 55 (1941), 57–8.

5 I.C. Jarvie, *The Revolution in Anthropology* (London, Routledge & Kegan Paul, 1964); "Academic Fashions and Grandfather Killing – In Defense of Frazer," *Encounter*, 26 (April 1966), 53–5; "The Problem of the Rationality of Magic," *British Journal of Sociology*, 18 (March 1967), 55–74. *The New Golden Bough* (New York, Criterion, 1959) is Theodor H. Gaster's version of *The Golden Bough. Myth, Legend, and Custom in the Old Testament* (New York, Harper & Row, 1969) in his updating of *Folk-Lore in the Old Testament*. Much less remains of the original in the latter than in the former.

6 John B. Vickery, *The Literary Impact of The Golden Bough* (Princeton, Princeton University Press, 1973); Mary Douglas, "Judgments on James Frazer," *Daedalus*, 107 (Fall 1978), 151–64; Sabine MacCormack, "Magic and the Human Mind: A Reconsideration of Frazer's *Golden Bough*," *Arethusa*, 17 (Fall 1984), 151–76.

7 Northrop Frye, *Anatomy of Criticism* (Princeton, Princeton University Press, 1957), pp. 108–9; Lionel Trilling, "On the Teaching of Modern Literature" (1963), in *Beyond Culture* (New York, Viking, 1965), pp. 15–18.

1 Childhood and youth

1 "Speech on Receiving the Freedom of the City of Glasgow" and "Memories of My Parents" may be found in *C & E*, pp. 117–51; subsequent references to these will be given in the text within parentheses.

2 His brother, Samuel McCall Frazer (1855–1914), worked in the family business but was something of a failure. Of the two sisters, the elder, Christina ("Tiny"), died unmarried in 1911, and Isabella, who died in 1945, married J. E. A. Stegall, Frazer's classmate at Trinity and later Professor of Mathematics for fifty years at University College, Dundee.

3 Diary in possession of Margaret, Viscountess Long, and used with her kind permission. Viscountess Long is Frazer's great-grandniece (the granddaughter of Ninian Frazer, the son of Samuel Frazer).

4 *C & E*, p. 135. The subtitle is " A brief sketch of the principal writing materials used in all ages, with a chapter on how and when we began to write."

5 *FGB*, p. 20: "He [Frazer] was not a brilliant conversationalist, for his shyness imposed great formality upon his contacts with others; and even with friends – he had no familiars – he was apt to demand chapter and verse for the most trivial observation."

6 For the comparison between Sterne and Frazer in a different context, see J. Z. Smith, pp. 11–13.

7 *The Chemist and Druggist*, 20 January 1900, 90–1.

8 Bronislaw Malinowski, "Sir James George Frazer: A Biographical Appreciation," in *A Scientific Theory of Culture and Other Essays* (New York, Oxford University Press, 1960; orig. pub. 1944), pp. 181–6.

9 A catalogue of Daniel Frazer's books, made in 1875, is mentioned in the catalogue of JGF's library (TCC Frazer 20:1) but has not survived.

10 See Andrew L. Drummond and James Bulloch, *The Scottish Church 1688–1843* (Edinburgh, St Andrew Press, 1973).

11 Frazer describes his father politically as "an ardent Liberal and a warm admirer of Mr Gladstone." Frazer, according to Downie, was largely an innocent in politics, but such political opinions as he had were those of an old-fashioned Liberal (*FGB*, p. 19). It is striking that he spends a single sentence on his father's politics but many pages on his social class and religion.

Whatever Frazer's political sophistication or lack of it, his politics suited his college's, for the Senior Combination Room of Trinity was Liberal in the second half of the nineteenth century. Thus Henry Sidgwick, in his journal (5 July 1886): "Dined in Hall and was surprised to find the great preponderance of Unionist sentiment among the Trinity fellows – a body always, since I have known Trinity, preponderantly Liberal." TCC Add. MS c. 97:25 (93).

12 A. H. Quiggin, *Haddon the Head Hunter* (Cambridge, Cambridge University Press, 1942), chap. 1.

13 *FGB*, p. 20.

14 "I am . . . absolutely ignorant of all the material side of savage life, the arts, manufactures etc. . . . My studies have all been in the other branch of savage life, the mental and social side, the customs, superstitions etc." Frazer to von Hügel, 16 December 1893. MS: Cambridge University Museum of Archaeology and Anthropology. Quoted by permission of the Curator.

15 For New Guinea: Frazer writes to Francis Galton, 10 October 1897: "You may remember that some years ago I spoke to you of an expedition to New Guinea, which my friend Prof. Haddon and myself had some thoughts of making. That scheme has been for the present at least abandoned" (MS: University College Library, London; quoted by permission).

16 He made no secret of the fact that he was no Christian, as the letter of 22 December 1900 to his friend Solomon Schechter, quoted in Chapter 10, makes clear. Downie (*FGB*, p. 21) does not think that Frazer was an atheist, but his reasons speak exactly to the ambivalence that I see at the heart of his absorption in religion: "Frazer was never definite or committed enough to qualify as an atheist." Stanley Edgar Hyman also calls attention to Frazer's ceaseless search for solid ground on the question of religion (*The Tangled Bank*, New York, Atheneum, 1962, pp. 251ff).

17 For an amusing anecdote about Frazer's total lack of musicality, see *FGB*, p. 19.
18 For Frazer's unsuccessful application in 1881 for the chair of Humanity (i.e., Latin) at the University of Aberdeen, see Chap. 2. Here one may note the words of one of his referees at that time, the Rev. E.W. Blore, Vice-Master of Trinity and Frazer's old tutor: "I have had several opportunities of testing your powers in our Examinations, and I have further had the knowledge that your success on these occasions has not been due to the very careful training which English Public-School boys receive, but to your own power and love of learning. At a very early period of your career here, I ventured to prophesy your success as against those who had started with much greater advantages than you had" (TCC Frazer 16:90).
19 The dedication in the Pausanias thanks Ramsay for his "sympathetic and stirring teaching" that has afforded Frazer "years of happy commune with the great of old" (*Paus*, I, v). Frazer won the prize (awarded by the members of the class) for Greek and Latin at Glasgow.
20 An excellent example of this "amateur" humanistic spirit is seen in Frazer's comments to Malinowski, in a letter of 8 March 1922, on the then soon-to-be-published *Argonauts of the Western Pacific*, to which he contributed a preface. Although he spends some time on Malinowski's ideas on magic, most of the long letter is devoted to matters of language and style. He praises Malinowski for having printed all native terms in parentheses: "this helps the reader greatly. But I think that you might perhaps with advantage have used them somewhat more sparingly, substituting in many cases the English equivalent, where this would not involve ambiguity. The frequent occurrence of barbarous and (to a European) unintelligible words is a stumbling-block to any but a very serious reader." The attitudes of the old and new anthropology toward language could hardly be more tellingly juxtaposed (MS: British Library of Political and Economic Science, Malinowski Collection, General Correspondence, File F; quoted by permission of the Librarian).
21 It may be relevant that Veitch also came from a Free Church background (*DNB*).
22 *Knowing and Being* (Edinburgh, Blackwood, 1889), p. 3.
23 For Kelvin see the obituary, by "J.L.," in the *Proceedings of the Royal Society*, series A, appendix 1908, "Obituary Notices of Fellows Deceased," esp. pp. xxix–xxxiii.
24 Cf. his ironic aside at the expense of relativistic physics in *The Worship of Nature* (1926), p. 12, n. 1. On 28 December 1919 Frazer wrote to his friend M.J. Lewis: "Have you followed the discussion of Eckstein's [*sic*] theories and do you understand them? His own exposition in the *Times* [on 28 November 1919] appeared to me cloudy and confused to the last degree, in the worst German style, and I mistrust a man who cannot express himself clearly: confused speaking or writing implies confused thinking. But of course I have no pretension to understand the high abstractions of mathematics" (TCC Frazer 1:28).
25 MS: Sir Robert Marett; quoted by permission.
26 During the five years he spent at Glasgow Frazer won first prize for Latin (1869–70); the prize for general eminence in Latin, Professor Muirhead's Foundation prize for written examinations on Tacitus, the *Aeneid*, and the *Pharsalia*, and a prize for the examination on Latin books read over the summer (1870–1); the junior logic prize, the prize for general eminence in mathematics, and the prize for reading in Reid and Whately (1871–2). I wish to thank the Archivist of the University of Glasgow for this information.

2 Trinity undergraduate

1 D.A. Winstanley, *Later Victorian Cambridge* (Cambridge, Cambridge University Press, 1947), pp. 210, 211, n. 3. The survey of university history is largely derived from Winstanley.
2 For example, T.R. Glover, *Cambridge Retrospect* (Cambridge, Cambridge University Press, 1943); [Leslie Stephen], *Sketches from Cambridge* (London, Oxford University Press, 1932); Thomas Thornely, *Cambridge Memories* (London, Hamish Hamilton, 1936).
3 This does not, of course, mean that Frazer did nothing but read; according to Downie, and quite in keeping with his generally eighteenth-century style, he fenced, rode, and walked as a young man (*FGB*, p. 20); he was at least enough of a cricketer to pose for a photograph in his flannels. In his mature years his main exercise was walking.
4 Thornely, p. 26.

5 Then as now, Trinity was the largest and wealthiest college in the university. In 1874, when Frazer went up, Trinity had more than one-quarter of all undergraduates (583 out of 2229) and more than the next two largest colleges (St John's and Trinity Hall), which together had only 557.

6 Frazer's tutor was E. W. Blore, not Image, but the latter befriended Frazer, as we know from the letters given in the text. For Image and his generous temperament, see A. E. Housman, "J. M. Image," *Cambridge Review* (28 November 1919), rpt. in *Selected Prose*, ed. John Carter (Cambridge, Cambridge University Press, 1962), pp. 151–3. Frazer's reading list is TCC Add. MS. b. 17:102.

7 Personal communication from Professor W. M. Calder III, of the University of Colorado. Frazer read Lucan in connection with the Professor Muirhead prize competition in Glasgow in 1870–1 (see Chap. 1, n. 26); no information exists as to when he might first have read the other late authors.

8 Personal communication. For Wilamowitz's school reading to the age of eighteen, see his *My Recollections*, trans. G. C. Richards (London, Chatto & Windus, 1930), pp. 77–85; W. M. Calder III, "Three Unpublished Letters of Ulrich von Wilamowitz-Moellendorff," *Greek, Roman and Byzantine Studies*, 11 (1970), 139–70, esp. the first and second letters, offers details on Wilamowitz's reading at the age of twenty-one.

9 TCC Frazer 29.

10 MS: University College London Library; quoted by permission.

11 Here is one list: snow-soft, cold-kind, yellow-skirted, sable-stoled, silver-buskined, star-proof, sin-worn, vermeil-tinctured, sky-robed, smooth-dittied, white-handed, love-lorn, empty-vaulted, flowry-kirtled, silver-shafted, night-foundered, close-curtained, solemn-breathing, sun-clad, amber-dropping, tinsel-slippered, rushy-fringed, coral-pav'n, rosy-bosomed.

12 I wish to thank Mrs Margaret Farrar, assistant for college muniments in the Trinity College Library, who checked the details of JGF's residence.

13 Frazer was not innumerate: he won a mathematics prize at Glasgow and in the annual Trinity examinations, for 1877, he received first-class marks in "mathematics and classics." The mathematical competence in question was probably at secondary-school level.

14 First classic was Alfred Hands Cooke, a zoologist, who also won the Chancellor's Classical Medal. The board of examiners consisted of T. E. Page, J. S. Reid, R. D. Archer-Hind, T. H. Orpen, A. F. Kirkpatrick, and W. M. Gunson.

15 James Reid, one of the examiners, in his letter supporting Frazer's application in 1881 to become Professor of Latin at Aberdeen, wrote: "In the year 1878, when Mr Frazer took his degree, I was one of the Examiners for the Classical Tripos, and in common with the other Examiners was greatly struck by the width and accuracy of his reading. Mr Frazer's translation papers were, I think, quite the best which I have seen done in any Examination" (MS: TCC Frazer 16:93).

16 TCC Add. MS b. 17:104.

17 TCC Add. MS b. 17:105.

18 W. R. Scott (in the *DNB*) says of Nicholson that after 1877, "accompanied by his friend (Sir) James George Frazer, he went to Heidelberg, where he attended lectures, chiefly on law, at the university."

19 TCC Adv. McTaggart 4 (between 490 and 491).

20 *The Growth of Plato's Ideal Theory*, p. vi; subsequent references will be given in the text within parentheses.

21 *C & E*, p. 126. He does not say when Ward suggested that he read Tylor, but he calls Ward his "friend," and although they knew one another since about 1875, they became close only after Frazer won the fellowship. The early 1880s seems reasonable.

22 This information on fellowships courtesy of Mr T. C. Nicholas, Fellow and former Senior Bursar of Trinity College.

23 I am indebted to Professor Wynne Godley, of King's College and the Department of Applied Economics at Cambridge, for this information.

24 I wish to thank Miss E. McNeill, Librarian and Keeper of the Records for the Middle Temple,

for the information on Frazer's legal training. Daniel Frazer's "keen appreciation of legal rights" may have been behind his pressure on his son to read law.

25 Olwen Ward Campbell, "Memoir" of James Ward, in James Ward, *Essays in Philosophy* (Cambridge, Cambridge University Press, 1927), p. 70.

26 TCC Frazer 28:190 preserves Ward's testimonial for Frazer in the latter's bid to become librarian of the Royal Geographical Society. The letter is dated 26 February 1885 and begins: "I have known Mr Frazer during the last ten years."

27 The acknowledgment of Tylor is to be found in the discussion following Frazer's 1885 lecture, "On Certain Burial Customs Illustrative of the Primitive Theory of the Soul," *GS*, p. 49; that to Smith in *C & E*, p. 126.

28 The testimonials are preserved as TCC Frazer 16:89–96.

29 The diary is TCC R. 8. 43.

30 Campbell, "Memoir," p. 75.

31 In 1958 P. W. Filby composed "Life under the Golden Bough," an amusing reminiscence of his experiences as one of Sir James's amanuenses from 1937 to 1939. It was published in the *Gazette of the Grolier Club*, n.s., no. 13 (June 1970), 31–8. When it was reprinted as "Life with the Frazers" in the *Cambridge Review*, 105 (30 January 1984), 26–8, the editor of that journal added this note: "It was in Sir James Frazer's rooms in Trinity on a broiling hot day during the vacation of 1879 that *The Cambridge Review* was initiated" (p. 28).

32 He maintained this custom of spending part of each summer in Scotland with his family throughout most of his life.

33 The point is also made by H. J. Rose in his obituary in *Classical Review*, 55 (1941), 58.

34 Sheldon Rothblatt, *The Revolution of the Dons* (London, Faber & Faber, 1968), p. 153.

35 See Beatrice Webb, *My Apprenticeship* (London, Longmans, 1926); Jane Ellen Harrison, "The Influence of Darwinism on the Study of Religion," in A. C. Seward (ed.), *Darwin and Modern Science* (Cambridge, Cambridge University Press, 1909), pp. 494–511; Martin J. Wiener, *Between Two Worlds: The Political Thought of Graham Wallas* (Oxford, Clarendon Press, 1971), pp. 8–13.

36 John Holloway, *The Victorian Sage* (New York, Macmillan, 1953).

3 The vista of anthropology

1 See Introduction, n. 3, for the references to the three works by Evans-Pritchard.

2 Frank M. Turner, *Between Science and Religion: The Reaction to Scientific Naturalism in Late Victorian England* (New Haven, Yale University Press, 1974); J. W. Burrow, *Evolution and Society: A Study in Victorian Social Theory*, rev. edn (London, Cambridge University Press, 1966); Reba N. Soffer, *Ethics and Society in England* (Berkeley, University of California Press, 1978).

3 As B. M. G. Reardon remarks, "The issue of science *versus* religion was most prominent from about 1862 to 1877, when both sides were in the mood for conflict." [*From Coleridge to Gore* (London, Longmans, 1971), p. 13.]

4 A third among the antinaturalists, Myers, was an undergraduate at Trinity in the 1860s, but does not count for Frazer. Myers was a pioneer in psychic research.

5 The memoir is R. St John Parry, *Henry Jackson O.M.* (Cambridge, Cambridge University Press, 1926).

6 In 1904 when the possibility of lecturing at a Baptist theological seminary arose, and in 1910 when he was financially pressed and thought of leaving the college – see Chap. 11.

7 Parry, p. 43; for his reading of McLennan, p. 11.

8 For Ward's place in the histories of psychology and philosophy, respectively, see R. S. Peters (ed.), *Brett's History of Psychology* (London, Allen & Unwin, 1962), pp. 675–84; and the Ward commemorative number of *The Monist*, 36 (1926), 1–175. Frank M. Turner has a good chapter on Ward.

C. A. Mace, "James Ward," *Encyclopedia of Philosophy* (New York, Macmillan, 1967), VIII, 288, writes: "Ward's psychology, however, was soon outmoded by the spectacular development of the new psychologies, behaviorism and psychoanalysis, and by the rapid expansion of a scientific psychology based on experimental and biological methods. It was outmoded by the separation of scientific psychology from the philosophy of mind."

9 JGF to Marett, 17 May 1911, TCC Add. MS c. 56b:200. Ward, elected an Apostle in 1876, was a brilliant talker and much more sociable than Frazer.

10 When, in 1922, he came to summarize the history of anthropology ("The Scope and Method of Mental Anthropology," in *GS*, pp. 234–51), Spencer's name does not appear.

11 See the "Preface to the Second Edition," *GB*[2], I, xvi.

12 TCC MS O. 11.41.

13 See, e.g., Noel Annan, *The Curious Strength of Positivism in British Thought* (London, Oxford University Press, 1959).

14 *Mill on Bentham and Coleridge*, intro. by F. R. Leavis (London, Chatto & Windus, 1950).

15 As R. R. Marett does: *Tylor* (London, Chapman & Hall, 1936), p. 69.

16 Quoted by Gladys Bryson, *Man and Society: The Scottish Inquiry of the Eighteenth Century* (Princeton, Princeton University Press, 1945), pp. 87–91; most of this extract appears in J. Z. Smith, pp. 114–15, n. 18, where I first saw it. The passage comes from Stewart's "Account of the Life and Writings of Adam Smith, LL.D.," rpt. in Sir William Hamilton (ed.), *The Collected Works of Dugald Stewart, Esq. F.R.S.S.* (Edinburgh, Constable, 1858), X, 32–7.

17 See, e.g., the opening of Jane Ellen Harrison's "The Influence of Darwinism on the Study of Religion," in A. C. Seward (ed.), *Darwin and Modern Science* (Cambridge, Cambridge University Press, 1909), pp. 494–511: "The title of my paper might well have been 'The Creation by Darwinism of the Scientific Study of Religions.'"

18 Orderly yes but rectilinear no. Frazer often took exception to those who, like Lewis Henry Morgan, believed that social evolution took only one path, and that all societies therefore passed through a single, inevitable set of stages. For one of a number of demurrers on this matter, see "The Scope and Method of Mental Anthropology" (1922): "But whether or no human evolution started from a single point, it has certainly run very different courses in different ages and in different parts of the world. It is not merely that the rate of progress has varied in time and place, but that the products, that is, the races, have varied in kind from each other. Hence we cannot arrange the existing races of mankind in a progressive series, and say that in the course of nature the lower would necessarily, though slowly, develop into the higher" (*GS*, pp. 238–9). He probably found this idea of "staggered" evolution (*évolution en échelons*) first in Renan.

19 What A. R. Radcliffe-Brown called the "if-I-were-a-horse fallacy." See E. E. Evans-Pritchard, *Theories of Primitive Religion*, p. 24.

20 Herbert Spencer, *An Autobiography*, 2 vols. (London, Watts, 1904), II, 488.

4 Pausanias and Robertson Smith

1 William Robertson Smith, *The Religion of the Semites*, rev. edn (London, A. & C. Black, 1894), p. ix.

2 The full title is *C. Sallusti Crispi Catalina et Jugurtha*.

3 Although a school text, it was noticed in Germany. TCC Frazer 22:2–3 contains a translation (in Frazer's hand) of a review by August Schindler from the *Deutsche Literaturzeitung* (2 May 1885). Schindler is extremely laudatory, calling the book a "beautiful edition of Sallust" and praising its editor's tact, diligence, and ingenuity.

4 J. P. Postgate (1853–1926), Fellow and classical lecturer, Trinity College; Professor of Comparative Philology, University College, London; editor of *Classical Review* and *Classical Quarterly*: editor of Propertius, Lucan, and Tibullus.

5 Pausanias was edited by C. G. Siebelis in 1822–8 but the text Frazer used was the product of forty years of effort by J. H. Schubart, who edited it in 1838, 1854, and 1875. Since Frazer, the text has been edited by H. Hitzig and H. Bluemner (1896–1910), F. Spiro (1903), and M. H. Rocha-Pereira (1973–81).

6 George A. Macmillan (1855–1936), publisher, director of the Macmillan Company.

7 MS: BM Add. MS 55257.

8 One reason Macmillan gave in this first letter for his interest in a translation of Pausanias was that "some years ago [I] had an idea of undertaking it myself."

9 BM Add. MS 55418 (1), pp. 169–70.

10 (Sir) Sidney Colvin (1845–1927), literary and art critic, Fellow of Trinity, Director of the Fitzwilliam Museum, Cambridge.

11 BM Add. MS 55418 (1), p. 427.

12 BM Add. MS 55418 (1), p. 963.

13 The biography is J. S. Black and George Chrystal, *The Life of William Robertson Smith* (London, A. & C. Black, 1912).

14 *The Religion of the Semites* is the name of the first of the three series of Burnett Lectures that Smith gave from 1888 to 1891 on the religious institutions of the ancient Semites. His health failed before he could revise the second and third series for publication.

15 TCC Frazer 1:40.

16 He contributed the following articles to the *Britannica*: "Penates," "Pericles," "Praefect," "Praeneste," "Praetor," "Priapus," "Proserpine," "Province," "Saturn," "Taboo," "Theseus," "Thesmophoria," "Thespiae," and "Totemism." "Theseus" and "Thespiae," although signed by Frazer, do not appear in Besterman's bibliography.

17 Black and Chrystal, pp. 494–5.

18 TCC Frazer 28:188–91.

19 Trinity College Council Minutes, Domestic, 1882–1897, p. 59, 22 May 1885: "The meeting unanimously resolved to permit Mr J. G. Frazer to retain his fellowship subject to the provisions of Statute XV S.10 for a period of five years." The minutes for this period contain only a record of decisions taken and do not present the content of discussions. For this and subsequent extracts from the Council Minutes, I wish to thank Dr Timothy Hobbs, Sub-Librarian of Trinity College.

20 In a letter of 23 July 1929 to Karl Pearson, Frazer wrote: "I believe that Francis Galton and my ever-lamented friend Robertson Smith used their powerful influence to ensure the renewal and were successful" (MS: University College London Library).

21 The talk was published in *JAI*, 15 (1885–86), 64–101; rpt. in *GS*, pp. 3–50. Subsequent references will be made to the reprint and given within parentheses in the text.

22 J. Z. Smith, Pt I, Chap. 3, offers a different analysis of this essay.

23 Matthew Arnold, "Heinrich Heine," in *Lectures and Essays in Criticism*, ed. R. H. Super (Ann Arbor: University of Michigan Press, 1962), pp. 107–32.

5 Mythography and ambivalence

1 Salomon Reinach, "The Growth of Mythological Study," *Quarterly Review*, 215 (October 1911), 423–41; *"genuit Frazerum"* occurs on p. 438.

2 JGF, "Taboo," *Encyclopaedia Britannica*, 9th edn (Edinburgh, A. & C. Black, 1888), XXIII, 15–18; rpt. in *GS*, pp. 80–92.

3 *Ibid.*, *GS*, pp. 86–7.

4 See Herman Kogan, *The Great EB* (Chicago, University of Chicago Press, 1958), chap. 4.

5 Lord Bryce, "William Robertson Smith," *Studies in Contemporary Biography* (London, Macmillan, 1902), pp. 311–26.

6 For example, Henry Sidgwick, in his journal, recounts meeting Smith at dinner on 19 February 1885: "Met Robertson Smith there: the little man flowed, entertained, domineered, almost as usual." TCC Add. MS c. 97:25 (30).

7 See Douglas Bush, *Mythology and the Renaissance Tradition in English Poetry* (Minneapolis, University of Minnesota Press, 1932).

8 Frank E. Manuel, *The Eighteenth Century Confronts the Gods* (Cambridge, Mass., Harvard University Press, 1959); Burton Feldman and Robert D. Richardson (eds.), *The Rise of*

Modern Mythography 1680–1860 (Bloomington, Indiana University Press, 1972).

9 Henry M. Hoenigswald, "On the History of the Comparative Method," *Anthropological Linguistics*, 5 (1963), 1–11.

10 Hans Aarsleff, *The Study of Language in England 1780–1860* (Princeton, Princeton University Press, 1967).

11 Quoted in Basil Willey, *More Nineteenth Century Studies* (London, Chatto & Windus, 1956), p. 143.

12 See H. G. Hewlett, "The Rationale of Mythology," *Cornhill Magazine*, 35 (1877), 407–23, for a bemused survey of contemporary views. Curiously Hewlett did not know, or did not mention, Tylor's theory of animism announced in *Primitive Culture* in 1871.

13 F. Max Müller, "Comparative Mythology," in *Chips from a German Workshop*, 2 vols. (New York, Scribners, 1869), II, 1–142.

14 *Ibid.*, II, 77.

15 Richard M. Dorson, "The Eclipse of Solar Mythology," in T. A. Sebeok (ed.), *Myth: A Symposium* (Bloomington, Indiana University Press, 1958), pp. 25–63.

16 Andrew Lang, *Modern Mythology* (London, Longmans, 1898).

17 John Burrow, *Evolution and Society*, rev. edn (Cambridge, Cambridge University Press, 1966), p. 114.

18 Only the desire to keep this sketch to manageable proportions makes it seem as if anthropology sprang into existence in Britain in 1871. For an excellent review of developments at mid-century and earlier, see the introduction by George W. Stocking, Jr., "From Chronology to Ethnology: James Cowles Prichard and British Anthropology, 1800–1850," to J. C. Prichard, *Researches into the Physical History of Man* (Chicago, University of Chicago Press, 1973).

19 See Margaret Hodgen, *The Doctrine of Survivals* (London, Allenson, 1936).

20 Appropriately enough, for Tylor frequently calls savagery "the childhood of the human race."

21 E. B. Tylor, *Primitive Culture*, 2 vols. (London, Murray, 1871); I quote from the sixth edition, of 1920, I, 285.

22 Concerning this phrase Marett writes testily: "There never was such a thing." *Tylor* (London, Chapman & Hall, 1936), p. 119.

23 E. B. Tylor, *Anthropology*, rev. edn (London, Macmillan, 1924), p. 387.

24 JGF, "William Robertson Smith," *Fortnightly Review*, 55 (June 1894), pp. 800–7; rpt. in *GH*, p. 284. Cf. Frazer's letter of 4 November 1892 to H. Montagu Butler, the Master of Trinity: "I am certainly of opinion that the College should not lose an opportunity of securing a bust of the late Mr J. F. McLennan. He was a very powerful and original thinker, and his researches into the early history of society have been epoch making. He was one of the founders of the study of primitive society, and in respect of natural ability, acuteness, and soundness of judgment I am inclined to think that he ranked first" (TCC Frazer 1:7).

25 E. E. Evans-Pritchard, *A History of Anthropological Thought*, ed. André Singer (London, Faber & Faber 1981), pp. 62–3. Another important essay is the introduction by Peter Rivière to the reprint of McLennan's *Primitive Marriage* (Chicago, University of Chicago Press, 1970).

26 Evans-Pritchard, p. 68.

27 The tendency inevitably produced a reaction. Here is Haddon [*Man*, 2 (1901), no. 124]: "Totemism has too long been a 'blessed word,' and the time has arrived when strong protest must be made against the use of the term. There are many animal and plant cults in the world, totemism is one of them; indeed, it is probable that what is described as totemism among one people may be different from what is called totemism elsewhere. . . . It is entirely unwarrantable to speak of every animal cult as totemism."

28 JGF, "Preface," *GB*, I, ix. Some of what follows is taken from my essay, "Frazer on Myth and Ritual," *Journal of the History of Ideas*, 36 (1975), 121.

29 "Preface," I, viii.

30 *Ibid.*

31 JGF, "William Robertson Smith," *GH*, pp. 278–90.

32 *Ibid.*, pp. 283–4.

33 Stanley A. Cook, a disciple and friend, states flatly that Smith was always a Christian, and that

"he had no sympathy with . . . any thorough-going humanism or rationalism" *Centenary of the Birth on 8th November 1846 of the Reverend Professor W. Robertson Smith* (Aberdeen, The University Press, 1951), p. 16.

34 William Robertson Smith, *Lectures on the History of the Semites*, 2nd edn (1894; rpt. 1972), Lectures VII–X.

35 Robert Alun Jones, "Robertson Smith and James Frazer on Religion: Two Traditions in British Social Anthropology," in George Stocking, Jr. (ed.), *Functionalism Historicized* (Madison, University of Wisconsin Press, 1984), p. 36.

36 TCC Add. MS c. 30:45.

37 Frazer, in a letter of 18 November 1888 to Smith [UL Add. 7449 (c) 236], writes of conversations with Rouse about totemism and exogamy.

38 TCC Add. MS c. 30:46.

39 J. S. Black and George Chrystal, *The Life of William Robertson Smith* (London, A. & C. Black, 1912), pp. 517–18.

40 *Ibid.*, pp. 518–19.

41 In 1887 he published a pamphlet entitled *Questions on the Manners, Customs, Religions, Superstitions, etc., of Uncivilized or Semi-Civilized Peoples* that he circulated to workers in the field. Reissued in 1889 and later expanded, this questionnaire obviously was not the "general work." The casual allusion in Pausanias ii.27.4 cannot have been the fresh evidence that interested him anew in the story.

42 Ernest Renan, "Le prêtre de Némi," in *Drames philosophiques* (Paris, Calmann-Lévy, 1888), pp. 253–400.

43 "J'ose même dire que parmi vos grands écrivains il n'en est aucun avec lequel je me sente lié d'une sympathie aussi étroite et aussi profonde qu'avec Renan." JGF, *Sur Ernest Renan* (1923), rpt. in *GS*, p. 267. The comparison with Renan is also made by H. J. Fleure in *Obituary Notices of Fellows of the Royal Society, 1939–1941*, 3 (1941), 899–900.

44 *GS*, p. 277.

45 TCC Frazer 20:1(181).

46 See, e.g., Smith's ferocious review of vol. 1 of Renan's *Histoire du peuple d'Israël*, *English Historical Review*, 3 (January 1888), 127–35; rpt. in *Lectures and Essays of William Robertson Smith*, J. S. Black and George Chrystal (eds.) (London, A. & C. Black, 1912), pp. 608–22.

6 *The Golden Bough*

1 BM Add. MS 55943, pp. 49–51.

2 To be designed by his good friend John Henry Middleton (1846–96), classical archaeologist, architect, and art historian (Director of the Fitzwilliam Museum, Cambridge). See *Paus*, I, viii.

3 Per the contract, dated 19 December 1889, in the Macmillan corporate archives, Basingstoke.

4 TCC Frazer 22:4 is a scrapbook compiled by JGF containing twenty-five reviews, but not including Joseph Jacobs, "Recent Research in Comparative Religion," *Folk-Lore*, 1 (1890), 384–97. As a member of the Folk-Lore Society he would have received *Folk-Lore* and therefore would have read Jacobs's long, temperate, and informed notice.

5 Comparisons to Tylor and/or McLennan are to be found in the reviews in the *Manchester Guardian, Pall Mall Gazette, Political World, Allhabad Pioneer,* and *Oxford Magazine*. Along with Jacobs, already cited, other mixed or less-than-enthusiastic reviews appear in the *Classical Review, Academy,* and *Speaker*.

6 Such as Jane Ellen Harrison. In *Reminiscences of a Student's Life* (London, Hogarth, 1925), pp. 82–3, she misleadingly implies that the first edition was greeted as a landmark by all classicists.

7 For example, in his 1908 inaugural lecture at Liverpool, *The Scope of Social Anthropology*, rpt. in *PT* (rev. edn, 1913), pp. 159–76.

8 Charlotte S. Burne, "Some Simple Methods of Promoting the Study of Folk-Lore, and the Extension of the Folk-Lore Society," *Folk-Lore*, 5 (1887–8), 64–5.

9 Herbert Read in his survey (*English Prose Style*, rev. edn, London, Bell, 1952) of the development of prose in English offers an extract from *The Golden Bough* (on pp. 191–2) as an example of the continuation in the twentieth century of the latinate classical "high style."

10 J. Z. Smith brings together in the notes to chap. IV all the evidence concerning the reception and standing of Frazer's theories by historians of religion in general and of Roman religion in particular – see esp. nn. 42–5, 58, 82, 86.

11 *GB*, I, 255.

12 *GB*, I, 290.

13 *GB*, I, 278.

14 *GB*, II, 338–9.

15 *GB*, II, 363.

16 *GB*, II, 363, 364, 370.

17 *GB*, I, 347–8.

18 *GB*, I, 348.

7 Smith dies; Frazer marries

1 TCC R. 8. 44 (1).

2 For Plataea, see *Paus*, V, 13; for Thespiae, V, 142; in the 1895 diary [TCC R. 8. 44 (3), entry for 12 October] Frazer expresses his disappointment that the excavation he had seen in 1890 has been covered up; for Epidaurus, Nauplia, Mycenae, Tiryns, Argos, Piraeus, Munychia, Kephisia, Marathon, and Rhamnus, vol. 7 of the 1895 diary (December) makes it clear that he was revisiting these places to see whether anything new had been turned up. If it had, he was carrying the proofs of the first volumes of Pausanias with him and made changes on the spot.

3 TCC R. 8. 44 (1), fols. 105–6.

4 *GB²*, III, 247–8 and n. 4.

5 TCC Adv. c. 21. 71.

6 TCC Adv. d. 21. 2. Only three other volumes can with certainty (from dated flyleaf inscriptions) be placed in Frazer's 1890 trunk. These, preserved in the Wren Library, are the annotated two volumes of *GB* – TCC Adv. c. 21. 67–8 – and Wilhelm Gurlitt, *Über Pausanias* (Graz, Leuschner & Lubensky, 1890) – TCC Adv. c. 21. 25.

7 For Jane Harrison, see J. G. Stewart, *Jane Ellen Harrison: A Portrait from Letters* (London, Merlin, 1959); Robert Ackerman, "Jane Ellen Harrison: The Early Work," *Greek, Roman and Byzantine Studies*, 12 (Spring 1971), 113–36.

8 BM Add. MS 55431 (2), p. 579.

9 BM Add. MS 55432 (2), p. 683.

10 TCC Frazer 1:6. Frazer's fellowship had been renewed on 23 May 1890, while he was in Greece. Under that date TCC College Council Minutes: Domestic, 1882/3–1897, says: "It was unanimously agreed that Mr J. G. Frazer, author of the Golden Bough and other works should be continued as a Student Fellow for a further period of five years counting from M[ichael]mas next." I wish to thank Mr T. C. Nicholas for his help on this and other matters pertaining to Frazer and Trinity.

11 *GB*, I, 285–6.

12 See *FGB*, p. 22. In a note here Downie explains: "This is how Lady Frazer related the incident to me. She was no Latin scholar, but knew Italian, hence the strange form *fortiore*." In telling the story, however, Downie manages to mislocate the error from Pliny to Ovid – his mistake, not Lady Frazer's.

13 Pausanias proved equally slow going for Hitzig and Bluemner. The first volume of their *Pausaniae Graeciae Descriptio* (Leipzig, Reisland) appeared in 1896, but there were not to be nine more volumes. The rest of the edition consists of volume two, in two parts (1901, 1904), and volume three, likewise in two parts (1907, 1910). Allowing for the considerable preparation necessary before the publication of the first volume, it therefore took the two of them much longer, in man-years, than it had taken Frazer, working on his own. They spent a long time on the text, he a long time on the commentary.

14 Macmillan's rejection [BM Add. MS 55445 (1), pp. 1266–8], on commercial grounds, came despite a generally favorable reader's report by Prof. H.E. Ryle (BM Add. MS 55952, pp. 97–100).

15 JGF, *Passages of the Bible Chosen for Their Literary Beauty and Interest* (London,A. & C. Black, 1895), vi–viii.

16 The letters are dated 11 January 1889 (UL Haddon 3), 18 July 1889 (UL Haddon 3), 22 July 1889 [UL Add. 7449 (c) D237], 18 July 1890 (UL Haddon 3), 29 January 1891 (UL Haddon 3), and 27 July 1892 (UL Haddon 3058).

17 A.C. Haddon, "The Ethnography of the Western Tribe of Torres Straits," *JAI*, 19 (1890), 300. Nonanthropologists need to know that "Torres Straits," without the definite article, referring not to the body of water but to the islands in it, has become standard usage in the anthropological literature.

18 A.H. Quiggin, *Haddon the Head Hunter* (Cambridge, Cambridge University Press, 1942), p. 82.

19 *Ibid.*, p. 297.

20 *Ibid.*, p. 93.

21 *Ibid.*, p. 97; the letter has not been preserved.

22 Haddon, "Notes on Mr. Beardmore's Paper," *JAI*, 19 (1890), 466: "Mr J.G. Frazer having provided me before I left home, with several copies of his 'Questions,' I gave one to my friend, Mr Beardmore, when I visited him at Mowat, in August, 1888."

23 Edward Beardmore, "The Natives of Mowat, Daudai, New Guinea," *JAI*, 19 (1890), 459–66.

24 Quiggin, p. 81.

25 A.C. Haddon and A.H. Quiggin, *History of Anthropology* (London, 1910), p. 3; as noted in Quiggin, p. 81.

26 Quiggin, p. 92.

27 The Frazer–von Hügel correspondence, which lasted from 1888 to 1908, is in the archives of the University Museum of Archaeology and Anthropology, Cambridge.

28 Personal communication. Both James and Downie (his source) cite the name of Lilly Frazer's father incorrectly. The Frazer marriage certificate (St Catherine's House: 1896 – Cambridge 3b. 1023) clearly names him as "Sigismund de Boys," and his occupation as "gentleman." Leaving aside the mistake in the name, if we accept Downie's portrait, it is easy to believe that she gave herself the particle and changed her father's occupation from merchant to gentleman. The witnesses to the marriage were Frazer's friend J.S. Black, and his brother-in-law J.E.A. Stegall. Her age on the marriage certificate is thirty-five (i.e., seven years younger than J.G.), but on the more credible death certificate she is eighty-six (one year younger). Further evidence against Lilly Frazer's being Jewish is supplied in a love poem "To My Wife" that Frazer wrote in one of his notebooks (BM 45496, fol. 105v), dated 7 June 1921. In loosely retracing her life, he speaks of her as educated "–within the convent garden."

29 Sir J.R.M. Butler and Mr T.C. Nicholas.

30 Although Downie prides himself on finding the clue to Lady Frazer's ancestry which E.O. James pursued in his *DNB* obituary, he was misinformed about her children. He "suspected" that she had had a daughter (*FGB*, p. 23); in fact she had two children. Lilly Mary Grove was a teacher of French, a writer, and a translator, and held the *Docteur ès lettres* from the Sorbonne, having written a thesis in 1908 on Robert Louis Stevenson. She died suddenly in early 1919, perhaps a victim of the postwar influenza pandemic. C[harles] Grenville Grove (born 1878) was an occasion for concern to both Frazers for many years, as (in their view) he seemed never to come to much. He married a Swedish woman, lived in Stockholm, and was a professional translator, rendering a large number of scientific and other works from Swedish, the first appearing in 1914 and the last in 1947.

31 Her book, *Dancing* (London, Badminton Library, 1895), is now regarded by historians of the dance as a pioneering classic.

32 *FGB*, chap. 2.

33 The Wren Library holds most of Lady Frazer's voluminous personal correspondence.

34 Thus, e.g., even Sarah Campion, who as the Frazers' last secretary was locked in combat with

Lady Frazer virtually every day, acknowledged that *everything*, however rude or nasty, the latter did was to further her husband's interests. "Autumn of an Anthropologist," *New Statesman*, 41 (13 January 1951), 34–6.

8 *Pausanias's Description of Greece*

1 For allowing him to see and use unpublished materials, he thanks Charles Waldstein, director of the American School in Athens; Th. Homolle, director of the French School; Cecil Smith, former director of the British School; and Percy Gardner of Oxford (*Paus*, I, ix).

2 It is impossible to say how much anthropology is appropriate, for to some tastes none is ever wanted. Although Frazer mostly restrains himself, he sometimes offers too much by any standard: e.g., III, 55, 192, 240. and 368.

3 For A. W. Verrall's contempt for archaeology (and anthropology), which he called "stuffage," see J.G. Stewart, *Jane Ellen Harrison: A Portrait from Letters* (London, Merlin, 1959), pp. 56–7.

4 Charles Whibley, "The Oldest Guide-book in the World," *Macmillan's*, 77 (April 1898), 415–21; "A Greek Baedeker," *Academy*, 53 (2 April 1898), 363–4; [J.P. Mahaffy], *Edinburgh Review*, 188 (October 1898), 358–77; Konrad Wernicke, *Wochenschrift der klassische Philologie*, 15 (1 October 1898), 1081–7; Percy Gardner, "Frazer's *Pausanias's Description of Greece*," *Classical Review*, 12 (1898), 465–9; *Saturday Review*, 28 (1898), 209–10; "Mr Frazer's Pausanias," *Cambridge Review*, 20 (4 May 1899), 306–7; H. Blümner, *Göttingische gelehrte Anzeiger* (1899), 66–79; Georges Radet, *Revue de l'histoire des religions*, 45 (1902), 84–90.

5 This was said in conversation by both Profs. Peter Levi and the late Eugene Vanderpool, of the American School in Athens.

6 Aside from the articles noted below, in nn. 11 and 12, as Habicht explains (n. 8), the main polemic was only initiated by Wilamowitz, in "Die Thukydideslegende," *Hermes*, 12 (1877), 326–67. When the defenders of Pausanias asked that the charges be substantiated, Wilamowitz preferred that his students and followers fight the battle. Most vehement among these was August Kalkmann, *Pausanias der Perieget* (Berlin, Reimer, 1886); Frazer's copiously annotated copy is in the Wren Library (TCC Adv. c. 21.24). Other anti-Pausanians include C. Robert, *Pausanias als Schriftsteller, Studien und Beobachtungen* (Berlin, Weidmann, 1909); G. Pasquali, "Die schriftstellerische Form des Pausanias," *Hermes*, 48 (1913), 161–223; L. Deicke, *Quaestiones Pausanianae* (Göttingen diss., 1935).

7 As might be expected, Frazer was not the only one who saw the campaign against Pausanias as wrong-headed. Of the pro-Pausanians perhaps Wilhelm Gurlitt [*Über Pausanias* (Graz, Leuschner & Lubensky, 1890)] was the most notable, and Frazer in his introductory essay uses many of Gurlitt's arguments.

8 Christian Habicht, "Pausanias and His Critics," in *Pausanias* (Berkeley, University of California Press, 1986), appendix 1; "An Ancient Baedeker and His Critics: Pausanias' *Guide to Greece*," *Proceedings of the American Philosophical Society*, 129 (1985), 220–4.

9 Some examples of direct disagreement with Wilamowitz: II, 57, 173, 214, 222, 287–8, and 288.

10 *Paus*, III, 180; Wilamowitz's essay is "'Ελευθέριον ὕδωρ' *Hermes*, 19 (1884), 463–5.

11 For Wilamowitz on Pausanias' style ("der Stil so zerhackt und verzwackt, so altbacken und muffig ist"), see his survey, "Die Griechische Litteratur des Altertums," in Paul Hinneberg (ed.), *Die Kultur der Gegenwart* (Berlin and Leipzig, Teubner, 1905), I, 163. JGF writes: "[Pausanias'] is a loose, clumsy, ill-jointed, ill-compacted, rickety, ramshackle style, without ease or grace or elegance of any sort." *Paus*, "Introduction," I, lxix.

12 JGF offers an instructive comparison between the highly colored depictions of part of an itinerary from pseudo-Dicaearchus with the stolid plodding of Pausanias. He concludes that, whereas the former may be more pleasurable to read, precisely because of his rhetorical gifts he is less reliable, especially as a guide to the sort of idiosyncratic aspects of a bygone period that Pausanias, in his dogged antiquarianism, gives us. The former is merely deft, whereas the latter is invaluable. *Paus*, "Introduction," pp. xlii–xlix.

13 JGF never forgave Wilamowitz. For a startling expression of anger thirty years later, see his letter to A. E. Housman in Robert Ackerman, "Sir James G. Frazer and A. E. Housman: A Relationship in Letters," *Greek, Roman and Byzantine Studies*, 15 (1974), 339–64; and Robert Ackerman and W. M. Calder III, "The Correspondence of Ulrich von Wilamowitz-Moellendorff with Sir James George Frazer," *Proceedings of the Cambridge Philological Society*, no. 204, n.s. 24 (1978), 31–40.

14 Despite their disagreements, JGF continued to think highly of Doerpfeld as a man, and Doerpfeld remained friendly likewise. On 8 May 1900 Frazer writes to Macmillan: "I think you will like to see the enclosed letter from Doerpfeld. Considering how often and strenuously I have controverted his views, his testimony to the usefulness of my book is very generous as well as very valuable. . . . I need hardly observe that his recommendation of my big book to the young German students, who accompany him on his annual tours, is the very best introduction that my book could have to the learned circles in Germany."

15 *Paus*, II, 528–9.

16 Stanley Edgar Hyman, using Kenneth Burke's dramatistic terminology, is excellent on the "scenic" element in Frazer in *The Tangled Bank* (New York, Atheneum, 1962).

17 *Paus*, I, viii.

18 *Paus*, II, 461–2.

19 Sales data from the Macmillan corporate archives, Basingstoke.

20 "Mr. Frazer's Pausanias," 306.

21 Gardner, p. 467. Radet, p. 84, praises the translation warmly, noting that Pausanias' clumsiness and dullness need precisely the grace and vigor that Frazer supplies.

22 *Paus*, "Preface," I, x. Frazer liked this paragraph enough to reprint it, as "My Old Study," along with other "gems," in *Sir Roger de Coverley and Other Literary Pieces* in 1920 and then again in *GH* in 1927.

9 Baldwin Spencer, Andrew Lang, and Edmund Gosse

1 Information on both children from the National Union Catalogue of Printed Books.

2 *FGB*, p. 26.

3 Sir J. R. M. Butler and Mr T. C. Nicholas.

4 TCC Add. MS b. 36:33. Thomas Taylor had translated Pausanias into English in 1794.

5 See Ann Thwaite, *Edmund Gosse: A Literary Landscape, 1849–1928* (London, Secker & Warburg, 1984).

6 Thwaite, p. 260; Frazer in a letter (22 September 1919) to Gosse written on the occasion of the latter's seventieth birthday reminisces about their first meeting in Trinity.

7 Frank E. Manuel, *The Eighteenth Century Confronts the Gods* (Cambridge, Mass., Harvard University Press, 1959); George Stocking, Jr., "From Chronology to Anthropology: James Cowles Prichard and British Anthropology, 1800–1850," introduction to J.C. Prichard, *Researches into the Physical History of Man* (Chicago, University of Chicago Press, 1973).

8 In the following discussion of Lang I follow Peter G. Baker, "The Mild Anthropologist and the Mission of Primitive Man" (Cambridge diss., 1980), chap. 5.

9 A. W. Howitt, "On Some Australian Beliefs," *JAI*, 13 (1883–4), 185–98; "On Some Australian Ceremonies of Initiation," *ibid.*, 432–59; "The Jeraeil, or Initiation Ceremonies of the Kurnai Tribe," *JAI*, 14 (1885–6), 301–25; "On the Migration of the Kurnai Ancestors," *JAI*, 15 (1885–6), 409–21.

10 Andrew Lang, *Myth, Ritual and Religion* (London, Longmans, 1887), I, 8.

11 Lang, *Cock Lane and Common-Sense* (London, Longmans, 1894), p. 338.

12 George Stocking, Jr., "Animism in Theory and Practice: E. B. Tylor's Unpublished 'Notes on Spiritualism'" *Man*, 6, n.s. (1971), 88–104.

13 *Folk-Lore*, 6 (1895), 79–81.

14 E. B. Tylor, *Primitive Culture*, 3rd edn (London, Murray, 1891), II, 310.

15 Letter to Mrs Hills (MS: Brotherton Collection, University of Leeds), quoted in Baker, p. 247.

16 Lang, *The Making of Religion* (London, Longmans, 1898), p. 220.

17 *Ibid.*, p. 329.

18 *Ibid.*, p. 331.

19 For a different version of Lang's religious position see Edward Clodd, *Memories* (London, Chapman & Hall, 1916), p. 211.

20 For an example of this, see Lang's "Australian Problems," in *Anthropological Essays Presented to Edward Burnett Tylor* (Oxford, Clarendon, 1907), p. 212, where, on a related topic (exogamy), Lang remarks: "As far as I am aware, nobody except M. Van Gennep . . . has tried to meet my argument or even made it the subject of an allusion."

21 For the chronology, see JGF, "On Some Australian Ceremonies of the Central Australian Tribes," in *GS*, p. 201; JGF's obituary of Fison is rpt. in *GH*, pp. 291–301.

22 *GS*, p. 201.

23 R.R. Marett and T.K. Penniman (eds.), *Spencer's Scientific Correspondence with Sir J.G. Frazer and Others* (Oxford, Clarendon, 1932), pp. 82–3; hereafter *SSC*.

24 *SSC*, pp. 24–5; the next quotation is from p. 26.

25 *SSC*, pp. 30–7.

26 *SSC*, p. 35.

27 *SSC*, p. 36.

28 At Frazer's request Francis Galton called a special meeting of the Institute on 14 December at which Spencer spoke.

29 *SSC*, pp. 39–40.

30 *SSC*, pp. 41–2.

31 *GB²*, I, 62.

32 *Ibid.*

33 A..A. Goldenweiser, "Totemism: An Analytic Study," *Journal of American Folklore*, 23 (1910), 179–293. This highly critical monograph was the first evaluation of Frazer's theories by an "outside" (i.e., non-British) scholar, one not caught up in the polemical atmosphere in which this entire generation wrote. Although Goldenweiser also vigorously criticized Lang and Tylor, this essay marked the beginning of the end of Frazer's being taken seriously as a theorist on totemism.

34 Andrew Lang, "The Golden Bough," *Fortnightly Review*, 69, n.s. (1901), 235–48; "Mr. Frazer's Theory of the Crucifixion," *ibid.*, 650–62; *Magic and Religion* (London, Longmans, 1901), *passim*.

35 Baker, p. 198, n. 58.

36 *SSC*, p. 29; E.B. Tylor, "Remarks on Totemism, with Especial Reference to Some Modern Theories Respecting It," *JAI*, 28 (1898), 138–48.

37 The Tylor–Frazer correspondence is TCC Add. MS b. 37: 308–16.

38 He was so pleased with the interleaved volumes that he had Macmillan run off a similar set of the second edition when later he came to revise it.

39 But see the letter from Maurice Macmillan to JGF [BM Add. MS. 55496 (1)], 28 September 1909, when Frazer asked the firm to publish John Roscoe's work on the Baganda. After saying that they would wish to see the MS before making a commitment, Macmillan writes: "I have no doubt whatever . . . that the book will have scientific value. A mere collection of anthropological facts, however, although it may be of great value to professed anthropologists, does not necessarily make a book which could command a sufficient sale to pay the expenses of production, as we found in the case of books by [A.W.] Howitt, [W.W.] Skeat, and [W.H.R.] Rivers which we have brought out during the last few years. At the same time I need not tell you that we are inclined to view more than favourably any manuscript which comes to us with your commendation."

40 *Athenaeum*, 25 June 1898, p. 320, on *Scenes of Child Life in Colloquial French*, by Mrs J.G. Frazer: "These are capital dialogues, quite as good as those Mrs Frazer published last year."

10 The second edition

1 *GB²*, I, xxi–xxii.

2 *GB²*, I, xv.

3 H. Hubert and M. Mauss, "Essai sur la nature et la fonction du sacrifice," *L'Année Sociologique*, 2 (1897–8), 29–138.

4 *GB²*, I, xx.

5 See E. E. Evans-Pritchard, "Frazer (1854–1941)," in *A History of Anthropological Thought*, ed. André Singer (London, Faber & Faber, 1981), pp. 132–52; for a different view, see Bronislaw Malinowski, "Sir James George Frazer: A Biographical Appreciation," in *A Scientific Theory of Culture and Other Essays* (New York, Oxford University Press, 1960; orig. pub. 1944), pp. 196–201.

6 *GB²*, III, 197.

7 *GB²*, III, 198.

8 MS: Jewish Theological Seminary of America, New York; quoted by permission of the Librarian, Mr M. Schmelzer.

9 E.g., "Among recent books on the speculative side of anthropology, both disciples and opponents confess the pre-eminence of Mr J. G. Frazer's 'Golden Bough,' in the second and greatly amplified edition. Since Mr Tylor's 'Primitive Culture,' now thirty years old, we have had nothing so learned as 'The Golden Bough'; and, till Mr Tylor gives us the new book on which he is understood to be engaged, Mr Frazer need fear no rival." "Anthropology – A Science?", *Quarterly Review*, 195 (1902), 180–200; quotation from p. 195.

10 *Folk-Lore*, 12 (1901), 219–43; the eight reviewers were E. W. Brabrook, G. L. Gomme, Moses Gaster, F. B. Jevons, Alfred Nutt, and Charlotte S. Burne, along with Haddon and Lang.

11 Nutt, *ibid.*, 239.

12 St Andrews University Library MS 3618, quoted by Peter G. Baker, "The Mild Anthropologist and the Mission of Primitive Man," p. 258.

13 Lang's best-known, if rather sneering, wisecrack is that Frazer's sort of analysis, in which everyone and everything turns out to be a vegetation deity, reminds him of the now-vanquished solarists, who found the sun everywhere. "The solar mythologists did not spare heroes like Achilles; they, too, were the sun. But the vegetable school, the Covent Garden school of mythologists, mixes up real human beings with vegetation." *Magic and Religion* (London, Longmans, 1901), p. 239.

14 Malinowski, pp. 182–3.

15 MS: TCC Frazer 1:19.

16 The diaries are in the possession of Mr Alan Clodd, Edward Clodd's grandson, and extracts from them are used with his kind permission. The laborious task of transcription was carried out by Peter G. Baker, who generously allowed me to use his texts.

17 TCC Add. MS c. 58:15; review of *Magic and Religion* in the *Daily Chronicle*, 26 July 1901, p. 3.

18 TCC Add. MS b. 36:42.

19 J. G. Stewart, *Jane Ellen Harrison: A Portrait from Letters* (London, Merlin, 1959), p. 37.

20 Henry James (ed.), *The Letters of William James*, 2 vols. (London, Longmans, 1920), II, 139–40; italics William James's. The two sentences about Lilly Frazer are published here for the first time, by permission of the Houghton Library, Harvard University.

21 TCC Add. MS b. 36:202. No memorial volume appeared; instead a Lang lectureship was established.

22 The translation by F. W. Kelsey of August Mau, *Pompeii, Its Life and Art* (London, Macmillan, 1899).

23 BM Add. MS 55463 (2).

11 The Hebrew world

1 A. C. Haddon, [Presidential Address], *Report of the British Association for the Advancement of Science . . . 1902* (London, Murray, 1903), pp. 738–52. The published version amply acknowledges Frazer and Spencer.

2 MS: UL Haddon 3054.

3 *Ibid.*

4 TCC Add. MS b. 37:308.

5 Norman Bentwich, *Solomon Schechter* (Cambridge, Cambridge University Press, 1938).

6 *Ibid.*, p. 87. Bentwich quotes (p. 88) from a letter that has not survived from Frazer (to Mrs Schechter?) after Schechter's death: "I am proud to have been recognized among the most intimate friends of such a man, great in his intellect and learning, greater even in the warmth of his affections and his enthusiasm for every high and noble cause. To have enjoyed his friendship is an honour which I shall always prize."

7 Downie, *FGB*, p. 25.

8 Although Downie is mistaken about Lilly scheming against Schechter, that does not mean that she did not try to exclude others of J. G.'s friends. Downie's story about her trying to keep Haddon out (*FGB*, p. 123) is corroborated by H. D. Skinner, "Christ's College in 1917–1918," *Christ's College Magazine*, 60 (May 1967), 39. I wish to thank Paul Naiditch for this reference.

9 For an example of the anti-Semitic tone of the Senior Combination Room at Trinity, see J. McT. E. McTaggart, TCC Add. MS c. 184, no. 179.

10 "Passionately" because, according to Phyllis Abrahams, daughter of Israel Abrahams, Schechter's successor at Cambridge, sometime during the Beilis case a letter to the press was drafted, to be signed by leading British academics, assailing the charges as false and the trial as a frameup. Abrahams was sitting and talking excitedly about it with J. G. when Lilly entered, angry that he should be distracting her husband from his work. This once, however, the mild-mannered J. G. resisted. He is said to have cried out, "Leave me alone, woman! This is a matter of life and death!" Letter from Phyllis Abrahams (13 September 1970) to Downie, communicated by Downie to me.

11 MS: Library of Congress. The full text is published in Robert Ackerman, "Sir James G. Frazer and A. E. Housman: A Relationship in Letters," *Greek, Roman and Byzantine Studies*, 15 (1974), 339–64.

12 TCC Adv. c. 20–3.

13 Peter G. Baker, "The Mild Anthropologist and the Mission of Primitive Man" (Cambridge diss., 1980), pp. 389–92.

14 "Folk-Lore in the Old Testament," in *Anthropological Essays Presented to Edward Burnett Tylor* (Oxford, Oxford University Press, 1907), pp. 101–74.

15 See William F. Moulton, *James Hope Moulton* (London, Epworth, 1919). Probably because W. F. Moulton was a member of the council of the Cambridge Philological Society, his younger brother J. H. was admitted to membership while an undergraduate, on 12 November 1885: see *Proceedings of the Cambridge Philological Society*, no. 12 (1885), 19. Frazer became a member on 1 March 1884: *ibid.*, no. 4 (1884), 8.

16 Black's letter is neither as long nor as interesting as Jackson's, but he too agrees that Frazer should accept. MS: TCC Add. MS b. 35:66.

17 TCC Add. MS c. 30:47.

18 TCC Add. MS c. 34:3.

19 TCC Add. MS c. 30:48.

20 The Literary Fund file contains as application in Gosse's hand setting out the facts regarding Frazer's income; a letter from Gosse making the case for Frazer's literary and scholarly eminence and describing him as existing "in a condition of urgent poverty"; and a letter from Professor George Darwin corroborating that the Trinity fellowship dividend had indeed dropped steeply and suddenly to £175 in 1898, with no prospects for improvement soon. Darwin also says that at one point the Frazers had been reduced to keeping no servant, with only a charwoman in to do the rough work two hours a day. However, they now have a servant once again (Royal Literary Fund – file A/RLF/I:2563). For the Civil List pensions, see Nigel Cross, *The Common Writer* (Cambridge, Cambridge University Press, 1985), p. 85.

21 (1) "Artemis and Hippolytus," *Fortnightly Review*, n.s. 76 (1904), 982–95; rpt. in *The Magic Art, GB*[3] (1911), I, 24–40. (2) "The Beginnings of Religion and Totemism among the Australian Aborigines," *Fortnightly Review*, n.s. 78 (1905), 162–72, 452–66; rpt. in *T & E*, I, 139–72.

22 House of Commons Accounts Papers 1904–5; 1905 (201) xliv. 139. For Gosse's role in selecting and sponsoring recipients of Civil List pensions, see Ann Thwaite, *Edmund Gosse: A Literary Landscape, 1849–1928* (London, Secker & Warburg, 1984), pp. 350, 452.

23 Henry Ling Roth received a £70 pension in 1902 and Frazer's friend Lorimer Fison received a £150 pension in 1905.

24 Thwaite, p. 428.

12 *Lectures on Kingship* and Liverpool

1 The only writer on Frazer who even mentions, much less appreciates the importance of, *Kingship* is Stanley Edgar Hyman, *The Tangled Bank* (New York, Atheneum, 1962), pp. 203, 205, 236, 263.

2 Charles Seltman, "Arthur Bernard Cook, 1868–1952," *Proceedings of the British Academy*, 38 (1952), 295–302.

3 A. B. Cook, *Zeus*, 5 vols. in 3 pts. (Cambridge, Cambridge University Press, 1914, 1924, 1940).

4 Jane Harrison, in reviewing the first installment of *Zeus*, remarked that its author had only one failing – he lacked "*l'art de se faire valoir.*" "Zeus and Dionysos," *Spectator*, 114 (27 February 1915), 304.

5 "The Golden Bough and the Rex Nemorensis," *Classical Review*, 16 (1902), 365–80.

6 MS: TCC Frazer 1:58.

7 In his response Cook wrote (on 16 October 1902): "Still, I cannot help feeling that there are very few men whose love of truth would enable them to meet an attack on their cherished theory as frankly and fairly as you have done." TCC Add. MS b. 35:226.

8 JGF says as much in a letter to Hermann Diels, 6 February 1903; MS: Sammlung Darmstaedter 2b 1890 (41), Staatsbibliothek Preussischer Kulturbesitz, Berlin. I wish to thank Dr I. Stolzenberg, Manuscript Librarian, for permission to quote.

9 "Zeus, Jupiter and the Oak," *Classical Review*, 17 (1903), 174–86, 268–78, 403–21; 18 (1904), 75–9, 325–8, 360–75. "The European Sky God," *Folk-Lore*, 15 (1904), 264–315, 364–426; 16 (1905), 260–332.

10 Cook did not value literary form highly in works of scholarship. Jane Harrison said that he believed that it was "'the collection of facts that matters,'" whereas she believed that facts were nothing unless they were interpreted. Finally she despaired of getting him to understand the importance of clarity in exposition. J. G. Stewart, *Jane Ellen Harrison: A Portrait from Letters* (London, Merlin, 1959), pp. 169–70.

11 "The Golden Bough and the Rex Nemorensis," 380.

12 MS: TCC Add. MS b. 35:211. For another statement of Cook's intellectual imagination and his generosity in helping others, see Stewart, p. 102.

13 *Kingship*, p. 83.

14 This vision of prehistoric enlightened rascality is entirely compatible with Frazer's own Liberal politics. He believed in individual effort and distrusted strong centralized government and political ideologies.

15 *Kingship*, pp. 150–2.

16 *Ibid.*, p. 196.

17 R. R. Marett, "From Spell to Prayer," *Folk-Lore*, 15 (1904), 132–65; rpt. in *The Threshold of Religion* (London, Methuen, 1909). For Marett, see his delightful autobiography, *A Jerseyman at Oxford* (London, Oxford University Press, 1941); H. J. Rose, "Robert Ranulph Marett, 1866–1943," *Proceedings of the British Academy*, 29 (1943), 357–69.

18 As Marett remarked in his review of *Kingship* [*Man*, 6 (1906), no. 29], Frazer's headings of homeopathic and contagious magic are doubtless useful enough for classificatory purposes, "But we are as far as ever from the inwardness of the magical act."

19 MS: TCC Add. MS b. 36:189.

20 Marett reviewed nearly every one of Frazer's important publications: for a nearly complete list see the bibliography compiled by T. K. Penniman in the Marett Festschrift, edited by L. H. D. Buxton, *Custom Is King* (London, Hutchinson, 1936), pp. 303–25.

21 R. R. Marett, [rev. of *The Northern Tribes of Central Australia*], *Oxford Magazine*, 23 (23 November 1904), 100; not in Penniman.

22 Marett's review of the first edition of *Adonis Attis Osiris* in *Man* (6, 1906, no. 114) begins: "This book is, from the literary point of view, a masterpiece." Although he goes on to take

predictable exception to some of the theoretical passages, his overall enthusiasm for the book was typical of that of the general public.

23 In the entry under the second edition of *Adonis* (1907) Besterman notes the retrospective decision to make it part of the third edition of *The Golden Bough*, which involved the pasting-in of a cancel half-title page. Frazer also composed a separate prospectus outlining the scope of the entire third edition.

24 *T & E*, I, x.

25 Thus, Lilly Frazer to Victor Gollancz, secretary to the Academy, on 15 November 1902: "Alas! unlike you we fossilize here and a day in town is an event for us, so I would go up with Mr Frazer for the whole day" (MS: British Academy Archives).

26 Although not a matter of university statute, the custom in Cambridge was not to award an honorary doctorate to resident Fellows or lecturers. After he left for Liverpool his name was proposed for a degree, but he returned too quickly for an honor to be conferred, and then for various reasons he was passed over until 1920. See letter of J. J. Thomson to Lord Rayleigh of 20 May 1908 in Lord Rayleigh, *The Life of Sir J. J. Thomson O.M.* (Cambridge, Cambridge University Press, 1942), p. 108. I wish to thank Mr Paul Naiditch for this reference. I wish also to thank Dr Dorothy Owen, Keeper of the Archives of Cambridge University, for explaining to me (the absence of) the rule about the award of degrees to resident senior members of the university.

27 There is a hint in a letter to Clodd of 28 June.

28 Cf. a journalist in the *Liverpool Daily Post* on 12 November 1907, commenting on three new appointments, of which Frazer's is the most noteworthy, who concludes that these men were attracted by "the absolute freedom of teaching and learning to be found in this University." (Archives of the University of Liverpool, S. 2508; for this reference I wish to thank Mr A. A. Allan, Assistant Archivist.)

29 See Frederic G. Kenyon, *The British Academy: The First Fifty Years* (London, Oxford University Press, 1952).

30 MS: British Academy Archives. I wish to thank Mr P. R. Williams, Deputy Secretary of the Academy, for his help.

31 R. R. Marett and T. K. Penniman (eds.), *Spencer's Scientific Correspondence with Sir J. G. Frazer and Others* (Oxford, Clarendon, 1932), pp. 112–14; letter to Schechter, 6 May 1908 (MS: Jewish Theological Seminary of America).

32 Sir John Murray (1841–1914); his voyage of exploration on the *Challenger* took place 1873–6. Frazer was serious enough about his scheme for a research institute to send copies of his inaugural lecture, marked at the appropriate place, to each member of the Cabinet (letter to Macmillan, 21 May 1908). After he had returned to Cambridge he learned from Marett that Oxford might revive the plan for a Western Australian expedition. Responding to Marett on 11 March 1909 (TCC Add. MS b. 36:195) he mentions his approach to Murray; he also suggests that interest from Oxford might spur the Liverpudlians into action, but it was not to be.

33 *The Times*, 5 December 1932, p. 17: "For the last 18 years of Roscoe's life in Uganda, Frazer gave him unstinted help and encouragement." See also JGF's obituary, "Canon John Roscoe," *C & E*, pp. 73–9. BM Add. MS 45449 (99–100) contains JGF's notes of a conversation, presumably in Cambridge, with Roscoe on totemism and exogamy in Uganda on 19 November 1896.

34 JGF's letters to Roscoe are TCC Add. MS b. 37:33–64, 66–74, 76–106, 108–44, 146–71; TCC Frazer 16:77–78 are a letter and notes on Africa from Roscoe to JGF.

35 JGF–Roscoe, 19 July 1907 (TCC Add. Ms b. 37:35).

36 Roscoe's early ethnography: "Notes on the Manners and Customs of the Baganda," *JAI*, 31, n.s. 4 (1901), 117–30; "Further Notes on the Manners and Customs of the Baganda," *JAI*, 32, n.s. 5 (1902), 25–80; "Kibuka, the War God of the Baganda," *Man*, 7 (1907), no. 95; "The Bahima, a Cow Tribe of Enkole in the Uganda Protectorate," *JAI*, 37, n.s. 10 (1907), 93–118; "Nantaba, the Female Fetich of the King of Uganda," *Man*, 8 (1908), no. 74; "Notes on the Bageshu," *JAI*, 39, n.s. 12 (1909), 181–95; rev. of W. S. Routledge, *With a Prehistoric People*, *Man*, 10 (1910), no. 63.

37 Macmillan brought out *The Scope of Social Anthropology* as a pamphlet in 1908, and it was republished in 1913, as part of the volume containing the second edition of *Psyche's Task*. All citations from the text are taken from pp. 166–70 of this latter version.

38 MS: Sammlung Darmstaedter, 2 b 1890 (41), Staatsbibliothek Preussischer Kulturbesitz, Berlin; I wish to thank Dr I. Stolzenberg, Manuscript Librarian, for permission to quote.

39 MS: Archives of the University of Liverpool. Although he was never subsequently in residence at Liverpool, he gave the substance of *Psyche's Task* as a course of four public lectures in the spring of 1909, and he gave two lectures on "Totemism and Exogamy" in March 1910 and two more, on "Demeter and Persephone as Goddesses of the Corn," in November 1911. Frazer did not resign the chair until 1922. This information courtesy of Mr A. A. Allan, assistant archivist of the University of Liverpool.

40 MS: TCC Frazer 1:30.

41 Lilly made J. G. pay in other ways as well. In a long letter (dated 30 November 1908) to Henry Jackson, who was away ill, J. M. Image sends all the Trinity and Cambridge gossip. Embedded here is the following item: "Frazer I haven't yet seen. On dit that one of the conditions attaching to the return was that he should dine in the domestic circle – not in Hall." MS: Henry Jackson collection, Lilly Library, Indiana University, Bloomington, Indiana.

42 MS: TCC Frazer 1:60.

43 *Psyche's Task* (1909); revised and enlarged, it was reprinted in 1913 along with his inaugural lecture of 1908, and then reissued in 1927 under the better title of *The Devil's Advocate*. I am happy to thank Theodore Besterman here for unraveling this and many other bibliographical knots.

44 *PT*, p. vii.

45 *PT*, pp. 1–2.

46 *PT*, p. 44.

47 *PT*, p. 47.

48 *T & E*, IV, 121; IV, 280.

49 *T & E*, III, 9–10; cp. I, 346–7.

50 Haddon's unguarded reaction to *T & E*, as noted in Clodd's diary of 18 June 1910: "He [Haddon] agrees that *Totemism* will not add to Frazer's reputation – Haddon says he is a literary man, not a man of science: & he doesn't know human nature, allowing theories to obsess him." There is, in addition, JGF's copy of a letter of 3 November 1898 from A. W. Howitt (BM Add. MS 45451, 25–6), written when the latter was seeing Spencer off to England: "Of one thing, however, I am absolutely sure – that no Australian black ever went through the mental process of reasoning about the totem in the manner described by you. He did not think totemism out before he adopted it in the beginning. It was a growth, not a manufacture, but what it grew from is lost beyond all recall. One thing is firmly fixed in my mind – that if we look at these customs with our own eyes we shall never see what the savage sees, and if we think them out from our own mental standpoint, we shall never reach his own."

51 *T & E*, I, xiv.

52 *T & E*, IV, 14.

53 For *Totem and Taboo*, see Ernest Jones, *Sigmund Freud: Life and Work* (London, Hogarth, 1955), II, 392–404, where he acknowledges that most people in the psychoanalytic movement then thought the work a fantasy. Its reputation has not grown in the ensuing years.

54 This is an appropriate place to amend Downie's treatment of the relations between Frazer and Freud. Per *FGB*, p. 21, to Frazer he was "that creature Freud"; further, "when Freud sent him a copy of *Totem and Taboo* Frazer did not acknowledge the book or look further in that direction." "That creature Freud" is presented as *ipsissima verba*, and it is easy to imagine Frazer uttering the remark. But we actually have a reference to Freud (although Frazer cannot be bothered to name him), and his reaction is one of bemused condescension, not fear and loathing. It comes in the postscript to a long, chatty letter of 8 April 1920 to Roscoe (TCC Add. MS b. 37:134). Others may analyze the significance in Frazer's getting the title wrong of *Totem and Taboo*: "I have got a new book *Totemism and Taboo* [*sic*], the translation of a book by a German or Austrian psychologist, who borrows most of his facts from me and

tries to explain them by the mental processes, especially the dreams of the insane! Not a hopeful procedure, it seems to me, though he seems to have a great vogue with some people."

55 The subject of an essay by another of Robertson Smith's friends and disciples: Stanley A. Cook, "Israel and Totemism," *Jewish Quarterly Review*, 14 (1902), 413–48.

13 Frazer and his critic Marett

1 JGF to George Macmillan, 1 April 1910; Lilly Frazer to M. J. Lewis, 13 June 1910 (TCC Frazer 1:31).

2 Three anecdotes: (1) T. C. Nicholas, who was elected to his fellowship at Trinity in 1912, told me in 1984 that when he returned to Cambridge in 1919 after war service, he and his young wife were invited to dine at the Master's. Among the other guests were the Frazers. Because Mrs Nicholas' mother was deaf and wore such a hearing aid, she knew that deaf people sometimes were embarrassed by these large, unwieldy devices. When the gentlemen had retired to their port and cigars she therefore thought to dispel any possible awkwardness on Lady Frazer's part by mentioning her mother's experience. To this amiably intended overture Lady Frazer responded fiercely, "Can you not find *anything* else to talk about?", reducing Mrs Nicholas to tears.

(2) A dinner in honor of the speaker is regularly given the night before the Frazer Lecture. In 1973 Sir E. E. Evans-Pritchard told me that he attended the dinner held in Oxford in (he thought) 1926. He said that Lady Frazer, whose hearing aid was inoperative that night, insisted on being kept *au courant* with the conversation by having a *précis* shouted down her ear trumpet, which slowed things down considerably. When a joke or witty remark was uttered, however, she required not only that it be repeated but that the entire table laugh once again with her. Evans-Pritchard called it one of the longest nights of his life.

(3) Sir Raymond Firth told me in 1985 that it was Lady Frazer's habit to point her hearing aid at you until she deemed that enough had been said, then shut it off and turn away.

3 TCC Frazer 1:31.

4 MS: Henry Jackson collection, Lilly Library, Indiana University, Bloomington, Indiana.

5 JGF to Andrew Bennett, 16 February 1911; MS: St Andrews University Library.

6 The first two sets of lectures were published as *The Belief in Immortality* in 1913. With this book Frazer began the practice of reading (from the proofs) parts of his upcoming books as lectures at Trinity College.

7 Much of the following discussion is either taken or adapted from my essay, "Frazer on Myth and Ritual," *Journal of the History of Ideas*, 36 (1975), 115–34.

8 For the general movement to irrationalism, see Lancelot L. Whyte, *The Unconscious Before Freud* (New York, Basic Books, 1960); from Noel Annan, *The Curious Strength of Positivism in British Thought* (London, Oxford University Press, 1959), it is clear that Frazer exemplified the mainstream of British thought, no matter how far out of step he was with Continental developments.

9 R. R. Marett, *The Birth of Humility* (Oxford, Clarendon, 1910); rpt. in *The Threshold of Religion*, 2nd edn (London, Methuen, 1914), pp. 169–202.

10 Along with the physiological psychology of James and Lange, Marett is thinking of Gustave Le Bon's *The Crowd: A Study of the Popular Mind* (London, Unwin, 1896).

11 The letters: TCC Add. MS c. 56b, 198–200. For Marett's criticism of Frazer, see Franz Steiner, *Taboo* (London, Cohen & West, 1956), chap. 8, whence the title of this chapter.

12 *The Birth of Humility*, p. 12 (= *Threshold*, p. 181).

13 Richard M. Meyer, "Mythologische Studien aus der neuesten Zeit," *Archiv für Religionswissenschaft*, 12 (1910), 270–90.

14 In fact, p. 20.

15 See T. O. Beidelman, *W. Robertson Smith and the Sociological Study of Religion* (Chicago, University of Chicago Press, 1974).

16 W. Robertson Smith, *Religion of the Semites*, 2nd edn, rev. (London, A. & C. Black, 1894), p. 16, Cf. Voltaire (*Essai sur les Mœurs*, I, 50), who observed a century earlier concerning the

Romans and their religious tolerance: "Car il n'eût point de dogmes, il n'y eût point de guerre de religion."

17 JGF, "William Robertson Smith," *GH*, p. 281.

18 *GB*, I, xiv.

19 *Religion of the Semites*, pp. 17–18.

20 *Ibid.*, p. 18.

21 *GB*³, XI, 315. Cf. JGF, *The Belief in Immortality* (1913), pp. 24–5: "the more we penetrate into the inner history of natural religion, the larger is seen to be the element of truth contained in Euhemerism."

22 *GB*³, VI, 158.

23 "Song is a later invention than the dance, to which it is in its beginnings secondary and certainly not indispensable." C. M. Bowra, *Primitive Song* (London, Weidenfeld & Nicolson, 1962), p. 243.

24 *GB*³, IX, 374.

25 R. R. Marett, "Magic or Religion?" *Psychology and Folk-Lore* (London, Methuen, 1920), pp. 168–95, esp. pp. 190–1; orig. pub. in *Edinburgh Review*, 219 (1914), 389–408.

26 See Downie, *FGB*, p. 22, for anecdotes illustrating Frazer's puritanical standards of personal rectitude.

27 *GB*², I, xv–xvi.

28 Apollodorus, *The Library*, trans. J. G. Frazer (London, Heinemann, 1921), I, xxvii.

14 The third edition

1 TCC R. 8. 44, vol. 4, fol. 83v = *Paus*, V, 223.

2 *Adonis*, p. v.

3 *Adonis*, pp. v–vi.

4 Frazer's clearest statement regarding his lifelong practice of enhancing his sources may be found in the preface to the first volume of *Anthologia Anthropologica* (London, Lund Humphries, 1938), p. viii.

5 His discipline is still imperfect because Chapter 9 of the section on Osiris, "The Doctrine of Lunar Sympathy," is totally irrelevant to the argument.

6 L. R. Farnell, [review of *Adonis*], *Hibbert Journal*, 5 (1906–7), 187–90, calls for the judicious use of "proximate" or "adjacent" anthropology only.

7 *Adonis*, p. 25; see also pp. 164, 215–16, 227.

8 See "Gibbon at Lausanne," in *C & E*, pp. 47–52.

9 For Jesus as myth, see Grant Allen, *The Evolution of the Idea of God* (London, Grant Richards, 1897) and "Immortality and Resurrection," in *The Hand of God* (London, Watts, 1909); J. M. Robertson, *Christianity and Mythology* (London, Watts, 1900), and *Pagan Christs: Studies in Comparative Hierology* (London, Watts, 1903).

10 *Adonis*, p. 202.

11 *Adonis*, p. 202 n. 2

12 *Oxford Magazine*, 29 (4 May 1911), 289.

13 *Magic Art*, I, viii.

14 Frazer having visited Nemi in 1900, his description in the third edition is much more elaborate and circumstantial than it had been. For a cynical reading of the meaning of this expanded version, see Edmund Leach, "Reflections on a Visit to Nemi," *Anthropology Today*, 1 (April 1985), 2–3.

15 *Magic Art*, I, ix.

16 *Magic Art*, I, 111 and n. 2; my italics.

17 *Taboo and Perils*, p. 214.

18 *Taboo and Perils*, p. 217.

19 *Athenaeum*, 15 July 1911, 77.

20 *GB*², II, 56.

21 *Man*, 8 (1908), no. 9.

22 C. S. Myers, "Charles Gabriel Seligman, 1873–1940," *Obituary Notices of the Fellows of the Royal Society*, 3 (1939–41), 627–38.

23 TCC Add. MS b. 37:190.

24 C. G. Seligmann, "The Cult of Nyakang and the Divine Kings of the Shilluk," *Fourth Report of the Wellcome Tropical Research Laboratories, Khartoum*, vol. B, pp. 216–32 (the quotation is from p. 232); Seligman's typescript of 1 February 1911 to JGF is published in *Anthologia Anthropologica*, I, 508–15.

25 For example, fifteen of the twenty-four books that Frazer reviewed between 1922 and 1926 were on Africa.

26 E. E. Evans-Pritchard, *The Divine Kingship of the Shilluk of the Nilotic Sudan* (Cambridge, Cambridge University Press, 1948).

27 After a thorough review of the evidence for Frazerian sacral regicide J. Z. Smith (pt. 2, "Rex Sacrorum," with the notes) concludes that enough trustworthy evidence exists to permit a disinterested observer to conclude that the Frazerian pattern did and does exist in Africa (p. 330). For a more recent review, see Gillian Feeley-Harnik, "Issues in Divine Kingship," *Annual Review of Anthropology*, 14 (1985), 273–313; I wish to thank Sir Edmund Leach for this reference.

28 H. Hubert and M. Mauss, "Essai sur le sacrifice," *L'Année Sociologique*, 2 (1897–8), 29–138; "Théorie générale de la magie," *L'Année Sociologique*, 7 (1902–3), 1–146; and J. E. Harrison, *Prolegomena to the Study of Greek Religion* (Cambridge, Cambridge University Press, 1903) and *Themis* (Cambridge, Cambridge University Press, 1912).

29 *Spirits of the Corn*, I, vii.

30 *Ibid.*, I, viii.

31 *Ibid.*

32 *Ibid.*, II, 40; II, 94.

33 *Scapegoat*, p. 412 n. 1.

34 Noeldeke was Ordinarius for Oriental languages at Strasbourg. His long letter has survived in an imperfect and incomplete copy (made by JGF and Lilly) in BM Add. MS 45451, 83–5. For a translation I am indebted to Dr Siegfried de Rachewiltz.

35 MS: University Library of Tübingen, Md. 782, Fasz. 70; quoted courtesy of the University Library of Tübingen.

36 *Balder*, I, v–vi.

37 This is the jumping-off point for Margaret Murray's *The Witch Cult in Western Europe* (Oxford, Clarendon, 1921) and her subsequent books.

38 *Balder*, I, viii–ix.

39 John Roscoe, "Kibuka, the War God of the Baganda," *Man*, 7 (1907), no. 95, whence the quotation below.

40 *Adonis* (1914), II, 197. For Budge, see *Osiris and the Egyptian Resurrection* (London, P. L. Warner, 1911), I, 40, 67, 320.

41 *Adonis* (1914), II, 198.

42 *Adonis* (1914), II, 197–8.

43 *Balder*, II, 88.

44 *Balder*, II, 312.

45 *Balder*, II, 315.

46 Royalty arrangements from the Macmillan corporate archives, Basingstoke. The percentages for his later works were as follows: GB^a, 15% (10% in the US); FOT, 25% (10%); FOT^a, 15%.

47 All sales figures from the Macmillan corporate archives, Basingstoke. Between November 1922 and December 1933 Macmillan printed 33,510 copies of the abridged *Golden Bough*. I wish to thank Mr T. M. Farmiloe of the Macmillan Company for permission to consult these files.

15 Honor to the king

1 Early reviewers suggested that a cumulative index volume would make the series much more useful, and this was done in 1915; it was, however, entirely a mechanical matter of collation and proofreading.

2 MSS: Cecil and Clare (Cornford) Chapman; quoted by permission.

3 Cornford marked the launch of the fund with an advertisement in *The Times* (21 May 1914, p. 15).

4 BM Add. MS 58428. Raleigh must have had a change of heart; his name appears on the list of supporters in A. E. Housman's address in 1921.

5 Warren G. Dawson (ed.), *The Frazer Lectures 1922-1932* (London, Macmillan, 1932), pp. ix-x.

6 I wish to thank Miss E. McNeill, Librarian and Keeper of the Records of the Middle Temple, for information about the Frazers' status and residence there.

7 Downie told me that when Frazer received the O.M. he had to go to Buckingham Palace in midwinter for the investiture (the honors list appears on New Year's Day). He prudently wore long woolen underwear under his court dress. In the coach on the way, however, his court dress went awry, which caused his sensible underwear to appear. When the coach arrived and the palace footman opened its door, Lady Frazer was discovered tucking in the errant combinations. The footman closed the door until the process had been completed.

8 Downie (*FGB*, p. 66) tells of the Frazers, attending church in the Temple, being asked to move to accommodate a party of the royal family. Lady Frazer refused because, she said, Sir James was an Honorary Bencher of the Temple and thus outranked the royal duke. Although the story contains several factual inaccuracies, her refusal is believable. I wish to thank A. S. Adams, Reader Services Librarian of the Middle Temple Library, for help.

9 TCC Frazer 1:32; William Wyse (1860-1929), a classical lecturer and Fellow of Trinity, was an old friend of Frazer's. Toward the end of his life his health failed and he became embittered, and his letter must have shown this. Whatever Lilly may have thought of Wyse, he remained a friend of J. G.'s: see JGF's *Times* obituary, "Mr. William Wyse," rpt. in *GS*, 254-7.

10 Frazer's copy of the four-volume *The Holy Scriptures of the Old Testament Hebrew and English* (Berlin, British and Foreign Bible Society, 1903) in the Wren Library (TCC Adv. c. 20-3) is covered with marginalia. Each time he finished a book of the Bible he made a note of it on the last page of the text: thus, "Finished reading Genesis in Hebrew, Wednesday, 18th April 1906." His progress through the Scriptures may therefore be traced with assurance. He reread Genesis and then went straight through the Old Testament from 1906 to 1909, and then immediately started again. In 1915 he was on his last traverse. The imbalance between Genesis and the rest of the Bible must owe something to the fact that he read that book no fewer than five times (the last time "mostly without a dictionary"). Like many other would-be readers of the Bible, his attention flagged during the Pentateuch, for he completed Exodus and Leviticus three times and Numbers and Deuteronomy only twice each. He read Joshua, Judges, and Kings four times and the Later Prophets and miscellaneous Writings generally only once.

11 "Ancient Stories of a Great Flood," *JRAI*, 46 (1916), 231-83.

12 "The War: Declaration by British Authors," dated September 1914 (Gilbert Murray Papers 26:1, Bodleian Library); JGF to Murray, 14 October 1914 (Bodleian).

13 The entire affair is described in G. H. Hardy, *Bertrand Russell and Trinity* (Cambridge, Cambridge University Press, 1972; orig. pub. 1942).

14 MS: Cecil and Clare (Cornford) Chapman; quoted by permission.

15 MS: TCC Frazer 1:28.

16 MS: TCC Frazer 1:33.

17 An exception is her amusing and far-sighted book, based on personal experience, *First Aid for the Servantless* (1913).

18 In this Balkan vein he also wrote "The Cursing of Venizelos" for a short-lived periodical called

The New Europe in February 1917 (rpt. in *GS*, pp. 205–11), but although political at least this piece had a basis in folklore.

19 JGF to Murray, 6 February 1918. (Gilbert Murray papers 35:177–8, Bodleian).

20 See Malinowski, *A Diary in the Strict Sense of the Term*, trans. N. Guterman (New York, Harcourt Brace, 1967), pp. 108, 134, 212, 216, 272.

21 Malinowski, "Baloma: Spirits of the Dead in the Trobriand Islands," *JRAI*, 46 (1916), 353–430; for collective consciousness, see p. 423, n. 1, where Malinowski acknowledges his indebtedness to Durkheim but complains that concepts like "collective representations," "collective soul," etc., are untenable. He concludes that "The postulate of a collective consciousness is barren and absolutely useless for an ethnographical observer." I wish to thank Sir Edmund Leach for this identification, as well as that in the next note and the reference in n. 24.

22 The "leading field ethnographer" was W. H. R. Rivers and the "Egyptologist" G. Elliot Smith.

23 TCC Add. MS b. 36:175.

24 See Robert J. Thornton, "'Imagine Yourself Set Down. . . . ': Mach, Frazer, Conrad, Malinowski and the Role of Imagination in Ethnography," *Anthropology Today*, 1 (1985), 7–14.

25 "Preface" to *Argonauts of the Western Pacific* (London, Routledge & Kegan Paul, 1922): rpt. in *GS*, 391–8; the quotation is on p. 392.

26 See Raymond Firth, "Bronislaw Malinowski," in Sydel Silverman (ed.), *Totems and Teachers* (New York, Columbia University Press, 1981), pp. 101–39; for his near-dictatorial relationship with his students see Firth, "Malinowski as Scientist and as Man," *Man and Culture* (London, Routledge & Kegan Paul, 1957), pp. 1–14.

27 Sir Raymond Firth told me in December 1985 that Malinowski introduced him to Frazer in 1924. Upon hearing that Firth was a New Zealander, Frazer asked whether he knew anything about the Maoris. Firth had not long before attended a service in a native Maori church, and briefly described what he had seen. To which Frazer's reply was, "I am not interested in that." Frazer said this politely and meant only that he was interested exclusively in taboos and other beliefs and not in such "nonprimitive" behavior; the incident illustrates what Firth called Frazer's social "gaucherie" and also his mental rigidity by that time.

28 For his flattery see *Totems and Teachers*, p. 112; for his "somewhat contemptuous affection for Frazer," p. 123.

29 TCC Add. MS b. 36:179.

30 TCC Add. MSS b. 37:59ff.

31 Sales figures from Macmillan corporate archives, Basingstoke. The immense success of the one-volume abridgment of *The Golden Bough* in 1922 encouraged Frazer to produce a one-volume epitome of *Folk-Lore* in 1923, and this sold well too.

32 Beyond this subjective criterion, there is the further implicit negative constraint that he will omit topics on which he has written elsewhere, such as the figure of the scapegoat or the festival of Purim.

33 *FOT*, I, viii.

34 *FOT*, I, 8.

35 *FOT*, III, 306.

36 Marett, "The Interpretation of Survivals," *Psychology and Folk-Lore* (London, Methuen, 1920), p. 120; orig. pub. in *Quarterly Review*, 231 (1919), 445–61. Citations are to *Psychology and Folk-Lore*.

16 Return to the classics

1 For the inception of the Loeb Library, see W. M. Calder III, "Ulrich von Wilamowitz-Moellendorff to James Loeb: Two Unpublished Letters," *Illinois Classical Studies*, 2 (1977), 315–22.

2 Macmillan's refusal is conveyed in a letter of 12 October 1910 to Lilly Frazer, BM Add. MS 55500 (2), p. 886: "We considered the whole scheme very carefully some weeks ago and came

to the conclusion that it had not much to commend it from what we might call the scientific point of view, and even less from the point of view of practicable publishing. That Mr Frazer should have a salary of £300 [*sic*] a year for a term of years is no doubt a very desirable object, but we do not feel that this particular scheme would help his reputation."

3 Calder, 319.

4 MS: W. H. Heinemann.

5 *Ibid.*

6 Especially those of Richard Wagner, who had found and edited the hitherto-missing epitome of *The Library* in 1891 and then edited the entire work in the Teubner series in 1894.

7 *Library*, p. xvii.

8 Gosse's review in *The Sunday Times* was reprinted as "Gods and Heroes" in *More Books on the Table* (London, Heinemann, 1923), pp. 29–35.

9 In a letter to Clodd of 14 November 1921 (MS: Harry Ransom Humanities Research Center, The University of Texas at Austin) he says, "I am glad that you like Apollodorus. All the same I regret the time I spent on him."

10 *Library*, p. xxvii; the two definitions that follow are on pp. xxvii-xxix and xxix.

11 *Ibid.*, p. xxxi.

12 MS: W. H. Heinemann.

13 JGF to Clodd, 11 April 1919 (TCC Add. MS b. 35:195).

14 TCC Frazer 1:28.

15 This and following quotations from TCC Frazer 1:34. She neglects to mention that Trinity had a good reason for turning down the request, namely, that space was at a premium because of the numbers of men returning after the war. From a letter to Roscoe of 29 January 1920 (TCC Add. MS b. 37:132), in which J. G. speaks of the "extraordinary pressure on rooms caused by the great increase in the number of students," it is clear that he understood and was not crushed by the rejection; once again she is dramatizing. I wish to thank Dr Timothy Hobbs, Sub-Librarian of Trinity College, for checking the Council minute book.

16 Warren R. Dawson (ed.), *The Frazer Lectures 1922–1932* (London, Macmillan, 1932), p. x.

17 MS: W. H. Heinemann.

18 MS: W. H. Heinemann.

19 On 5 December 1920 (TCC Add. MS b. 37:147) this is the anthropological news to Roscoe: "The South African Government is about to appoint to a Chair of Social Anthropology in the University of Cape Town, and I have been asked to act on the Advisory Committee, along with Haddon, Rivers, and Marett. Do you happen to know of any likely candidate? I fancy that A. R. Brown (formerly of Trinity) is standing for it. He is in South Africa and wrote to me for a testimonial some time ago. I sent him one, but he did not take the trouble to acknowledge it. He is an able but eccentric man."

20 A postscript to the letter of 12 October (TCC Add. MS b. 37:141) says: "My Wife tells me that the name you mention is [J. H.] Driberg. I do not know anything about him, but no doubt you have good means of judging. N. W. Thomas is, I think, out of work, but I do not esteem him highly as an anthropologist."

21 Housman's address is printed in *The Frazer Lectures*, pp. xii–xiii; Frazer's response, which was printed and sent to all supporters of the fund, is to be found in *GH*, pp. 365–6.

22 These reviews are reprinted in *GS*, pp. 297–418.

23 *FGB*, p. 25.

24 JGF to Roscoe, 27 January 1924, TCC Add. MS b. 37:166; 25 July 1924, Add. MS b. 37:170.

25 *Classical Review*, 44 (1930), 235.

26 For their continuing friendship see the postscript to JGF's letter to Macmillan, 29 January 1926.

27 *Fasti*, I, xvii.

28 See the reviews, universally favorable, by H. J. Rose, *Journal of Roman Studies*, 19 (1929), 235–9; Salomon Reinach, *Revue Archéologique*, 31 (1930), 225; A. Ernout, *Revue Philologique* (1930), 429–31; J. Toutain, *Journal des Savants* (1931), 105–20. Both Reinach and Toutain were old friends, Toutain having translated two of Frazer's books into French.

29 The translations are by Thynne (1833), Butt (1833), Taylor (1839), Riley (1851), and Rose (1866); of these, Riley's is by far the ablest.

30 Seneca, *Controversiae*, II, 2, 12 (ed. Winterbottom): "verbis minime licenter usu est [Ovidius] nisi in carminibus, in quibus non ignoravit vitia sua sed amavit."

31 Quintilian, *Institutio Oratoria*, X, 1, 98 (ed. Butler): "Ovidi Medea videtur mihi ostendere, quantum ille vir praestare potuerit, si ingenio suo imperare quam indulgere maluisset." For more of Quintilian's comments on Ovid, see *Inst. Orat.*, X, 1, 88, 93. I wish to thank Dr John O'Meara of Dublin for the references to both Seneca and Quintilian.

32 For a different view of Ovid's poetical language, see L. P. Wilkinson, *Ovid Recalled* (Cambridge, Cambridge University Press, 1955), p. x: ". . . their [the eighteenth-century translators'] vocabulary tends to be artificial, whereas Ovid's was usually plain and direct, or to be outmoded now, whereas Ovid's was in the main contemporary. I do not mean that his diction was not poetic; but it was not quaint or recherché or archaic."

33 *Fasti*, II, 37.

34 *Ibid.*, II, 38.

35 *Ibid.*, II, 335.

36 *Ibid.*, II, 354.

37 *Ibid.*, II, 356.

17 Aftermath

1 On this occasion JGF gave a brief inaugural address, in French, that repeats his often-expressed view that folklore consists of survivals (rpt. in *GS*, pp. 286–7).

2 For this item and the next, UL Add. MS 7654 F46, F47.

3 (Sir) Harold Nicolson, *Diaries and Letters 1930–1939*, ed. Nigel Nicolson (London, Collins, 1966), pp. 74–5; the jazz and poultry farming are facetious references to the squawks made by some of the hearing aids of the time when they acted up.

4 *FGB*, pp. 119–27; P. William Filby, "Life under the Golden Bough," *Gazette of the Grolier Club*, n.s., no. 13 (June 1970), 31–8; Sarah Campion, "Autumn of an Anthropologist," *New Statesman*, 41 (13 January 1951), 34–6.

5 Lionel Trilling ["On the Teaching of Modern Literature," in *Beyond Culture* (New York, Viking, 1965), p. 15], misreading the essay, credited Frazer with having foreseen the Nazi threat. In fact the menace in the East is that posed by the Bolsheviks ("Condorcet," *C & E*, p. 85, which is also the source of the quotation).

6 Besterman told me in 1974 that Lady Frazer was the "anonymous donor" he mentions in the preface: *A Bibliography of Sir James George Frazer O.M.* (London, Macmillan, 1934), p. ix.

7 Downie (*FGB*, p. 120) was paid £5 a week (then a good wage), which meant that Lady Frazer was able to save about one-third of the Drapers' £400 annual grant. He is incorrect when he says that the grant was for £750 a year – see the notes of Drapers' Company Finance Committee for 26 February 1940, which recapitulates the history of the grant. (I wish to thank Mr R. R. Brown, education officer of the Drapers' Company, for sending me copies of the entire Frazer file.) *Aftermath* is dedicated to the Drapers' Company. In addition Lady Frazer secured at least one grant from the Anglo-Jewish philanthropist Sir Robert Mond, to whom *Totemica* is dedicated: "To Sir Robert Mond, the generous friend of learning and worthy scion of his noble race."

8 For an account of the writing of these two works, see *FGB*, pp. 122–4.

9 *Aftermath*, p. v.

INDEX

Aberdeen, University of, 29–30, 53, 65
Academy, 97
Addison, Joseph, 23, 187, 260, 291
Adonis, 105, 107, 169, 246
Aeneas, 103
Allen, Grant, 120, 152
Anaitis, 249
Andreas, F.C., 249
Anthropological Institute, 40, 65, 86, 121, 159, 209, 262
Antoninus Liberalis, 286
Archer, William, 194
Archiv für Religionswissenschaft, 226–7
Argos, 111
Aricia, *see* Nemi
Aristotle, 286
Arnold, Matthew, 31, 68
Arunta tribe, 154, 156–7, 175
Athenaeum, 97, 115, 157, 175
Athenaeus, 135
Attis, 105, 107, 169
Author, 148

Bailey, Cyril, 292
Bain, Alexander, 40, 50, 51
Baker, Peter G., 159
Balder, 95, 105, 108, 200, 231, 251
Balfour, A.J., 259
Baron, Salo, 182
Bayle, Pierre, 74
Beardmore, Edward, 121
Beilis, Mendel, 183, 330 n.10
Bell, George, 53
Bentham, Jeremy, 43, 47, 48, 49, 50
Bergson, Henri, 260
Besterman, Theodore, 305
   A Bibliography of the Works of Sir James George Frazer, O.M., 291, 309–10
Bevan, A.A., 248–9
Black, A. & C., 63, 119, 204–5

Black, J.S., 63, 70, 90, 91, 188, 230, 249, 263
   F's letters to, 90–1
Blore, E.W., 29, 317 n.18
Boas, Franz, 242
Bodleian Library, 302
Boni, Giacomo, 174
Bradley, F.H., 40, 50, 225
British Academy, 209
British Association for the Advancement of Science, 180
British Museum, 209
Browning, Oscar, 29
Bryce, James, Viscount, 259
Budge, E.A. Wallis, 233, 253, 254
Burkitt, F.C., 182
Burne, Charlotte S., 101, 170
Burrow, John, 77
Butcher, S.H., 283
Butler, H. Montagu, 115, 172
Butler, Samuel, 36

Caird, Edward, 15, 34
Calder, William M., III, 21
Calvin, John, 8
Cambridge Philological Society, 188
Cambridge Review, 32, 139, 319 n.31
Cambridge Ritualists, 3, 170, 234
Cambridge, University of, 191, 192, 207, 223, 260, 270, 332 n.26
Campion, Sarah, 308
Carlyle, Thomas, 9, 33, 42, 75
Carnegie Trust, 270
Cervantes, Miguel de, 8, 9
Chesterton, G.K., 194
Church Missionary Society, 210
Church of Scotland, Free ("Free Church"), 9, 58–9, 83
Cicero, 286–7
Clark, R. & R., 117
Classical Review, 200

341

Clifford, W. K., 34, 36
Clodd, Edward, 120, 146, 152, 172, 173, 177
  diaries of, 329 n.16, 333 n.50
Codrington, R. H., 122
Coleridge, S. T., 43, 75
Colonial Office, 270, 283
Colvin, Sir Sidney, 56
Comte, Auguste, 15, 33, 42, 44, 47, 51, 71, 83, 157
Confessions (St Augustine), 176
Conon, 286
Conrad, Joseph, 223
Conway, R. S., 200
Cook, A. B., 3, 183, 197–200, 241, 331 n.10
  Zeus, 197, 198
Corinth, 128
Cornford, F. M., 3, 183, 258, 264, 284, 288
Cowell, E. B., 250
Cowper, William, 68, 187, 283
Crabbe, George, 187
Creighton, Mandell, 182
Cults of the Greek States (Farnell), 195
Cumont, Franz, 165, 167, 259
Cynadra, 135

Daily Mail, 194, 196
Darwin, Charles, 33, 77, 262
Daulis, 236–7
De Quincey, Thomas, 89
Delphi, 128
Demeter and Persephone, 107, 246
Diana, 95, 109, 201, 231, 255
Dickens, Charles, 9
Didsbury College, Manchester, 188, 217
Diels, Hermann, 213, 214, 259
Dinka, 244
Dionysius Halicarnasensis, 279
Dionysus, 105, 107, 246
Doerpfeld, Wilhelm, 128, 133, 136–7, 259, 327 n.14
Donaldson, J., 30
Doré, Gustave, 111
Dostoyevsky, Fyodor, 213
Downie, R. A., 2, 261
  description of JGF, 10, 303, 317 n.3
  on JGF and Freud, 333 n.54
  on JGF's religious views, 316 n.16

personal relations with Frazers, 8, 221, 307, 340 n.7
  and Lady Frazer, 116, 124, 145, 182, 290, 337 n.8
  JGF: Portrait of a Scholar, 308
Drapers Company, 306
Druids, 95, 115
Dryden, John, 187
Durkheim, Emile, 1, 225, 259, 338 n.21

Edmonds, J. M., 283
Eliot, George, 33
Eliot, T. S., 105
Encyclopaedia Britannica, 57, 62, 70, 71, 85, 119, 140, 205
  Robertson Smith, editor of, 59, 60
Epidaurus, 111, 128
Essays and Reviews, 75
Eustathius, 135
Evans, Mary Ann, *see* Eliot, George
Evans-Pritchard, Sir E. E., 80, 245, 334 n.2

Faunus, 298
Ferguson, Adam, 46
Filby, P. William, 307–8
Firth, Sir Raymond, 269, 334 n.2, 338 n.27
Fison, Lorimer, 153, 291
Folk-Lore, 98, 170, 198, 200, 202
Folk-Lore Society, 101, 152, 170, 305
Fortnightly Review, 117, 119, 171, 172, 173, 174, 206, 218
Fowler, W. Warde, 115
Frazer, Christina (JGF's sister), 316 n.2
Frazer, Daniel (JGF's father), 5–9, 28, 33, 316 n.11
Frazer, Elizabeth (Lilly) de Boys Grove, Lady Frazer (JGF's wife)
  anecdotes about, 330 n.10, 334 n.2
  and Downie, 2, 116, 182
  and JGF Lectures, 284–5
  and JGF in France, 288–9
  last years, 303–8
  Leaves from the Golden Bough, 302
  and Liverpool, 162, 207–8, 214–15, 222
  and Manchester, 190
  meets and marries JGF, 124–5, 141
  personality, 125–6, 147, 210, 334 n.2
  relations with JGF, 142, 146, 173, 221,

222, 235, 260–1, 263; Gosse, 143,
191–2; Macmillan, 143, 161–3, 205,
302; Schechter, 182
and Trinity College, 145, 215, 333
n.41
unhappiness in Cambridge, 192, 207–
8, 215, 223, 286, 290, 332 n.25
William James on, 175
in World War I, 265–6
Frazer, Isabella (JGF's sister), 316 n.2
Frazer, Sir James George
life:
early years (1854–74), 5–16; Trinity
College (1874–8), 19–23; studies
law (1878), 28–9; Trinity
fellowship (1879), 25–8; friends
and early influences (Jackson, 38–
9, Ward, 39–40, Spencer &
utilitarians, 41–51); edits Sallust
(1884), 53–4; starts Pausanias
(1884), 55–8; meets Robertson
Smith (1884), 58–62; early
anthropological work, 62–7;
Golden Bough (1890), 95–8;
travels to Greece (1890), 98, 111–
12; Pausanias (1890–8), 113–20;
death of Smith (1894), 117;
friendship with Haddon (1890–2),
120–4; second trip to Greece
(1895), 236; marriage (1896), 124–
6; publishes Pausanias and leaves
Trinity (1898), 141–2; friendship
with Gosse, 148; attacks from
Lang, 151–3; friendship with B.
Spencer, 154–8; *Golden Bough*
(1900), 160, 162; eye trouble, 173;
friendship with Schechter, 182–3;
studies Hebrew, 183–4; rejects
Didsbury College, 188–91; Civil
List pension, 193; *Lectures on
Kingship* (1905), 200–1; friendships
with Cook and Marett, 197–203;
Totemism & Exogamy (1910), 206–
7; professor at Liverpool, 207–9;
returns to Cambridge, 213–15;
Golden Bough (1911–15), 239–40;
moves to Temple, London (1914),
258; knighthood (1914), 260–1;
wartime activities, 262–6;
friendship with Malinowski, 266–
9; friendship with Roscoe, 269–70;

Folk-Lore in the OT (1918), 270;
returns to classics (1918–29), 278–
80; F.R.S. (1920), 288;
inauguration of Frazer Lectures
(1922), 288; leaves Temple (1922),
286; abortive attempt to return to
Cambridge (1924), 289–90; moves
to Queen Anne's Mansions,
London (1925–8), 290; in Paris
(1928–9), 301; blindness (1931),
303; slow decline (1931–41), 303–
7; death (1941), 308
writings:
Aftermath, 57, 306, 307; *Ancient
Stories of a Great Flood*, 262, 273,
274; *Anthologia Anthropologica*,
307; *The Library*, 139, 234, 278,
279, 280–3, 286, 292, 294, 295,
296; *Belief in Immortality*, 240,
262–3, 282, 284, 287, 291, 293,
301; *Condorcet on . . . Human
Mind*, 304; *Creation & Evolution
in Primitive Cosmologies*, 306;
["Early Accounts of the American
Indians"], 177; *Essays of Joseph
Addison*, 187, 260; [*The Fasti*], 32,
139, 278, 286, 292–300, 301, 303;
Fear of the Dead, 304; "Folk-Lore
in the OT," 57, 185, 186, 271; *Folk-
Lore in the OT*, 57, 132, 262, 270–
7, 278, 281, 293, 297; *Folk-Lore in
the OT* (abridged edn), 289, 293;
Garnered Sheaves, 303; *Golden
Bough* (1890), 81, 85, 90, 92, 95–
110, 113–15, 128–9, 131, 132, 133,
137, 140, 149, 154, 166, 199, 229,
230, 252; (reviews of) 98, 170,
171–4; (sales of) 113; *Golden
Bough* (1900), 141, 149, 151, 158,
159–62, 164–79, 188, 192, 198, 199,
222, 234 (reviews of) 170–2, 198–9;
Golden Bough (1906–15), 107, 177,
187, 188, 193, 205, 207, 224, 236–
57, 258; (sales of), 256–7; *The
Magic Art*, 239, 240–1, 257; *Taboo
& Perils of Soul*, 239, 241–3; *Dying
God*, 107, 239, 243, 244; *Attis
Adonis Osiris* (1906), 203–6, 236–8,
246; *Attis Adonis Osiris* (1914),
107, 240; *Spirits of Corn & Wild*,
240, 246–8; *Scapegoat*, 183, 240,

Frazer: writings (*cont.*)
248; *Balder the Beautiful*, 231,
240, 250–1, 253, 254–5, 258; *Index*,
240, 262; [abridged edn], 257, 289,
292–3; *Growth of Plato's Ideal
Theory*, 21, 25–7, 302–3; *Gorgon's
Head*, 260, 291–2, 303; *Graecia
Antiqua*, 302; *Lectures on . . .
Kingship*, 187, 193, 197, 200–1,
204, 211, 216, 241; *Letters of
William Cowper*, 187, 260;
"Memories of My Parents," 5, 8,
306; *Myths of the Origin of Fire*,
301; "On Certain Burial Customs
. . . Theory of the Soul," 22, 40,
65–7, 262, 304; *Passages from the
Bible*, 119–20, 141, 204; *Pausanias
and Other Greek Sketches*, 138,
236; *Pausanias's Description of
Greece*, 13, 32, 55, 86, 96, 97, 112–
14, 116–17, 118, 127–41, 178, 188,
270, 288, 292; (translation), 54–7;
(reviews of) 139–40; "Pericles,"
62: "Philosophy" (notebook), 28,
41–51; *Psyche's Task*, 11, 215–17,
242, 252; *Questionnaire on the
Manners . . . of Uncivilized or
Semi-Civilized Peoples*, 120, 269,
323 n.41; [Sallust edn], 53–4, 55,
65; *Scope of Social Anthropology*,
211–13; *Sir Roger de Coverley*,
260; "Speech . . . Freedom of the
City of Glasgow," 5, 306; *Studies
in Greek Scenery*, 138; *Sur Ernest
Renan*, 93; "Taboo," 57, 62, 70,
200; "Totemism," 57, 62, 63, 205;
Totemism, 57, 63, 119, 149, 155,
206, 207, 217; *Totemica*, 306, 307;
Totemism & Exogamy, 57, 62, 63,
205, 206, 207, 215, 217–20, 221,
222, 223, 228, 239, 266, 292, 306,
307; (reviews of) 328 n.33;
Worship of Nature, 291
Frazer, Katherine (JGF's mother), 5, 9,
11–12, 160
Frazer, Samuel (JGF's brother), 261–2,
316 n.2
Frazer & Green, 5, 6, 149, 191
Frazer Anthropological Research Fund,
258–60, 284
Frazer Lectures, 284, 288

Freud, Sigmund, 48, 51, 213
Totem und Tabu, 62, 217, 219–20,
333 n.54
Frye, Northrop, 3

Galton, Sir Francis, 22, 34, 36, 65, 147,
208, 209, 221
Gardner, Percy, 140, 162
Gaster, Moses, 170
Gaster, Theodor H., 2, 99
Gibbon, Edward, 22, 239, 275
Gifford, Adam (Lord Gifford), 224
Gifford Lectures, 224, 260
Gillen, F.J., 154; *see also* Spencer, W.
Baldwin
Glasgow, University of, 12, 192
Godley, A.D., 279
Gosse, Sir Edmund, 11, 148, 188, 192–
3, 208, 260, 282, 286
JGF letter to, 194–6
and Royal Literary Fund, 143, 162,
191, 222, 223, 303, 330 n.20
Gow, James, 55
Gower, Lord, 259
Graetz, Heinrich, 182
Grimm, Jakob and Wilhelm, 212
Grove, Charles Baylee, 124, 145
Grove, Charles Grenville (JGF's
stepson), 124, 144, 285, 325 n.30
Grove, Lilly Mary (JGF's
stepdaughter), 124, 144, 265, 284,
285, 325 n.30

Haddon, A.C.
early life, 10
JGF letters to, 120–4, 180–1
as JGF lecturer, 288
friendship with JGF, 170, 180–2,
259
on Lang and JGF, 173
position in Cambridge, 123–4, 208
and Seligman, 244
trip to New Guinea with JGF, 11, 65,
86, 147
Haman, 168, 248–50, 251
Hamilton, Sir William, 46
Hardy, G.H., 264
Hardy, Thomas, 39, 106, 194
Hardy, W.B., 283
Harris, J. Rendell, 182
Harrison, Frederic, 34, 36

Harrison, Jane Ellen, 3, 33, 137, 174, 183, 246
  Mythology and Monuments of Ancient Athens, 112
Hartland, E. Sidney, 147, 148, 152, 173, 194
  Frazer Lecturer, 288
Hartley, David, 40
Hawkins, A. H. 259
Hegel, G. W. F., 15
  Hegelianism, 14, 34, 35, 39, 267
Heine, Heinrich, 9, 25, 38, 67–9, 86, 183
Heinemann, W. H., 278, 280, 293–4
Heraea, 134
Herakles (Euripides), 135, 136
Herder, J. G. von, 74, 86, 237
Herodotus, 72, 82, 134, 279
Hesychius, 135
Heyne, C. G., 74
Hitzig, H., and Bluemner, H., 117, 118, 132
Homer, 72, 74, 128, 283
Housman, A. E., 183, 288
Howitt, A. W., 228, 291, 333 n.50
Hubert, H., and Mauss, M., 165, 230, 246
Hume, David, 46, 74, 184
Huxley, Thomas Henry, 34, 36, 75
Hyman, Stanley Edgar, 2, 233

Icaria, 138
Image, J. M., 20, 24
Independent Review, 291
Innes, H. McLeod, 285
intichiuma ceremonies, 155, 160, 144
Isaeus, 286
Ishtar, 249

Jackson, Henry
  as JGF's friend, 40, 53, 64, 223–4, 281
  as JGF's teacher, 38–9, 43, 44
  JGF's letters to, 85–90, 147, 188–9, 190, 223, 263
  letter to JGF, 189–90
Jacobs, Joseph, 98
James, E. O., 124
James, William, 174, 175, 203, 226
Jarvie, I. C., 2
Jewish Theological Seminary, 183

Jones, Robert Alun, 84
Journal of the Anthropological Institute, 210
Jupiter, 200

Kant, Immanuel, 15
  neo-Kantianism, 14
Keats, John, 189
Kelvin, Lord (William Thomson), 14, 15
Kennett, Robert, 183
Kenney, E. J., 296
Kephisia, 111, 138
Khent-Amenti, 254
Kibuka, 253, 254
King's College, Cambridge, 29
Kingsley, Charles, 33
Kipling, Rudyard, 288

Lactantius, 279
Lagarde, P. A. de, 58
Lang, Andrew, 15, 63, 157, 194, 283
  Cock Lane and Common-Sense, 151–2
  Magic and Religion, 171–4
  Making of Religion, 152–3, 159, 173, 174
  Myth, Ritual and Religion, 150–1, 159
  against solarism, 76–7, 100, 149–51
  relations with JGF, 170–5, 180, 214, 235, 329 n.13
Lange, C. G., 226
Larchfield Academy, 12
Lévy-Bruhl, Lucien, 225, 228
Lewes, G. H., 36, 47
Lewis, M. J., 214, 221, 261, 263, 264, 265
Lityerses, 246
Liverpool, University of, 162, 207–14, 332 n.28, 333 n.39
Livy, 75
Locke, John, 43
Loeb, James, 278, 279, 294
Loeb Library, 278–80, 281, 286, 292–4
London School of Economics, 268, 287
Long, George, 53
Long, Margaret, Viscountess, 4
Lotze, R. H., 58
Lund Humphries, 307
Lupercalia, 298–300

McDougall, William, 225, 228
Mackenzie, Alexander, 12
Mackie, Sir Peter, 270, 283
McLennan, Donald, 69
McLennan, J.F., 1, 80–1, 82, 98, 100, 322 n.24
Macmillan, Frederick, 118
Macmillan, George, 54, 55–7, 67, 69, 92, 95–8, 113–14, 116–17, 118–19, 131, 132, 138, 141, 143, 145, 148, 149, 155, 159, 160, 161, 174, 176, 177, 178, 184, 185, 192, 193, 205, 207, 215, 222, 256–7, 262, 273, 278, 289, 290, 292, 293–4, 297, 302, 305, 307
Macmillan, Maurice, 118
Malinowski, Bronislaw, 100, 126, 161, 259
  as JGF lecturer, 288
  as protégé of JGF, 161, 266–9
  on JGF and Lang, 172, 174, 198, 214
  letters to JGF, 266–8
  portrait of JGF, 4, 8
  Argonauts, 268, 287, 317 n.20
  Diary, 266
Man, 210, 253
Mannhardt, Wilhelm
  as influence on JGF, 81–2, 105, 107, 177, 233, 248, 252, 299
Mantinea, 111, 128
Marathon, 111, 137
Marett, R.R., 15, 201–3, 224–35, 246
  animatism, 202
  "Birth of Humility," 225
  JGF lecturer, 288
  on *FOT*, 276–7
  as social psychologist of religion, 201–3, 224–9, 241
Mau, August, 176
Maurice, F.D., 33
Mayhew, Henry, 212
Meyer, Richard M., 226, 230
Middleton, J.H., 141, 148
Mill, John Stuart, 34, 40, 42, 43, 44, 48, 49, 50
Milton, John, 22
Montesquieu, Baron Charles de, 46, 47
Moore, Tom, 8
Morgan, Lewis Henry, 1, 320 n.18
Morley, John, 34, 45–6
Morris, William, 140

Moulton, J.H., 188, 189, 330 n.15
Müller, F. Max, 75–6, 81, 88, 100, 151, 230
Mueller, K.O., 74
Munro, H.A.J., 29
Munychia, 111
Murray, A.T., 283
Murray, Gilbert, 3, 100, 120, 263
Murray, Sir John, 210, 332 n.32
Murray, Lady Mary, 174
Mycenae, 111, 135
Myers, F.W.H., 36, 319 n.4

Nature, 157
Nauplia, 111
Nemi (Aricia), 92–3, 95, 102, 108, 335 n.14
Nicholas, T.C., 334 n.2
Nicholson, J.S., 25, 64
Nicolson, Sir Harold, 303
Niebuhr, B.G., 74
Nietzsche, Friedrich, 21, 213
Nilus, Saint, 154
Noeldeke, Theodor, 248–50
Northcliffe, Lord, 194
Nutt, Alfred, 170–1

Old Testament: Esther, 168, 249; Genesis, 184, 272, 273, 274; Numbers, 275; Pentateuch, 275; Prophets, 184, 274
Olympia, 111, 134
Order of Merit, 260
Osiris, 105, 107, 169, 254
Oxford, University of, 162, 288

Page, T.E., 18, 278, 286
Pagenstacher, Dr (JGF's eye doctor), 173, 177
Pausanias, 54, 82, 136
Piraeus, 111
Plataea, 111, 128
Pliny, 115, 249, 291
Plutarch, 67, 279
Polemo of Ilium, 134
Porphyry, 279
Postgate, J.P., 54
Potter, Beatrice, 33
Pre-Raphaelites, 140
"Primal Law" (J.J. Atkinson), 219
Purim, 168–9, 239, 249

Quiggin, A. H., 123
Quintilian, 296

Rackham, H., 283
Radcliffe-Brown, A., 100, 339 n.19
Raleigh, Sir Walter, 259
Ramsay, G. G., 13
Ray, Sidney, 122
Reconstruction of South-Eastern Europe (Savic), 265–6
Reinach, Salomon, 70, 71
Renan, Ernest
  as influence on JGF, 38, 109, 212, 213, 237
  JGF on, 269, 289, 323 n.43
  Robertson Smith on, 93–4
  Le prêtre de Némi, 93
Rhamnus, 111
Ridgeway, Sir William, 262
Ritschl, Albrecht, 58
Rivers, W. H. R., 218
Robertson Smith, William, *see* Smith, William Robertson
Romanes, George, 36
Roscoe, John, 8, 214, 218, 233, 245, 259, 290
  and euhemerism, 253–4
  as JGF lecturer, 288
  relations with JGF, 210–11, 266, 269–70, 287
Rothblatt, Sheldon, 33
Rouse, W. H. D., 89
  and Loeb Library, 278, 280, 283, 286, 292
Rousseau, J. J., 90
Royal Institution, 215, 265
Royal Literary Fund, *see* Gosse, Sir Edmund
Royal Society, 209, 270, 283
Ruskin, John, 33, 213, 215
Russell, Bertrand, 263–4

Sacaea, 167, 239, 249
St Andrews, University of, 224
Saturnalia, 167, 168, 239
Schechter, Solomon, 169, 182–3, 330 n.6
Schlegel, Friedrich and Wilhelm, 74
Schliemann, Heinrich, 128, 134
Scholem, Gershom, 182
Schubart, J. H., 113
Scott, Sir Walter, 8, 9

Scottish Enlightenment, 46
Seligman, Brenda Z., 244
Seligman, Charles G., 244–6
Seneca, 296
Shilleto, A. R., 140
Shilluk, 244–5
Sidgwick, Henry, 25, 34, 36, 49
Skeat, W. W., 161, 165
Smith, Adam, 15, 46
Smith, G. Elliot, 267
Smith, William Robertson,
  arrives at Trinity College, 59
  editor of *Encyclopaedia Britannica*, 59–60
  and JGF, 58–63
  as ritualist, 226–30, 232
  Religion of the Semites, 53, 58, 70, 84, 90–1, 98, 117, 170, 186, 226
Société du Folklore Français, 301
Society for Psychical Research, 151–2
Sorbonne, 288
Sparta, 111, 128
Spencer, Herbert, 36, 47, 65, 84, 150
  as influence on JGF, 11, 22, 27, 38, 40–4, 201
Spencer, W. Baldwin, 149, 154–7, 160, 181, 228, 245
  and F. J. Gillen, 155, 159, 165, 174, 203, 209, 210, 218, 244
Steed, Wickham, 174
Steffen, Captain (archaeologist), 135
Steggall, J. E. A., 32, 316 n.2
Stewart, Dugald, 46, 47
Strabo, 249
Swift, Jonathan, 187
Symons, A. J., 194

Tacitus, 82
Taylor, Charles, 182
Taylor, Thomas, 148
Taylor, Tom, 223
Thammuz, 107
Thebes, 128
Theocritus, 283
Thespiae, 111
Thompson, W. H., 29, 64
Thomson, Sir J. J., 260, 301
Thomson, William (Lord Kelvin), 14, 15
Thornely, Thomas, 19
Tieck, Ludwig, 74
Times, The, 194, 204

Times Literary Supplement, The, 196,
    289
Tiryns, 111
Torres Straits expedition, 122, 244
Trilling, Lionel, 3
Trinity College, Cambridge, 3, 318 n.5
    animosity to Lilly Frazer in, 125–6
    Bertrand Russell at, 263–4
    College Council, 67, 263–4
    JGF as Fellow in, 27, 28, 64–5, 115,
        144, 162, 321 n.20, 324 n.10
    JGF as lecturer in, 193, 304
    JGF's friends in, 39, 54, 59, 148
    JGF in folklore of, 115–16, 145, 308
    JGF as undergraduate in, 16, 17–24,
        38
    JGF's love for, 141, 142
    JGF tries to return to, 285–6, 290–1,
        301, 339 n.15
    politics of, 316 n.11
    Robertson Smith at, 59–60
Trinity Hall, 19
Tripos, classical, 17–19, 23–4, 318
    nn.14, 15
Tristram Shandy (Sterne), 248
Troy (Hissarlik), 128, 134
Turner, J.M.W., 96, 97, 102–3, 108–9,
    237
Tylor, E.B., 1, 38, 47, 58, 63, 65, 67,
    77–80, 82, 83, 84, 98, 100, 150,
    225, 231, 267
    Anahuac, 77
    Anthropology, 79
    Festschrift, 184, 262, 271
    Natural History of Religion, 184
    Primitive Culture, 27, 29, 39, 53, 77,
        79, 96, 152
    animism, 79
    cognitionism, 40, 79–80, 231

relations with JGF, 159–60, 175, 180,
    181
relations with Lang, 152, 171, 173

"Ulysses" (Tennyson), 88, 89
Uncle Vanya (Chekhov), 166

Van Gennep, Arnold, 225
Veitch, John, 13–14, 22, 43
    Knowing and Being, 14
Verrall, Margaret, 112
Virbius, 95, 109
Virgil, 103
Von Hügel, Baron Anatole, 51, 124
Von Ranke, Leopold, 15

Wace, A.J.B., 302
Wallace, Alfred Russel, 36
Ward, Mrs Humphry, 171
Ward, James, 36, 38, 260
    early life, 39–40
    and JGF, 27, 29, 64, 89, 203, 225, 228
Wellhausen, Julius, 58
Westermarck, Edward, 252, 259, 288
Whewell, William, 42
White, John F., 59, 61, 68, 147, 194
Whittaker & Co., 53
Wilamowitz-Moellendorff, Ulrich von,
    133–7, 292, 327 n.13
Wilberforce, Samuel, 75
Wilken, G.A., 181
Wissowa, Georg, 259
Wolf, F.A., 74
Wordsworth, William, 9, 13
Wright, William, 59
Wyse, William, 261, 304–5

Zakmuk, 167, 168

ATHENEUM

PUBLISHERS

597 FIFTH AVENUE   NEW YORK CITY 10017

Title: THE 100% NATURAL, PURELY ORGANIC,
         CHOLESTEROL-FREE, MEGAVITAMIN,
         LOW-CARBOHYDRATE NUTRITION HOAX

Author: Dr. Elizabeth M. Whelan and
        Dr. Fredrick J. Stare

Publication Date: September 25, 1984

Price: $7.95 paperback

THIS BOOK *is sent to you with our com-*

pliments. Should you publish any men-

tion of it, we would be grateful for two

clippings of your article. Please do

not review the book before its

publication date.